LEVEL THREE LEADERSHIP

SECOND EDITION

LEVEL THREE LEADERSHIP

Getting Below the Surface

James G. Clawson

The Darden Graduate School of Business Administration
University of Virginia

Prentice
Hall

Upper Saddle River, New Jersey 07458

Library of Congress Cataloging-in-Publication Data

Clawson, James G.
    Level three leadership : getting below the surface / James G. Clawson.—2nd ed.
        p.   cm.
    Includes bibliographical references and index.
    ISBN 0-13-032943-6
    1. Leadership.   I. Title.
HD57.7.C545   2002
650.1′3—dc21   2002000086

Acquisitions Editor: Melissa Steffens
Editor-in-Chief: Jeff Shelstad
Assistant Editor: Melanie Olsen
Editorial Assistant: Kevin Glynn
Media Project Manager: Michele Faranda
Marketing Manager: Shannon Moore
Marketing Assistant: Christine Genneken
Managing Editor (Production): John Roberts
Production Editor: Renata Butera
Production Assistant: Dianne Falcone
Permissions Coordinator: Suzanne Grappi

Associate Director, Manufacturing: Vincent Scelta
Production Manager: Arnold Vila
Manufacturing Buyer: Michelle Klein
Cover Design: Bruce Kenselaar
Cover Illustration/Photo: Brian Bailey/Stone
Composition: Impressions Book and Journal Services, Inc.
Full-Service Project Management: Impressions Book and Journal Services, Inc.
Printer/Binder: Hamilton

Pearson Education LTD.
Pearson Education Australia PTY, Limited
Pearson Education Singapore, Pte. Ltd
Pearson Education North Asia Ltd
Pearson Education, Canada, Ltd
Pearson Educación de Mexico, S.A. de C.V.
Pearson Education–Japan
Pearson Education Malaysia, Pte. Ltd

10 9 8 7 6 5 4
ISBN 0-13-032943-6

To Alex Horniman, who declares that excellence is a neurotic lifestyle, knows whereof he speaks, and taught and continues to teach me much, and to Doug Newburg, who continues to stretch boundaries in his unique way.

Brief Contents

Preface   xix
Acknowledgments   xxv

PART I   INTRODUCTION   1

Chapter 1   The Leadership Point of View   3
Chapter 2   The Changing Context of Leadership   8
Chapter 3   General Model of Leadership in Organizations   24
Chapter 4   Levels of Leadership   42
Chapter 5   The Moral Foundation of Extraordinary Leadership   54
Chapter 6   A Leader's Guide to Why People Behave the Way They Do   66
                An Abbreviated List of Personal Defense Mechanisms   88

PART II   SELF   91

Chapter 7   Six Steps to Effective Leadership   93
Chapter 8   Leadership and Intelligence   110
Chapter 9   Resonance, Leadership, and the Purpose of Life   122

PART III   STRATEGIC THINKING   141

Chapter 10   Strategic Thinking   143
Chapter 11   Personal and Organization Charters   159

PART IV   LEADING OTHERS   175

Chapter 12   Leading Others   177
Chapter 13   Leading Teams   190

PART V   LEADERS AS DESIGNERS   207

Chapter 14   Leading Organizational Design   209
Chapter 15   Leading Change   227

PART VI   CONCLUSION   245

Chapter 16   Summary   247

PART VII   SUPPLEMENTARY MATERIALS   255

Level Three Leadership Program Workbook   257

Survey of Managerial Style   275

Life's Dream Exercise   287

Leadership Steps-Assessment (LSA)   291

Team Self-Assessment   305

Assessing the Moral Foundation of Your Leadership   308

Balancing Your Life   310

Energy Management Exercise   319

Life's Story Assignment   322

Leadership Theories   325

Appendix   344

Select Bibliography   347

Index   351

Contents

Preface   **xix**

    Background   xx

    General Organization of the Book   xxi

        Structure of the Book   xxi

        Themes in the Book   xxii

    What's New in This Edition   xxiii

Acknowledgments   xxv

PART I   INTRODUCTION   1

CHAPTER 1   The Leadership Point of View   3

    The Leadership Point of View   4

    Seeing What Needs to Be Done   4

    Understanding the Underlying Forces at Play   5

    Initiating Action to Make Things Better   6

CHAPTER 2   The Changing Context of Leadership   8

    Hunter-Gatherers   9

    Aristocratic Society   9

    The Industrial Revolution and Bureaucratic Society   11

    The Present Paradigm Shift   14

CHAPTER 3   General Model of Leadership in Organizations   24

    Leading Strategic Change   26

    Key Elements of Leadership   27

        The Leader   28

        Task: What Should We Do?   29

        Others: Working Together with Followers   29

        Organization: Designing the Right Context   29

        The Environmental Context   30

    Results: Outcomes of Leadership   30

    Relationships Are the Key   30

    How the Diamond Model Relates to Other Models of Leadership   32

    Leadership Potentialities   32

    Leading Ethically   33

The Diamond Model and What Chief Executive Officers Do   33
Basic Definitions   35
Visioning, Commitment, and Management Skills   36
Target Levels of Leadership   39

CHAPTER 4   Levels of Leadership   42

Body, Head, and Heart   43
Connecting the Three Levels to Scholarly Views   46
Learning Level Three Leadership   46
The Strong History of Level One Leadership   48
The Focus and Impact of Level Three Leadership   49
The Dark Side of Level Three Leadership and Engagement   50
Organizational Implications   51
Applying Level Three Leadership at Both the Individual and
     Organizational Levels   52

**CHAPTER 5   The Moral Foundation of Extraordinary
                         Leadership   54**

Morality, Ethics, and Legality   54
Morality and Leadership   55
The Moral Foundation of Effective Leadership   57
The Normal Distribution of Employees' Value Added   59
Universality of the Moral Foundation of Level Three Leadership   62

**CHAPTER 6   A Leader's Guide to Why People Behave the Way
                         They Do   66**

The Beginnings   67
Our Genetic Endowment   69
Solidifying the Tendencies   70
Memes   72
Motivation   73
The Rational-Emotive Behavior Model   74
Events   75
Perceptions and Observations   75
VABEs   76
External Conclusions   78
Internal Conclusions   79
Feelings   79
Behavior   81
An REB Example   81
Meaning Chains   82
REB and Leading Change   82
The Self-Concept   83
Defense Mechanisms   84

An Abbreviated List of Personal Defense Mechanisms   88

Healthy, Productive Defense Mechanisms   88
Moderately Healthy Defense Mechanisms   88
Unhealthy, Unproductive Defense Mechanisms   89
Dangerous Defense Mechanisms   89

PART II   SELF   91

CHAPTER 7   Six Steps to Effective Leadership   93

1. Clarifying Your Center   95
   Clarifying What You Stand for: Engagement   96
   Developing Character: Ends Versus Means   97
   Meditation   97
2. Clarifying What Is Possible   98
   Clarifying Mental Images of What Can Be   98
   Scenario Building   100
3. Clarifying What Others Can Contribute   100
   Basic Assumptions About Others   100
   Identifying the Critical Skills   101
4. Supporting Others So They Can Contribute   102
   Information Age Organizational Structures   102
   Empowering Systems Design   104
5. Being Relentless   104
   Life As a Motorboat or a Wood Chip   105
   Developing Commitment   105
6. Measuring and Celebrating Progress   106
   Focusing on the Right Measures   106
   Focusing on the Glass Half Full   107

CHAPTER 8   Leadership and Intelligence   110

Not One Intelligence, But Many: Gardner's Research   111
Intelligence Quotient   112
Emotional Quotient   112
   Recognizing Your Own Emotions   114
   Managing Your Emotions   115
Social Quotient   116
   Recognizing the Emotions of Others   116
   Listening   116
   Empathy and Caring   117
   Helping Others Manage Their Emotions   117
Change Quotient   118
   Recognizing the Need to Change   119
   Understanding and Mastering the Change Process   119
   Emotional Comfort with Change   119

CHAPTER 9 Resonance, Leadership, and the Purpose of Life 122

Dreams 124
   Internal Dreams 124
   Flow 125
   The Universal Search for Resonance 127
Preparation 129
   The Energy Cycle 129
   The Search for Ideas 130
   Managing Your Energy 131
Setbacks, Obstacles, and Successes 132
Revisiting the Dream 134
Resonance 137

PART III STRATEGIC THINKING 141

CHAPTER 10 Strategic Thinking 143

Definitions 143
Strategic Domains 145
Fundamentals of Strategic Thinking 145
   Fit Model 146
   Growth Model 150
   Intent Model 151
   Ecological Model 152
   Strategy As Revolution 153
Developing Strategic Thinking 154
   Scenario Building 155
   Broad Reading 155
Essential Elements of Strategic Thinking 156

CHAPTER 11 Personal and Organization Charters 159

Charters 159
   Mission 161
   Vision 165
   Values 167
   Strategy 168
   Operating Goals 170

PART IV LEADING OTHERS 175

CHAPTER 12 Leading Others 177

Sources of Power 178
The Currency of Reciprocity 180

The Role of Trust and Respect   183
General Approach to Influence   184
   Purpose   184
   Clear Communication   184
   Invitations   185
Level Three Influence   186

CHAPTER 13 Leading Teams   190

What Makes a Team?   191
Team Life Cycles   191
   Forming: Initiation and Orientation   192
   Norming: Exploration of Procedure   192
   Performing: Stabilization   193
   Reforming: Reassessment   193
Team Roles   194
   Task Driver   195
   Process Facilitator   196
   Creative Visionary   196
   Practicality Pusher   196
Inspired Vision That Creates . . .   197
. . . A Powerful Sense of Mission   197
Getting the Right People   197
Distributed Leadership   198
Extraordinary Coordination   199
Creative Support   199
Moral Foundation for Respect   199
The Right Roles for the Right People   200
Participation   200
The Right Measures   201
Virtual Teams   202

PART V LEADERS AS DESIGNERS   207

CHAPTER 14 Leading Organizational Design   209

A General Model of Organizational Design and Its Impact on Results   210
   Background Factors   210
   Leadership Philosophy   211
   Organizational Design Decisions   212
   Systems Design   214
Organizational Culture   220
Organizational Results   222
Organizational Glue   223

CHAPTER 15 Leading Change   227

A General Model of Change   227

The Role of Outside Help in Managing Change   230

Clarifying Disconfirming Data   231

Building a Change Team   232

Designing and Leading Change Experiments   233

Relentlessly Reinforcing Results with the Vision   234

Classic and Current Change Models   234

Roles in the Change Process   235

Responses to Change—Dying Little Deaths   236

The Many Faces of Denial   236

Levels in Change   239

John Kotter's Model of Change   240

The Four P's   240

The MIT Model   240

PART VI CONCLUSION 245

CHAPTER 16 Summary   247

Summary of Basic Principles Introduced in This Book   251

PART VII SUPPLEMENTARY MATERIALS   255

Level Three Leadership Program Workbook   257

General Leadership Model   258

Strategic Challenges I'm Facing   258

Leadership Implications
    of My Strategic Challenges   259

Self-Assessment on the Six Steps
    to Effective Leadership   261

Charter for My Organization   262

Charter for My Work Group   263

Charter for Myself   264

Keep, Lose, Add   265

Managing Personal Change and Blind Spots   265

Systems and Processes That Need Redesigning   266

My Life's Dream   267

Activities in Which I Resonate   268

Ways to Bring Resonance to Work   268

Ways I Want to Improve
    My Leadership Language   269

Leading Change   270
Intelligence Self-Assessment   271
Building Commitment   272
What Do I Want to Do This Year?   273
Central Point   274

Survey of Managerial Style   275

Survey of Managerial Style   276
Section I: General Information   276
Section II: Management Style Items   276
Scoring and Interpreting Your Data   278
Leadership and the Survey of Managerial Style (SMS)   279
Scoring Your Data   280
SMS Scoring Form   281
Survey of Managerial Style Profile   282
Interpreting Your Profile   282
Interpretive Alternatives   284
Suggestions for Strengthening
    Your SMS (VCM) Profile   284

Life's Dream Exercise   287

Identifying Your LDext   288
Identifying Your LDint   289
Implementing Your Life's Dream (LDint)   290

Leadership Steps Assessment (LSA)   291

Part I: Descriptors/Adjectives   292
Part II: Descriptive Phrases   293
Part III: The Theory   294
Part IV: Scoring Procedure   296
Part V: Displaying Your Scores   297
Part VI: Interpreting Your Scores   297
Clarifying Your Center   297
Clarifying What's Possible   298
Clarifying What Others Have to Contribute   299
Supporting Others So That They Can Contribute   300
Being Relentless   301
Measuring and Celebrating Progress   301
Conclusion   302
LSA Data Collection   303

Team Self-Assessment   305

Assessing the Moral Foundation of Your Leadership **308**

Balancing Your Life **310**

Energy Management Exercise **319**
    Energy Action Items 320
      Reflections *321*

Life's Story Assignment **322**
    My Life's Story in 400 Words or Less 323
    My Life's Story Key Events Table 324

Leadership Theories **325**
    1. Trait Approach 325
      The "Great Man" Theory of Leadership *325*
      Stogdill's Leadership Traits *325*
      Maccoby's Leader *327*
      John Gardner *328*
      Jim Collins *328*
    2. Behavior Approach 329
      Mintzberg's Ten Managerial Roles *329*
      Kotter's Leadership Factor *329*
      Stewart's Three-Part Theory of Management *331*
      Kouzes and Posner's Leadership Challenge *331*
      Results Focused Leadership *332*
    3. Power and Influence Approach 332
      Two Faces of Power *332*
      Winter's Theory of Leadership *333*
      The West Point Way of Leadership *333*
      Social Exchange Theory *333*
      Strategic Contingencies Theory *334*
    4. Situational Approach 334
      Hersey and Blanchard's Situational Theory of Leadership *334*
      House's Path-Goal Theory of Leadership *335*
      Fiedler's Contingency Model of Leadership *335*
      Leadership Substitutes Theory *335*
      The Multiple-Linkage Model *336*
      Cognitive Resources Theory *336*
    5. Charismatic Approach 337
      House's Theory of Charismatic Leadership *337*
      Attribution Theory of Charisma *338*
      Self-Concept Theory of Charismatic Leadership *338*
    6. Transformational Approach 339
      Warren Bennis' Theory of Leadership *339*
      James MacGregor Burns' Theory of Leadership *340*
      Bass' Theory of Transformational Leadership *341*

Tichy and Devanna's Transformational Leadership Process   *342*
Schein's Model of Organizational Culture and Leadership   *343*

APPENDIX   Cases That Apply   344

Introduction   344
   Self   344
   Task and Strategic Thinking   344
   Leading Others   345
   Leading Teams   345
   Leaders As Designers   345
   Managing Change   345

Select Bibliography   347

General Perspectives   347
Individual Perspectives   347
Strategic Thinking (Task Vision)   348
Creativity   348
Interpersonal Perspectives   348
Organizational Perspectives   349
Managing Change   349

Index   351

Preface

I cannot resist a suggestion which embodies all of my hopes for the school. It is that nothing will ever induce us to lay aside instruction in the ethical foundations of American business. Without a firm attachment to unimpeachable integrity, in our business as well as in our personal affairs, we build on shifting sands and there can be no future for any of us.
—COLGATE W. DARDEN, JR.

This book is about learning to make a difference as a leader. It promotes the view that many leaders, especially those raised and trained and experienced in Industrial Age organizations, have learned to lead at what I call Level One, focusing on behavior and often ignoring or undervaluing opportunities to influence people at Level Two, their thinking, and at Level Three, their values and basic assumptions about how the world operates. As a consequence, many managers have a superficial impact on the people with whom they work, which manifests as a perceived lack of leadership and lackluster results. The goal of this book is to provide practical principles of leadership that get beneath the surface, that intend to influence others' thinking and feeling rather than just their behavior. In this, the book attempts to present a practical perspective of leadership rather than a theoretical one. There are no summaries of common leadership theory, yet bits and pieces of many of them are woven into the story presented here. In that sense, this book draws on the literature—what we say we know about leadership today—and it greatly reflects the experience of several faculty at the Darden Graduate School of Business, University of Virginia, who have been involved in designing and teaching leadership programs for master of business administration (MBA) and executive education students for several decades.

The book is intended for practicing managers who, on their own or in connection with ongoing studies in executive MBA or executive short courses, want to learn more about effective leadership. It is also intended for MBA students thinking about the same issue, yet this is not, in the usual sense, a textbook. It is not about summarizing all the leadership theories; rather, it's about integrating theory and practice and creating a model and a set of related perspectives and concepts about how one can become a better leader in one's own life, work group, and organizations.

BACKGROUND

The book is based on consulting, research, and teaching experiences from several faculty of the Darden Graduate School of Business Administration at the University of Virginia in Charlottesville, Virginia, whose mission is "to better society by developing leaders in the world of practical affairs" and whose students, we hope, tend to be known for an action orientation, an enterprise perspective, determination, vision, judgment, integrity, and social responsibility. The ideas here have been tested in the MBA and executive education classrooms of the Darden School over the last 15 years.

The Darden School faculty take a student-centered, practical approach to education, that is, we believe that each class should begin with and build from the level of the students' understanding of the issues and intricacies presented in a series of cases. Cases are descriptions of actual business situations where the authors focus on the situation rather than demonstrating any particular theory or point of view. Real (as opposed to "armchaired") business cases form the basis for virtually all of the class work at the Darden School.

Students, all with more than two years of work experience after college, are required to prepare, on average, one case for each of three 85-minute classes each day. The discussion typically begins with a student speaking to the case as well as she can and then develops into an active debate including all members of the class. I have not included any of the cases from our various programs here, although several are referred to, and I am developing a case book to accompany this volume. The cases used in class were not intended to be used as illustrations of theory as orchestrated by an instructor or as presented by student study teams. Rather, they provided data and scenarios that invited personalized discussion, demand decisions, and action plans. This allows students to confront and learn to deal with actual business situations (as presented in the cases) as viewed by a group of highly active, intelligent peers.

Typical discussions include overviews of the key issues and problems, analysis of the underlying forces and realities, choices of action, and discussions of how to implement action decisions. Business-related cases are available from Darden Educational Materials Services (DEMS) at the Darden School; from Harvard Case Services (HCS) at the Harvard Business School, and from the Ivey School in London, Ontario, Canada; and other sources, including the *Case Research Journal*.

To assist the students in their wrestling with these business cases, faculty often write and disseminate technical notes, which are short briefs of relevant theories, concepts, frameworks, and principles. We use these notes to avoid lecturing in class. We hold the expectation that students can read and determine in the process what is useful and what doesn't fit their experience. These technical notes help students get through the current literature more rapidly and consolidate thinking on a number of topics; they provide frameworks for the students to help them make sense of cases or a series thereof.

Students read these conceptual treatises and choose whether and how to apply them to any succeeding case that they may encounter. The case method avoids rote memorization for an exam's sake. The use of technical notes avoids "reinventing the theoretical wheel," a common criticism of case method, so that students can wrestle with the practical applications of current theory. Technical notes also give a flexibility that assigning texts doesn't; one can pick and choose the conceptual frameworks one wants to use without having to assign a book for each.

We desire to have students develop their own theories-in-use that will *stick with them* over time. Thus, although the technical notes tend to focus less on abstractions and more on practical applications, they are decidedly *not* atheoretical. The notes are filled with theories and portions of theories, concepts, and principles gleaned from multiple sources including the academic literature, our faculty's own research, and the faculty's practical experience in working in and consulting in industry. This book is derived in part from these technical notes.

The book also draws on the work of a wide range of scholars and authors in the field of leadership and managing change. There is no intent here to substitute for those primary sources but only to summarize where appropriate for those who want the core concepts without the supporting discussion and databases. Consequently, most chapters will have footnotes for further references that readers may pursue if they wish.

GENERAL ORGANIZATION OF THE BOOK

This book does not purport to present a summary of the various theories of leadership. Other volumes, notably Gary Yukl's *Leadership in Organizations* (Prentice Hall, 2002) do that task very well. Rather, my goal here was to present a set of practical principles of effective leadership as they seem to be emerging in these difficult times that mark the transition from the Industrial Age to the Information Age. I have included a section at the back of the book, however, that gives a very brief (usually one page or less) summary of some of the key points for a variety of current leadership theories.

The book generally follows the structure of the general leadership model (sometimes referred to as the diamond model because of its shape) presented in Chapter 3. This framework attempts to incorporate aspects of many previous leadership theories into a single, broad structure that can be examined in part or as a whole and provides the largest overarching theme of the book. This model includes four basic elements—self, task, others, and organization—and various relationships among them. All of these elements and their relationships appear in an environmental context and combine to produce a set of leadership outcomes.

Structure of the Book

The book follows the rough outline suggested by this diamond-shaped model. The first section introduces the major paradigm shift between the Industrial Age and the Information Age, the general model of leadership employed in the book, and some important concepts on ethical behavior in leadership. The second section focuses on characteristics of individual leaders that are important to positive leadership outcomes. The short, third section addresses strategic thinking and the importance of a prospective leader developing strategic-thinking skills. The fourth section explores the connection between the leader and the followers and introduces concepts of leading others and leading teams. The fifth section examines the importance of leadership as manifest in the design of organizations and their systems and of leadership in managing change. The book ends with a summary chapter and then some additional materials that include a workbook we often use in executive education seminars, some recommendations for additional reading, and exercises.

The end of each chapter contains a summary list of the principles of effective leadership introduced in that chapter. Some of these principles may not seem like principles. In general, I've included summaries and concepts as well as "if one does x, then y will occur" principle statements. Although this list may tally what I see as the important ideas in each chapter, they do not provide a substitute for engaging the logic and reasoning in the chapters themselves. Again, this is not about memorizing ideas but about considering leadership more deeply and how one might become better at it rather than know more about it.

The chapters also include a series of questions for readers' personal reflection. These questions are intended to help the interested reader reflect on the key ideas in that chapter. Taken seriously, these questions become a series of exercises from which one can learn more about oneself and one's leadership philosophy. They provide a gateway to a deeper level of thinking about leadership than simple reading might yield.

Themes in the Book

The major theme running throughout the book is what I call Level Three leadership. I describe how much of management for the last hundred years has focused on behavior, which I call Level One, to the exclusion of followers' values and basic assumptions, which I call Level Three. Level Three leadership can be taken generally as an attempt to get below the surface in leading and managing others. This effort, and it is an effort, means first, an awareness of some of the complexity of human behavior and second, trying to use that complexity to have a deeper, longer-lasting impact on those around you. It means thinking about how people think and about what they value and how that influences their behavior—much more than just telling them what to do. Throughout, I assert that effective leadership is Level Three leadership, aware of and able to deal with employees' basic beliefs and values.

To the extent that one works at influencing those basic values and assumptions, leadership has a markedly moral aspect. We find it difficult to discuss leadership with our students and executive program participants without addressing the ethical and moral overtones. The Darden School was one of the first in the country to require an ethics course in its MBA program and has long been a leader in ethical research and teaching in business. The Olsson Center for the Study of Business Ethics at the Darden School has been at the forefront of this field as well. The chapter on ethics and leadership summarizes some of the concepts and principles that we have used successfully for many years at the school and that relate powerfully to most people's intuitive understanding of what it means to be an effective leader.

A third theme in the book is the value of strategic thinking and its relationship to leadership. The book invites readers to become more strategic thinkers and makes the argument that without strategic thinking, people in leadership positions don't really have anything to say to their followers. This stretches the common view of leadership and invites students to develop a broader set of skills. It also implies another theme in the book.

A fourth theme that appears in the book is the integrative nature of leadership. We don't believe it is accurate or effective to talk about leadership in isolation; rather, any discussion of leadership must address questions of strategy, managing change, and ethics. For several years, our required capstone course in the MBA program was called Strategy, then Leadership and Change, and finally Leading Strategic Change. When one talks about leadership, one *has* to talk about strategy, managing change, and the ethical underpinnings of both. The reader will find here, then, forays into each of these areas as closely related to leadership. We do not say that these explorations constitute complete courses or examinations of strategy, managing change, or ethics by any means, but they are intended to signal clearly the interrelatedness of these four areas.

Finally, a fifth theme is a very personal one. Consistent with the notion of Level Three leadership, I invite the reader to engage the leadership process personally and to consider the demands and consequences of leadership behavior. I am more interested in contributing to those who want to work at *becoming better leaders* than in talking *about* leadership in the abstract. In our course work, we always include many descriptions of individual leaders that consist not only of their business activities but also of how they manage their lives and the balance between self, family, work, health, and social life.

Readers may ask if the principles presented here are not uniquely American and therefore generally not relevant to Europe, Latin America, Africa, and Asia. I can say only that having lived abroad in Hong Kong and Japan and having worked off and on over the years in South Africa, England, France, Australia, and Southeast Asia, the models, concepts, ideas, and thoughts contained here have proven to be stimulating and provocative for all those audiences. Certainly their application varies from country to country and from region to region. The goal has been to present ideas in a general framework that works like a four-wheel-drive vehicle, able to negotiate rough terrain in various parts of the world but rugged enough to stand the strain. For example, the concept of Level Three leadership, leadership that intends to influence followers' values, does not specify what those values might be, yet it does invite Asians, Latinos, Europeans, and Africans as well as North Americans to consider the potential impact one might have if one were able to connect with others at this deeper level. In this sense, I believe the framework introduced here to be sturdy enough to work around the world. So far, for me, it has.

WHAT'S NEW IN THIS EDITION

The second edition includes several new pieces. The chapter on why people behave the way they do provides a foundational model of human behavior that was missing in the first edition. The chapter on organizational charters expands some ideas only briefly introduced in the first edition. The chapters on strategy, resonance, leading others, leading teams, organizational design, and leading change have all been updated to include emerging research and perspectives. The workbook section includes new instruments for assessing leadership and team characteristics as well as a summary of leadership theory that has been added to give students of leadership a quick overview of the major perspectives out and about.

At the same time, the central thrust of the book remains the same: helping you explore your values, assumptions, beliefs, and expectations about what it means to be an effective leader—and suggesting ways to grow and develop your leadership skills. One of Jack Welch's leadership principles was "Control your destiny or some one else will." He implies accurately, I think, the need to understand the role of leadership in our society and, more important, to develop leadership skills in ourselves.

Acknowledgments

Many of my colleagues have contributed ideas and frameworks to the thinking that resulted in this book. Although the book draws on their experience, I wish to make it clear that I do not speak for them or presume to put words in their mouths. By teaching, consulting, and working together, we share ideas and approaches. I wish to acknowledge the tremendous impact these people have had on me. This list would include but not be limited to Alex Horniman, Bill Zierden, Eileen Hogan, Paul McKinnon, Jack Weber, Lynn Isabella, Robin Johnson, Jay Bourgeois, Joe Harder, Martin Davidson, Jeanne Liedtka, John Rosenblum, Ed Freeman, Sherwood Frey, Elliott Weiss, Robert Carraway, and others. To a large degree, the conceptual material contained herein is the product of being in their midst. Somehow, in that context, using the pronoun *I* seems inappropriate. I have learned too much from them and benefited too much from their experience to claim ownership of many of the ideas presented here. Early reviewers took exception to the use of *we,* so when it felt necessary to assert an individual point of view, I have used *I.* Any faults of the book and in the way the principles and concepts are presented lie with me; any conceptual strengths are the result of collaborative effort in an unusual community of scholars and teachers.

Can leadership be taught? I don't suppose it can in its entirety; surely some things are well developed or inherited by the time students arrive at college or graduate school or have spent 10 to 20 years in business settings. Yet our experiences with these materials, some of them over the last 20 years, suggest that students can learn a lot about what leadership is and isn't, can develop skills that will help them to be more effective in leadership situations, and can create plans that will continue this development after a course (long or short) is finished.

As you know, the literature on leadership is enormous and growing rapidly. If this book can distill some practical personal and professional leadership concepts and help students and practicing managers and leaders to develop a stronger desire to make a difference in society and to do that in a powerful, ethical, and Level Three way, then the book will have served its purpose.

In addition to my Darden School colleagues in general, I would like to acknowledge many people over several years who have contributed specifically to this project. I am grateful for their effort and contributions. First, thanks to Bill Zierden and Alex Horniman, who invited me to join this remarkable community and for their contributions to my life. Next, to Paul McKinnon, with whom I worked for three years and in conversations with whom this book was conceived. Doug Newburg, Curt Tribble, and Jeff Rouse have contributed enormously to my understanding of the principles of resonance and managing energy.

The work of secretaries and research assistants over the years may not be as obvious, so I'd like to thank in particular Mary Darnell and Barbara Richards, for unflagging support and assistance; Christine McCabe and Maki DePalo, for their help on various aspects of the manuscript; the Darden School editing department, including Steve Smith, Elaine Moran, and especially for this edition, Jenny Nowlen, for their timely work; and the Darden School and the International University of Japan for their support while writing. Most of all, I wish to acknowledge the consistent support and encouragement of my wife, Susan, without whose love and dependability and willingness to fill in elsewhere this book would not even have been possible.

James G. Clawson
Charlottesville, Virginia

About the Author

James G. Clawson is a professor at the Darden Graduate School of Business Administration, University of Virginia, where he teaches in the MBA, executive education, and doctoral programs. He has also taught at the Harvard Business School, Northeastern University, the International University of Japan, and in various countries as a consultant throughout Europe, Africa, Australia, Asia, and North America. Dr. Clawson earned a DBA from the Harvard University Graduate School of Business Administration, an MBA at Brigham Young University, and a B.A. from Stanford University. His areas of research include leadership, managing change, mentoring, management development, and career management, and he is an active consultant in these areas to a variety of public and private sector organizations.

Introduction

CHAPTER

1

The Leadership Point of View

The task of a great leader is to get his people from where they are to where they have not been. . . . Leaders must invoke an alchemy of great vision. Those leaders who do not are ultimately judged failures, even though they may be popular at the moment.

—HENRY KISSINGER

Anyone can take a leadership point of view. It doesn't depend on your title, level, or status in an organization. Whether you do or do not is up to you. Your title does not determine whether you will be a leader. To say that the people with the senior titles in an organization are its leaders is to misconstrue position with leadership. Clearly, a seniority invites a person to be a leader, but it does not guarantee that the person will fulfill that role. Many people with titles are not leaders, and many people without titles are strong leaders.

Society tends to regard people who occupy leadership positions as leaders. If one is president of an organization, we think of that person as the organization's leader. In fact, this may or may not be true. We've all met many people with leadership titles who were not strategic thinkers, who had little influence, and who weren't sure where they were going—or how to get there! Some of the most powerful leaders in history, for example, Mother Teresa, Jesus, and Gandhi, never held titular offices, yet they influenced millions of people. At the same time, some people holding powerful leadership positions were—and are—viewed as weak, ineffectual, and having little influence. In the private sector world, boards of directors are constantly reviewing and shuffling incumbents in senior management positions, looking for someone with strong leadership skills—and removing those whose track record did not, on some dimension, measure up.

Your point of view, in large part, determines your attitude about leadership. Many options exist for your point of view: that of a follower, an administrator, a bureaucrat, or even a contrarian. As we watch and listen to people, the point of view they are employing, whether consciously or not, becomes apparent. People who take the follower's point of view, for example, tend to ask questions like, "What do you want me to do?" "How will you measure me?" "What resources do I have to do the job?" "Can you give me more authority to match my responsibility?" or "Can you remove

TABLE 1-1　Language Cues of Various Points of View	
Point of View	*Language Cues*
Follower's POV	What do you want me to do?
	Will you give me more authority?
	I need you to clear the obstacles for me.
Bureaucrat's POV	That's not my job.
	I'll pass that on to so-and-so.
	Our procedures don't allow that.
	We've never done it that way.
	This hasn't been approved.
	I can't do that without my supervisor's permission.
Administrator's POV	What did they do last time?
	We've never done it that way.
	Let's see, what was the rule on that?
	How can we maintain our present position?
Contrarian's POV	That'll never work!
	We tried that before.
	That's a terrible idea.
	You won't be able to fund it.
	You'll never be able to do it in time.

the obstacles I face?" Bureaucrats tend to say, "That's not my job!" or "Our procedures require you to fill out this form." Table 1-1 provides more such examples. The language for each point of view is consistent with the underlying mental framework that the person takes toward the surrounding world. Perhaps you've heard some of these language clues in your daily experience.

THE LEADERSHIP POINT OF VIEW

The leadership point of view (LPV) is something different from these and consists of three elements:

1. *Seeing* what needs to be done
2. *Understanding* the underlying forces at play in a situation
3. *Initiating* action to make things better

I won't say that adopting and employing the LPV is necessarily easy, but I will say it is demanding and powerful. It demands broad, strategic thinking; careful analysis and insight; and planning mixed with lots of courage. It requires being willing to focus your attention, your efforts, and your time and energy (see Table 1-2).

SEEING WHAT NEEDS TO BE DONE

Most people rely on someone else to tell them what needs to be done. The problem with this approach is that eventually someone has to make that decision. How does one decide what to do next? What the priorities should be? These questions have no

TABLE 1-2   The Leadership Point of View
1.   Do you *see* what needs to be done?
2.   Do you *understand* the underlying forces at play?
3.   Are you willing to *initiate action* to make things better?

easy answers, and the truth is that some time, somewhere, someone has to say, "Well, let's go left instead of right." It may be that the higher-level people in some organizations have better information, better experience, and better judgment, and that they are better prepared to make those decisions. In my experience, though, this is not necessarily true. If a more senior position in an organization comes open, who will be chosen to fill it? Usually, the person perceived to have done the best job at the last level in the organization is the one who gets promoted. So we might ask, "When does one begin to take the leadership point of view, that is, to begin looking around and deciding what needs to be done and then exercising courage to get it done?" If you wait until you have a title that designates you as a leader, the odds are it's too late. You've spent too many years waiting for others to tell you what needs to be done to make a sudden professional and psychological jump to figuring that out for yourself— and others.

You may say, "Well, my boss has more data than I do." This may be true, but in today's world, it is increasingly less likely. Later, I'll introduce the notion of "infocracies," organizations empowered by access to business data through ever more sophisticated networks. Today, with the Internet, intranets, and other forms of mass media, we have access to oceans of information. The challenge is to develop the vision, perception, wisdom, and judgment to sift the information that is relevant to you and your organization, the information that contains implications for your future, from all that data and then to clarify and expose those implications for those around you. Your boss has no magic wand. She is faced, as are you, with scanning the environment, sifting through these oceans of information, and making choices about what's important and what's not. If you think you'd like more responsibility but you don't enjoy or aren't motivated to do this kind of mental homework, I invite you to rethink your ambitions. Leaders by their nature—and, I say, by definition—are charged with seeing what others commonly do not. This vision does not come overnight. It's the result of lots of reading, lots of scanning, lots of conversations, and lots of thinking. If you look around your work and cannot see what needs to be done to make the place a beehive of productivity and value creation, look again. And again. And again.

UNDERSTANDING THE UNDERLYING FORCES AT PLAY

One of the reasons the suggestions of junior- or middle-level people are dismissed is that they have made their proposals from a limited perspective and have not taken into account the broader issues that the more senior people have. This has been very apparent in some of my client experiences in which middle-level employees were called on to identify problems and offer solutions. The accepted proposals showed a more in-depth analysis of current conditions and situations and what aspects of the organization might be affected if these were changed. You cannot responsibly propose a new plant without considering the costs. You cannot propose expanding a facility without understanding local zoning regulations and the size of the local labor pool. Sometimes what seems obvious to one employee is sheer folly to another who sees the big picture. Leaders have to be continually broadening their vision and deepening their insight into the global, societal, market, competitive, consumer, and related issues that surround any organization. If they miss these or any underlying forces, their choices for what to focus on and what to do will be met with surprises, unanticipated obstacles, and probably failure. This is true also for senior people who have strong opinions not based on analysis. Sometimes subordinates must obey senior leaders while being convinced that their leaders don't see the whole picture. So the malaise of seeing less clearly or comprehensively is not limited to lower levels of an organization. Again, your title does not guarantee your leadership.

Can you ever understand all that is required to make informed leadership choices? Probably not. You can stack the odds, though, by doing your homework, by soliciting other viewpoints, and by developing your judgment as to what works and what doesn't. Leaders must operate in conditions of uncertainty, and that reality implies the need for even more careful analysis and ultimately for some faith and courage. The fields of risk analysis and quantitative analysis in business schools help leaders-to-be to assess conditions and think about alternatives and potential outcomes. And although paralysis by analysis is not a good thing, many would-be leaders merely shoot from the hip and hope for the best. If you take a real leadership point of view, you'll do what you can to ensure you understand what's going on in a situation before you jump in. Some Americans believe that the worst thing is to do nothing, but sometimes, if you understood what was going on, you would realize it was the best thing. Although inaction is often deadly, so, too, can be "Fire, Fire, Fire, Aim!"

INITIATING ACTION TO MAKE THINGS BETTER

The final aspect of LPV is the courage to initiate action to improve the situation. Again, most people are unwilling to do this. Perhaps it's because they are comfortable and don't want the hassle. That's one reason leaders make the big money: They do things that others cannot or will not out of fear of being criticized or hurt in some way. To adopt the LPV is indeed to put yourself in a crucible. Those who are comfortable with the current way of doing things will not like you suggesting changes, particularly if you're not seen as a leader. "Who are you to say?" they may comment. "What gives you the right?" If you've done your homework, you won't have to rely on that tired, old saw, "Because I said so, and I'm the boss." Instead, you can lay out your vision of why this is important (what you see) and explain why your solution addresses all the forces at play (political, economic, environmental, consumer, employee, etc.) and in the process persuade people to your way of thinking. This takes courage. Plain guts. What if you're wrong? You may be. What if they don't agree with you? I'm sure at least one contrarian won't! At that point the weight of real responsibility will settle on your shoulders and you'll know what it means to be a true leader, not just one in title alone.

CONCLUSION

Don't wait for someone else to tell you what to do, no matter what your level in an organization. Learn as fast as you can. Strive to open your eyes to see what needs to be done. Don't wait for someone to point it out to you. By then, it may be too late—as they announce either the closing of your division or the sale of your section or the outplacement of your department's services to a subcontractor. Look around. Look beyond your present circle of responsibilities. Devote time weekly to thinking about where your organization should be going. At a minimum, you'll be a much better conversationalist at receptions and in the hallway. More likely, you will come to be viewed as a person who goes beyond the current job, beyond the bureaucratic mind-set, to a proactive view of the business as a whole—the stuff of which leaders are made.

The times, as Bob Dylan wrote, are a-changin'. In some ways things are different, and in some ways they are the same. The next chapter will explore the challenges of these changes for leaders and would-be leaders.

2

The Changing Context of Leadership

Ten short years. . . . The one thing that we have done consistently is to change. . . . It may seem easier for our life to remain constant, but change, really, is the only constant. We cannot stop it and we cannot escape it. We can let it destroy us or we can embrace it. We must embrace it.

—MICHAEL EISNER, DISNEY 1994 ANNUAL REPORT

Things aren't what they used to be, especially when it comes to understanding what it means to be an effective leader. Most observers agree that there have been three major worldwide paradigm shifts in management: one caused by the prehistoric shift from hunting and gathering to farming, one caused by the Industrial Revolution, and one caused by the Information Revolution, which is now changing the way that we think about business, the way we organize to do business, and the problems and dilemmas that business presents.[1] The changes we face today are as significant as those experienced during those previous transitional phases.

Understanding and becoming effective in this emerging new context requires a fundamental shift in management thinking and modes of leadership. Principles of organization and leadership that worked well for the last 100 years are being replaced with principles based on new assumptions about people, economies, and how to organize. Understanding this new paradigm is essential to becoming a leader in the world of today leading to tomorrow. Many of the basic assumptions about leadership and management that you may have been taught earlier could be ill suited to the realities of business in the emerging information age. Your perspective on the world around you and the way in which you plan and execute your business will surely determine your success. If you don't understand these new realities, you'll be at a disadvantage compared with your peers and competitors.

Because we were all born in a world dominated by the bureaucratic mentality—filled with pyramidic organizations that operated on such principles as "one man, one boss," "follow the chain of command," and "success means climbing the corporate ladder"—it is often difficult to grasp and appreciate the nature of the changes taking place around us. Most of us learned the bureaucratic mind-set at an early age and have had it reinforced over years of experience. At one level, we see corporations combining and dividing, growing and dying, much as they have for a long time. At a second level, we can observe that the reasons for those combinations and divisions, for the growth and decline, are changing. And at a third level, we can begin to identify the fundamental differences underlying the belief systems supporting those causes. Although it can be difficult to see what's happening in the larger picture of today's world, if you are willing to extend yourself and perhaps to reexamine some long-held beliefs, you have a chance to add new concepts, principles, and ideas to your present skill sets that will enhance your efforts to lead. If you take that opportunity, you'll be a more effective leader.

If you understand the dynamics and implications of this turbulent transitional period between the Industrial Age and the new, emerging Information Age and can put your personal efforts at leadership in that context, you'll be better prepared for making the change, for understanding the seeming chaos about you, for influencing those around you, and for helping, not hindering, your organization's efforts to make the transition as well. And that's what this book is about: enhancing your ability to influence others amidst changing times.

HUNTER-GATHERERS

The hunter-gatherer era was dominated by our race's focus on food for survival. Tribes were relatively small and widely separated to allow sufficient territory for subsistence. Because all this happened before recorded history, we do not have detailed accounts of life and leadership among hunter-gatherer groups. We have learned a lot from archeological studies, though, and are able to infer some things about society among these small tribes. At about 11,000 B.C. a blossoming of human creativity, innovation, and population growth took place. Best-selling author Jared Diamond calls this transition the beginning of "farmer power."[2] When humans learned to farm, they no longer had to roam the countryside looking for food. Instead, by cooperating and concentrating their efforts, they could generate enough food to last them through the winter and with some to spare so that they could turn their attention to other pursuits such as music, art, religion, writing, tool making, and so on. Only a few moments of reflection is needed to imagine how the nature of leadership, the skills that would be respected, and the organization of the human groups changed dramatically then. Tribes could grow in size and complexity. Spare time would increase. Those with a seasonal perspective, with an understanding of horticulture instead of hunting, became leaders, and society was increasingly organized around stability and responsibility rather than bravado and daring. Well-known organizational theorists Paul Lawrence, Nigel Nicholson, and Rod White have written about these prehistoric roots of modern management thought.[3] Land ownership became an important feature of the new agrarian society, and this gave rise to the elements of aristocracy, the dominant management model, as written history emerged in the world.

ARISTOCRATIC SOCIETY

From the cultural bloom at 11,000 B.C. until the nineteenth century, much of society around the world was stratified according to the aristocratic model.[4] The word *aristocracy* comes from Greek and means "rule by the best"—which meant those born to noble families, that is, families who owned land—for farming. In Japan, for example, wealth was determined by the number of bags of rice (*koku*) one's land could produce. With few exceptions, societies around the world prior to 1800 assumed that royal birth meant royal abilities and royal rights to power and authority. One's birth determined one's likely standing in society, one's wealth, and one's ability to influence events. This meant that societal and organizational power and authority were distributed largely according to family lineage. The random process of birth selected the next generation's kings and queens and emperors and empresses. In the effort to consolidate power and authority, great houses in Europe and Asia sought alliances through political and military means as well as arranged marriages, hoping to bind their fortunes and build greater stability in society. Table 2-1 lists the major characteristics of the Aristocratic Age.

Structurally, the aristocratic model meant that certain families tended to rule and dominate the social and political landscape. At a second, mental level, it meant that people accepted the noble families being the rightful rulers as a matter of course. At a third level, the tacit, central assumption in the aristocratic paradigm was, practically speaking, "Father knows best." Royal fathers were the center of political and economic activity in most of the world. Fathers who were also titular heads of states, nations, and great estates made the decisions and the laws, arbitrated disputes, and administered justice and punishment. Fathers dreamed of conquest, alliance, or economic expansion and then established the funds for and recruited others to fulfill those dreams. Their sons—the princes—held hopes of ascending to the father's throne by right of primogeniture, which was recognized by the people for the most part.

The aristocratic model had many positive aspects. It gave stability to society because people knew their place in the world virtually from birth, and were molded and educated to accept and grow in that place. With enormous wealth and lots of leisure time, monarchs and royal families searched for interesting employment and entertainment. Artists, musicians, sculptors, and writers all benefited from this search and thus were able to add to the world's treasures. The aristocracies supported the development of some of the world's greatest literature, philosophy, art, and music.

Despite these good points, the aristocratic model had many disadvantages. It left millions of people feeling disenfranchised. Although many accepted their supposedly natural position as servants or subjects, others longed for a more fluid, free society. The revolutions for freedom and independence in the eighteenth century were manifesta-

---

TABLE 2-1   Characteristics of the Aristocratic Era

- Orderly society
- Limited information
- Limited transportation
- Homogeneous followers
- Limited opportunities
- Limited education
- Limited technological advances
- Male dominated
- Limited resources

---

tions of humankind's dissatisfaction with a model of society that was beginning to seem increasingly confining, unfair, and anachronistic. The aristocratic system tended not to recognize individual talents if the person possessing these talents was not in the proper class. It limited education to a few; inhibited the movement of talent into key positions in a multitude of organizations; inhibited the distribution of wealth in a fair and equitable way; and, perhaps most important, was not flexible enough to meet changing times. All of these factors contributed to burgeoning dissatisfaction among the underprivileged classes.

THE INDUSTRIAL REVOLUTION AND BUREAUCRATIC SOCIETY

The aristocratic model's limitations led to the political upheavals of the late eighteenth century, including revolutions in the Americas and France. Powerful as the political changes were, an equally profound but quieter change was gathering momentum. In the second half of the eighteenth century and the first half of the nineteenth century, the invention of the steam engine, the discovery of petroleum, and the development of mass manufacturing techniques for clothing, guns, shoes, utensils, and tools revolutionized the economic world. This transformation made a host of durable goods available to an ever-wider subset of the population and created a new, more powerful merchant class. The Industrial Revolution also caused a major shift in the nature of leadership in organizations as it became clear that the aristocrats could no longer keep up with the changes that were occurring or be counted on to provide the best leaders for the new organizational forms that were taking shape.

These realities, along with the increasing economic and political gaps between the noble class and the working classes, created a tension between the old system and the emerging new reality. Wars of independence in the United States, France, and Russia were the earthquakes that occurred along the fault line of this tension between the old and new ways of thinking and were symptomatic of an aristocratic paradigm giving way to a new worldview.

The Industrial Revolution forced a paradigm shift to a new model of management for society in which common people were given authority and power by virtue of their abilities and skills. The powerful positions in the new companies began to be occupied increasingly by people who were more familiar with the techniques of manufacture and wealth creation than the political and societal niceties of the elite. Power began to be distributed according to one's earned position, not one's birthright. The French word *bureau*—meaning "office"—was joined with -*cracy* to convey the novel idea that power was fixed to the office one held and not one's last name. This was a key difference between the old and new paradigms: power accrued to the office, not to the individual. Yet today, of course, vestiges of the aristocratic model still linger, although in both England and Japan as well as elsewhere, these remnants are under increasing scrutiny and are considered outdated and expensive residues of a previous world order.

A very important contributor to the notion of bureaucracy as we know it today was Frederick the Great, who needed to find quick and efficient ways of molding uneducated poor people into effective fighting units. His efforts to assign specific jobs to members of teams, to develop uniforms and systems of rank, and to centralize decision making all provided strong models for future organization designers.

This transition from the Aristocratic Age to the Industrial Age was a major paradigm shift. However, the word *shift* might imply a speedy change, whereas the process seems painstakingly slow when viewed from the vantage point of the span of a single lifetime; most people are born, live, and die in one dominant model. But when we look at the structure of society over several generations, paradigm shifts representing dramatic disruptions in the stability of society, including its patterns of thought and organizational forms, become clearly apparent.

Ironically, one of the best summaries of the new bureaucratic system was written by a man born into the highly cultured, upper middle class of Europe in 1864: the German sociologist Max Weber. By that time, the Industrial Revolution had been gaining momentum for almost a hundred years, so the world into which Weber was born was already largely industrialized. Weber summarized the key assumptions that represented a break with the aristocratic system and clarified the way that the bureaucratic system had already begun to take hold. In *The Theory of Social and Economic Organization,* Weber took great pains to describe carefully his view of the new *legitimate* authority as opposed to aristocratic authority. His writing was considered a milestone in describing the shift from aristocratic thinking to bureaucratic thinking because it clarified the view of what largely had already happened.

In describing the new bureaucratic system, Weber concluded that a new order of society was growing out of a widely accepted set of laws "which are formally correct and have been imposed by accepted procedure"[5] and were very distinct from the aristocratic view. The key components of this new idea of legitimate authority were

1. Legal norms or laws or rules are established by mutual agreement.
2. Laws should be equally applied to all.
3. People in authority occupy an office.
4. Members of societies or organizations obey the laws, not the whims of the office incumbent.
5. Members are free and owe obedience only to the impersonal order of laws, not to the individual incumbent.
6. Organizations and their offices have spheres of competence and authority and can compel people only within those bounds.
7. The offices in the organization are arranged hierarchically so that higher offices have more authority or legitimate power than lower offices.
8. Appointments to office should be based on expertise.
9. Reward for work comes in the form of a set salary. (Weber waffled a little here by noting that salaries should be related to a person's office *and* to their social status.)
10. Management should be separate from ownership.
11. Individuals do not carry rights of office; when they leave office, their authority is gone.
12. The authority of an office must be documented.
13. The incumbent of each office is subject to "strict and systematic discipline" in the control and management of his office.[6]

The institutionalization of the bureaucratic model produced enormous momentum and commitment throughout societies worldwide. Although aristocracies depended on the good health and skills of the heirs, bureaucracy allowed organizations to continue even without a particularly key family member or individual. Bureaucracy changed the aristocratic transfer of power by allowing nonfamily members to fill the offices of power subject to the rules of the organization. Hence, institutions could be created and continue in existence even though their individual members and surnames changed with time.

In bureaucracies, power and authority are distributed according to the office or the structural relationships of the offices in an organization. When promoted, one receives additional power, authority, and usually wealth. Decision making is often consolidated at the top of these organizations, and implementation of those decisions is assigned to the middle and bottom. Organizations have continued to come and go as they did in the aristocracies, and people have continued to think of the established organizations as the right ones, but the basic assumption underlying the bureaucratic model has been just a variation on the aristocratic model's third basic assumption: Rather than father knows best, the boss knows best.

Although similar to the aristocratic model in some respects, the bureaucratic model has expanded the range of individuals who could fill the power roles. As in the aristocracies, new bosses have been primarily men, but now not necessarily the sons of previous bosses. The new leaders have been better educated than others and often more experienced, thus lending a general credence to the underlying tenet that the boss knows best. Employees and middle managers in most bureaucracies have looked to the executive ranks for vision, guidance, control, encouragement, rewards, and information about the nature and status of the organization. Raw data has flowed up, analysis and decision making has taken place at the top, and instructions and orders have flowed down.

This common pattern has spawned a range of bureaucratic phrases such as "We don't pay you to think, just do it" and "That's on a need-to-know basis only" that have become common, everyday expressions for most of us. They have become a part of our everyday language, so much so that we seldom question them; we take them for granted as the way things are. This tacit acceptance, in fact, reflects the reality that the new paradigm had taken hold and is no longer thought of as a change.

Bureaucracies, which worked very well for over a century, have been a powerful influence and produced many positive changes. Talented people have had greater freedom of upward socioeconomic movement than in the aristocratic model. Bureaucracies have provided a structure for mobilizing large labor pools. The development of new industries has no longer been dependent on the whims of aristocratic individuals. Bureaucratic society as a whole has been more flexible to meet the challenges of changing times. Bureaucracies have dampened the effects of ignorance improperly promoted and, more important, have reduced the dissatisfaction associated with the aristocratic model (although bureaucracy supplanted aristocracy in many ways with a new resentment for those with "new" money).

Bureaucracies have also generated a stream of organizational research and theory building, much of it based on a desire to reduce the variance between job description and human performance. Much of Frederick Taylor's work on scientific management, along with the dominant leadership models of the bureaucratic era, revolved around finding ways to fragment, prescribe, and control human behavior.[7] The goals of management during these times included standardizing human behavior and minimizing variance in human work. It was, in Gareth Morgan's term, the "machine company."[8]

With bureaucracies, as with many systems, sources of historical success became the seeds of future decay. The system of assumptions and principles that formed bureaucracies have generated some unfortunate outcomes. The ability to continue business without a particular individual and eventually to create institutions as more or less fixed parts of society has led some organizations to focus more on survival as an objective of their existence, diverting their efforts from customer-service goals. Fitting people into predefined job descriptions has tended to alienate them from their work; to encourage a one-way, top-down communication pattern; and to discourage learning activities. In their worst form, some bureaucracies came to serve few if any beyond their employees. Bureaucracies have also allowed moderate or lesser talents to remain and hide within their labyrinthine structures. Sometimes, the new, prescribed legal order of things codified by Weber has blurred the view of good people properly promoted so that they couldn't *see,* much less contribute to, customer needs. Bureaucracies have also had the propensity to discourage creativity and entrepreneurial behavior in favor of low-risk, previously conceived and planned behavior. These problems of bureaucracies have come to the fore recently with a vengeance, as North American and European firms wrestle with their underlying principles in the face of technological breakthroughs and ferocious competition spawned by an emerging paradigm.

THE PRESENT PARADIGM SHIFT

Today, rapid change is the order of things. In many respects, this is a function of the turbulence caused by the move from the Industrial Age into the Information Age, but it also represents the nature of a society connected by instant information and ready means of travel. During the twentieth century, we saw the development of electricity, petroleum products and fuels, nuclear energy augmented by wind and sun, and unanticipated volumes of technological breakthroughs in chemistry, physics, machinery, genetics, biochemistry, miniaturization, nutrition, energy use, data transfer, computers, and hundreds of other fields. The pace of change represented by these breakthroughs and innovations seems to have accelerated in the last 50 years. Most managers agree that the relationship between time and change in our society is exponential (see Figure 2-1), that things are changing at an ever-increasing rate. Of course, no system can maintain an exponential rate of change, because eventually it approaches a vertical line, but during the transition period between the Industrial Age and the Information Age, the rate of change has been enormous.

The task of keeping current in any field has become overwhelming. There are more books to read, more theories to comprehend, more sensors creating more data, more observers drawing more conclusions, more TV channels, and more access to political, scientific, and socioeconomic situations than ever before. Citizens of many countries can watch at their leisure the inner workings of foreign governments around the world as they happen. Our ability to integrate the disparate tidal waves of information and new knowledge is overtaxed.

The implications of this information and change explosion for our generation and succeeding ones are many and enormous. Perhaps first on the list is the realization that although our parents may have had the luxury of continuing their careers in the same fields over the course of a typical 40-year career, our generation does not. We cannot expect to finish our careers doing the same things we started out doing. In almost every field, new materials, tools, theories, techniques, substitutes, and ways of organizing mean that *we must all be constant learners* or we'll soon be obsolete and out of work.

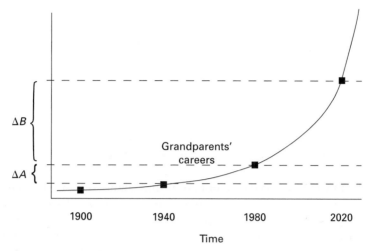

Exponential change over two 40-year career spans.

FIGURE 2-1   Commonly Accepted Rate of Change in Society

Now more than ever before, lifelong learning is critical to survival. Expect that whatever you learn now will soon be displaced and replaced and that you must be engaged in not passively but actively seeking to gain an advantage by learning more quickly than others. Reading, thinking, ingesting, digesting, pondering, struggling, skimming, researching, and investigating with a sense of urgency have become the *normal* way of life, the necessary means of keeping up. This is especially true in leadership, in developing the ways you think about and manage your influence on others.

A new framework for organizations that differs significantly from that of bureaucracies is emerging in response to these dramatic changes. Organizations are re-forming around information systems and the communication systems that support them. Power now is emanating from people who have access to and can digest volumes of information. As with the previous paradigm shift, this shift is not instantaneous, although it is happening much more swiftly than the previous shift from the Aristocratic Age to the Industrial Age. The causes for this new shift, like the last one, are rooted in technological change.

Many aspects of the new Information Age shape our thinking about organizations and leadership. In this new age, power revolves around the people who coordinate resources to meet customer needs. Information becomes the key competitive and managerial advantage, as markets and customer demands change much more rapidly than before. Companies such as Wal-Mart and BancOne have used information systems as powerful strategic weapons in building competitive positions that are difficult for others to assail. With increasing size and shortening time lags between customer orders and expected fulfillment, internal cycle times of product development and then of getting products to market are much shorter than before. These phenomena, in turn, mean that management can no longer know and understand what needs to be done at each interface between the organization and its environment.

Managers are turning increasingly to employees to get relevant data and to make decisions in order to respond to demands and challenges more quickly than bureaucratic structures would allow. This trend gave rise to a popular term of the late 1980s and early 1990s: *empowerment.* Organizations unable to wield bureaucratic structures effectively to compete are turning to their employees and trying to empower them to make decisions, to take responsibility for corporate results, and to show initiative in recognizing and solving the problems confronting their firms. Although this flattening of organizations is a natural outcome of the Information Revolution, many managers still see it as an isolated fad that they can choose to ignore or treat superficially; they don't understand the larger context in which these changes are occurring.

As information networks proliferate, the boundaries of any organization begin to blur; thus, recent writers have begun describing the emergence of boundaryless or virtual organizations that exist primarily in concept but whose edges or limits are hard to find. Large numbers of part-time employees, commingled computer systems that automatically place orders to stock shelves, and alliances between competitors and vendors of all kinds are examples of this emerging phenomenon in corporations. In an interview with *Industry Week,* Mike Malone, co-author of *The Virtual Organization,* described the redistribution of power that takes place in these new organizations this way:

> The biggest [example of the disappearing perquisites of power] is the position at the top of the corporate hierarchy on a permanent basis with levels of people reporting to you, that very set pecking order. In this sort of fluid organization [the virtual organization] a lot of that disappears. The idea of empowering the people out there on the edges of the company to deal with the suppliers and deal with the customers, you're stripping power away from yourself, but you're still retaining a lot of responsibility. And you have to know what's going on out there, but you may not have much ability to control what's happening because you have to trust those people to make the right decision. And it's a very difficult position to find yourself in. The trade-off is that managers always talk about how they wish they had more time to spend on being visionaries; well, now they're going to get the chance. Long-term strategic planning suddenly becomes the primary job of people at the top, along with holding this amorphous company together.[9]

One concern raised by these new, emerging organizational forms is the danger that employees will lose a sense of participation, of being part of a larger whole. If people don't see whom they work for and don't understand the larger picture of how their work fits into an ethereal, virtual organization, they may not be able to commit enough energy to contribute world-class effort. Effective leaders in these new organizations will be able to find ways to hold the people in these organizations together. Traditional kinds of organizational glue are becoming less adhesive. In this respect, many private sector companies are learning from nonprofit organizations, which historically have pioneered structures that deal with fluid employee roles and fuzzy boundaries.

Another symptom of this paradigm shift was the wave of de-layering or flattening of organizations in the 1980s and 1990s in which the ranks of middle managers were eliminated. Their very existence was a legacy of nineteenth-century railroad companies, which had a big impact on the rise of bureaucracy in general. They built multiple layers of management primarily to move information coming from many geographically diverse sources through the organization, processing it, refining it, summarizing it, and passing it on to the top. A decision was eventually made, which then traveled back through these organizational layers and was disseminated to the ranks.

Modern information systems are rapidly replacing these vertical organizational forms. Customers' use of similar systems in dealing with competitors also means that an organization doesn't have the time to follow that involved chain; rather, many organizations are learning to become instantaneously responsive. As a result, the need for a vertical hierarchy of decision makers is disappearing.

These pressures are turning more and more companies to experiment with and deploy empowered, team-oriented structures. As the middle levels are being cut out, people at lower ranks of the organization are gaining authority to commit the resources of the firm to meet customer needs. Not coincidentally, this trend parallels a similar one in the political realm, as so many countries recently have exerted their independence from former protectors and dictatorships. Centralized systems are breaking down all over the world as people at all levels are confronted with frenetic technological change, instant information, and the need to act.

As we saw in the transition from the Aristocratic Age to the Industrial Age, organizations are continuing to come and go and reform, so no new insight there. Further, most people are beginning to accept mentally the emerging reality that change is a fact of life and that the new, flatter organizations are the right ones (although many still resist this recognition). But at the third level, the newly emerging assumption about management is not that father knows best or that management knows best but rather that *people close to the work know best*. These are the people who know the key customer-serving processes best and who know what needs to be done to manage those processes to the best effect. Although some executives and managers who still adhere to the bureaucratic mind-set are resisting this realization, the de facto reality is that the power to make effective decisions is migrating to these key process contributors.

Organization designers are struggling to find structures that recognize and accept this new reality. Business executives in the nation's largest corporations are now talking about speed, boundaryless organizations, project teams, concurrent engineering, and the importance of listening rather than telling. In the late 1980s, for instance, Jack Welch, chief executive officer (CEO) at General Electric, initiated an enormous corporate change called "WorkOut" intended to help the business leaders of his divisions get in touch with the ideas and perspectives of people at various levels. As 1 of 24 national consultants hired to assist this effort, I saw how Mr. Welch was working to transform his company from an Industrial Age bureaucracy into an Information Age organization. Welch has not been alone in this effort as more and more of his peers in industry after industry have sought to do the same.

Everywhere there is a new interest in the key information-based processes that produce goods and services and in the organizational structures that support them. Enlightened corporate executives are examining how these processes work, and they are looking for ways to speed up the production and creative processes with higher quality *and* increased levels of customization to meet customer needs. Those who were raised in bureaucracies and are uncomfortable with the new context tend to be reluctant, recalcitrant, and resistant to understanding what they need to learn to be effective in the new surroundings.

One wonders what the emerging organizational forms of the Information Age (or as it's also known, the Post-Industrial Era) for distributing power will be called because they will not be bureaucracies. Although they will have some lingering bureaucratic characteristics, they will look more like neural networks. Whether they are called *team forms, empowered organizations, circles of influence, virtual organizations, infocracies, custocracies, boundaryless organizations,* or *fluid collections of processes,* they will be the face of the new paradigm. It may be that we will settle on Peter Senge's simple but powerful term, *the learning organization.*[10] For me, the term *infocracy* seems to capture the idea that information has become the basis of power in these new forms. It is not the family or the office but rather the information explosion that has caused the shift in the distribution of power in these new organizations.[11] Whatever the new approach is called, it will be characterized by widely distributed power and structures that recognize much better the value of all organization members receiving, processing, and making decisions from new and exploding oceans of information.

In these new structures, leadership power will migrate in what will seem to older managers like chaotic fashion to the people who are close to the key challenges of each organization and who have the talent and abilities to resolve them. Employees in surviving companies will ignore and avoid the historical, formalized ways of functioning; titles will become less meaningful, while relationships between people assigned to different areas or functions will become more so. Management will support rather than direct teams, and the artifacts of steeply stratified bureaucracies (like executive parking places, dining rooms, washrooms, suits and ties, isolated offices, one-way performance evaluation, and disparities between employee and executive compensation) will continue to shrivel and disappear. Organizational boundaries will continue to blur as vendors and customers alike demand and tolerate organizational representation, data, mainframe access, team membership, and influence on what used to be internal decisions. Alliances made possible by vastly superior communications will continue to grow in number around the world. The very notion of what is internal and external to an organization will continue to fade.

The paradigm shift from bureaucracy to infocracy has been described and predicted by many others, one of the first being Warren Bennis, who wrote an article entitled "The Coming Death of Bureaucracy" in a 1966 article in *think* magazine.[12] In it, he characterized bureaucracies as having well-defined chains of command, standardized operating procedures for dealing with virtually every contingency, divisions of labor based on specialization and selection, promotion systems based on technical competence, and high levels of impersonality when dealing with employees. Bennis went on to identify four threats that spelled their demise: rapid and unexpected changes, growth to the point that historical procedures would no longer work, increased complexity in modern technology, and growing discontent with the impersonality of management–employee relationships.

The new organizations replacing bureaucracies, Bennis wrote, would be temporary in nature and would shift rapidly to meet changing demands. He called them "organic-adaptive" structures. In them, employees would be highly motivated but would have less commitment to a particular work group because these connections would change rapidly. Organizational designs would evolve to the point that they would encourage play and creative thinking rather than repressing them as organizations struggled to keep pace with environmental changes. Today, as we watch the transformations taking place in organizations around us, we cannot help but be impressed with Bennis's prescience. Others have described this transition as well.[13]

Figure 2-2 offers a visual representation of the paradigm shift we have been discussing. The diagonal lines separating the three major paradigms described here are intended to show the gradual nature of the shifts; however, the shift from bureaucracy to infocracy will surely happen much more quickly than the shift from aristocracy to bureaucracy. New fuels and new sources of information will be key stimulants to the shift. The models used to distribute power in organizations are shown at the bottom of the figure along with their basic assumptions about who knows what to do.

The new information-based paradigm requires new thinking, values, systems, skills, and certainly kinds of leadership. Members in the new organizations also will have to develop broader ways of thinking about their work. No longer will they be able to say, "That's not my job," and expect to either have a job or a company that will survive. They will have to find ways of sending information from the bottom up while not replacing means of sending from the top down. Managers and employees alike will have to realize that every employee has something to contribute that may go beyond the formal job description. Less and less will leadership be an exercise in conveying the message, "Listen up folks, here's how we're going to do this!" We will have to think about inclusive answers instead of exclusive ones. We will learn to function with so-called fuzzy logic and and/also answers instead of clear logic and either/or answers. The employees and leaders who thrive in these new organizations will be comfortable with these less certain cognitive strategies.

The new paradigm also demands that leaders develop some novel core values and skills. The leaders of the future will have to place greater value on listening than on talking. Leaders will learn to value cooperation more than competition; talent, more than title; teamwork, more than individual effort and glory. They will have to

FIGURE 2-2   Management Paradigm Shifts in Human History

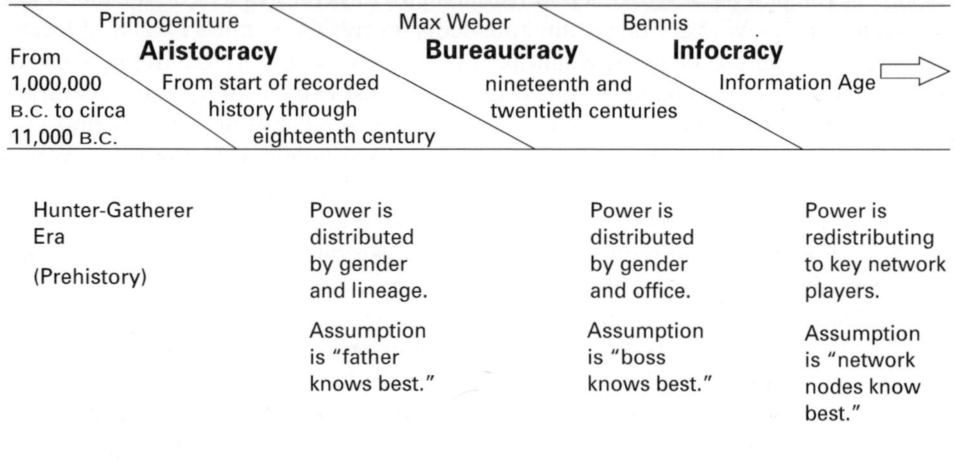

	Primogeniture	Max Weber	Bennis
From 1,000,000 B.C. to circa 11,000 B.C.	**Aristocracy** From start of recorded history through eighteenth century	**Bureaucracy** nineteenth and twentieth centuries	**Infocracy** Information Age ⇨
Hunter-Gatherer Era (Prehistory)	Power is distributed by gender and lineage.	Power is distributed by gender and office.	Power is redistributing to key network players.
	Assumption is "father knows best."	Assumption is "boss knows best."	Assumption is "network nodes know best."

value service to customers more than (but not at the exclusion of) profits and accept, deep down, the fact that customers come before profits, that profits come after customers, and that without customers there are no revenues or profits. Collins and Porras, in their soon-to-be-classic book, *Built To Last,* call this orientation "purpose beyond profit."[14] Many of us, striving for positions of leadership, will have to, as Davidow and Malone put it, "reverse our thinking": rather than trying to create customers for our present products, we will have to value and understand customer needs and then reorganize our firms to meet those needs more quickly and with higher quality than others.

The leaders in this new context will have to learn to value fixing things that aren't yet apparently broken. This is what Hal Leavitt means in part by introducing the notion that new leaders will create problems as much as they find or solve them.[15] The new leaders will value anticipation. They will value risk-taking. They will value new ideas. They will have to *develop a value for change,* a deep-seated belief in and trust in the change process, and an enthusiasm for embracing it. Hugh McColl, CEO at the (then) NationsBank, has taught the motto, "We will savagely embrace change."[16] It's a philosophy that effective leaders in the new paradigm will understand and live. They will have to relinquish their love of stability and control and the present distrust for surprises; they will learn to love learning, to love change, to love diversity, and to love the feeling of having to be alert and ever-present in order to see and respond to surrounding changes.

The emerging paradigm will also require the design and implementation of new organizational systems. Leaders will implement and experience new organizational forms, like the spaghetti organization in Denmark reported by Tom Peters.[17] They will implement spherical performance evaluations (which go beyond the groundbreaking 360-degree evaluations done in some companies now) performed by team members, subordinates, *and* customers and suppliers and community citizens, rather than single superior officers. These spherical evaluations will include relevant data from all who have stakes in a person's or a team's contributions to the organization. We will see working hours shift to meet the needs of customers and team members, not predictable working hours in our time zone as standardized by bureaucracies. We will see computer data links worldwide at all levels of organizations, not just at the pinnacles.

The new paradigm is dependent in many ways on speed of travel and of information transfer. Without these, the knowledge necessary to build loyal and trustworthy alliances and partnerships would break down. We will see increasingly sophisticated accounting and tracking systems that match cost causes with total costs rather than spreading costs across departments. We will see promotion systems that allow for changes in the strategic and competitive tactical demands facing firms. We will see recruiting systems that focus increasingly on social skills as much as or more than technical skills (which can be taught and developed more easily).

Infocracies will require new internal organizational skills. Employees and managers alike must be better at listening, eliciting, discussing, encouraging, recognizing feelings, influencing informally, persuading rather than commanding, using foreign languages and computers, focusing on customer-oriented priorities, and searching out causes. Paradoxically, they will be better at attending to more by attending to less, that is, by *focusing* in a way that one can see *more* of what is happening. The new paradigm will require employees and managers who are more facile at intercultural understanding and communication, better at seeing what people have to offer than what they look like. They will become more adept at sharing, at taking personal risks in order to model, at praising rather than criticizing, at helping rather than telling, and at observing—and when necessary, intervening in—processes. We must learn how to be patient up front to be more effective later on. More empathy is required—in other words, the ability to see the world the way others see it—and less sympathy, trying to solve others' problems with our own core of beliefs and values.[18]

The new leaders will be learners, people who are open to new ideas, who value change. The new leaders will be trustworthy, respectworthy, and changeworthy. They will value what others can do, and they'll know how to highlight and build on that. They will be clear on who they are and what they stand for, because without a central pool of guiding principles, the changes ahead of us would overwhelm. Unlike aristocratic and many bureaucratic leaders, they will be deeply respectful of the value and dignity of individuals in and near their organizations.

The new leaders of tomorrow will be able and eager to see ever larger pictures of systems within systems. They will respect the individual regardless of race or gender or religion for what she can do and how she does it. They will be designers and initiators, people who are always looking for a better way, always willing to fix things that aren't yet broken, but with a specific purpose in mind. The new leaders will be and/also thinkers instead of either/or thinkers.[19] The new leaders will be coaches and caretakers, teachers and students, workers as well as managers, and role models as well as instructors.

Timing is important in all of this. Trying to move too soon is as deadly as moving too late. Consider the Nash Metropolitan, a compact car designed for urban traffic and ease of parking, with lots of storage space, high gas economy, and sturdy construction. Unfortunately, it was introduced in the early 1950s rather than 1973 when the energy crisis taught people worldwide the value of such cars. The picture telephone was introduced about the same time but is only now coming into its own as a desired technology. Companies that succeed in the new paradigm will have a good sense of timing and will be able to take account of the parameters in their industries that either facilitate or inhibit the introduction of the new paradigm. Unfortunately, too often the usual error will be in changing too late, and the usual inhibiting factor will be senior or middle-level management.

CONCLUSION

The world is changing rapidly around us, and it's not going to slow down in the near future. Organizations are scrambling to invent new structures and systems to respond to these changes, and they are discovering that the changes are so profound that they require new thinking, values, skills, designs, and leadership. This book is about what that leadership might look like and the organizations that those leaders will design and implement. Our goal is that you will begin to prepare in earnest for the changes that you will encounter during your career and lifetime. The next chapter introduces a simple conceptual framework to help provide a structure for the book and help you to think about how to plan for and develop new skills of leadership.

PRINCIPLES OF EFFECTIVE LEADERSHIP INTRODUCED IN THIS CHAPTER

1. As the millennium turned, we were and are in the midst of a major paradigm shift in the way business is done, the way organizations are structured, and the way leadership works.
2. The Information Revolution is creating new organizational forms, *infocracies*, that are flatter; more dependent on fast, accurate information; demand more participation from all members; and must respond more quickly than ever before.
3. The Information Age demands new kinds of leadership that are substantially different from the leadership of the bureaucratic, Industrial Age.
4. Many leaders trained and experienced in the Industrial Age will find it difficult to let go of old leadership habits and to learn new ones.
5. Effective leaders in the new Information Age will understand and be masters of the change process.
6. Effective leaders in the new Information Age will be able to coordinate diverse sub-units of ethereal, boundaryless organizations that often defy description.
7. To be an effective leader in the new Information Age, one must learn new skills and develop new perspectives.

QUESTIONS FOR REFLECTION

1. What kinds of changes have you noticed in your work and organization over the last several years?
2. What role does accurate, current information play in your ability to do your job, to become a more effective leader, and to shape your organization in the future? How well are you able to collect, understand, and utilize that information?
3. Which people in your organization seem to be working on an old, bureaucratic paradigm, and which seem to be moving ahead with fresh thinking?
4. Where does your organization rank with its competitors in your industry in terms of moving into the Information Age? Are you ahead? In the middle of the pack? Behind?
5. What is your emotional reaction to the changes you see taking place around you? Do you feel threatened or invigorated? Why?
6. What would it take to get your organization moving firmly into the Information Age?

NOTES

1. Although there are many places where one can find support for this premise, one good one is Edwin C. Nevis, Joan Lancourt, and Helen G. Vassallo, *Intentional Revolutions* (San Francisco: Jossey-Bass, 1996).
2. Jared Diamond, *Guns, Germs and Steel* (New York: Norton, 1999).
3. All three authors presented papers at the Academy of Management 2000 meetings in Toronto. Subsequently, Nicholson has published *Executive Instinct* (New York: Crown Business Publishers, 2000), an exploration of our genetic tendencies in leadership. White wrote a paper with Barbara Decker Pierce entitled "The Evolution of Social Structure: Why Biology Matters" (*Academy of Management Review* 24, no. 4 (199): 843–53) explaining their thinking.
4. Human groups, like chickens with their pecking order and many other groups in the animal kingdom, always stratify themselves. We have yet to find a human group that is not stratified. The only question seems to be "along what criteria?"
5. Max Weber, *The Theory of Social and Economic Organization* (New York: Free Press, 1947), 131.
6. Ibid., 332–34.
7. Frederick Taylor, *Principles of Scientific Management* (New York: Harper, 1911).

8. Gareth Morgan, *Images of Organization* (Newbury Park, CA: Sage, 1986).

9. "Think in Reverse," *Industry Week* (July 19, 1993), 14. Interview with Bill Davidow and Mike Malone, authors of the book *The Virtual Organization* (New York: Harper Business, 1992).

10. Peter Senge, *The Fifth Discipline: The Art and Practice of the Learning Organization* (New York: Doubleday Currency, 1990).

11. James G. Clawson, "The New Infocracies and Their Leadership Implications," *Ivey Business Journal,* June–July 2000.

12. Warren Bennis, "The Coming Death of Bureaucracy," *think,* New York, IBM, 1966.

13. For example, see Gifford Pinchot and Elizabeth Pinchot, *The End of Bureaucracy & the Rise of the Intelligent Organization* (San Francisco: Berret Kohler, 1994).

14. James C. Collins and Jerry I. Porras, *Built to Last* (New York: Harper Business, 1994).

15. Harold Leavitt, *Corporate Pathfinders* (Homewood, IL: Dow-Jones Irwin, 1986).

16. From a private conversation with a NationsBank executive.

17. Tom Peters, *The Tom Peters Seminar* (New York: Vintage, 1994), 29.

18. Jim Collins, *Good to Great* (City: Publisher, 2001).

19. See, for example, Charles Handy, *The Age of Paradox* (Boston: HBS Press, 1995).

3

General Model of Leadership in Organizations

A Diamond in the Rough

In a learning organization, leaders are designers, stewards, and teachers. They are responsible for building organizations where people continually expand their capabilities to understand complexity, clarify vision, and improve shared mental models–that is, they are responsible for learning.

—PETER SENGE, *THE FIFTH DISCIPLINE*

The chief executive officer of a Fortune 500 company realizes that the way his company has been managing its hundreds of thousands of employees isn't working anymore.

The woman in charge of a major telecommunications company seeks to revise the culture of her firm so that it can compete in the next century.

An Asian member of a global project team developing a new product worries that the approach the team is taking won't work.

A single parent facing evening responsibilities wonders how to manage homework and "life's lessons" conversations with headstrong teenagers.

Each of these people faces a similar set of challenges. They are surrounded by a turbulent environment as described in the previous chapter, they need to find ways to influence people who may not be interested in being influenced, they operate inside of structures that have a history and a momentum, and they need results. Each of these people needs to find ways of developing influence. Although the scope of their influence varies widely, many of the characteristics they need to develop are the same. Together, they all need to become more effective leaders. It would help if they had a relatively simple, generally applicable, and powerful model of what leadership is and how to go about improving their leadership abilities. Finding this model may not be easy; there are many to choose from.

Many studies over the last 100 years have focused on various aspects of leadership. Some have looked at the traits of well-known leaders in various fields in an attempt to find the commonalities among them. When this effort led to a list of traits several hundred items long, researchers focused on the fit between leaders and the situations they were in, resulting in the so-called contingency theories. Recently, writers have commented on the importance of values, the ways in which women lead, the importance of leadership that recognizes diversity, and the relationship between leadership and a firm's strategic challenges. As we move into a new millennium, we need a model of leadership that takes an eclectic approach, including the major leadership principles we've discovered in this century and yet providing for a powerful, flexible application of those principles in a range of settings. This chapter presents such a model.

Why would we need yet another model of leadership? Well, first, it's clear that we live in a rapidly changing world that needs leaders at every level of society— international, national, local, neighborhood, and family. We need leaders in businesses at all levels regardless of their overall size. We need these leaders because until we all become perfectly and uniformly able to perceive the meaning of present and future events clearly and to act on them effectively, leaders help us to see things differently, to organize our efforts, and to accomplish tasks that we might not be able to accomplish otherwise. Yet the various leadership models available seem to omit various aspects of leadership that one needs to consider in today's environment. Some emphasize individuals; others emphasize situations and coworkers; others emphasize strategies; and still others, organizational design. We need a model that can allow for all these various aspects of leadership. The one presented here is more of a Jeep than a Cadillac, designed for flexibility, rough terrain, and alternative explorations and tough enough to take the impact of various settings and circumstances.

If you have read this far, you must be somewhat interested in leadership and presumably in becoming a leader. This is not true for everyone. Some people don't think of themselves as organizational leaders. They feel uncomfortable trying to influence others, too shy, or more interested in doing work than in getting involved in office politics. Let me suggest an alternative way to think about this question, and that is to ask whether you'd like to have more positive influence on those around you. You may be thinking of thousands of employees, a few team members, colleagues in a professional firm, other citizens on a local committee, or members of your family. If the answer to that question is yes, then you can learn something here that will help you develop that influence. *Leadership* is not a dirty word. It simply means seeing what needs to be done, understanding the underlying forces, and then having enough courage to do something about it. If you have a flexible but powerful way of thinking, a robust mental model about developing influence, your efforts will be more effective.

LEADING STRATEGIC CHANGE

Our model begins with a key concept: Leadership has meaning only if it has a direction and a means of achieving that direction. In other words, leadership without a strategy is aimless, and leadership without the ability to manage change is powerless. To address leadership, one must address the questions of strategic thinking and of managing change. In essence, leadership is really about leading strategic change. So, if we begin with the leader or leader-to-be, the first question this person needs to answer is "Leadership for what?" That is the strategic question. Once the person has developed that answer, the next question is "How can we get there?" And this question usually involves two domains: others, that is, the potential followers, and the organization or the setting in which the leader and the followers work. One way to diagram this three-way view is shown in Figure 3-1. The potential leader must address all three initiatives or vectors to solve her fundamental problems of "what?" and "how?" These three directions of attention, if you will, provide the basis for our comprehensive, four-wheel-drive sport utility vehicle model of leadership. Thus, although we speak of leadership, of strategy, and of managing change, we could also speak of—and, I argue, *should* speak of—leading strategic change as a more comprehensive concept. How these domains overlap can be simply shown as in Figure 3-2.

FIGURE 3-1   Three Key Leadership Initiatives

FIGURE 3-2   The Interrelated Domains of Strategy, Leadership, and Change

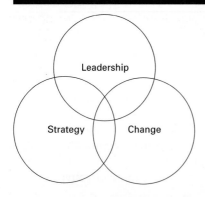

KEY ELEMENTS OF LEADERSHIP

With these three leadership initiatives in mind, we can see the fundamental elements of a model that they imply. First, there is the leader; second, strategic tasks to work on, selected from among all the possible tasks one could do. The tasks a leader chooses to focus on are influenced, as are all the elements in the model, by environmental forces. These include labor markets, the economy, political forces, and other influences in the world. Third, there are others, people whom leaders attempt to influence; and fourth, organizations, in which most work in the world is done. Aligning these along our initiatives, we get a model that resembles a diamond as shown in Figure 3-3. The northern ball is the individual leader and his characteristics. The eastern ball is the set of tasks that leader has chosen to address. The north–east axis represents the leader's strategic-thinking methods. The western ball is the target audience, the people whom the leader intends to influence. The north–west axis represents the methods of influence that the leader employs. The southern ball is the organization with all of its characteristics, including structure, systems, and culture. The north–south axis represents the leader's design methodology, how he creates and shapes the organization in which they work.

Our basic model contains some other elements. The east–west axis between the others and the task represents the view that the employees of the organization have of the leader's strategic goals. If the leader is clear on strategy and effective in communications, this axis will be strong. However, if the leader has either weak strategy (and therefore, nothing to communicate) or weak influence on the others, they will probably not see the leader's vision, and the east–west axis will be broken.

The south–west axis represents the bond between the employees and the organization. This relationship might be a mercenary one in which employees simply exchange

---

FIGURE 3-3 The Diamond Model of Leadership

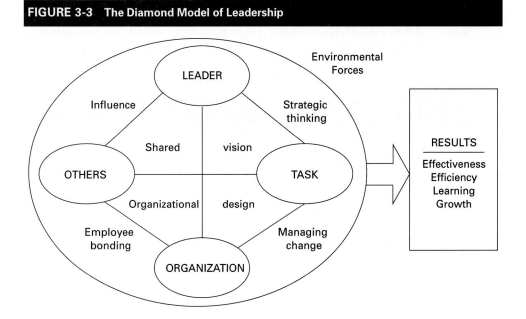

time and talent for money, or it might be a committed relationship in which employees are highly invested in the organization. The organization's various systems and their impact on employees will have a big influence on the connection between employees and the organization, hence the importance of leaders as organizational designers.

The south–east axis represents the connection between the organization and the leader's strategic objectives. In a rapidly changing world like the one described in the last chapter, strategic challenges will be constantly evolving. Because it takes time to design an organization and then create that design, there is, almost by definition, a constant gap between the current organization and the current strategy. This highlights the need for constant management of change. I find that this model-based explanation goes a long way to help people understand why management keeps making so many changes: The changing world demands it.

The relationships among these four basic elements point out that leadership is not just a result of any one of them but of how all of them work together. In other words, leadership is not just about the qualities of the leader: One must consider the strategy envisioned, the relationships with the followers, and the organizational context in which the leader will attempt to influence those followers. In this view, leadership is the result of a confluence of the characteristics of these four main domains and of the relationships between and among them, a total of at least 11 essential factors. Each of these factors, the four basic elements and their relationships, as much as the traits of any potential leader, will influence the outcomes of a situation and help determine whether there will be positive results. Let's examine each of the elements in greater detail.

The Leader

Clearly, the leader, the person—*you*—have characteristics that will influence your ability to create a successful leadership outcome. Each individual leader brings to a situation a variety of personal characteristics including preferences, skills, values, goals, education, interpersonal style, and psychological makeup. These attributes shape the leader's abilities to observe, to make sense of and deal with the environment, to understand and relate to followers, to manage change, and to define and work toward a goal. Many leadership theories focus on individual characteristics, but the approach here is that what you bring to the situation is only one—albeit an important one—of a set of factors that will affect its outcomes.

A number of models and assessment instruments have been designed to outline the characteristics of effective leadership. As mentioned earlier, leadership researchers gave up on the trait model after the number of relevant traits exceeded several hundred. However, many companies still routinely develop what they call leadership competency models, lists of traits felt to be important in their particular culture. Some companies use their own assessment instruments; others use off-the-shelf assessment instruments to try to identify an individual's leadership profile and its appropriateness for their organization. The Center for Creative Leadership in North Carolina probably has the largest leadership-focused database. It is able to compare an individual profile with the thousands it has on file. Jim Collins suggests two essential characteristics: dogged determination and humility.[1] Yet no matter who you are as a leader, the question remains: "What do you think we should do?"

Task: What Should We Do?

The individual leader's view of the tasks, of what the organization should be working on, sets the agenda for an organization and is critical to the leadership outcomes in that situation. One way we often introduce this issue in executive education groups is to ask, "What are the strategic challenges facing your organization?" Group answers to this question point out how consistently or inconsistently employees see the tasks that face them. Clearly, one leader's view of those tasks can vary from another's, and outside observers may see yet another set of tasks or challenges that the organization ought to be addressing. An individual's ability to read and assess what is taking place around her guides her conclusions about what is important and what the organization could and should do. This vision of what needs to be done, what can be done, or what should be done will shape virtually all of the leader's behavior and, thus, the agenda for the rest of the organization. The vision a person has of the challenges facing an organization are clearly a function of that person's vision and of the "realities" facing the organization. I put the word *realities* in quotes because those issues only become realities when leadership recognizes and places priority on them.

Depending on what the leader sees, on what the leader believes he can do, and how the leader behaves, the situation might be transformed from a no-change situation into one in which dramatic and positive things begin to happen. Leadership has a lot to do with sensing, seeing, and appreciating what is taking place around one, with seeing what tasks should be addressed. But, of course, no leader can do this alone.

Others: Working Together with Followers

Leadership doesn't happen without followership, so any map or model of leadership must include the others, or followers. The leader's employees and colleagues also bring to the situation a set of characteristics, values, preferences, experience, skills, goals, educational background, and concerns. Environmental pressures affect them as well as the leader but perhaps in different ways. Their personal and collective characteristics help determine whether the leader will be able to develop an influential relationship with them, and the quality of that relationship will in turn do much to determine whether the followers will develop a view of the tasks facing the organization similar to that held by the leader. If the others don't trust or respect the leader, it will be difficult for them to develop commitment for and energy to work on the leader's view of what can be or should be.

Organization: Designing the Right Context

As the leader and employees develop convergent views of what the firm should be doing, the organization's structure and the systems that hold it together become increasingly important. The organizational context can either enable the leader and the employees to move ahead on their objectives or constrain them from realizing their vision. If the organization's structure and systems do not fit the demands of the task that has been defined, the organization and its leadership will be at a severe disadvantage. Effective leaders are constantly working with questions of whether the organizational context is favorable to the task or mission they have defined. Stan Davis, in his book *Future Perfect*,[2] asserts that all organizations are obsolete by definition because of the time lag between the development of a strategic vision and the implementation of an organization to work toward it. By the time the organization is in place, especially in a turbulent environment, the strategic picture has changed, and the organization must itself change to try to keep up. Peter Senge reinforces this message with his concept of the learning organization in *The Fifth Discipline.*[3] Unless one has developed a learning organization, he notes, it will be unable to keep up with the rapidly evolving world as we now know it. Similarly, if the employees' attitudes and abilities are not matched to or aligned with the organization's systems and structure, their efforts to achieve the goals of the firm will be diluted and diffused.

The Environmental Context

All leadership situations occur within an environmental context that includes political and legal forces, labor market realities, financial vicissitudes, increasingly diverse demographics, advancing technology, investor inquiries, and competitive pressures, among other things. Although these forces are often overlooked or only given cursory attention, they impact all other elements of a leadership situation, individually and in concert. Effective leaders are adept at scanning and interpreting these external forces and their impact. The previous chapter described the importance of these environmental changes in setting a context for one's attempts to lead or influence others.

RESULTS: OUTCOMES OF LEADERSHIP

In the end, leadership is about results, about outcomes, which might include effectiveness, efficiency, growth, learning, and morale. Effectiveness is an important outcome measure because it tells us whether we've accomplished our purpose. Effectiveness measures might include profitability, new product development, client studies completed, and so on. Efficiency is a useful measure because it reminds us of the costs associated with every outcome and encourages a consideration of the value of the cost–benefit perspective. Growth and learning are indicators of health. If the people and the organizations in the leadership situation are not larger and better educated as a result of the leadership experience or not feeling engaged in and feeling rewarded by it, we might question the effort's value. Selecting the right measures of leadership situation outcomes becomes an important issue in and of itself. Many companies have recognized the value of a "balance scorecard" set of result measures that recognizes the importance of market relationships, internal efficiencies, and learning and growth as well as financial returns.[4]

RELATIONSHIPS ARE THE KEY

The four basic elements—the leader, a set of strategic challenges or tasks, the followers, and the organization—set in an environmental context, form the key building blocks of leadership outcomes. But although these elements' characteristics provide the basic raw materials of a leadership situation, it is the *relationships* among them that determine how it will all turn out. Consider again the diamond-shaped model shown in Figure 3-3.

The north–east axis, the line between the leader and the task—the challenges facing the organization—represents the relationship between them. This relationship is the substance of what the leader sees as critical and forms the crux of his vision of what the organization should be doing. If this axis is broken (that is, if the leader has not developed a vision of what needs to be done and set some priorities for himself and the organization), the leader has no purpose, no direction, no outlet for attempts to lead or influence. In short, a leader cannot get somewhere if he doesn't know where he wants to go. The relationship between who the leader is and the array of tasks from which the leader may choose defines the leadership agenda, what the leader will choose to focus on and work on.

The north–west axis, the line between the leader and the others, represents the relationship between them. We can analyze and examine the quality of those relationships and determine if they are healthy or broken. If they're broken, that is, if the leader doesn't have influence with the followers, no matter how clear the vision (the north–east axis) is, not much in the way of leadership will happen.

The south–west axis, the line between the others and the organization, represents the quality of their connection. If this relationship is basically a mercenary one in which people trade time and talent for money, it will be more difficult to lead toward world-class performance, for instance, than if that relationship is a committed one in which the systems and processes of the organization encourage a deeper attachment to it.

The south–east axis, the line between the organization and the task, represents the match between the various aspects of the organization (structure, systems, processes, culture, etc.) and the strategic challenges it faces. If the organization is ill structured to meet those challenges, creating a positive leadership outcome will be difficult.

The east–west axis, the line between the others and the task, represents the view the followers take of what they are trying to do. If there is a gap between what the leader sees (the north–east axis) and what the followers see (the east–west axis), a positive leadership outcome will be hard to achieve. If the leader's view of the task and her relationships with the followers (the north–west axis) are strong but the east–west link is broken, again, a positive leadership outcome will not be an easy thing to accomplish.

Finally, the north–south axis represents the leader's connection to the organization. If the leader's style and skills don't match the way the organization is formed, one or the other will have to change. If the leader is a good organizational designer and a master of managing change, this axis will be strong. If the leader comes from the outside and has a style that is at great variance with the characteristics of the organization, a positive leadership outcome is unlikely to result. I've seen a situation where an outside leader came in and was clearly at odds with the culture, structure, costing systems, and other features of the organization, and even though he was hired to make changes, the organization eventually rejected him as a body might a poorly conducted transplant.

Each of the circled elements portrayed in Figure 3-3, including the environment that surrounds the whole of it, has a variety of features or characteristics that affect the outcome of the leadership opportunity. Leaders who ignore any of them may not get the results they hope for. Further, understanding the relationships between and among those elements is essential to understanding leadership.

Margaret Wheatley, in her provocative book *Leadership and the New Science,* makes an important point:

> One evening, I had a long, exploratory talk with a wise friend who told me that power in organizations is the capacity generated by relationships. It is a real energy that can only come into existence through relationships. Ever since that conversation, I have changed what I pay attention to in an organization. Now I look carefully at how a workplace organizes its relationships: not its tasks, functions, and hierarchies, but the patterns of relationship and the capacities available to form them.[5]

Although Wheatley is speaking of human relationships, I'm convinced that the observation holds as well for the relationships between elements of the diamond model outlined here. The connections are where the interesting insights into leadership effectiveness lie.

HOW THE DIAMOND MODEL RELATES TO OTHER MODELS OF LEADERSHIP

The diamond framework presented here is flexible enough to incorporate many of the features of the main leadership models out and about today but in a way that is simple and useful for the practicing manager. The diamond model allows a focus on the leader's individual characteristics, giving room to include the useful elements of the great leader theories, as well as on leader–follower relationships. It also contains a strong contingency flavor in that it asserts that the fit between the leader and the surrounding situation is a critical part of a positive leadership outcome. The model includes the importance of leaders as designers in shaping the organizations in which they attempt to influence. Although the model doesn't give all of the details related to each element or of the relationships that connect them, it does point out the key areas of attention that leaders need to be aware of and understand.

LEADERSHIP POTENTIALITIES

Leadership situations or opportunities can be viewed from another important perspective. Margaret Wheatley notes that every situation in relationships and in organizations can be seen in a number of different ways, and in fact, the way one views the situation can determine its outcomes. Wheatley compares these organizational or relational situations to photons, the tiny particles of light that emanate from the sun. Photons are remarkable in that how you look at them determines what you will see. If you conduct an experiment that tests to see if they are waves of energy, they look like waves of energy. If you look at them expecting to see tiny particles of mass, you'll see tiny particles of mass. Physicists speak of photons as having different *potentialities;* that is, they have the potential to be seen as energy or matter.

Like photons, each leadership situation contains a myriad of potentialities. Which one will emerge depends on how the people in that situation see, understand, and behave in that situation. This makes leadership that much more important. If a leader is able to see a different potentiality in a situation than others do and to convince them of the possibilities, then a different outcome may result. This view is consistent, by the way, with long-understood and accepted perspectives on how humans create their own realities. We know that people filter what they see and accept from all of the sensory stimuli that surround them. That filtering process determines what people will pay attention to and spend their energy on.[6] The potential leader's challenge is to see various potentialities rather than one or two and to find ways to help those potentialities come to life.

Our basic model allows for that variety of potentialities. One can see the situation from the eyes of the leader or the eyes of the followers, from the context of the organizational structure and other systems, from the point of view of the various tasks that lie ahead of the organization, and so on. Depending on what one sees and where one focuses one's energy, one can envision and perhaps create many different leadership-based outcomes to almost any situation.

LEADING ETHICALLY

I have already said that leadership is not an isolated phenomenon but rather occurs in connection with other aspects of organizational life, namely, strategy and managing change, and that these three domains are all part of the same overall phenomenon. We must add ethics to that picture.

Every leadership situation is an ethical situation. Leadership involves the use of power and influence, and this fact raises a long series of questions about when, how, and why one seeks to gather and to exercise this influence. Who agrees it is one person's right to influence others? Who decides what kinds of influence are acceptable? How do the followers view the leader's efforts to influence them? Is it right or wrong for the leader to do this? Do we have the right measures for assessing the outcomes of attempts to lead? Who decides that? To what extent do we attempt to influence our environment or allow it to influence us? Figure 3-4 shows how strategy, managing change, and ethics might map onto our general leadership model.

THE DIAMOND MODEL AND WHAT CHIEF EXECUTIVE OFFICERS DO

If the diamond model is an accurate depiction of leadership activity, it should correspond well with empirical studies of what leaders do. An important corroboration of this idea comes from a study by Farkas and Wetlaufer as reported in the *Harvard Business Review*.[7] The authors gathered data on 160 chief executive officers (CEOs) of major companies on several continents and concluded that they used five basic leadership foci: strategy, box, human resources, change, and expertise. The strategy CEOs emphasized the importance of setting a strategic direction for their firms. The box CEOs focused on building organizational control systems and measurements that defined what employees could or could not do. The human resources CEOs focused on building human relationships and developing mini-CEOs through their relationships. The change CEOs centered their attention on managing change in their organizations in an attempt to keep them current with their environments. And the expertise CEOs

FIGURE 3-4 **The Overlap Between the Diamond Model and Other Business Disciplines**

focused on developing particular skill mastery in their organizations to create a competitive advantage.

These modern CEO styles map easily onto our general model as shown in Figure 3-5. The strategy focus aligns with the north–east axis in the model. The human resource focus corresponds with the north–west axis. The box approach parallels our south–west axis, and the change approach gives attention to the south–east link (redesigning the organization so that it fits the demands of the strategy tasks chosen as priorities). The expertise approach maps onto both the north–south and the north–west axes because these CEOs built expertise into their organizations. This high degree of overlap suggests that the diamond model of leadership is flexible enough to relate to and help explain the skills needed in leadership situations as defined and implemented by chief executives all over the world.

Leadership is the ability and the willingness to influence others so that they respond willingly.

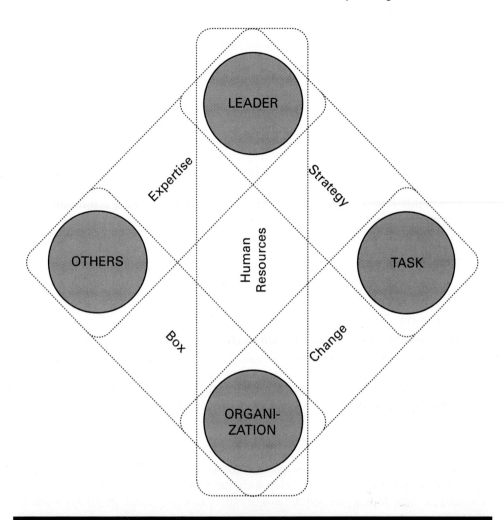

FIGURE 3-5   **The Relationship Between the Diamond Model and Wetlaufer's Model of Leadership Types**

BASIC DEFINITIONS

All of this modeling is fine and good, but in the end we need a short, clear definition of what leadership is and how it works. Models help us think about leadership; the words we use to define it reveal what we mean by the building blocks of those models. Earlier, we said that the leadership point of view consisted of seeing what needs to be done (the north–east axis), understanding the underlying forces (analyzing all of the elements in our model), and initiating action to improve things. Let's add to that perspective by establishing some working definitions. First, I assert that *power* is the ability to make something happen. Power in organizations is the ability to get others to do what you want them to do. There is nothing fancy about this definition; it simply states that when you make a change in something, you are exerting power in that thing. This definition is similar to the physics definition of work, mass times acceleration. If you exert power, you get something done; you move a person, an organization, a project from here to there.

Leadership, I say, is something different and has three key components. *Leadership* is first, the ability to influence others; second, the willingness to influence others; and third, the ability to do that in a way such that they respond willingly. Unless a person chooses freely to respond, it's not leadership. Thus, although leadership includes the use of power, not all uses of power are leadership. Consider the three components of this leadership definition.

First, there is the ability to influence others. This can be taught. In fact, in *The West Point Way of Leadership,* the author notes that one West Point commandant once said that he could make a leader out of anyone who was not a schizophrenic.[8] People learn their influence tactics relatively early in life. Perhaps they learned that whining or bullying or asking or persuasion will get them what they want. Whatever approach we use, we have learned those tactics over the course of our lives. Sometimes they may work; other times they may not. Politicians have become masters at this domain of study and art.

Visioning, Commitment, and Management Skills

The ability to influence others could be clustered into three areas that we could collectively call VCM: visioning; garnering the commitment of others; and monitoring, measuring, and managing progress toward the vision. The visioning cluster includes gaining a historical perspective, identifying trends in the present, and perceiving their outcomes in the future; a concern for what might be and could be; the ability to identify signposts along the way that point one way or another; and in some sense, the ability to dream, to see clearly a picture of the future you'd like to see and to articulate that to others.

The skills that cluster around garnering the commitment of others include your communication style, patterns, and abilities; your level of trustworthiness and the quality of the relationships you develop with others; and the ability to listen, to understand, and to respect the goals and dreams of others so that you can find ways to match them with your own.

And the monitoring, measuring, and managing skills cluster includes the ability to design and follow significant measures of what you're trying to accomplish. These are necessary if the organization begins to drift from your vision. They also help you to praise and to celebrate those who are contributing to progress toward the goal.[9] This tripartite view of leadership skill development is shown in Figure 3-6. Each of these skill clusters includes specific behaviors that you can learn. If you wish, you can, by studying these skills and practicing them, increase your ability as a leader. Whether doing so will have the desired effect depends on some other factors that we'll discuss later.

The second element of our leadership definition is willingness. Some people with the ability to be leaders choose not to exert influence for a variety of reasons. Sometimes it's because they are uncomfortable being in the center of the stage, laying out their thoughts and beliefs for others to see and accept or reject. Sometimes their reluctance is based on an ethical belief that self-determination is paramount above all else. Regardless of the reason, each of us has to decide whether we will accept or seek leadership responsibilities. Steve Covey writes about "circles of influence" and "cir-

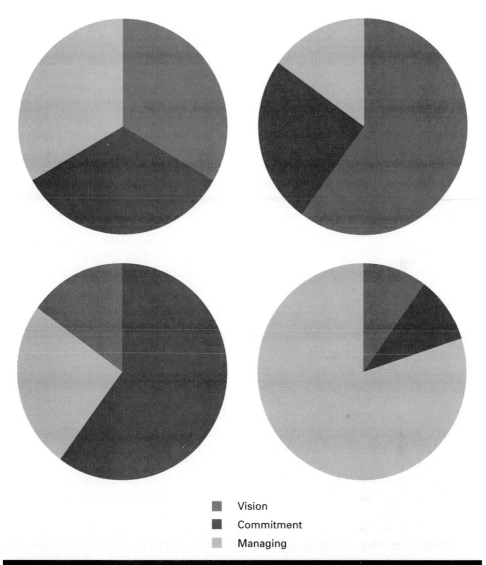

Vision
Commitment
Managing

FIGURE 3-6   The VCM Model of Leadership and Various Clusters of Leadership Skills

cles of concern."[10] He argues persuasively that people are more effective when their circle of influence is larger than their circle of concern. (See Figure 3-7.) His point is that if we would worry more about the things we can influence instead of the things we cannot, we would be more influential in our lives and cause more good to come about. If you are reluctant to think of yourself as a leader, you might rather think of things you'd like to see changed and the people who might help you do that. In this view, you'll soon realize that you're in a leadership role regardless of your title or lack thereof.

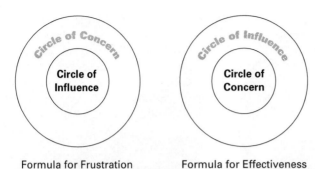

Formula for Frustration   Formula for Effectiveness

FIGURE 3-7 **Stephen Covey's Circles of Concern and Influence**

While working for seven and a half years as the chief operating officer of a large nonprofit organization involving 2,800 people and eight different operating units, I learned a lot about the practical aspects of leadership. One thing I discovered was that in some respects leadership is like a crucible that either refines or incinerates a person's soul and being. At times it feels like being the figurehead on the prow of a clipper ship, with your arms and legs pinned against the hull, your face and chest exposed to the elements and the flotsam and jetsam of the sea and crashing repeatedly into the waves, with nothing to buffer or protect you except your own determination to persist and reach your goal. This aspect of leadership, the loneliness and vulnerability to attack and criticism, justified or not, often causes otherwise capable people to shrink. Even in smaller group settings, the process of exposing one's thoughts and feelings and beliefs and analyses to others can be daunting. Clearly, to be a leader, one must develop some mental toughness and the ability to endure criticism. Ultimately, to be a leader, one must be willing to attempt to influence others.

The third key element of this definition lies in the willingness of the followers to follow. When the agency of the followers is compromised or removed, that is, when followers are forced or coerced into doing something, leadership ceases to exist and something else takes its place. If you threaten people with their jobs and thereby force them to do what you want, you may indeed be exerting power, but by this definition, you're not leading but rather coercing. Call it dictatorship. Call it force. Call it what you will. If you get people to do what you want them to do without them knowing about it, you've moved into the realm of manipulation. And that, I say, is not leadership either. Leadership is about winning more than the behavior of people; it is about winning their minds and hearts. If the followers don't choose to follow, then someone may be exerting power, but that person is not a leader.

People in positions of potential leadership, like CEOs or vice presidents or supervisors, sometimes borrow authority from their titles and order people to do things on threat of their livelihoods. My first business school instructor, Stephen Covey, likened this many years ago to using a crutch to walk; unable to influence on one's own merits, the person who borrows power from her title to force people to do things is using a leadership crutch. Although the desired short-term job may get done, in the end such methodologies undermine one's ability to lead others.

I have already made a distinction between manipulation and leadership. The deceit involved in manipulation removes the element of follower willingness. If people don't know what you're getting them to do, how can that be leadership? The question becomes, "If the followers knew what you were doing, how you were doing it, and what your motives were, would they still follow you willingly?" If the answer is yes, then you don't need to use manipulative techniques, and you can claim to be a leader. If the answer is no, I wouldn't consider you to be a leader, and, I argue, neither would your followers.

TARGET LEVELS OF LEADERSHIP

> Leading strategic change can occur on at least three levels: organizational, work group, and individual.

I must now introduce one more important aspect of leadership, which I'll call "target level." When people talk about leadership, they most often think of the organizational or institutional level and refer to the titular heads of companies or foundations or institutions as their leaders. True, organizational leaders have a broad impact; their decisions can affect thousands of lives. Yet much research and experience suggest that we need leaders at many levels in organizations.[11] Each of the people introduced in the list at the beginning of this chapter is a potential leader. Each will surely continue in his or her responsibilities; the question will be—to what level of effectiveness and influence? Surely, each work group within an organization needs leadership to guide and manage its daily activities. We can also think of individual or self-leadership.[12] If we are unable in some sense to lead ourselves, how can we presume to lead others?

One can apply the general model in Figure 3-3 to organizations, to work groups, and to individuals. These three levels of attention are important, and I invite you to remember them throughout the discussion in the remainder of the book. The concepts later introduced about the ethics of leadership, the need for strategic thinking, and the ability to influence others and to redesign structures to unleash potential all relate to each of these levels.

CONCLUSION

As you reflect on the model in Figure 3-3 and contemplate your own leadership goals and aspirations, please note that leadership is the *result* of a situation in which people have worked together voluntarily with energy to accomplish some purpose. In this view of leadership, leaders respect the dignity of their followers and recognize the importance and power of self-determination. They work openly rather than covertly to convince, persuade, and guide others to a view of what needs to be done and, in so doing, build commitment to that view. This approach has necessary and strong, underlying ethical foundations. However, leaders often attempt to influence others in environmental and organizational contexts that can severely handicap their efforts.

The view of leadership presented here incorporates a broad view of leadership potentials or situations that has a respect for various forces at play including the characteristics of the leader, the followers, the organization, and the environment as well as the array of strategic possibilities it presents. This view is optimistic about the internal capacities of the followers and the leader's confidence in and acceptance of his own role in guiding those capacities. This view asserts that leadership begins to happen when a person recognizes all of the elements of the situation and is willing to work to unlock the potential in each of those elements to make something happen. This view also asserts that leadership requires significant personal attributes, intense effort, and a deep sense of respect for the environment and people. It requires an ability to see and formulate strategy, an ethical foundation on which to build relationships, and a clear sense of appropriate measures and the ability to manage change.

All of these features take place at three levels, that of the individual, the work group, and the organization. An effective leader understands this and is aware and active at all three levels, willing to influence organizations and work groups and to lead strategic change but also willing to initiate equally disruptive change in herself.

PRINCIPLES OF LEADERSHIP INTRODUCED IN THIS CHAPTER

1. Leadership is the result of much more than the personal characteristics of the potential leader. Leadership includes defining a task (setting a strategy), the quality of relationships with followers, designing organizations, and managing change within the organization as well as one's relationships with followers to achieve the outcomes desired in the task/strategy.
2. Leadership is different from exercising power. Whereas power is getting others to do what you want them to do, leadership involves ability (skill in influence), willingness to be in the leadership role, and influence that creates a voluntary response. Many people who have the skills to lead choose not to because they don't want to accept all of the pressures and difficulties of the leadership role.
3. One cannot talk about leadership without talking about strategic thinking, managing change, and ethics. Effective leaders are strategic thinkers, masters of the change process, and ethically grounded.
4. Leadership involves a cluster of skills around creating a vision, another cluster of skills around garnering commitment, and a third cluster of skills around managing progress toward the vision.
5. Leadership occurs at three levels: the organization, the work group, and one's self.

QUESTIONS FOR REFLECTION

1. To what extent do your efforts to influence others rely on your position or title (exercising power)? If your title or position were taken away, would others listen to you? Why or why not?
2. How much time do you spend in strategic thought, creating a vision for yourself, your work group, or your organization? What would you need to do to increase this time?
3. How comfortable are you with the change process? Do you understand it? Do you feel like you are a master at managing it?
4. Why is it important for a potential leader to have a clear vision or dream to become an effective leader?
5. Recall a person who has been in authority over you who has used power rather than leadership as defined here to influence you. How did you respond to that person? What were your thoughts about that experience? What did you learn from that experience?

NOTES

Note: To quickly access all *Harvard Business Review* reprints listed here, go to www.hbsp .harvard.edu/hbsp/adv_search.asp, insert the reprint number in the Product Number field, and click Search.

1. Jim Collins, *Good to Great* (New York: HarperCollins, 2001).
2. Stanley M. Davis, *Future Perfect* (Reading, MA: Addison-Wesley, 1987).
3. Peter Senge, *The Fifth Discipline: The Art and Practice of the Learning Organization* (New York: Doubleday, 1990).
4. Robert S. Kaplan and David P. Norton, "Using the Balanced Scorecard as a Strategic Management System," *Harvard Business Review,* reprint 96107.
5. Margaret Wheatley, *Leadership and the New Science* (San Francisco: Berrett-Koehler, 1992), 38–39.
6. See Peter L. Berger and Thomas Luckmann, *The Social Construction of Reality* (New York: Doubleday, 1966).
7. Charles M. Farkas and Suzy Wetlaufer, "The Ways Chief Executive Officers Lead," *Harvard Business Review,* reprint 96303.
8. Larry Donnithorne, *The West Point Way of Leadership* (New York: Currency Doubleday, 1993).
9. James Kouzes and Barry Posner, *The Leadership Challenge* (San Francisco: Jossey Bass, 1987).
10. Stephen Covey, *Seven Habits of Highly Effective People* (New York: Simon & Schuster, 1992).
11. See John Kotter, *The Leadership Factor* (New York: The Free Press, 1988), for a discussion of what he calls the "little '1' leadership" needed everywhere in organizations.
12. See Charles Manz, "Self Leadership," *Academy of Management Review* 11, no. 3 (1986): 585.

CHAPTER

4

Levels of Leadership

For every thousand hacking away at the leaves of evil,
there is one striking at the root.
—HENRY DAVID THOREAU

Before we begin to address the various aspects of the general model, we need to consider an important set of ideas that have to do with the difference between focusing on the superficial and focusing on the deeper, more powerful aspects of leadership. Leadership is about affecting human activity, and human activity can be thought of as occurring at three levels: observable behavior, conscious thought, and basic values and assumptions. Behavior is simply what others do, that which we can observe. People speak and act. They make gestures and movements that we can see and hear. This is what I call Level One activity.

At Level Two, people have conscious thoughts that they may or may not reveal to us. Although we may not be aware of these, the person having them certainly is. Our attempts to lead others may or may not pay attention to what others are thinking.

At a deeper level that I call Level Three, people hold a set of values, assumptions, beliefs, and expectations (VABEs).[2] These values and beliefs have developed over time and have become so much a part of the person that they may be only partially visible or available to them. These VABEs are therefore semiconscious or partially conscious collections of how we think the way the world should be. Levels One, Two, and Three are shown in Table 4-1, where the heavy dashed line denotes a separation between what we can see and what we cannot.

Because it is seemingly difficult to understand Levels Two and Three, we often deal with people only at the level of their behavior; it is simpler and seemingly more accurate. In fact, many theorists and observers argue strongly that leaders can deal only with Level One and that attempts to influence Levels Two and Three are an unethical invasion of privacy. This would be a Skinnerian view. B.F. Skinner, the famous psychologist, conducted research and wrote extensively arguing that we could condition animals and people to behave in certain ways by managing the mechanisms by which they were rewarded.[3] You may remember that he put (among other things and in his work's simplest form) a chicken in a box with a button, and when the chicken pecked on the button, it was rewarded with a kernel of corn. By reinforcing the pecking behavior with the corn, Skinner was able to teach the chicken to peck in a certain

TABLE 4-1 Basic Levels of Human Activity	
Level One:	Behaviors
OBSERVABLE	
NOT OBSERVABLE	
Level Two:	Conscious thoughts
Level Three:	Values, assumptions, beliefs, and expectations

way. Skinnerians, then, tend to argue that leadership should focus on behavior and neither consider nor worry about what goes on inside a person.

Of these three levels, behavior is the most readily available because it is visible to us. Levels Two and Three are available to us only through two means: when others decide to reveal themselves to us and through our observations of their behavior, which allow us to infer what the underlying VABEs might be. Both of these methods are imprecise. We cannot always be sure that what someone says is an accurate reflection of what they are thinking or experiencing. They may be hesitant to tell us the truth, or they may not be very clear in their own minds about their own cognitive processes. When we observe people, if we are careful, we may get some very good clues about why they behave the way they do. In fact, sometimes our observations may give us a more clear picture than if we just listened to what they said. People don't always behave consistently with what they say they believe.

The model presented in this book is decidedly not Skinnerian. Rather, recognizing the levels of conscious thought and of somewhat vague but strongly held values, I assert that effective leadership must take into account Levels Two and Three. Unless one does, one has little hope of understanding why people behave the way they do and of influencing them in profound ways, ways that move beyond monitoring and constraining behavior.

BODY, HEAD, AND HEART

Because behavior is decidedly physical and observable, we can liken Level One to the body. Some companies and managers have explicitly stated their wish that employees would check their thoughts and emotions at the door and just do their jobs. In essence, this philosophy is focused on Level One and attempts to manage behavior in isolation. A commonly quoted joke is that companies are frustrated because they hire workers and people keep coming to work. Henry Ford once complained that he kept trying to hire a pair of hands and they kept showing up with bodies and heads attached. I assert that most managerial systems since the beginning of the Industrial Revolution have focused on Level One, with much less attention on Levels Two and Three. Frederick Taylor's work on time-motion studies around the turn of the century, for instance, focused largely on managing employees' behavior of employees and assigned little importance to their inner thinking and feeling.[4] The underlying assumption here is that people are like machines, so the goal of these managerial systems was to minimize variance from work objectives by managing people to behave in the most efficient manner.

Increasingly, in a changing world with enormous volumes of information available to employees at every rank, the centralized control mentality is outdated and unworkable. People keep bringing their heads and their hearts to work, and these influence their behavior constantly. Further, as competition increases, corporations are concerned about building high-performance work places where employees at all levels are committed and engaged in serving customers, where their heads and hearts are focused on high-quality work. The present approach argues that unless management can tap into the potentials at Levels Two and Three, it will be unable to compete with the best of their competitors. The work won't be as high quality as it otherwise would be unless the whole employee is engaged in it. Focusing on Level One is insufficient for getting this kind of commitment.

Effective leadership also needs to influence Level Two, that of which we are immediately aware in ourselves, our conscious processes. We think thoughts and choose whether to communicate them and, if we do, whether to communicate them accurately. We are aware of Level Two activity within ourselves, and we presume it in others. We can liken Level Two to the mind because that's where it takes place. Would-be leaders who ignore what people think are undermining their own capacity for influence.

Level Three refers to the deep-seated beliefs that we hold about what has become so true in life for us that we take it for granted and no longer need to think about or reflect upon it. Level Three includes our hierarchy of priorities, our list of what we value more than other things. It includes our summary of the shoulds and oughts in the world, the way the world and the people in it should behave.

Our Level Three VABEs are by nature highly cultural and family specific. The circumstances of where we were born and grew up, the quality of our relationships with our parents and what they taught us—in fact, all of our life's experiences—have contributed to the set of VABEs we hold as adults. More about this in a later chapter.

In a sense, our VABEs are like limestone caverns. The interior of these caverns is dark and wet. Over time, tiny drops of limestone-laden water drip from the ceilings and land on the floors. As they do, evaporating partially each time, a small deposit is left. After millions of repetitions, these deposits form into stalactites and stalagmites. Some of these structures are thin and easily broken. Others are thick and may even have formed into solid columns extending from ceiling to floor. Our VABEs are like these limestone structures. Some are pretty weak, whereas others are central pillars to our personality and views of the world. Further, some have become so familiar to us that we no longer notice them. These stalactites and stalagmites and pillars make up the structures of our personality–yet we ourselves may not see them clearly.

To see our own Level Three VABES, we often need assistance. Like fish swimming in water or birds flying in air, we have come to take for granted these fundamental VABEs and assume them to be true. Honest conversations with others, particularly people who are skilled in recognizing VABEs when they see them, can be very helpful for both parties in clarifying what a person's–or an organization's–VABEs are. This does *not* mean that you have to be a psychologist to be a Level Three leader. Psychology is the study of where a person's VABEs come from. Management and leadership have to do with *recognizing* what the VABEs are and then working with that person or organization to accomplish some goals with those VABEs.

VABEs come in a variety of forms. We can think of VABEs of distinction, VABEs of association, and VABEs of strategy. Distinction VABEs help us to perceive and understand the difference between one concept and another.[5] We have come to believe, for example, that one country's boundaries begin here or end there. Yet looking at the ground, we see no lines, just continuous dirt. That country, France perhaps, is an assumption of distinction. Association VABEs reflect our priorities and values. "France is good," we may think, or "France is bad." Finally, strategy VABEs have to do with action. "If I turn left, we can get there faster," we may believe, or "If I lie, no one will find out."

VABEs are usually clearest and most available for examination when they are stated as declarative normative sentences. For example, "People should tell the truth," "The early bird gets the worm," "Be respectful to your elders," or "Don't spit in public." And so forth. The basic structures of distinction, association, and strategy VABEs are shown in Table 4-2.

We carry thousands of VABEs with us. Some of these we have inherited from others (see a later chapter on the concept of memes), whereas others we have developed from our unique experience. Some of them are relatively weak, and others are quite strong and central to our way of living. The collective structure of our VABEs forms the nature of our personalities in a powerful way. Even so, it may not be so easy to recognize another person's VABEs.

VABEs are often manifest at Level One when people act or speak. Whenever you hear a person say "should" or "really oughta wanna" or "Good Xs do it this way," your personal VABE radar should go "beep, beep, beep" because that person has just revealed to you a portion of their VABEs. If you watch and listen, you can pick up a lot about a person's VABEs. Clearly, not everyone is completely congruent, so there may also be a gap between what a person says and what she does. This gap between espoused theories or VABEs and actual behavior has been the subject of much research and practical speculation.[6]

Level Three, then, is a gray area between conscious thought and the subconscious, an area that may be available to us, about which we seldom think and into which we seldom delve, and yet that controls our lives, our thinking, and clearly our judgments about what we view to be right or wrong. We can liken Level Three to the heart although there is no physiological evidence that our values, assumptions, beliefs, and expectations in any way reside there.

Please note that these three levels of human activity are closely intertwined. Clearly our VABEs affect our thinking, and clearly our thinking affects our behavior. Others argue that our behavior affects our thinking and feeling—this would be the view taken by the Skinnerians. The effective Level Three leader will be aware of these recursive influences and strive to work with all three levels, not just one. A singular focus on behavior ignores two-thirds of what makes people do what they do. See Figure 4-1 for a visual diagram of the relationship among behavior, thoughts, and VABEs.

TABLE 4-2 Basic Structure of VABEs	
Distinction VABEs	This is X.
Association VABEs	X is (good, bad).
Strategy VABEs	If A, then likely B.

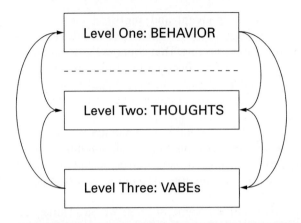

Figure 4-1 Levels of Human Activity

CONNECTING THE THREE LEVELS TO SCHOLARLY VIEWS

This three-level view of human activity is relatively straightforward and well under-stood by scholars and many practicing leaders. In discussing the development of lead-ership in ethnic and organizational cultures, for instance, Ed Schein, one of the world's principal authorities on the subject, introduces what he calls three levels of cultural manifestations: (1) artifacts, the visible structures and processes of a culture; (2) espoused values, the conscious justifications for behavior; and (3) basic underlying assumptions, the "unconscious, taken-for-granted beliefs, perceptions, thoughts, and feelings" that drive culture.[7] If you're interested in exploring this further, Schein's book contains an excellent description of how these underlying basic assumptions are formed and shape individual and organizational behavior. Our three-level leadership model parallels Schein's cultural model nicely.

LEARNING LEVEL THREE LEADERSHIP

If you accept the assertion that human activity occurs at three levels and that leaders should pay attention to all three, the question emerges, "How do I learn how to do this?" The first step has to do with learning to recognize your own VABEs and those of others. Developing a skill at observing and inferring is critical to perceiving VABEs. If we recollect that the issue of "what do you see?" is the first step in developing an LPV, then we can see the importance of developing better vision. If we can see what others overlook, we have a head start on developing influence. Second, we may have to unlearn some of the VABEs we have developed thus far in life, particularly in this era of paradigm shift from a bureaucratic to an infocratic society. This is difficult for many people. By definition, they've become comfortable with their VABEs. And to a large degree, our present VABEs have worked for us so far in life. I agree, however, with the best-selling author Mihalyi Csikszentmihalyi, who notes that becoming a truly free adult means transcending some of the VABEs that we have come to accept as true in our limited experience.[7] So long as we are unwilling or unable to reexamine our core, columnar VABEs, we are unlikely to change our view of the world and the way we behave in it. Third, we will need to develop skills of influence based on our new insights about why people behave the way they do. Our habits of communication based on our historic VABEs may no longer be functional. Finally, because organizations reflect the VABEs of their leaders, we will need to reexamine our roles and strategies in designing and leading change in organizations. The rest of this book introduces you to many of these new skills.

Many people in leadership positions subscribe to a Level One definition of leadership. They are uncomfortable with tinkering with a person's mind or personality and believe it an ethical issue to focus only on behavior. For them, the carrot-and-stick approach is tried and true: Entice them with carrots and if they don't respond, beat them with sticks. Again, this is a distinctly Skinnerian view in which human thought and value are thought to be indiscernible content and thus irrelevant to a leader's goals. Although I agree that it makes sense to reward people for desirable behavior and that it is folly to hope for one behavior while intentionally or unintentionally rewarding another, I also note that, although people will work for rewards and may adjust their behavior to get those rewards, people also value different rewards.[8] Extra pay to one person is an incentive, whereas for another, job fulfillment is what motivates him. People will indeed exchange time and some effort for financial return—in some cases, for a pitifully small financial return. Much of the research about operant conditioning in psychology and about its cousin, expectancy theory in management, has attempted to clarify the connections between reward and behavior. Even expectancy theory, which asserts that motivation to effort is generally a function of a person's belief that they can do a task times their belief that they will be rewarded for doing that task times the value of that reward to them, begins to question the strictly Skinnerian view.[9] If a person doesn't value the reward, expectancy theorists would note, the motivation of the individual declines rapidly. We'll discuss this more in the chapter on why people behave the way they do.

The often overlooked implication of the carrot-and-stick approach (which, by the way, implies that the object of attention in the middle is a mule) is that one has to begin to take into account what is happening inside the person in addition to observing her external behavior. Expectancy theorists therefore want to know which rewards people value and why. This leads us to a decidedly non-Skinnerian viewpoint: Leaders must understand and work with more than behavior; effective leaders must work at Levels Two and Three.

People are different from machines and animals in many ways—our abilities to think and to value one thing above another, for example—although leaders for at least 100 years have often taken a mechanistic view of organizations.[10] I believe that human behavior is so closely connected to both thoughts and VABEs that if we hope to understand why people behave the way they do, we must understand something about their thought processes and their hierarchies of values and basic assumptions about the way the world *ought* to be.

Further, my definition of leadership (the ability and the willingness to influence people so that they respond voluntarily) implies that in true leadership–followership situations, the followers' *willingness* is essential to effective leadership. If that is the case, then we must be concerned with what people think and feel. Otherwise, we cannot tell if we are leaving the realm of leadership and beginning to move into strong-over-weak power relationships where the durability of the employees' willingness to comply with the leader's wishes comes into question. If the leader retreats or goes away, what do the followers do and why? If the rewards offered by the leader go away, what do the followers do and why? Do they choose to continue doing as they were asked? If so, perhaps leadership is truly occurring. If not, perhaps what was happening was not leadership but some other kind of power relationship.

THE STRONG HISTORY OF LEVEL ONE LEADERSHIP

Level One leadership has been a dominant model in history: The strong have controlled the weak. Yet I assert that it is not very powerful—indeed, it may not even be leadership. When we focus only on the behavior of others and ignore and downplay an understanding of what they are thinking and believing and feeling, we retreat from leadership as influencing others to respond willingly and move toward an exchange- or coercion-based relationship. Were the kings of medieval Europe leaders or dictators? Did people do what they bid because they feared for their lives or because they shared a common value set? In power-based dominance relationships in business, employees are frequently aware that management personnel, the self-proclaimed leaders, are not interested in them as people but only as cogs in the bureaucratic machinery or as means to a goal. Consequently, their level of engagement in the work and their commitment to fulfill it will decline. If and when this kind of relationship is tested by events or situations that hit at or question what the employees think or believe, their loyalty to the Level One leader will be severely threatened. Their stamina for continuing as asked will seep away. Their willingness to contribute creative thought and passionate effort will be drained off. And if treated like this for long periods of time, employees will become what the system has systematically encouraged them to become, mentally and emotionally disengaged from their work, bringing their bodies to the job but leaving their minds and hearts at the entrance, out of gear and idling in neutral.

For a long period of time, longer than you and I have been alive, Level One leadership, the traditional approach, worked remarkably well. Worldwide economies were expanding, labor was relatively inexpensive and easy to find, and the relative stability of domestic markets allowed managements to view labor as a commodity like buildings and equipment. In this light, the formation of the labor unions can been seen as a reaction to this impersonal approach. Nevertheless, the system worked, and companies grew and were profitable.

Today, though, as outlined earlier, the environment has changed so dramatically—and continues to do so—and competition has grown so fiercely that management teams can no longer compete successfully with that kind of mercenary, Level One relationship with their employees (represented by the south–west axis of our basic leadership model). Everywhere now, people are looking for ways to create high-performance workplaces. Unfortunately, many managers attempting this retain their old management principles and end up applying the new, emerging leadership techniques superficially, at Level One. One observes this in the application of the latest management fad, whether it be TQM, empowerment, or self-directed work teams, without concomitant changes in the other aspects of the organizational reality such as reward and systems, training, structures, operating cultures, and leadership approaches.

This creates a credibility gap in the minds of the employees when leaders are seen as saying one thing and doing another or not "walking the talk." The resulting "knowing-doing gap" is so large and common that it has become the topic of books.[11]

Many of the new management systems attempt to deal at Levels Two and Three. If they are applied in a Level One way, though, they often fail, and those who tried then say, "See, I told you. This won't work." A Level One leader attempting to implement a Level Three program is likely only to create more cynicism among employees. The observance of a gap between new programs and old, persistent styles of managing breeds alienation in the work force. Level gaps (between Level One leaders and Level Two or Level Three programs) also inhibit the kind of trust and respect employees need to fully engage in the organization's work.

THE FOCUS AND IMPACT OF LEVEL THREE LEADERSHIP

Level Two and Level Three leadership recognize the importance of potential followers' thoughts and values. Level Three leadership assumes that effective leadership speaks to peoples' hearts and is able to engage them in profound ways almost regardless of compensation. Although Level One leadership focuses on getting movement out of people, Level Three leadership seeks to get engagement. Level Three leadership recognizes that today's generation of workers, at least in the industrialized world where poverty and famine are for the most part peripheral issues, are looking for more than a monthly paycheck; they're looking for meaningful work that is worthy of not only their time and talent but also of their creativity and heartfelt commitment. Sadly, many employees worldwide have come to believe that work and engagement are incompatible.

Level Three leadership recognizes that in a service-oriented economy, they cannot and will not deliver customer satisfaction, much less delight, unless they can engage people at that third level. In a Level One leadership organization, the myriad moments of truth, when service or product is delivered to the customer, will be found by the customer to be unsatisfying and irritating.[12] The fast-food drive-in window employee operating at Level One delivers the sack of food with a fake smile and no eye contact and, when questioned about the four missing items, says, "I put them in there; you must not be seeing them," and then gives an impatient look because you are holding up the line. Level One employees are going through the motions. In a world where competition is growing and some companies are learning how to organize large numbers of employees to care about what the customer thinks and feels, the alternatives will be more attractive to customers who are tired of dealing with employees who are engaged only at that first level.

Level Three leadership seeks to understand the basic assumptions and values of employees and to match them or educate them toward harmony with the goals and strategic directions of the firm. This relationship is represented by the east–west axis of our basic leadership model. Level Three leadership recognizes the importance of dealing with people at this level and rejects that leaders need only focus on behavior rather than on what people are thinking and feeling. Level Three leadership assumes that employees' behavior is closely intertwined with their thoughts and feelings.

Clearly, Level Three leadership requires a different perspective. Would-be Level Three leaders must develop new skills, including the ability to infer people's thoughts and emotions. The central invitation of this book is to begin to develop these skills so you can begin to influence at Levels Two and Three. Are you willing to learn how to engage people not only in their behavior but also in their hearts and minds? If you find yourself whispering to yourself, "I don't care what they think or feel; I just want a good day's work for a good day's wages," we invite you to pause and reflect on the consequences of your approach. Will you be able to organize a high-performance workplace with a series of exchange-based mercenary relationships? Will you be able to develop an organizational culture of excellence and quality if your management team is constantly worried about controlling and guiding employees' behavior when they're not there? Can you expect to create an organization characterized by extraordinary performance if you work only at Level One? What does it take to get employees to give their all and then some?

You may be thinking that lots of people don't *want* to be engaged in their work; they want only to put in their hours, collect their paycheck, and go home. That's Level One thinking. A Level Two or Level Three question might be to ask yourself, "Go home to what? What is it that motivates these people? Do they drudge through work and then go home and begin yelling enthusiastically during the match at their local bowling or softball league?" If so, a Level Three leader would go on to ask, "How can I get them to play softball at work?" If you followed your employees around before and after work, would you ever find them working hard, even passionately, to accomplish some goal? What would that goal be? If you can imagine them doing *something* with passion, you might ask yourself, "How can I get some of that passion here at work?" Maybe some employees go home to nothing. Maybe their level of activity at home is even lower than at work in a Level One organization. If this is the case, the odds are you aren't going to be able to make a significant change in their lives. Perhaps then you need to consider reexamining and perhaps redesigning a recruiting system that has invited these people to work in your organization.

THE DARK SIDE OF LEVEL THREE LEADERSHIP AND ENGAGEMENT

There is a potential dark side to Level Three Leadership and the high levels of engagement it invites. When people work on something that they believe in and value, they often work very hard. When they work on something that they believe in and are focused on the goals of the effort, they can work so hard that they begin to do damage to themselves, working excessively and burning out. This can extend to others, to coworkers and subordinates who are asked to do more than they can or should. More and more literature is appearing that describes this phenomenon, and our guess is it will continue to grow as the pace of the world, the volume of information available to us, and the pressures of stiffened competition continue. If you're interested in this topic, you might read *Workaholics* by Marilyn Machlowitz (Addison-Wesley, 1980), *Working Ourselves to Death* by Diane Fassel (Harper, 1990), or *The Addictive Organization* by Anne Wilson Schaef and Diane Fassel (Harper, 1990). Robert Reich's book, *The Future of Success* (Knopf, 2001), makes a similar point: People are working harder and longer today than a decade before but for less time off and relatively even wages.[13] Although Level Three leadership can lead to extraordinary results and deeply committed relationships between individuals and their companies, it can also lead to exhaustion.

Working with people at Levels Two and Three initially requires more effort and more involvement on the leader's part, but it promises a more committed group of followers and higher quality of production. When the work group gets to the point that it can function without the boss's oversight at a very high level of productivity and quality, the need for leadership involvement begins to diminish. Level Three Leadership is front-end loaded; you make a significant investment up front learning and focusing on co-workers' Level Three values, but when you understand that and can align those values with the work, your need to monitor and manage drops significantly.

ORGANIZATIONAL IMPLICATIONS

So far, we have discussed Level Three leadership primarily from individual and interpersonal perspectives (see Table 4-3). We can also speak of three levels of activity in a broader, organizational sense. A Level One (behavioral or superficial) focus in organizational leadership is reflected in the use of the latest fads or techniques. Level One leaders read about the latest technique in the literature and try to apply these techniques over the top of their existing organizations without a consideration of how these new techniques affect all of the other interrelated systems, structures, and cultures of the organization. Sometimes it manifests itself in commissioning expensive educational programs–but never attending personally.

Level Two at the organization includes its structure, key systems, and formal design. These consciously, historically designed aspects of the organization are the result of conscious thought; hence we can align them with Level Two.

The way in which an organization's design factors combine with the people who work in it create an organization's culture. The leadership style of the people in charge creates a set of values, assumptions, beliefs, and expectations about how people in the organization should behave, which we call the *organizational culture*. Level Three resides in the organization's culture, the set of commonly held values and operating principles that people have come to take for granted as the "way we do things around here." These cultural realities may or may not line up with the formal organization and its subordinate designs. When it doesn't, the designers experience unintended consequences.

Level Three in the organization, like in the individual, is not quite on the level of consciousness. Some employees may be able to talk about aspects of the extant culture; others may not be clear enough about it to articulate it—although they act according to it. Using Chris Argyris's terms, Level Two is the espoused theory of the organization, whereas Level Three is the theory in action.[14] These elements are shown in Table 4.4. They differ somewhat from Ed Schein's characterization, yet for our purposes here they illustrate the point that what managers do (trying to apply the latest fad in the literature), how they think about the organization (its structure and processes), and what they believe deeply about how to manage and organize are all potentially very different things.

TABLE 4-3   Levels of Organizational Activity

Level One:	Managerial fad (short-term programs)
Level Two:	Intentional organizational design (structure and systems)
Level Three:	Organizational culture and operating values

TABLE 4-4	Levels in Personal and Organizational Analysis	
Level	*Personal*	*Organizational*
One	Behavior seen on camera	Artifacts, buildings, physical things
Two	Conscious thoughts	Espoused theories, the "talk," fads
Three	Values, assumptions, beliefs, and expectations	Theories in action, the "walk," and underlying assumptions

APPLYING LEVEL THREE LEADERSHIP AT BOTH THE INDIVIDUAL AND ORGANIZATIONAL LEVELS

Level Three leadership works in both individual relationships and in the organization's management. In both instances, it assumes that high performance only comes when the central features of Levels One, Two, and Three are all aligned. When there are variations between the directions and main thrusts across these three levels, between what people or organizations do, think, and feel, inefficiencies are introduced and leadership becomes diffused and ineffective.

Increasingly in today's turbulent world, leaders must learn to influence people at Level Three if they want to be effective. The titular power bases of bureaucracies continue to melt. Personal influence is increasingly more important. Although Level One is seemingly faster and there are two centuries of momentum for dealing with people at this level, the growing importance of customer service moments of truth and the explosion in worldwide competition demand that an organization's employees participate in a world-class effort—often an effort based on high levels of engagement at all levels—if it is to survive and thrive. Although the up-front costs of learning to influence people at Level Three may be more time consuming than operating at Level One, the long-term benefits include more deeply committed employees and co-workers, higher-quality work, more satisfied customers, and a higher probability of surviving. The downside is that Level Three leaders must learn to recognize and manage in themselves and others the dangers of overworking and burnout. This observation leads us to a consideration of the moral aspects of Level Three leadership, which are addressed in the next chapter.

PRINCIPLES OF EFFECTIVE LEADERSHIP INTRODUCED IN THIS CHAPTER

1. Level One leadership that focuses only on behavior ignores two major sources of motivation for most people: what they think and what they believe and feel.
2. Level Three leadership that is aware of and influences people's values and basic assumptions has the potential of being far more powerful than Level One leadership.
3. Although Level Three leadership does not imply that one must be a psychologist (who studies where values and assumptions come from), it does imply that effective leaders will be skilled in recognizing and clarifying VABEs in those they work with.

4. VABEs affect thoughts and thoughts affect behavior, and the reverse is probably also true. Consequently, effective leaders will pay attention to all three levels.
5. Historically, most leaders in the Industrial Age have targeted Level One. In the new Information Age, effective leaders must be aware of and understand and target Levels Two and Three.
6. Levels One, Two, and Three apply to organizations as well as to individuals. Most organizational leaders focus on Level One and ignore the realities of Levels Two and Three.

QUESTIONS FOR REFLECTION

1. What are your boss's VABEs? Your co-workers'? Can you write these down? If you listened more carefully, could you figure them out?

2. What are your basic values and assumptions about the way your organization should be working? Can you write these down? That is, can you see the Level Three culture of your organization clearly enough to put them on paper?

3. Identify the ways during the past week that you've behaved as a Level One Leader—at home, at work, and in your avocation. What impact did these behaviors have?

4. How could you have behaved as a Level Three leader during the episodes you identified in question 3?

NOTES

1. Some scholars may find this terminology weak, yet over a dozen years it has proven very effective in executive education settings as a means for consolidating several ideas and making them memorable.

2. See B. F. Skinner, *Beyond Freedom and Dignity* (New York: Bantam, 1971).

3. See Frederick Winslow Taylor, *The Principles of Scientific Management* (New York: Harper & Brothers, 1911).

4. See Richard Brodie, *Virus of the Mind* (Seattle: Integral Press, 1996).

5. See, for example, Chris Argyris, *Reasoning, Learning, and Action* (San Francisco: Jossey-Bass, 1982).

6. Ed Schein, *Organizational Culture and Leadership* (San Francisco: Jossey-Bass, 1992), 17.

7. See Mihalyi Csikszentmihalyi, *The Evolving Self* (New York: Harper Perennial, 1993).

8. See Steven Kerr's classic article, "On the Folly of Rewarding A While Hoping for B,"

Academy of Management Journal 18 (1975): 769–83.

9. See, for example, Robert Merton, *Social Theory and Social Structure* (New York: Free Press, 1957), and Edward E. Lawler III, *The Ultimate Advantage: Creating the High-Involvement Organization* (San Francisco: Jossey-Bass, 1992).

10. See Gareth Morgan, *Images of Organizations* (Newbury Park, CA: Sage, 1986), Chapter 2, for a good summary of this phenomenon.

11. Jeffrey Pfeffer and Robert I. Sutton, *The Knowing-Doing Gap* (Boston: Harvard Business School Press, 2000).

12. See Jan Carlzon, *Moments of Truth* (New York: HarperCollins, 1987), for a nice discussion of the importance of moments of truth in service industries.

13. Robert Reich, *The Future of Success* (New York: Alfred Knopf, 2001).

14. See, for example, Argyris, *Reasoning, Learning, and Action.*

The Moral Foundation of Extraordinary Leadership

What you do thunders so loudly in my ears, I cannot hear what you say.
—RALPH WALDO EMERSON

All leadership has a moral dimension, and this is a Level Three consideration. Because leadership is about influencing others, it begs the questions of whether it is right to do so and if so, what means one should employ. Some people feel very strongly that they have no right or desire to influence others and prefer that they be left alone to determine the path of their lives without external pressures. In an increasingly crowded, connected, and hostile world, controlling one's own life is becoming increasingly difficult. Decisions made by strangers minutes or miles or continents away affect us in many ways. Yet this dilemma remains: Within our sphere of contacts and acquaintances, we choose whether or not to try to persuade others to change the way they behave and, if you accept the premise of the previous chapter, the way they think and believe as well.

MORALITY, ETHICS, AND LEGALITY

Let us make a distinction for the moment between morals, ethics, and legalities. *Morality* is the individual determination of what's right and wrong. An act may be immoral to a person while not viewed as unethical or illegal by the authorities. At the same time, what may be moral to one person may be immoral or unethical or illegal to others. Groups of people may or may not share views of what's moral and might attach others' judgments to those determinations. Typically, if a group judges a person's behavior to be immoral, they will ostracize that individual from the group.

   Ethics are the established and accepted guidelines of behavior for groups or institutions. Ethical considerations have to do with right and wrong as does morality, but in the context of a professional group's standards, and thus ethical behavior varies from group to group. To be a physician, for instance, you must accept the code of ethics set down by the licensing board of the medical profession. If you violate that code, you can lose your membership in that professional group. Where the criteria for membership in the professional group are fuzzy, as in business management where there is no comprehensive governing body as there is in medicine or law, the definition of ethical behavior becomes more problematic. As with morality, violation of the ethics established by a group usually results in expulsion from that group.

Legality obviously has to do with obeying the established laws of a society. Violating laws is illegal, but doing so may or may not be viewed by members of that society as immoral or unethical. For instance, many people violate the posted speed limits on major highways almost with impunity, obviously not believing that to do so is wrong or immoral or professionally unethical.

Although we can speak, given these definitions, of differences between morality, ethics, and legality, we can use a stakeholder perspective[1] to speak also of harms and benefits to others. If we can first identify all those who would be influenced by an act, the stakeholders in a situation, we could then begin to assess the consequences of the act to those people in terms of whether or not the act is harming or benefiting them. Does the attempt to influence another harm or benefit that person? If the act is harmful, we have a case that the act may be immoral.

MORALITY AND LEADERSHIP

Leadership creates many moral questions. We can begin, as noted previously, with the question of one's right to influence another. Is there such a right? Does another's influence in any way abridge what Thomas Jefferson called the "inalienable rights" that he and America's founders declared accrued to all humankind? Does everyone have a right to "life, liberty, and the pursuit of happiness" as well as freedom from influence? We live in a social world. Unless we live as hermits (and even then), we are unable to escape the repercussions of others' decisions. Whether we intend to or not, our choices affect others—the routes we take in traffic, the way we manage our garbage, the purchases we make. Some, perhaps including those who have been victimized in one way or another, resent the very notion of leadership, of one person intending to shape and guide another's behavior. Anyone who chooses to lead is choosing to influence others and should, we think, be aware of that role's moral responsibilities. Leaders will have an impact, and if that impact is negative, the leaders must bear at least part of the responsibility for the outcomes. This is another reason why, as I argued earlier, some people who may have the talent for leadership shrink from the opportunity.

Our earlier three-part definition of leadership has several moral positions in it. First, we said that individuals have the right to choose whether or not they wish to influence others. Many are not willing to do so and yet are thrust into positions of leadership. These people often wrestle with the emotional and moral burden of their roles, but because of the desire to be successful, they may continue in the position. Others choose to be in leadership positions yet are seemingly unaware and uncaring about the consequences of their choice. Because leadership has an impact, leaders should be aware of that impact and work at assessing whether or not it is harmful or beneficial and to whom.

Second, we also said that not all have the same ability to exercise that influence should they choose to try. Leadership ability varies, and one may choose to develop that ability or not. This usually includes finding a vision, a goal towards which the community should, in the eyes of the leader, work. The leader harnesses his skills to attaining that goal and in galvanizing the efforts of others engages them in this cause. Some with strong leadership abilities may choose, like Hitler and Stalin, goals that we would say are immoral. Others, like Gandhi, may choose more worthy goals. The use of one's skills as a leader invites one to consider the value of one's objectives.

Third, we said that leadership involves influence but not coercion, that true followers follow *willingly*. Leaders have, I believe, a moral obligation to use influence, not force. Further, I differentiate between the two so that when a person uses force, I argue they are no longer practicing leadership. They may be using power, but they are not leading.

So leadership has a very strong moral dimension, and many moral questions embedded in it. Level Three leadership purports to influence not only what people do and think but also what they believe and feel. This is in some sense an invasion of privacy, an exploration into the basic assumptions and values of another. Whether or not and how we go about this is also a moral issue. This recognition requires a few additional definitions.

> *Manipulation* is getting people to do what you want them to do without them agreeing to or knowing what you're doing.

Some view values-based leadership as a kind of manipulation. I see two kinds of manipulation: deceptive manipulation and coercive manipulation. Deceptive manipulation is when we maneuver events in ways that get people to do certain things when they are not aware of the forces influencing them. Coercive manipulation is when we maneuver events so that people are forced to choose what we want them to do when they would have chosen freely otherwise.

Both kinds of manipulation are, I say, immoral or wrong in the sense that they violate our definition of leadership—the followers are not following willingly. Only when people have full information and freedom to choose can they be enabled as followers. Further, manipulations involve violations of several moral principles (which I will outline later) that undermine our ability to lead. When people discover at some point, as they always do, that they have been manipulated or "had" or treated unfairly, their motivation and interest in following the so-called leader drops precipitously. Manipulation is not leadership. Manipulation is a leadership counterfeit that some people use believing that they are getting what they want out of a situation, but the net result is distrust, lack of respect, and weak relationships that will not produce quality over the long run. Manipulation is a short-term fix used by people who don't have the ability to lead as a way to cover up their own inadequacies.

THE MORAL FOUNDATION OF EFFECTIVE LEADERSHIP

If Level Three leadership involves moral issues, we need to find a basis for exercising it. I believe that there are four cornerstones to what I'll call the moral foundation of leadership. Without these four cornerstones, I don't believe that leadership will be effective or long lasting. These four pillars of leadership are truth telling, promise keeping, fairness, and respect for the individual.[2] We could actually distill these four ideas down to the last principle, respect for the individual, because if one had respect for another individual, one would not lie to them, break promises to them, or treat them unfairly. In a sense, then, these four principles are different windows onto the same core moral concept of integrity in relationships. However, I find it useful to look at respect for the individual in greater detail by considering the other three dimensions separately. In the end, though, one's answer to the question, "Are you showing respect for the individual?" is a good indicator of the other three.

> **The Four Cornerstones of the Moral Foundation of Effective Leadership**
> Truth telling
> Promise keeping
> Fairness
> Respect for the individual

Truth telling in leadership means telling the other the truth as you see it when it will have an impact on the other. Although saying that truth telling is a moral foundation for effective leadership may seem trite, I find that not all managers or would-be leaders believe this. In one seminar when senior managers of a major firm were gathered together to discuss leadership and influence, they were considering the question, "Should one tell the truth in business?" As the discussion progressed, the group became violently divided on this question—so much so that at one point individuals were literally standing on chairs and pounding the table and pointing and shouting at their colleagues across the room. Those who argued in favor of truth telling, whether it be to employees or customers or suppliers or the press or the parent company or whatever stakeholder, said that business is based on trust and that if the ability to trust another (either to behave consistently or to behave with our best interests at heart) erodes, the ability to do business disappears. People may do one deal, but they won't do two. Those who argued against truth telling, said that if you told people the truth, (e.g. how much you're making on a deal, the quality of the product, etc.) you wouldn't be able to do any business, in part because deals are based on margins; margins are a product of people's perceptions and truth telling destroys perceptions.

> The truth, as you see it and communicate it to others, is a great crucible that burns out would-be leaders and hardens effective and true leaders.

I believe that truth telling is essential to effective leadership. If you are unwilling to tell people the truth, you will not be able to lead them if for no other reason than they will be unable to respond to your ultimate goals *willingly*. The truth, as you see it and communicate it to others, is a great crucible. It refines relationships by cleaning out hidden goals, ulterior motives, suppressed resentments, manufactured conclusions, and uncertainties about the values of the other. Exchanging the truth as you see it is an essential part of the mutual, fair exchange that must occur for business to function.

People feel that they need to withhold the truth for a variety of reasons. Sometimes people feel pressured to withhold or distort the truth when there is bad news, either from an objective viewpoint, from a personal viewpoint, or from an imagined viewpoint of the other. This is, in part, true because we sometimes give data more evaluative power than exists inherently in it. In another view, though, data is just data. Some of it may be disconfirming to our present style of behavior, and some may be confirming, but in the end whether we accept it or reject it is entirely up to us. People are constantly accepting, rejecting, discounting, distorting, or ignoring the information that they receive. When we imagine that others will attribute to our data a negative, evaluative overtone or when we fear that the receiver will punish us for telling the truth as we see it, we are under influence to not tell the truth. On the other side of the relationship, we hope that potential leaders will note that if they cannot create an atmosphere around them where others are encouraged to tell the truth and find it safe to do so, the business will be making decisions based on late, faulty, or incomplete information far too often.

In relationships, feedback from others is data, neither moral nor immoral and neither right nor wrong until we respond to it, either accepting it or rejecting it or beginning to do something about it. The challenge for the person listening to another person's truth telling is to remain nondefensive, ears and hearts open, listening carefully to what is being communicated. Too often people get defensive immediately and miss the main message or its meaning. If you can also view the information you give to others in this light, you can learn to tell your truth more effectively.

Promise keeping is another cornerstone of effective leadership. Promises today often seem made to be broken. Management leaks to the press from confidential meetings, executives in offices of public trust are indicted for insider trading and other forms of fraud, and commitments to employees are routinely changed or broken outright. Worse, executives act willing to make whatever promises are necessary to keep the lid on a management situation and all too ready to abandon those promises a few short months later. Broken promises are destructive to trust and respect and ultimately to leadership. They are also characteristic of addictive behavior in which people promise without intention of following through to get what they want in the short run. To the extent that willing followership is a function of trust, promise keeping is an essential part of the moral foundation of effective leadership. People who make promises or commitments and then break them are like the shepherd who cried "wolf" too many times; before long the community didn't believe anymore. Potential leaders need to be careful of making commitments—and then careful of keeping the ones they make. Broken promises undermine potential leader–follower relationships quickly.

Fairness is also a part of the moral foundation of effective leadership because it ensures that the followers will get their share of the enterprise's rewards. When employees begin to perceive that they are not being treated fairly, their motivation to follow declines drastically. Much has been made recently about the gaps between first-line employees' and CEOs' salaries. Most reports indicate that in Japan, CEO salaries average about 9 to 10 times that of production employees. In Europe, the figure ranges from 9 to 15 times, whereas in the United States, the figure is closer to 25 times.[3] You may think that this is fair in that the senior managers are more experienced, better trained, add more value to the firm, are brighter and . . . any number of reasons. Whether or not these things are true, though, if the workers perceive an imbalance between their compensation and managers' up the organization, distrust will set in and productivity and performance will suffer. Why should one follow another whom one believes is not only likely but also proven to withhold fair compensation for value added and who is likely, therefore, to be exploiting the organization and its members for personal gain?

Fairness was less of an issue in traditional organizations than it will be in the new ones because information about the firm's health will be much more broadly distributed. If the employees don't know the financial picture of the firm, they might be managed or manipulated to accept lower wages and still work hard. In the new organizations, though, with large and readily available information networks, employees will have better information about the firm's (and industry's) financial standing, so it will be increasingly difficult to manipulate what stakeholders know about a firm and its distribution of resources.

The first three moral cornerstones of effective leadership can be distilled into the last, *respect for the individual.* If one is telling the truth, one respects the other well enough to be honest. If one is keeping one's promises, one respects the other. If one treats another fairly, one is showing respect for the individual: viewing and treating others as human beings with dignity who have and are adding value to the enterprise's mission. Respect for the individual means believing that everyone has some intrinsic worth and should be treated accordingly with courtesy and kindness. I'm reminded of the common Buddhist greeting in southeastern Asia, in which the greeter brings palms together in front, gives a slight bow, and says *namaste*—"I respect the part of god that is within you." Every person has something divine in them; Level Three leaders show respect for that.

This does not mean that all individuals should have equal influence on self or others, only that all should be treated with a basic human courtesy; because they live, they deserve to be treated with dignity. Paradoxically, treating people with respect accrues respect to the leader and thus enhances her circle of influence. Yet many so-called leaders, people in positions of influence, begin to lose sight of and respect for people in the lower ranks of the organization. They begin to judge employees' relative contributions to the firm's outcomes according to their rank and to treat people based on that judgment. Those whom they judge to be in the lower end of the distribution of contributors they treat with some disdain and perhaps even outright disrespect. This can have disastrous results.

THE NORMAL DISTRIBUTION OF EMPLOYEES' VALUE ADDED

In any given group of people, their performance will be distributed from high to moderate to weak. This is true of any organization. Regardless of the organization, members will vary in their contributions to the organization's mission. This distribution of performance will likely approximate a normal distribution, as shown in Figure 5-1, with

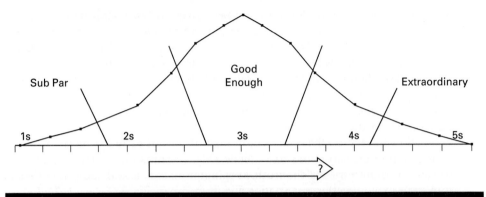

FIGURE 5-1

a small group of extraordinary performers, a large group of adequate performers, and a small group of subpar performers. One of the challenges for the effective leader is to move the good-enough group toward the extraordinary tail—but how? In other words, how can one shift the performance distribution to the right? Recognizing and using the moral foundation of leadership is key to this movement. Unless you are able to engage adequate people and get them to perform as 4s and 5s, your organization will continue to perform at the okay-but-not-great level. Unless you have a moral foundation in your leadership attempts, you will be unable to get more people to perform at the 4 and 5 level.

Let's test that assertion. Ask yourself, "If I tell my people or if we tell each other the truth half of the time, can we become an extraordinary team? If we keep our promises to each other half of the time, can we become world-class performers? If we treat each other fairly half of the time, can we become the competitor to beat in our business? If we show respect for each other half of the time, can we be world-class leaders?" My guess is that you answered no to each of these questions. If that's the case, then you agree that a moral foundation is essential to effective leadership.

Now, I agree that establishing the moral foundation does not guarantee that you will be able to shift the performance curve to the right; I do believe it enables that shift. We can think of leadership as having two main foci: the moral foundation and leadership skills. If the four cornerstones are not in place, one will not have the basis for growth. I assert that without that foundation, you can practice leadership skills (like strategic thinking, effective speaking, and good organizational design work) until you're blue in the face and still have no chance of improving the group's overall performance. On the other hand, if one has established the moral foundation, one must still exercise all of the leadership skills to get better performance. In this view, the moral foundation is a necessary precondition for an improvement in performance, and leadership skills are the motive force that actually gets the work done; the more leadership skills you pile on top of the moral foundation, the more efficiently you can get the distribution to shift.

You may think that the 2s and 3s in an organization are not motivated. As soon as you begin believing and operating on this principle, you begin to lose respect for those individuals, and your communications and actions will belie your beliefs. It may be that these people simply are not motivated by what's happening at work or the way in which that work is presented and organized. What if you were to follow these people home? You might find that many of them perform in nonwork activities with extraordinary quality, doing well in activities that engage them deeply. It may be as a rescue squad volunteer, clogger,[4] softball player, bowler, church administrator, or Little League coach. The challenge to the effective leader is to find ways to engage the employees' truly superior capabilities and then channel that energy in part toward the enterprise's goals.

One of the most direct ways of doing this, and therefore to develop Level Three Leadership skills, is to build one's leadership attempts on the moral rock described above, consistently telling the truth, keeping promises, treating people fairly and with respect. We can diagram this relationship as shown in Figure 5-2, with the four dimensions of the moral rock displayed below the normal curve of performance. Our observation is that the more leaders believe and behave in accordance with moral dimensions, the more powerful their relationships with their employees and the more extraordinary the performance of those employees will be. You can see in Figure 5-2 that each of the four cornerstones has been put on a 10-point scale. You might do a little self-assessment of your work group and rate your team on each of these four dimensions. A score of 10 means that you practice that dimension all or 100 percent of the time; a score of 5 would mean that you practice that dimension half or 50 percent of the time, and so on.

FIGURE 5-2

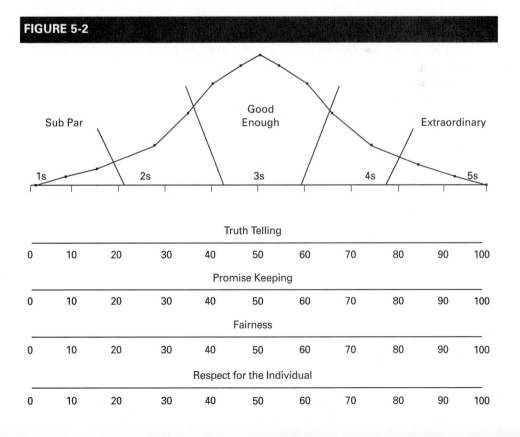

UNIVERSALITY OF THE MORAL FOUNDATION OF LEVEL THREE LEADERSHIP

Is the moral foundation of Level Three leadership possible for all? Does respect for the individual mean that we must like all of our employees or strive to have them like us? Is this a reasonable general approach? What do you think?

My answer is yes. Moral leadership is possible for all, and it does not require necessarily that you like each individual on your team. It does require that you recognize the potential of every individual and find it a worthy challenge to bring that potential to the fore. Sterling Livingston's classic article, *Pygmalion in Management,* cites the *My Fair Lady* story as a powerful example.[5] Dr. Higgins was able to bring out of Eliza that which others could not see and did not work to bring forth. The challenge of effective leadership is to bring out the best in others.

I acknowledge that many choose not to treat others with respect. We find many in our work who do not show respect for others and at the same time claim to be leaders of integrity. We believe that effective leadership is Level Three leadership and that it is built upon the moral foundation I have described here. This is what integrity means to us. People often claim integrity and defend their own possession of it vigorously yet never stop to examine what it is and how it plays out in dealings with suppliers, employees, and customers. *Integrity* means to be whole, to be unified. How can one not tell the truth and have integrity? How can one not tell the truth and have employees respond willingly to their attempts to influence? How can one break promises and claim integrity? How can one treat people unfairly and say that they are leaders with integrity?

This line of reasoning doesn't necessarily mean that all will like the leader or that the leader will like all the employees. There is plenty of room for disagreements within this framework and, at the same time, for mutual respect for each other and the basic beliefs upon which their relationship is built. Even though disagreements may exist, with the moral foundation in place, they are clear, on the table, and well understood. Time has been spent in showing respect for the other and in understanding all of the disagreement's aspects, and the issues are clear to both. Obviously, if the topic of dispute is major, it may lead to a parting of the ways, but the parting will be based on mutual understanding rather than manipulation, deceit, jealousy, or contempt.

Commitment to moral dimensions is evident in an effective leader's behavior. It emanates from a person's center so that in speeches, conversations, meetings, plans, and programs the four basic principles are evident. If you can get their attention, it's rather easy to have senior groups pause and assess themselves on these four dimensions, and when this happens, the group's insight jumps another level. In one senior management meeting, the people in the room were obviously not using the moral principles, and their company was therefore suffering from ordinary performance. One of my colleagues interrupted their discussion, introduced the moral dimensions, and then asked the group to rate privately its past and present behavior on each of the four dimensions on a scale of 1 to 10 as described previously. A few minutes later, the reported average score of the senior executives in the room was between 3 and 5. A lively discussion then ensued as to whether or not the group would be able to manage itself, much less the company, unless dramatic changes were made in the ways that they dealt with each other. This senior group began working immediately on improving their abilities to use the moral dimensions. They discovered that making that kind of Level Three change was not easy, yet each of them agreed that it was necessary if they hoped to move the company from ordinary to extraordinary performance.

This point is portrayed powerfully by survey results reported in *Industry Week* magazine. Two independent national polling firms conducted separate surveys of American middle managers from many industries over a 10-year span, in 1973 and 1983 (contact with the publisher revealed that the 1993 study was being held and used privately in consultation). In these controlled samples, two basic questions were asked: "Do you trust senior management?" and "Do you respect senior management?" In the 1973 results, the yes answers averaged about two-thirds. By 1983, the yes answers had fallen to about one-third. One wonders how one can manage, much less lead, a business if two-thirds of middle managers don't trust or respect senior management.[6] Although I haven't seen similar studies for 1993 and beyond, the question remains: At what level of trust and respect can a leadership team expect to get world-class performance from their employees?

Another indicator of the universal applicability and impact of morally founded leadership comes from my own research, in which surveys and interviews were given to over 100 matched pairs of superiors and subordinates in a large insurance company. Both individuals in the relationships rated how much the subordinate had learned in the relationship, a measure of the superior's influence on the subordinate at Levels Two and Three. In addition, measures of over 50 characteristics of the individuals and their relationship were included in the survey. The results indicated that the combined levels of *trust* and *respect* accounted for about three-fourths—yes, 75 percent—of the variance in the amount of learning in the relationship.[7] Both of these studies suggest that trust and respect are key factors in successful management and leadership relationships.

CONCLUSION

Effective leadership is built on a foundation of moral principles. If you ignore these principles, your attempts to lead will be undermined. On the other hand, if you can establish trust and respect among your colleagues by practicing the four cornerstones of moral leadership—truth telling, promise keeping, fairness, and respect for the individual—then you will have a foundation from which your attempts to lead can spring. Leading morally won't ensure dramatic results, but it will enable your other leadership skills to have influence.

PRINCIPLES OF EFFECTIVE LEADERSHIP INTRODUCED IN THIS CHAPTER

1. All effective leadership has a moral foundation.
2. Effective leaders tell the truth.
3. Effective leaders keep their promises.
4. Effective leaders treat people fairly.
5. Effective leaders have and show respect for the individual.

QUESTIONS FOR REFLECTION

1. Could you be an effective leader if you told your people the truth half of the time? If you kept your promises to them half of the time?
2. Rate your current work group on the four cornerstones of the moral foundation on scales from 0 to 10. (See the Self-Assessment Exercise that follows.)
3. What could you do to strengthen the moral foundation of your leadership base and of the leadership base of your organization?
4. How do you understand that the moral foundation of leadership relates to the concept of Level Three leadership?

NOTES

Note: To quickly access all *Harvard Business Review* reprints listed here, go to www.hbsp.harvard.edu/hbsp/adv_search.asp, insert the reprint number in the Product Number field, and click Search.

1. See Ed Freeman, *Strategic Management: a Stakeholder Approach* (Marshfield, MA: Pitman, 1984).
2. This concept was first introduced to me by my colleague, Alex Horniman, who developed it while head of the Olsson Center for Business Ethics at the Darden School. The ideas are also apparently used by Rich Teerlink, CEO of Harley Davidson, as noted in Tom Peters, *The Tom Peters Seminar* (New York: Vintage Books, 1994), 81.
3. See a Towers Perrin salary study reported in *Industry Week,* June 15, 1992, 29.
4. Clogging is a kind of group dancing.
5. Sterling Livingston, "Pygmalion in Management," *Harvard Business Review,* reprint 88509.
6. Bruce Jacobs and William Miller, "The Verdict on Corporate Management," *Industry Week,* July 25, 1983, 58.
7. James G. Clawson and Michael B. Blank, "What Really Counts in Superior Subordinate Relationships," *Mentoring International* 4:1 (Winter 1990): 12–17.

SELF-ASSESSMENT EXERCISE
THE MORAL FOUNDATION FOR EXTRAORDINARY
PERFORMANCE OF MY WORK GROUP

Rate your current work group on the following dimensions. Zero means "none of the time," 50 means "half of the time," and 100 means "all of the time." After you've made your rating, ask each member of your work group to give their ratings, anonymously if necessary, and then calculate the averages and reflect on or discuss the results.

Truth Telling

| 0 | 10 | 20 | 30 | 40 | 50 | 60 | 70 | 80 | 90 | 100 |

Promise Keeping

| 0 | 10 | 20 | 30 | 40 | 50 | 60 | 70 | 80 | 90 | 100 |

Fairness

| 0 | 10 | 20 | 30 | 40 | 50 | 60 | 70 | 80 | 90 | 100 |

Respect for the Individual

| 0 | 10 | 20 | 30 | 40 | 50 | 60 | 70 | 80 | 90 | 100 |

WORK GROUP AVERAGES:

TT = _____   PK = _____   F = _____   RFI = _____

Implications of these scores?

6

A Leader's Guide to Why People Behave the Way They Do

*To be autonomous means to act in accord with one's self—it means feel-
ing free and volitional in one's actions. When autonomous, people are
fully willing to do what they are doing, and they embrace the activity
with a sense of interest and commitment. Their actions emanate from
their true sense of self, so they are being authentic. In contrast, to be controlled means to act because one is being pressured. When controlled,
people act without a sense of personal endorsement. Their behavior is
not an expression of the self, for the self has been subjugated to the controls. In this condition, people can reasonably be described as alienated.*

—EDWARD DECI, *WHY WE DO WHAT WE DO*

Leaders influence people. Unless leaders understand why people behave the way they do, their efforts to influence others will have random, perhaps unpredictable, even alienating effects. You might get just the opposite of what you expected. For instance, perhaps you have been trying to get a subordinate to do something at work, and no matter what you do, she just won't respond. On the other hand, maybe your boss has been asking you to do something, and you resist. If you've ever asked yourself as a leader or a colleague, "Now *why* did he do that?" then you've wrestled with this problem. At home, at work, or at play, you have no doubt observed people doing things that were, to you, unexpected or unusual. You may have seen two people in very similar situations respond in very different ways. All of these incidents raise the question, for leaders, of why people behave the way they do. This is a very complex subject about which volumes have been and continue to be written. This chapter will introduce some fundamentals about what motivates people and under what conditions they will give their best efforts and then it will offer a summary framework that has proven pragmatic and powerful for leaders in a variety of situations.

Some people resist this process of analysis by saying that they are being asked to be psychologists rather than leaders. There is a difference. Both leaders and psychologists have to know something about human behavior, and both are encouraging change. In this, leaders who resist understanding human behavior focus at a very superficial level, behavior, and simply command, "Do this!" or "Do that!"—clearly a Level One approach. At the other extreme, many psychologists and psychiatrists attempt to understand the very building blocks of a person's personality, delving into significant and perhaps distant historical events. Our target lies in between. Effective leaders understand why the people they are trying to influence behave the way they do. Because mere compliance with commands is no longer an effective competitive mindset (getting workers to perform merely adequately and grudgingly will no longer set one apart from the competition), effective leaders' mental models of leadership go beyond giving orders and assuming compliance for monetary rewards. On the other hand, leaders are not trying necessarily to understand where a person's personality or psyche comes from, but they are trying to understand what that person's motivations *are* in the present. Ignorance of the fundamentals of human behavior leaves one with a limited set of generic influence models that may or may not have impact on any particular individual. Deeper understanding provides more options, gives one more potential tools, and frankly, makes one a more powerful leader.

THE BEGINNINGS

For the first nine months of existence, human fetuses are an integral part of another human being. Whatever preliminary awareness there may be of life, it is enveloped entirely inside another. When we are born, we begin a three- to six-month process of becoming simply aware of our individuality. As this emerging awareness dawns on us, at least five fundamental questions arise. These are not conscious questions in the sense of our thinking about them; rather, they represent issues that must be resolved one way or another. Their answers begin to shape our sense of individuality, our sense of place in the world and our fundamental stance in it.

1. When I'm cold, am I made warm?
2. When I'm hungry, am I fed?
3. When I'm wet, am I made dry?
4. When I'm afraid, am I comforted?
5. When I'm alone, am I loved?

When these questions are answered affirmatively, we tend to feel (rather than think) that we are cared for, that we have a place in the world, and that life—and more particularly, the key people in it—are supportive, confirming, and comfortable. We begin to learn that although we are not they, they are good. We start to ascribe to the objects of our attention (our parents) attributes of caring, concern, and dependability, which we generalize to other people in our life.[1]

When these answers are answered in whole or in part negatively, we tend to develop feelings that we are not cared for (as much as we want or need), that we may not have a place in the world, and that life and others in it are not supportive, confirming, or comfortable. Of course, no parent is able to be there all the time. Sometimes when we are cold, hungry, wet, afraid, or alone, mother does not come. And the uncertainty of this leads us to question the security of the world around us.

If these questions are answered negatively too often, we begin to develop holes in our personalities. By *holes,* I mean uncertainties, even fears, about our place in the world. Sometimes these holes are small, and sometimes they are quite large. Studies of chimpanzees conducted in France, for example, have shown that if a baby chimpanzee is left alone without motherly comfort yet supplied with more than enough shelter, warmth, light, food, and water, the baby will eventually die. Too many negative responses to human children's inchoate but deeply felt needs may lead them to a feeling of uncertainty or even betrayal. The noted English psychologist Melanie Klein calls this the "good breast/bad breast" phenomenon: Part of the time I get what I want, some of the time I don't, and that makes me angry with the very person who bore me. This can become a big psychological dilemma for a person, especially if the negative responses outweigh the positive ones.

These holes in our personalities can be very influential in our lives. If they are large enough, they can persist, perhaps even dominating our adult activities for decades or our whole lives. Let me give you an example. One day a student came to see me. She came in, shut the door, sat down, and began sobbing. I said, "What's the matter?" She said that she had just gotten the job of her dreams, making more money than she thought she could make, with the very company she had always wanted to work for. "Hmm," I said, "what's the problem?" She said that she had called her mother to report her success and that within 15 seconds the conversation had turned to her mother's charity work, her latest accomplishments, what she was working on, how many accolades she had received lately, and so on. Then this student said, "You know, it's been that way my *whole* life. Every time I've tried to talk to her about me, it quickly turns to being about her!"

This is an example of an apparent emotional hole in the mother's psyche. Even in the face of her own daughter's milestone achievement, she was driven to shift the conversation to her own unfulfilled needs for attention and recognition. We might well expect that this mother did not get sufficient positive responses to those five fundamental questions as a child. When she needed comforting, she didn't get it. When she needed loving, she didn't get enough of it. Probably, her mom or dad rewarded her with some attention when she made some achievement that pleased them. She learned that her checked-off to-do list was more important to them than who she was. With that hole inside her personality, she began searching for ways to fill it in through achievements, trying to find ways to obtain the love, affirmation, and comforting that she did not get as a child. This meant that when she became a mother, her child became another means of filling in those holes. Unwittingly, she used her infant to love her and to affirm her importance. And in the process, the child, my student, did not get what she herself needed.

We can observe elsewhere in adult life the behavioral result of these "holes" developed in infancy. When you meet someone at a cocktail party and the entire conversation revolves around their life, interests, hobbies, and goals, you might begin to wonder if he isn't trying to fill in a hole by keeping the spotlight of attention on himself, which is by now a habitual behavior. Maybe you have encountered situations such as I've seen where you are in a conversation with a small group when another person comes up and somehow changes the topic of conversation (regardless of what the group was talking about) to her own agenda. Melanie Klein[2] and Alice Miller[3] describe this "gift" that parents give to their children, the natural conflicts, small or large, of going from being totally and completely cared for to entering a world in which even those closest are inconsistent in their love and caring.

So my student's mother, not getting what she wanted as a child, grew up, married, and had children, including my student. She sought to affirm her own identity in the world, to fill in these holes, and this effort spilled over into her mothering. Consequently, she may not have given her children what they needed, perhaps instead seeking to get love and affection from them (perhaps manifest in language like "Don't you love your Mother?" instead of "Mommy loves you"), and they, in turn, began to develop holes because they were not getting what they needed. And so, a 30-year-old woman who graduated from a well-known professional school and got the job she always dreamed of for more money than she'd ever hoped for finds her good fortune hollow, empty, and a cause for sobbing.

The problem is that we cannot fill in these holes later in life. The attempt to do so is an unending source of frustration and emotional anguish. Miller makes this point, as does Gail Sheehy[4]. However many achievements we may attain, however much money we make, however many buildings we may construct, however many accolades and awards and prizes we may win, they will not fill these gaps left by parents who could not give what we needed at the time of infancy. We can, however, recognize them and in that recognition begin to make a "necessary passage" to let go of the desire to fill them. We can grieve the fact, if necessary, that we didn't get what we wanted or needed and then move on by learning to accept ourselves and our right as human beings to take up space in the world. In Klein's terms, we have to come to terms with the good breast/bad breast dilemma and reach a reparation of the conflict, acknowledging this reality, perhaps grieving at the recognition, and then getting on with our lives.

These fundamental five questions, however, imply a sixth question that lingers throughout our lives: "How can I get other people to do what I want?" Our developing personality and its holism (or "hole-ism") tends to help forge our strategies for influencing others. Perhaps we learned early on that bullying worked most of the time. Perhaps we learned that pretending to be pitiful elicited the results we hoped for. Perhaps we learned that being the best at anything would get us the adoration we craved internally. These and other strategies all have pros and cons associated with them. But these learned strategies for influencing others are not the end of the story.

Our Genetic Endowment

The object relations theorists and child psychologists represented in the previous section present a largely nurture-based view, namely, that people come into the world as blank slates upon which the tendencies of their lives are written by parents, friends, and other forces around them. Yet any parent will tell you that children have innate and unique tendencies. Clearly we have inherited a variety of characteristics from our parents. These include not only physical characteristics such as eye and hair color, metabolism, and body shape but also biochemical balances and emotional tendencies as well as more fundamental species-specific instincts or drives such as breathing, eating and drinking, reproducing, and socializing. Nigel Nicholson, of the London Business School, makes a case that many aspects of our human behavior, including the seemingly universal tendency to create hierarchies, are inherited traits that have been hard-wired into our DNA.[5] As we have recently mapped the human genome and continue research on the genetic basis for behavior, we will learn more about how much has been predetermined by our genetic endowments. It's a difficult and interesting question. It may be, for example, that we can no more teach a hard-nosed, autocratic leader to be kind and gentle than we can teach a person not to be allergic. Leaders are constantly faced with the questions, "To what degree can people change?" and "Will they follow my leadership?" If people cannot change, then leadership has no future. Most leaders in history—particularly business leaders, I assert—have been Level One leaders who targeted human behavior only.

As we grow and age, the interplay between our genetic endowment and our emerging personality traits begins to gel. If we are to understand the nature of leadership and its ability to impact humans, we must understand the relationship between our genetic tendencies and our view of the world that results from how we were raised.

Solidifying the Tendencies

Although much of the "drama," as Alice Miller calls it, takes place in the first three months to three years of life, some say that the basic tendencies usually gel sometime in the first decade of life. Morris Massey has hypothesized that what you were when you were 10 years old pretty much determines the basic values of your life that will shape your behavior.[6] By then, the basic answers to the five questions presented in the previous section have been repeated so many times that you have come to understand the world in terms of those answers. A personal example may help to explain. My father grew up in the Great Depression in the 1930s. His family grew vegetables in a small plot of vacant ground to have food to eat. Later in life, though, he made a small fortune building large motor hotels in Idaho. When we would go to visit him as adults, his idea of taking us out to dinner was "all you can eat for $4.99." Even though he had enough money to eat at any restaurant in the city without blinking an eye, he could not let go of this core value imprinted upon his personality in those formative years. Perhaps you have observed this kind of behavior in your own extended family where a person hangs on to values that seem to date from about age 10 or earlier yet no longer seem relevant to the present situation.

This phenomenon is commonly alluded to in the popular press by references to Generation This or Generation That (Baby Boomers, Generation X, Generation Y, etc.). The hypothesis is that the current generation (however difficult it is to define when one begins and another ends) has some common core tendencies that we, business and political leaders, should be aware of. To the extent that broad societal influences can imprint themselves on young, impressionable minds, there may be some truth to these portrayals. This raises the question of how, if at all, can we begin to see categories of humans and how they might be influenced by leadership. When we think about why people behave the way they do, we might note at least seven levels of similarity and dissimilarity:

1. *Humanity.* Some universally human characteristics do exist. In addition to our DNA, our bodily shapes, and the fundamentals of breathing, drinking, eating, and reproducing (all very strong instincts, by the way), other characteristics seem to mark all people: humor, smiling, laughing, socializing, playing, and so on. William Glasser has postulated that we all have five basic needs: survival, love and inclusion, power, freedom, and fun.[7]
2. *Regional culture.* Scandinavians, for instance, differ from Northern Europeans in predictable patterns, and Latin Americans differ from North Americans in certain ways as well.
3. *National culture.* People from the same nation have learned over the years to behave in some similar ways. Norwegians do things one way, whereas Swedes have chosen another; Mexicans can be differentiated clearly from Colombians according to some habits and customs.
4. *Subnational culture.* Inside most nations, regional units of similarity differ from other subnational regions. In the United States, for example, Southerners do things differently than Northerners or Westerners.
5. *Organizational culture.* Corporations also develop cultures. The predictable ways that employees of one company behave can often be contrasted with the predictable ways that employees of other companies behave.
6. *Family culture.* Regardless of where you live, your behavior is surely influenced by your family upbringing and principles. Some people litter and others don't, for example, largely based on their familial training.
7. *Individuality.* We know from studies of twins that even with the same genetic endowment and environmental upbringing, people will vary, will differentiate themselves. Each person has some unique features.

> Every human is like every other human in some ways, and in other ways, every human is unlike every other human.

Leaders must take into account all of these levels of similarity and dissimilarity, whether one is opening a new plant overseas or trying to motivate an underperforming employee to do better. There are ways in which we can treat all humans the same, yet there are ways that we must treat every individual differently–whether an employee in our own company or a business associate from another nation or global region. Every human being has a familial and a personal heritage that shapes what he or she says and does. Sorting out the differences and similarities along these seven levels becomes a leadership dilemma. Can I influence every Saudi the same way? Can I treat every Southerner the same way and expect strong followership behavior? Can I assume that all humans will work for money or for praise—and hope to get their best efforts? Unfortunately, many would-be leaders assume that their own set of values is universal, and they fall back on their own view of the world in their attempts to lead and influence others. This assumption is, in my view, one of the most persistent problems in leadership roles worldwide, but it is just one in the category of assumptions we make about how to lead and manage others. These assumptions, which are passed down from generation to generation much like genes, have been called *memes*.[8] Wise leaders will understand their memetic endowment as much as their genetic endowments. Let's now discuss these in more detail.

Memes

Memes are the ideas and beliefs that people develop and pass on to others over time. They live on from generation to generation and reproduce themselves, sometimes with mutations, in the lives of others. In some cases these ideas that seem to have a life of their own spread wildly, and in other circumstances they gradually die out. In this, memes are like viruses; they reproduce until their environment is no longer hospitable, and then they die.[9] "Waste not, want not" is a meme that developed during economically difficult times. "Never touch a person with your left hand" is a meme that spawned in nomadic nations without modern hygiene facilities. The stirrup is a meme that was born, spread, and ultimately changed the whole face of the world's political and military power structure.[10]

Memes are the mental building blocks (complementing the genetic physical building blocks) upon which we erect our behavior. We are quite aware of some of our memes. Other memes are so common and essential to us that they seem invisible, like water to fish swimming in a tank. Ideas that we take for granted, electricity, for one, were unknown for much of human history. At some point these ideas were born, propagated, refined, and passed on to successive generations.

Memes come in at least three varieties: distinction, strategy, and association. Distinction memes allow us to name things. *California* is a distinction meme. There is no line on the desert or mountain ground that shows where California begins and Nevada ends, yet we carry around with us the idea of California. "Lift weights and you'll get stronger" is a strategy meme. These are the if-then statements that we carry around about action-result linkages. "Thinner is better" is an association meme. Here, we apply a value to a distinction meme; we recognize the difference between fat and thin and make a judgment about which is preferable.[11]

One of the fundamental challenges in life and especially in leadership is to become more aware of our personal memes and to decide which we will perpetuate and which we will work to eradicate, in ourselves and in our progeny as well as in our associates and subordinates. If we do not undertake this reflective reexamination, we live our lives as little more than riders on spear-tips thrown by previous generations, carrying on their thoughts, beliefs, and assumptions about the way the world is and ought to be. To consciously transcend our memetic endowment, in ways that we cannot with our genetic endowment, is the mark of a truly mature adult and of a visionary leader.[12] Unless we see and examine the memes, conscious and subconscious, that guide our behavior and shape our motivations, we are not architects of our own lives, much less the lives of others; rather, we are the mere executors of previous generations' blueprints. Most leaders, however, take a decidedly simpler view of human motivation.

MOTIVATION

The vanilla leader's view of motivation generally includes two ideas—rewards and punishments. We hold a carrot out in front of somebody and expect that she will move ahead to get the carrot. If that doesn't work, then we stand behind and beat their backsides with a whip. If that doesn't work, we often throw our hands up in dismay and exclaim, "I just don't know how to get this person moving!" As Harry Levinson has pointed out what we really mean when we try this strategy, given the image of what stands between the carrot and the whip, is "I just don't know how to get this jackass moving."[13] But we deceive ourselves if we conclude that people are, like jackasses, necessarily unmotivated, lazy, stupid, or stubborn just because they won't do what seems so eminently rational to us.

One reason that the reward/punishment model does not always explain human behavior well is that one person's reward may be another person's punishment. When we extend the same carrot to everyone in the organization, only those who value that reward will respond. When we use the same whips (threats) on everyone in the organization, not everyone responds. Clearly, a person's values will greatly influence the effectiveness of any particular carrot or stick. If the person doesn't value the carrot or fear the stick, he is not likely to respond to its use. Expectancy theory gives us a partial answer to this question; it suggests that people are motivated to do things when they expect a reward that they value but are not motivated if they do not value the reward.[14]

Many leaders say that we should not concern ourselves with what goes on *inside* a person because we cannot observe or manage it. These are followers of B. F. Skinner, who first outlined the notion of behavior modification.[15] They consider people who do attempt to understand or explain such unobservable things to be charlatans and speculators. Rather, they say, managers should focus on the external behavior and then try to shape it by rewarding its desirable aspects and punishing the undesirable aspects. In one management seminar I attended, the instructor suggested that managers should not be managing people but rather their inputs and outputs. This was clearly a behavioral approach; it is, however, also a Level One approach.

My experience has been that most people who change jobs or leave corporations or withdraw from involvement in their work or organizations do so in large measure because their talents, interests, and abilities are being ignored and wasted. They see large gaps between who they are, what they want to be and can become, and what the organization asks of them. To me, the suggestion that managers should focus on the outputs rather than the people who create them is to further this alienation from organizational life and productivity—as suggested by the quote opening this chapter. This view of humans as merely resources continues the corporate tendency to dehumanize the work experience and perpetuates a meme that says, "People are homogeneous, predictable, replaceable parts." Frederick Taylor and others who subscribe to scientific management principles have kept this meme in the world.[16] People have proven to be much more complex than the principles of simple reward and punishment would suggest. But still, most managers seem to subscribe to the belief that they are in control of their associates' behavior.

This control theory meme has been clarified by William Glasser.[17] Many people subscribe, perhaps unwittingly, to control theory when they believe (1) that they respond to external stimuli (rather than choosing to respond or not), (2) that they can make other people do what they want them to, and (3) that it is their right or responsibility to reward or punish others depending on what those others do. This meme cluster carries with it many dysfunctional consequences including the central one of narrowing drastically one's range of choices in the world. We do not answer the phone because it rings (the first assumption); rather, we answer it because we choose to. Others do not make us angry when they do not do as we say (the second assumption); rather, we choose to be angry. When we lose sight of our own volition in selecting and responding to external stimuli by virtue of the memes within us, our range of options narrows, and we become pawns in the chess game of life. When this happens, we begin to lose our intrinsic motivation. Wise people recognize that all of our behavior is chosen—and leaders create more choices for people.

Glasser has also pointed out that there are four ways of behaving: (1) activity (what we say and do), (2) thinking, (3) feeling, and (4) physiology (our bodily reactions and chemistry). Total behavior, therefore, comprises all four components. The key point, he argues, is that we all choose how we behave in each arena, including the emotional one. If a loved one dies, for example, most people would say that we have no choice but to be depressed. Glasser points out that being depressed is a choice, too. With a different perspective, we might find contentment, peace, and even harmony at this time. Glasser clarifies the insight of the Stoic philosophers: It's not events that affect people but rather the view that people take of those events. Events do not control us, really, and neither do other people. We allow them to control us and our reactions.

> The truth is that we choose our responses to the world.

Understanding this responsibility for our own reactions is enormously freeing for most people. However, we can do so rationally only if we become aware of our memes, our personality holes, and, exercising courage, begin to pick and choose which ones we would like to retain and utilize. In doing that, we become freer, more autonomous, and more authentic. When others encourage that in us, we thrive. And there's the lesson for leaders to be: Finding ways to support others' autonomy engenders powerful followership, while persisting in the core beliefs of control theory weakens our ability to influence others.

THE RATIONAL-EMOTIVE BEHAVIOR MODEL

We need a model of human behavior that will take into account genetic and memetic endowments as well as our nurtured tendencies to help explain why people behave the way they do and then give us some practical tools to begin thinking about how to work with, how to communicate with, and how to lead others. This approach implies a model that recognizes thoughts and feelings along with behavior. The work of Albert Ellis[18] and other rational-emotive researchers provides such a foundation.[18] The rational-emotive behavior (REB) model shown in Figure 6-1 builds on Ellis's work and offers practicing managers a way of digging deeper, of understanding human behavior and its motivations, and of leading more effectively. The REB model includes several elements: events and our perceptions of them, values and assumptions we have about the

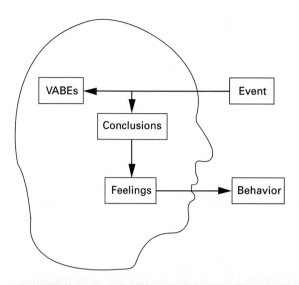

FIGURE 6-1   The Rational-Emotive Behavior (REB) Model

way the world should be (VABEs), conclusions or judgments about the present situation, feelings, and behavior (*activity,* in Glasser's terms).

Events

To paraphrase the common street meme, "things happen." People speak to us. Or don't. Doors open. Or close. We get feedback on our behavior. Or we don't. All of these things are events. We observe some of them, whereas we ignore or don't see others. What we see when we observe makes a big difference—as we've already suggested in our definition of the leadership point of view. Our understanding of science, especially particle physics, even suggests that how we observe can even change what we see. Studies of light have shown that depending on how you structure the experiment or observation, light appears either as matter or as energy. More commonly, two people watching the same event may very well come away with different perceptions and conclusions. We can see what people do and hear what they say. How we interpret those events makes a big difference in our behavior. This is in part because what a camera and microphone might capture may not be the same as what we perceive.

Perceptions and Observations

Observations and perceptions are not the same thing. An *observation,* as we use it here, involves simply what would be visible to an impersonal, unemotional camera's eye. An observation is a *description* as opposed to a *judgment;* for example, "John came in at 8:15 today." A perception, on the other hand, is a subset of what we might observe; it is what is left to our awareness after we've filtered out whatever it is that we filter out. Maybe we didn't notice what time John came in today at all. Maybe we didn't notice whether John was even at work today. So although a camera might record, without filtering, a series of events, we are constantly filtering and selecting what we will perceive.

Whatever it is that comes in through our perceptual filters is what we see, even though it may be a small part of what actually happened.

VABEs

When we observe something, we immediately compare that event with our personal set of VABEs about the way the world (including ourselves and our behavior) should be. If there is a gap between what we observe and what we expect, we have a problem. If there is no gap, things are as they should be, and we carry on without concern. These shoulds and oughts make up our value systems. When we say that a person should do this or should do that, we are expressing one of our VABEs.

Our VABEs develop early and over many years as outlined previously. We learn them from our parents, our friends, our teachers, and our experiences. Proponents of transactional analysis call them our parental tapes or scripts, the little messages that remind us of what our parents told us was right and wrong.[19] Our VABEs include more than just what others have taught us, however; they also include our own conclusions about the way the world and the people in it operate.

For instance, one person watching the people around him work diligently to further their own fortunes might conclude that people are greedy. If this person continues to see that kind of behavior generally, he might begin to hold this as a relatively central assumption about why people behave the way they do. This assumption would be even further solidified if the person behaved that way himself. Table 6-1 lists examples of

---

TABLE 6.1   Some Common VABEs

Always clean your plate.
Always cross at the crosswalk.
Submit your will to that of the group.
The next life is more important than this one.
There is no next life.
Kindness is good.
Kindness is foolish.
You can't trust a _____.
A good father would have _____.
Always obey the boss.
Question authority.
People should give their best efforts to the company.
People should save their best efforts for their personal lives.
If you want it done right, do it yourself.
If you want it done right, find the right team.
Professional people should wear suits and ties.
You should always call your boss by his or her name.
Never give a sucker an even break.
Always give the boss what he or she wants.
(Write in one or two that come to mind for you here.)

some common assumptions. Clearly, widely held VABEs will vary from culture to culture along the seven categories introduced earlier in this chapter. Some of these examples may seem normal to you, and others may seem foreign. That will depend on your culture, your upbringing, and your current set of VABEs.

This book's principal thesis is that an understanding of VABEs and how they shape behavior is essential to effective leadership. Some call this values-based leadership.[20] If you can understand a person's constellation of VABEs, you will have a much deeper understanding about why they behave the way they do. VABEs have some characteristics that are important to remember.

1.   *VABEs vary in strength.* Some of our basic beliefs are very important to us, and we put them at the *core* of our personalities. We all try to protect our core assumptions very carefully. Peripheral assumptions, the ones that are less important to us, are more easily changed. Figure 6-2 depicts the concept that core VABEs are more likely to shape our behavior than those at the periphery.

2.   *VABEs vary considerably from person to person.* Although one person may believe that a person should clean up her plate after dinner, the next person may not believe that at all. Surely many in a culture will share some broadly held societal values and assumptions. In fact, this is how we define a culture at one of the seven levels listed earlier. But if you accept the notion that assumptions vary from person to person, then it follows that to understand why a person behaves the way he does, you have to understand something about *that person's* assumptions, not just about your own or about what you think the culture's are. This points out what some authors have called the arrogance of the Golden Rule: Why should we expect that others want to be treated the way we want to be treated? They argue that the Platinum Rule would be "treat others as *they* want to be treated." The human race has not been very good at this since the beginning of recorded history.

3.   *VABEs apply to ourselves, too.* People have VABEs both about the way other people should behave (the external view) and about the way they themselves should behave (the internal view). We humans have a unique capacity to judge ourselves. We can observe our own behavior as well as others'. We have developed VABEs that describe a good self. This internal perspective of our VABEs we might call the ideal self, our vision of how we should be. Some parts of this ideal self are more important than other parts. The important parts we defend vigorously.

FIGURE 6-2   Centrality of VABEs and their Impact on Behavior

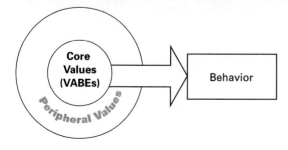

Inside us all, hidden from view, are vast arrays of connected values, assumptions, beliefs, and expectations. Some we hold strongly; some we exchange for others rather readily depending on the evidence and where we got them. Some we use to judge external events, and some we use to judge ourselves. And if we are wise, we will notice that our own VABEs do not necessarily match the VABEs of the person sitting next to us. Becoming aware of this opens a huge door of fascination and inquiry in life as we wonder, "Why does that person behave the way he does?" and "How might I best influence him?" Part of the answer lies in the connection between the observed event and one's VABEs.

External Conclusions

The key to understanding why people behave the way they do lies in the *comparison* of what they see and what they believe ought to be, the comparison between their perceptions and their VABEs. Events that take place around us do not determine what we do; rather, the comparison we make between what takes place around us and our personal, basic assumptions about what ought to be taking place is what motivates our activity.

Consider a simple example. Suppose that you and a friend are playing golf together. You both hit off the tee, and you both drive into the woods. You believe that, given who you are and your skill, you should not drive out of bounds. You compare your perception of what you have just done, driven into the woods, and realize that there is a disturbing gap between the two. At this point, another of your basic assumptions comes into play, for you believe that it is not becoming to a professional person to throw a temper tantrum, so you stifle your curse, work hard to control yourself, and keep the anger in. Yet you experience anger; your face may even grow flush. But you keep silent to maintain some vestige of control. Your friend, on the other hand, compares his basic assumption, "We all make mistakes. No one is perfect all the time, especially in golf" with his perception of his errant drive and walks calmly off the tee, trying to figure out what he did wrong. The events were the same, but the experience and the behavior were not. The comparison of similar events with different personal assumptions generated different behavior.

When we see something, we compare it with our VABEs in the space of a nanosecond. This comparison yields a number of options. If what we observe matches our expectations, then all is right with the world, and we go on. If there's a mismatch between what we expect to see and what we actually see, then we have a problem. We can ignore the disparity and go on as if nothing had occurred. We can fret and stew about the event and try to change it. Or we can reflect on our underlying VABE and consider changing it to match our observations. In this way, we are *all* scientists. In any event, in the fraction of a second that it takes to do this comparison, we reach a conclusion. These are the judgments we make about the situation, the people, and ourselves. If, for instance, we see our friend shoot a 110 in golf and we assume that "a good golfer always shoots 75 or under," then we are likely to conclude that our friend is a poor golfer.

Sometimes we jump to conclusions—that is, we make a judgment that may not be warranted by the evidence. One reason for this is that we tend to project our own meanings onto situations.[21] This is where the old saying "What Peter says about Paul tells you more about Peter than about Paul" comes from. Our tendency to project our own meanings on the world highlights again the usefulness of learning more about *our* assumptions and the assumptions of others. When a person jumps to conclusions, we can learn, if we are attentive, more about that person's basic assumptions, and this will help us greatly in our attempts to manage our relationship with that person.

Internal Conclusions

We can consider the observations we make about ourselves to be part of our *self-image.* We make self-judgments or conclusions by comparing what we believe we should be with what we see ourselves doing, that we are good fathers, good golfers, poor drivers, terrible poets, and so on. These conclusions can affect our behavior in a number of ways. We may become so convinced that we are or are not something that we stop trying to do anything differently. For example, we may assume that people who are good at something are good at it on the first try. If we try something and perform poorly, we may never try it again—and this could be a significant loss for ourselves and others. These self-fulfilling prophecies represent an internally directed, negative Pygmalion effect.[22] And our conclusions, external or internal, often cause powerful emotions within us. Figure 6-3 shows the relationship between these external and internal conclusions in the REB model.

Feelings

Whether our conclusions are internal (about ourselves) or external (about others), they tend to generate emotions. If we believe that people should tell the truth and we observe a person lying, then we conclude that this person is a liar and we become angry. If we believe we should be kind and we observe ourselves passing by a homeless person, we may conclude that we are not as kind as we should be, and we feel guilt. The next person, believing that people should make their own luck, might walk past the homeless person and feel nothing. Clearly, emotions are a big part of human behavior.

When our conclusions reflect a match between our observations and our assumptions, we usually experience the positive feelings—happiness, contentment, satisfaction, pride. When our observations violate or disconfirm our assumptions about either others or ourselves, we conclude that things or we are not right, or we experience negative feelings—sadness, discontent, anger, jealousy, disappointment. To an interested observer or would-be leader, these feelings are open windows to understanding why people behave the way they do.

The REB Model and the Missing Variable
Event + VABE → Conclusion → Emotions → Behavior

Often what we observe in others is their emotionally laden behavior. The REB model gives us a way of working backward to infer the underlying VABE(s) that must be in place for a particular event to have produced a particular emotional reaction. In this way the REB model structures an equation with one missing variable: the VABE that underlies emotional behavior. If we can understand all of the parts of this comparison dynamic—that is, the observations (what did you see?), the VABEs (what do you believe?), the conclusions (what conclusion do you draw from that?), and the feelings (how does that make you feel?)—then we can begin to understand why a person does what she does.

Because, as Skinnerians note, it is not easy to see what people are thinking or feeling, we have to be alert to detect the signals that others give us about themselves.

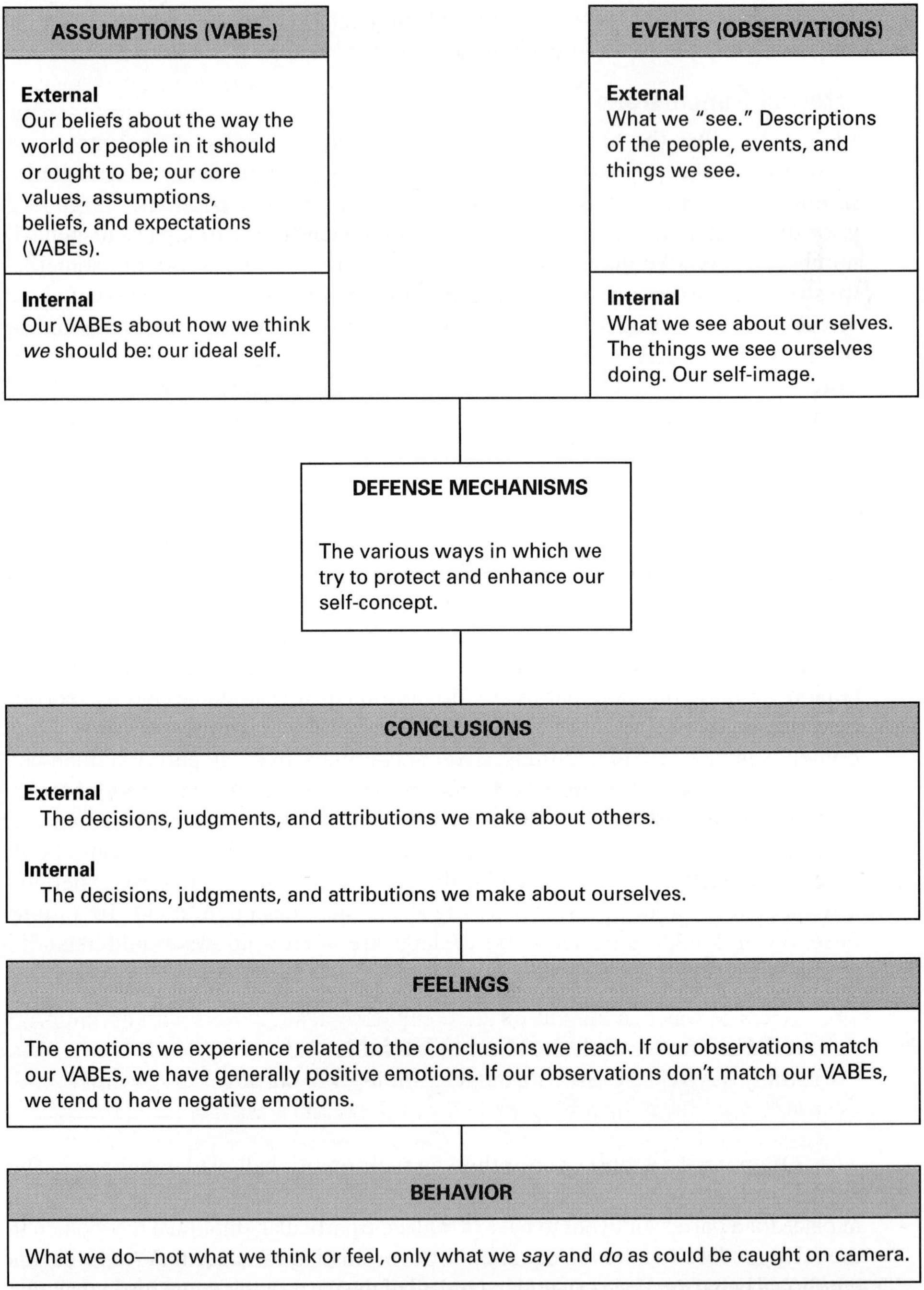

ASSUMPTIONS (VABEs)	EVENTS (OBSERVATIONS)
External Our beliefs about the way the world or people in it should or ought to be; our core values, assumptions, beliefs, and expectations (VABEs).	**External** What we "see." Descriptions of the people, events, and things we see.
Internal Our VABEs about how we think *we* should be: our ideal self.	**Internal** What we see about our selves. The things we see ourselves doing. Our self-image.

DEFENSE MECHANISMS

The various ways in which we try to protect and enhance our self-concept.

CONCLUSIONS

External
   The decisions, judgments, and attributions we make about others.

Internal
   The decisions, judgments, and attributions we make about ourselves.

FEELINGS

The emotions we experience related to the conclusions we reach. If our observations match our VABEs, we have generally positive emotions. If our observations don't match our VABEs, we tend to have negative emotions.

BEHAVIOR

What we do—not what we think or feel, only what we *say* and *do* as could be caught on camera.

FIGURE 6-3   The REB Model: Understanding Human Behavior

When we see a person who is obviously angry and we know what event triggered that anger, we can begin to infer what his underlying assumption might be. Usually, if a person is angry, his VABEs are contrary to the current event. If we care enough and can listen well enough, the person may even be willing to tell us outright what the underlying VABE was that triggered their feelings.[23]

Often, though, people are only vaguely aware of their VABEs, so they cannot describe their own VABE equation. They may be unclear about an assumption and, therefore, unclear about why they feel what they are feeling. In fact, if your experience is like mine, many people are quite unaware of their feelings, period. For simple issues, talking with a person may begin to reveal to both of you what the underlying assumptions and conclusions and emotions are. For more difficult issues, it may take someone more qualified, such as a psychologist or a counselor, to help understand the source of the feelings. When we can identify accurately the underlying assumption that, in comparison with an observation, caused a conclusion and generated a feeling, we will have a major insight into why people behave the way they do.

Behavior

Behavior is another result of the comparisons we make between events and our VABEs. *Behavior,* as we're using the term here, means simply what people say and do, that which we or a camera can observe. This includes what people say, their gestures, their facial expressions, and their eye movements as well as movements such as walking and running. When we see another's behavior, we reach conclusions about whether the person is behaving appropriately. In other words, her behavior becomes an event for us. The word *appropriately* implies that we have a judgmental filter, our VABEs, that determines what is fitting and proper and what is not. In trying to understand and influence others, if we ignore what lies behind their behavior, we are ignoring a powerful tool for understanding and working with that person.

AN REB EXAMPLE

With the basic elements of the REB model in place, let's see how it works to explain why people behave the way they do. Consider this short episode:

> George was coming out of the company's headquarters with an important guest when he saw Bill, one of his peer's subordinates and clearly in a hurry, on his way out. As he passed through the lobby, Bill cursed at the receptionist for not having his taxi waiting and stormed out the front door. George's client turned to George and remarked, "He's an interesting duck. How many more like him do you have around here?"

It's a small incident, one of hundreds we live through each day. If you were in George's shoes, what would you do? Before you read on, think for a moment. Interestingly, most groups will give a variety of answers, including:

1. Laugh it off and do nothing.
2. Go see Bill the next day and chew him out for behaving unprofessionally.
3. Chase Bill and demand an apology.
4. Go see Bill's boss the next day and demand that he reprimand Bill.
5. Offer an explanation to the guest. (What explanation would you offer?)

6. Reply "Oh, he's not one of ours, I can assure you."
7. Wait for a while to see if Bill will come to apologize. If not, go see him.

Perhaps you would do something not on this list. Where does all this variety of response come from? After all, it was the same, single incident. Well, if we use the REB model, we can begin to understand what is going on behind each of these alternative action plans. We first list the behavior and then try to infer logically what the underlying VABE must be for that behavior to have emerged.

Observed Behavior	Inferred VABE
Laugh it off and do nothing	Cursing at secretaries is no big deal, and important people understand this.
Go see Bill the next day and chew him out for behaving unprofessionally	You shouldn't reprimand your people in front of clients, and cursing at secretaries is unprofessional and unacceptable.
Chase Bill and demand an apology	You should reprimand people on the spot to have real results.
Go see Bill's boss the next day and demand that he reprimand Bill	Only a boss should reprimand a person.
Offer an explanation to the guest. (What explanation would you offer?)	Others, including clients, demand an explanation of poor behavior.
Reply, "Oh, he's not one of ours, I can assure you."	Lying to cover up one's shortcomings is an acceptable way to save face or maintain one's reputation.
Wait for a while to see if Bill will come to apologize. If not, go see him.	Most people recognize when they do bad things, and if you leave them alone, they will rectify the situation. We should give a person a chance to do well.

You can see that these VABEs are quite different and with some variation could mutate from person to person. The challenge is not to force people to all have the same VABEs; rather, from a leader's point of view, one wants to understand the VABEs of those she works with.

MEANING CHAINS

The point is not so much which action plan is right. All of the behavioral alternatives presented in the previous section would be right for the person who believes the VABE that led to them. Rather, the challenge is first to be able to *describe* this linkage between event and behavior. We can call this linkage the *meaning chain*. Meaning chains are like the value chains we use in strategic analysis. One must work to identify the chain and to assess each link's characteristics. This is especially true if we are trying to influence someone. Pausing to tease out another person's meaning chain does not require you to become a psychologist, but it does require you to be more careful about judging why people behave the way they do.

REB AND LEADING CHANGE

If we try to change a person's behavior by looking only at the behavior, we are guessing. For example, if you offer a subordinate more money if he will increase his sales, you are assuming that your subordinate wants more money strongly enough to change his behavior to get it. This is often true, but a person can use only so much money. And, believe it or not, some people value working relationships, the challenge of the work, the variety involved, and other features of their work more than they do the monetary compensations it brings. In fact, a series of studies have shown that people in general *lose* motivation when they are paid to do something.[24] This is evident in that volunteer organizations regularly have much higher levels of motivation and commitment than for-profit institutions.

So if offering a monetary reward doesn't seem to work to motivate someone, you might say, "If your sales aren't up by the end of the quarter, you're fired." This approach can lead to compliant behavior, obedience for the sake of avoiding punishment, or even passive-aggressive sabotage. The individual may compare the possibility of having to find new work with the cost of having to change behavior and conclude that she would rather find new work. Trying to change behavior in this way is like trying to move the tip of an iceberg without realizing that nine-tenths of the thing is underwater where you can't see it—just as invisible as a person's VABEs. With people, as with icebergs, a little informed exploration will often reveal the nature of what's hidden beneath the surface.

Suppose you are interviewing a moderate performer in your sales organization. After some conversation it becomes apparent that this person believes that people should not be pushy. Maybe he has had bad experiences with pushy people; perhaps he had pushy parents and is rebelling against their model of interpersonal style. Simply telling him to be more assertive is not likely to change his behavior. Unless you can help this person clarify his underlying VABE and compare its utility with the demands of the job at hand, you are not likely to make much progress. It may be that the person is willing to reexamine his VABE and work to change. If not, you both would be better off finding a different job fit for this person. Dealing with negative feedback is difficult for most of us. We tend to deny, discount, distort, or ignore disconfirming feedback. Why?

THE SELF-CONCEPT

The answer to the question I just posed is simple: because we all want to conclude positive things about ourselves. In fact, this may be the most fundamental human motivation of all. A well-known social scientist, S. I. Hayakawa, once noted that the basic purpose of all human activity is the protection, maintenance, and enhancement not of the self but of the self-concept or symbolic self.[25]

Our self-concept can be explained in three parts. First, the inward-looking set of assumptions about who we think we should be is the *ideal self*. Second, the inward-looking view of who we think we are is the *self-image*. Instead of observing an external event, we can see our own behavior—and this becomes the input to our VABE comparison. When there is a gap between our ideal self (self-oriented VABEs) and our self-image, when we behave in ways that we don't think we should, we reach a negative conclusion about ourselves, and our *self-esteem*, our feelings about ourselves, goes down. In other words, we can apply the REB model not only to external events but also to ourselves. These elements are diagramed in Figure 6-4. The more our self-image overlaps our ideal self, the better we feel about ourselves. The more distant our self-image is from our ideal self (either because the goals are too high or the behavior is too meager), the worse we are likely to feel about ourselves.

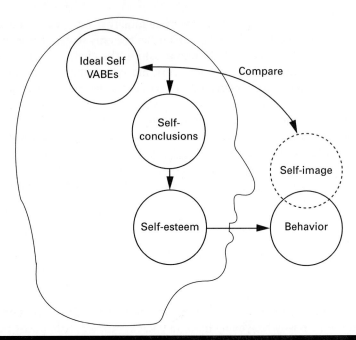

FIGURE 6-4 **An REB View of the Self-Concept**

DEFENSE MECHANISMS

Generally speaking, we don't like seeing gaps between who we want to be and who we are. So we figure out ways to protect ourselves from the psychological pain that comes with being aware of those gaps. These are known as *defense mechanisms.* Some are productive and motivate us to do something about the perceived gaps. Other ways are not so healthy or productive; we cover up the gaps or ignore them or try to make others' gaps bigger so ours won't seem so onerous. An abbreviated list of defense mechanisms appears at the end of this chapter.

We will go to extraordinary lengths to protect our self-concepts.

These mechanisms may be so strong that they let us be aware of only those perceptions that match our basic assumptions and, therefore, allow us to draw favorable conclusions about ourselves. In an extreme case, some abused children will even develop multiple personalities (enormous holes) to have someone inside themselves that they can like.

We activate our defense mechanisms when we are threatened. This occurs regularly in life and is appropriate, for it keeps us alive as well as also protected from responding to every little vacillation in feedback that comes along. The healthy defense mechanisms of the normal, functioning adult differ greatly from the unhealthy ones of an incapacitated psychotic. It is important to note that when a person's defense mechanisms are operating (or up, we might say), he is not likely to hear what you are trying to communicate. In coaching, teaching, or persuasion situations, this can be disastrous. If you want to influence others, you must learn to talk with them in ways that will tend to keep their defenses relaxed rather than activated.

CONCLUSION

What does all of this mean for a manager? Quite a bit. First, the issues we've discussed here suggest that one should be attentive to one's own motivations and memetic endowment. The simple statistics on the high failure rate of most so-called megamergers indicate that something far beyond financial expectation is going on. First, if one tends to build or merge or expand in the misguided attempt to fill some personal psychological hole, the consequences can extend to many others. Second, it means that to be more effective in dealing with, working with, and managing other people, one must be alert to the little tips of the psychological icebergs (VABEs) that we all carry around. They give us insight into why people behave the way they do. Third, it implies that unless we understand the core VABEs of a person, we are not likely to be successful in guiding her through a change process. Once a manager learns something of the central VABEs that a coworker or subordinate has (by listening, observing, or testing), the manager can assess whether or not the assumptions provide a basis for behavior that aligns with the organization's objectives. If a person's VABEs don't match those of the organization's culture, an extended coaching or mentoring period could be required, or it could mean looking for a better alignment in another organization.

Fourth, in smaller performance management settings, if a manager concludes that another's inappropriate behavior is based on assumptions that are fundamental to the individual's personality, the manager may begin thinking about alternative assignments for the individual because core values are not likely to change quickly. On the other hand, if the underlying assumption seems to be a peripheral one, the manager might hope to work with the individual to explore the usefulness of the assumption and its resulting behavior and perhaps initiate a change in the assumption and the behavior that grows from it. But as long as the manager ignores the VABEs that shape and generate behavior, he will be negating the human side of individuals and, worse, guessing at why they are behaving the way they are. Guessing is not managing.

This implies a simple but powerful model for coaching—as will be discussed in more detail in the chapter on leading change. First, do you *see* what the VABEs of the other person are? Can you write these down on paper? (This is a wonderful discipline for sharpening your thinking—many people think they understand something until they begin to write it down and discover that it's not so clear to them after all.) Second, can you *confirm* your assessment with the individual? Can you clarify and focus your tentative insights in informal conversations? "Gee, John, it seems to me that you seem to believe that if you want it done right, you have to do it yourself. Is that right?" If John confirms your observation, you can check that one off as accurate and go on to the next one. Third, you can set a time frame that you are willing to work on this, probably privately with yourself. What are you willing to give this change effort? Six months? Two years? Fourth, you can begin coaching—actively meeting with and discussing the functionality of the agreed-upon VABEs. "If you want it done right, do it yourself" is not a very functional managerial or leadership VABE. Is John willing to discuss this? Are you very adept at managing the conversation? Can you guide him to see how another approach might be more functional? Fifth, at the end of your tentative probationary period, you can decide whether you're making progress or not. If not, maybe a change will have to be made. If you are, perhaps you can continue your coaching with the hope that things will improve. Simply telling someone to delegate more, though, is not likely to produce a change.

A person's behavior, including response to leaders, is the result of many factors. People begin learning rapidly at birth. Depending on their familial support and their cultural surroundings, they begin to form a set of values, assumptions, beliefs, and expectations about how the world works by the time they are 10. Subsequent behavior, in general, stems from conclusions that emerge from a comparison of things seen with personal VABEs. These oughts and shoulds vary in their importance to a given individual as well as from individual to individual. These conclusions generate emotions in us that drive and shape our behavior.

We can apply the REB perspective to our views of ourselves as well as to our views of external events and other people—and this application affects our self-esteem. (See Figure 6-3 for an overview.) Various defense mechanisms attempt to shield our self-concept by protecting us from hurtful information—perhaps even if it's factual. Managers and potential leaders can use this framework to help understand why people behave the way they do. This involves watching for evidence of the VABEs that underlie a person's behavior. We can do this by listening, by observing, and by testing people's reactions to our proposals or conversations. Effective leaders will then explore ways to influence VABEs, for if they are able to influence at the VABE level, at Level Three, they will have a more lasting impact than if they simply target the external behavior (activity) exhibited by another. This is what it means to be a Level Three leader.

PRINCIPLES OF EFFECTIVE LEADERSHIP INTRODUCED IN THIS CHAPTER

1. Effective leaders are students of human behavior.
2. People develop their personalities early in life. Leaders may not be psychologists, but they do try to understand the personalities and psychological makeup of the people they hope to influence.
3. Human behavior is a function of genetic and memetic endowments. Unless one transcends these endowments, one is little more than a passenger on the tide of human history.
4. Human behavior is also a function of internal values, assumptions, beliefs, and expectations, or VABEs.
5. Although control theory summarizes a dominant model of leadership in the world, it provides a more powerful Level Three view of leader–follower behavior.
6. Leaders are good, descriptive observers of events around them; they *see* things.
7. We all compare events around us with our VABEs and reach conclusions based on those comparisons.
8. Our conclusions stimulate emotions within us.
9. Our conclusions and our emotions shape our behavior, but they are based on our VABEs.
10. The REB model explains not only external but also internal behavior, that is, self-judgment.
11. We all try to protect our self-concepts.
12. Effective leaders understand the VABEs of others and work to influence them, not just their behavior. This is the essence of Level Three leadership.

QUESTIONS FOR REFLECTION

1. What VABEs did my family teach me?
2. What are my core leadership VABEs?
3. How, if at all, am I behaving today to fill in holes from my past? What can I do to let go of this behavior?
4. How can I be more observant of others' VABEs?
5. Am I attentive to when others say "should" or "ought"?
6. How good am I at listening and inferring what others believe?
7. What are the core VABEs of the people closest to me? Can I write them down?
8. What are the core VABEs of the people I supervise? Can I write them down?
9. Which defense mechanisms do I tend to use the most? Are these functional or dysfunctional? Why or why not?

NOTES

Note: To quickly access all *Harvard Business Review* reprints listed here, go to www.hbsp .harvard.edu/hbsp/adv_search.asp, insert the reprint number in the Product Number field, and click Search.

1. For more detail on the object relations theory of human mental development, see N. Gregory Hamilton, *The Self and the Ego in Psychotherapy* (Northvale, NJ: Jason Aronson, 1996), and Jill Savege Scharff and David E. Scharff, *The Primer of Object Relations Theory* (Northvale, NJ: Jason Aronson, 1995).
2. Melanie Klein, *Love, Hate and Reparation* (New York: Norton, 1964).
3. Alice Miller, *The Drama of the Gifted Child* (New York: Basic Books, 1979; reprint, 1997) .
4. Gail Sheehy, *Necessary Passages* (New York: Bantam, 1984).
5. Nigel Nicholson, "How Hardwired Is Human Behavior," *Harvard Business Review,* reprint 98406. See also *Executive Instinct* (New York: Crown Business, 2000).
6. Morris Massey, *The People Puzzle* (Reston, VA: Reston, 1979).
7. William Glasser, *Choice Theory* (New York: HarperCollins, 1998).
8. Richard Dawkins, *The Selfish Gene* (Oxford, UK: Oxford University Press, 1976).
9. Susan Blackmore, "The Power of Memes," *Scientific American* 283, no. 4 (2000): 52–61.
10. Jared Diamond, *Guns, Germs, and Steel* (New York: Norton, 1999).
11. Richard Brodie, *Virus of the Mind* (Seattle: Integral Press, 1996).

12. Mihalyi Csikszentmihalyi, *The Evolving Self* (New York: Harper Perennial, 1993).
13. Harry Levinson, *The Great Jackass Fallacy* (Boston: Harvard Business School Press, 1973).
14. David A. Nadler and Edward E. Lawler III, "Motivation: A Diagnostic Approach," in *Perspectives on Behavior in Organizations,* ed. J. R. Hackman and E. E. Lawler (New York: McGraw-Hill, 1977).
15. B. F. Skinner, *Beyond Freedom and Dignity* (New York: Bantam, 1971).
16. Frederick Taylor, *The Principles of Scientific Management* (New York: Dover, 1998).
17. Glasser, *Choice Theory.*
18. Albert Ellis and Robert A. Harper, *A Guide to Rational Living* (Hollywood, CA: Melvin Powers Wilshire Book Company, 1997).
19. For example, Eric Berne, *Games People Play* (New York: Ballantine, 1964).
20. Gilbert W. Fairholm, *Values Leadership* (New York: Praeger, 1991).
21. Peter L. Berger and Thomas Luckman, *The Social Construction of Reality* (New York: Anchor, 1967).
22. Sterling Livingston, "Pygmalion in Management," *Harvard Business Review,* reprint 88509.
23. The skill of active or reflective listening is a big help here. It provides a means of enlarging the window onto a person's VABEs.
24. Edward Deci, *Why People Do What They Do* (New York: Penguin, 1995).
25. S. I. Hayakawa, *Symbol, Status and Personality* (London: Harvest Books, 1996).

An Abbreviated List of Personal Defense Mechanisms

HEALTHY, PRODUCTIVE DEFENSE MECHANISMS

Altruism   Helping others in a real, rather than imaginary, way that yields some instinctive gratification to the individual.

Humor   Pointing out the absurdities in life and oneself without hurting oneself as well as without hurting or excluding others.

Suppression   Postponement of consideration of difficult or painful information. One says, "I will deal with this tomorrow" and then does so.

Anticipation   Setting goals, realizing the gap between the present and the goals, and being willing to work toward those goals.

Sublimation   Channeling the emotions and motivations of difficult situations into other situations that promise some instinctive gratification.

MODERATELY HEALTHY DEFENSE MECHANISMS

Intellectualization   Rationalizing about situations and even developing solutions to them mentally but never doing what needs to be done to realize them. Paying undue attention to some things, particularly mental machinations, to avoid dealing with a situation.

Repression   Convenient forgetting of what may be difficult for the sake of not confronting the situation. For instance, a bereaved person may weep while having forgotten why. Compare with Denial.

Displacement   Transferring feelings toward a less important object or person. Practical jokes and wit with hidden hostile content are examples of displacement.

Reaction Formation   Behaving in the opposite of what one wants. Helping others when one wants to be helped; hating someone one loves.

Dissociation   Short-term dramatic changes in personality or behavior to deal with a situation: sudden carefree, happy-go-lucky behavior in response to the death of a loved one, for example.

Source: Adapted from George E. Vaillant, *Adaptation to Life: The Seasons of a Man's Life* (Boston: Little Brown and Company, 1977), 383–86.

UNHEALTHY, UNPRODUCTIVE DEFENSE MECHANISMS

Acting Out   Giving in to impulses to avoid dealing with a situation. This includes drinking, drug abuse, and the like.

Passive-Aggressive Behavior   Failures or procrastinations or other means of personal ineffectiveness performed in response to anger at others or situations. Internalizing situations that require an outward response.

Hypochondriasis   Translating concerns about the situation into physical ailments or sickness when there are none.

Schizoid Fantasy   Using fantasies to avoid dealing with a situation. Neither the fantasy nor the solution to the situation are affected.

Projection   Attributing one's own feelings and concerns to others.

DANGEROUS DEFENSE MECHANISMS

Distortion   Grossly reshaping reality to fit inner needs.

Denial   Refusal to be aware of reality.

Delusional Projection   False conclusions about reality and its relationship to the self.

Self

7

Six Steps to Effective Leadership

*Not much happens without a dream. And for something great to
happen, there must be a great dream. Behind every great achievement
is a dreamer of great dreams. Much more than a dreamer is required
to bring it to reality; but the dream must be there first.*

—ROBERT GREENLEAF, *SERVANT LEADERSHIP*

The topmost sphere in the general models presented in Chapter 3 refers to your characteristics as a potential leader. Our assertion throughout the book is that you can make a difference, but whether you want to do so—and on what scale over how large a circle of influence—is up to you. You can choose whether to influence one other, ten others, or millions of others and in what way.

Of course, each choice carries with it demands and consequences. If you choose to influence millions, you will have to spend your time among those millions, constantly working to gain their followership. This is a very different lifestyle than that of a person who wishes to influence only a few or none. Whatever lifestyle you choose will have consequences for you and those around you. It is important to remember, though, that it's all up to you.

Let's assume for the moment that you want to influence others, to be a leader. First, that's the wrong start. If you want to be a leader, you've put the cart before the horse, and your results are likely to be mixed or inconsequential. Truly effective leaders don't start out wishing to be leaders. The title, stature, and accoutrements of leadership do not wear well on those who seek them as the primary goal. Rather, you would be better off asking yourself, "What value do I want to add to society [my community]?" Or "What changes do I believe deep down are necessary to improve my organization, our world?" Truly effective and morally grounded leaders begin with a cause, a purpose, a goal that serves fellow citizens—and not with the goal of being the leader because the position appears attractive, powerful, respected, and well paid. In my experience, ultimately the so-called leaders who sought the positions mostly for the positions' sake end up being caretakers who do little and are not long remembered.

> Behaving as and becoming an effective leader is a secondary by-product of an intense commitment to a purpose.

Think about it. Reflect on people you know who have set goals to attain some position of authority and then made it. What did they do once they became the leader? Our guess is that their administrations were confused, ill directed, diffuse in policy and results, and not particularly powerful in accomplishing good for the society.

An effective leader has a powerful purpose or cause. In the relentless desire to accomplish that purpose, one becomes a leader, influencing others voluntarily to join in it. Without this purposeful base, so-called leaders are little more than caretakers, maintainers, self-aggrandizers, and, really, parasites on the rest of society. They seek title and prestige for their own gratification rather than to serve or improve those around them.

Still, as Nigel Nicholson points out, some are born to lead.[1] So whether you feel the need to lead or simply want to improve your leadership skills, we come to the question, "If you want to develop your leadership skills, how can you proceed?" I recommend six steps that can make you a more effective, powerful leader if you pursue them vigorously. The first step relates to developing an inner core that revolves around a purpose. I call it clarifying your center.

You'll notice that I use the present participle form of the verbs for all of the steps introduced in this chapter, the "-ing" forms. I do this intentionally to communicate the idea that none of these steps are binary processes, that is, you don't do them or not do them, and neither do you do them once and then are done with them. Rather, each is a process that involves a lifelong commitment to continuous improvement, constant polishing, revisiting, and adjusting. These six steps, shown in Table 7-1, become a way of life, not something you put on for a few moments to impress others or that, once achieved, are fixed forever.

One more point: Although what follows is six steps, I don't think of them as a recipe for becoming a leader. If these principles become a part of your life, I strongly believe you'll have the tools to be an effective leader. On the other hand, they are not principles that can be faked or used effectively in a half-hearted way. If you reflect on these principles and think about how they are connected, they can guide your efforts toward making things happen, toward implementing the leadership point of view.

TABLE 7-1   Six Steps to Effective Leadership

1. Clarifying your center
2. Clarifying what's possible
3. Clarifying what others can contribute
4. Supporting others so they can contribute
5. Relentlessness
6. Measuring and celebrating progress

1. CLARIFYING YOUR CENTER

James Allen once noted that "as a man thinketh, so is he."[2] Although we would argue for the inclusion of VABEs in this perspective, it does beg the questions "Who are you?" and "How does that core affect your leadership?" Your center, or core, and its content are crucial to your ability to lead. When your center is clear and focused, you are more likely to have a powerful influence on others. When your center is foggy and diffuse, you are less likely to be able to move others; physically, emotionally, socially, and organizationally, you'll be off balance and unable to provide dependable anchor points to others.

There are ways of physically demonstrating this. Students of the martial arts, for instance, learn to stand in a stable manner and in balance. They focus on their physical center of gravity, called the "one-point" in aikido. A physically centered person is very difficult to move. You can push and shove, and she stands stably without moving. The same is true of people who are centered socially and in general in life. As a former mentor once commented, they have "mass."

When you understand that being centered means that opposing forces, shifting currents of approval or disapproval, unstable foundations, and even censure by those you love will not unsettle or dissuade you or knock you off balance, then you will begin to develop a desire to clarify your center. As you do so, you will become more calm, more purposeful, more stable in the midst of turbulence around you. Although you can practice some physical techniques to develop this capacity, clarifying your emotional center is about determining what you believe in and value. Centering, therefore, is often a reflective, meditative exercise.

I suppose that one can never fully clarify one's center. We can never fully experience all of life, and life will constantly force us to revisit and perhaps polish, if not remold, our core values. We may think we know what we would do in a given, perhaps challenging, situation. We may hope so, but the truth is we will never really know for sure what we would do until we've encountered that situation at least once—probably several times.

Here's an extreme but poignant example. Although in Asia at the time, I did not serve in the military during the Vietnam War. Many of my classmates did. Since then, I've felt compelled to read about their experiences in such books as Mark Baker's *Nam,* which is a compilation of firsthand, eyewitness accounts of what it was like to prepare for, go to, fight in, and return from Vietnam.[3] One account is of a platoon of young Americans spending days on patrol in a free-fire zone, tired, hungry, scared, and pumped full of adrenaline, on a keen edge. At one point, they spotted an elderly Vietnamese man and a young woman on a motor scooter. They stopped the two, searched their bags, and found American canned fruit. They accused the man of stealing the fruit from American soldiers. The old man protested. As he did, two of the soldiers took the young woman, his granddaughter, out into the rice paddy and raped her. The rest of the platoon lined up. When the old man protested, someone shot him almost in half with automatic weapons fire. When they were all done with the girl, they killed her.

Most of us find this story appalling and disgusting. Most of us would like to think we know what we would do if we had been members of that platoon. We can imagine ourselves at 19 standing up to our platoon mates, saying, "Don't do this!" or "This won't happen here!" Perhaps we can imagine ourselves even being willing to lose our lives to not participate in or silently support the episode. Yet, truthfully, it is not really clear what we would do if threatened with death by our supposed friends, people with whom we'd trained, ate, and slept and whom we'd saved and been saved by. If we'd been attacked by young women and children with rifles and grenades before or if we were hungry and not thinking clearly or if we for any reason were unable to see a grandfather and his granddaughter as individuals worthy or respect, we might not do what we thought we'd do as we contemplated the situation from the comfort of our living rooms or classrooms. Thus, we need to be constantly clarifying our centers, thinking about, practicing, and behaving in accordance with our basic values.

We can explore and polish our centers, and we can resolve and reinforce our core resolves from time to time. If we have a desire to deal with various of life's situations one way rather than another, then it behooves us to constantly explore, examine, and refine our centers and to be as clear as we can be about what's there and how we will implement its content as we live.

Matsushita Seikei Juku is a leadership institute established in Kanagawa, Japan, by the founder of Matsushita Electric Company, Konosuke Matsushita. A truly remarkable individual, Matsushita and his leadership style have been the subject of several books.[4] His school of leadership was no less remarkable. In 1993, over 250 people completed applications to the school, yet only 5 were admitted to study, an application-to-admittance ratio of 50:1. The program of study lasts five years. The first year has no faculty and no courses. At the end of the first year, there is a one-question examination, and if you fail, you're out. The question is, "What is your life's purpose?" The underlying assumption is that to qualify for leadership, one must know one's life's mission; otherwise, how could one purport to lead others? It's a simple but powerful tenet.

Are you clear on what your life's mission is? Are you clear about what's at your center? Do you know what you stand for? If not, it will be difficult to lead. Are you willing to spend some time wrestling with this issue? If you were at the Matsushita Leadership Institute, you'd have a whole year with no other distractions to explore that single question. Are you willing to spend something less than that year answering it? The chapter on resonance was designed in large part to help you think about this fundamental question. Here are some additional suggestions for how you can begin to clarify your center.

Clarifying What You Stand for: Engagement

Many people go through life never clarifying their centers. They live and die having never tested their inner beliefs to see if and how they hold up under fire. In that, they have avoided leadership roles that will call their center into activity and hence never became leaders. One way to begin clarifying your center is to identify what engages you. We mean here more than what interests you, or as Stephen Covey would say, what "concerns" you.[5] What is it that captures your imagination, your leisure thinking moments, and your dreams? What is it that causes you to smile spontaneously, to increase your pulse, and to speak animatedly with others? What is it that motivates you and prepares you to expend tremendous energy, mental and physical, as you anticipate participating? We have included an exercise on your personal engagement planning in the workbook at the back of this volume.

Leadership is an act of engagement. —Alexander Horniman

These things begin to constitute your core. My colleague Alex Horniman is fond of saying that leadership is an act of engagement. When we are truly engaged in something, we begin to influence others without even trying. They begin to notice the energy and excellence with which we pursue our engagement, they begin to hear the animation in our voices, they begin to see our motivation, and all of this rubs off on them and they start wanting to be a part of it. In effect, we've begun to lead without ever being cognizant of or claiming a desire to be a leader. When we are truly engaged, leadership just begins to happen. Engagement is contagious; like a virus, it spreads, and others begin to feel it and are swept into it.

Identifying and examining your central engagements can help clarify your center's content. The process can even help you refine and redirect the content of your engagements, and it will be critical to your becoming more influential. Obviously, it's not something you can do in an afternoon or use as if it were a simple tool such as asking others where they come from. Clarifying your center by reviewing and refining your engagements will cause you to be constantly polishing your definition of who you are. The next step in that process is looking at the values that you hold, that is, looking at the *how* of getting to the realization of your core engagements.

Developing Character: Ends Versus Means

A person's character is the sum of her choices of goals and how to achieve them. This implies a moral dimension to leadership. One way to check the moral level of your leadership, that is, your respect for the follower, is to ask yourself if, given your behavior toward the other person, you would be willing to trade places with them immediately. If not, you might begin to ask yourself if you're behaving with respect for the individual.

A second method, commonly used by some, is to imagine that your dealings with this person were suddenly made into detailed headlines on the front page of the national newspaper you read. Would you be proud to have the story out for all to see? Or would you find yourself leaving out certain conversations, side deals, or actions in hopes of being better thought of? If you hesitate with either of these tests, we suggest you rethink your attempts to influence others and to reflect on what this hesitation might mean in terms of clarifying your center.

Meditation

A third method for clarifying your center is more metaphysical and involves meditating, praying, or practicing stress-reducing exercises. Physically centering, as one does in martial arts training, can also help. And interestingly, the physical practice of centering can help you strengthen your view of your center and of how to manage your life. My experience studying aikido, for instance, was very helpful in seeing new ways of thinking about my life and about my relationships. If you learn to sit or stand quietly for several moments, to focus your mind on breathing in through your nose and out through your mouth, and to let all other thoughts leave your mind, you will find that this exercise produces a remarkable sense of calm and peace. This physical–mental exercise will help you see more clearly what you believe and feel.

We've said that one is never finished clarifying one's center. It doesn't make sense, therefore, to wait to influence others until the center is *completely* clear. We still have to carry on with our lives even if we haven't reached a final realization or don't have it perfect at the moment.

The strategic corollary to clarifying your center is clarifying what's possible for you and your work group, organization, or society. If you clarify your center but have no view of what could be for those around you, not much will happen.

2. CLARIFYING WHAT IS POSSIBLE

If clarifying your center involves looking inward to the core, clarifying what's possible involves looking outward to the extreme. For most of us, this means stretching our horizons beyond what we usually see and apprehend. To clarify what is possible is to imagine in sharp detail what can and should happen for an individual or an institution in the future. In essence, this is strategic thinking. There is a chapter devoted to that topic coming up, but we can make some general comments at the moment.

In his book *Future Perfect*, Stan Davis claims that leaders have seen what they want to accomplish so clearly and understand the steps to that dream so thoroughly that they literally speak in the future perfect tense, noting, for instance, that when we have achieved our dream, we *will have done* A, B, and C.[6] It's as if the leader is working backward having seen, as Martin Luther King put it, the promised land. Most of us don't see the promised land or even the quadrant of the future in which it lies. Effective leaders have, and they therefore know where they're trying to go. You can call it strategic thinking or visioning or whatever you want, but effective leaders have an idea in their minds about what they are trying to do.

Clarifying Mental Images of What Can Be

Clarifying your mental images of what you or your organization can become is not easy. It requires getting out of present mental boxes, relaxing mental constraints (assumptions), and vigorously pursuing a mental mural painstakingly put together with thousands of mosaic thought tiles. Some may find this easy when it comes to imagining a romantic liaison or playing a major league baseball game or driving to the world's championship on the Formula One circuit. We can imagine tiny details of how we would behave in those exciting situations. Effective leaders have this same energy about their personal and organizational dreams and visions, and to become one of them, you need to develop this skill.

One of the biggest difficulties in developing mental pictures of the future is allocating time to the process. Most of us don't turn off the phone, close the door, and put our feet up and simply think hard about where we're going and how we're going to get there. In the rush to respond to the daily press of mail, phone messages, meetings, and emergencies, we spend our working lives, as Covey puts it, in

Quadrant I, working on urgent, high-priority items and, in so doing, losing sight of—and even the desire to gain sight of—the long view.[7] This is not to say, however, that strategic thinking and visioning is just a result of putting your feet up and thinking.

Another difficulty is keeping these future-oriented images current in our minds. We often glimpse the future and then lose sight of it in our daily routines. For instance, can you state from memory your organization's mission statement? If you have to pull out the card from your wallet, it doesn't count. The challenge here is to keep your future clearly in mind. If you can't, it will be difficult to allow that image to influence your thinking, much less the thinking of the people you interact with daily.

Further, can you see clearly where the organization should be in 5, 10, 20, 50, or 100 years? You may find these questions silly, particularly given the rapid change that characterizes the infocratic era. Many participants in my executive education classes do. They claim to wrestle with 30- and 90-day horizons, maybe a 360-day horizon, but they argue they can't see what's going to happen months down the road, much less years, given the increasing turbulence of the world.

Konosuke Matsushita, again, provides an interesting counterpoint. Asked in the late 1980s if he was concerned about the recent losses that his firm, Matsushita Denki (Panasonic Electronics), was sustaining, he said, "No, everything was on schedule." When asked how long his schedule extended, he replied, "250 years!" He had a vision of his firm, the firm he founded, that extended through ten 25-year periods. Each period had a set of goals and objectives that had to be accomplished to reach his view of what could be—of what was possible two and a half centuries into the dark curtain of the future. Although his firm was experiencing some short-term losses, the basic elements of that first 25-year period were on schedule and moving as planned. Surely he was interested in a profitable company, yet his primary focus was not on increasing quarterly profits but on the underlying elements and strategic pillars that would generate those profits over the long haul. In the meantime, Matsushita Denki has moved into the second 25-year period, having completed the goals of the first one.

I urge you to begin developing the habit of allocating time regularly to discipline your mind to think into the future, to imagine what could be, to play with the details, to follow the thin threads of reasoning that describe how those images could be brought to pass. This will not come to you in a flash; like physical, muscular tone, your mental imagining tone will come from repeated and vigorous effort. The chapter on strategic thinking will give you some additional guidance about how to go about this.

Reading is a great way to increase your stockpile of ideas. If you read widely, not just in your field, you'll begin to see connections among different disciplines and industries. Be willing to read in other fields so you can begin to identify trends and events that will impact yours. Recently, we had one participant in an executive program who reported that he read two books a night. Yes, two books a night! He began to develop this skill many years ago when he signed up for remedial reading because it was the only class his favorite high school instructor was offering that term. Although our friend was a normal reader, he learned techniques and insights into the reading process that now, after years of practice, leave him able to consume and understand close to

600 books a year. Can you imagine how this kind of input would inform and stimulate your mind in seeing what could be?

Scenario Building

I also encourage you to begin developing scenarios that will inform the paths you might take to your dreams. Peter Schwartz, in his book *The Art of the Long View,* describes this process very well. It differs from strategic planning and corporate planning and will be described more in the chapter on strategic thinking.

3. CLARIFYING WHAT OTHERS CAN CONTRIBUTE

One of the fundamental issues a potential leader faces is clarifying what the others, the potential followers, can do. Unless you can develop a view of how others can contribute to your objectives and vision, it's not likely that you'll be able to get their commitment. The breadth of that view varies from person to person, and it can make a big difference in your effectiveness as a leader. Two factors are critical in clarifying what others can contribute: first, your basic underlying assumptions about others, and second, clarity in identifying the critical skills you will need to reach your vision.

Basic Assumptions About Others

One common and dangerous outcome of the bureaucratic, industrial era has been that many managers think of their people in terms of the job descriptions they have. The corollary to this is thinking of people in terms of the job descriptions you'd like them to fill. This perspective constrains one from thinking about people's talents and imagining what they might contribute to a particular goal or agenda. This kind of bureaucratic thinking—based on the assumptions that we need to find people to fit into particular job descriptions and that management's task is to minimize variance from those jobs' performance—can be devastating to highly talented individuals. This is a Level One way of thinking about what people might contribute to an effort.

As argued earlier, this approach assumes that management knows exactly what needs to be done, that people can behave in a robotic way, and that the environment will be stable enough to avoid the need for quick response time and creative employees. Clearly, this is not the case in today's world.

A more powerful leadership approach is to assume that people have talents, can learn new ones, and have a basic desire to do well. Of course, these skills vary from person to person, and there will always be a need to monitor behavior. However, if one views, hires, trains, and manages people with an eye to developing their skills and judgment, one is increasingly able to rely on their abilities at work rather than on their job descriptions. Further, their insights on the job may, especially in turbulent times, be more informed and accurate than management's, several layers up the organization. This whole process of working with people's talents and accepting responsibilities for outcomes has been termed *empowering* and has become something of a trite phrase, in part because many managements give it lip service but don't really believe its underlying assumptions as just stated.

In a sense, clarifying what others could contribute by examining your own deep assumptions about the value that others bring to work is a part of clarifying your center. If your view of what others can do is limited, then your ability to clarify what others can contribute will be limited as well. If you are able to imagine and perceive people as growing, learning, and developing beings and are willing to invest in that growth, you can get a very different kind of response. What you see about people certainly helps to determine how they will respond. If we treat people like robots, they will begin to behave like robots. If we treat people with expectations of higher contributions, they will begin to make higher contributions.

Identifying the Critical Skills

Another challenge to reframing how we look at people and conceive of what they have to offer is knowing what we need to accomplish our purposes. Most people look primarily at technical skills when assessing fit between a job and a candidate. Again, this is Level One thinking. Consider a different approach.

The FMC plant in Aberdeen, South Dakota, builds missile-launching canisters for the U.S. Navy. This facility was organized by an unusual and very effective leader, Bob Lancaster, who worked hard to develop a different kind of working environment. When the facility needed a new welder, management used the basic assumptions of their new organization to find the next new employee. The traditional, Level One approach would be that a company would advertise for a welder, accept applications with résumés summarizing experience, and then pick the most qualified candidate based on experience, references, and maybe an interview.

At FMC Aberdeen, though, a different set of underlying assumptions and, correspondingly, a different set of identified critical skills came into play.[8] First, the organization's process was more important than its technical skills. According to this logic, a collection of highly qualified people who couldn't work well together would be less effective than a group of moderately talented people who could. The second assumption was that social skills were harder to teach than technical skills, that is, that it was easier to teach welding than it was to teach teamwork, learning, self-esteem, and other related interpersonal talents. The third assumption was that people trained in one technical way of doing things, and perhaps reinforced by a union experience that encouraged focusing on a narrow range of skills, would have difficulty learning new ways of organizing their work.

With these three assumptions in mind, the management of FMC Aberdeen realized that the critical skills they needed were self-esteem (so employees were able to receive feedback without getting defensive), a learning attitude (so they were interested and even eager to learn new skills and techniques), team spirit (so they were willing to share in the work and responsibility for results), and a pride in quality (so they wanted to find ways to improve results). Consequently, they developed a recruiting and screening process that lasted four hours and focused on these principles *rather than on the technical skills of welding.*

After using this process, they screened out virtually all of the experienced welders who had applied for the job and ended up hiring a woman who had never welded before in her life! They chose her because she was bright, interested in learning, socially well adjusted, willing to take feedback, and clearly a team player. As it turned out, she became a master welder within a short period of time and then went on to learn a wide variety of the rest of the technical skills listed in the plant's pay-for-skill compensation system. Management was convinced that if they had hired a seasoned welder, maybe with union experience, they would have had difficulty teaching that person new, now more important social skills and a wider range of technical skills. Although it took several weeks before the new welder could perform well, within the first year the value added to the firm was far beyond what it would have been had they hired a welder.

How could this happen? A big part of the answer was in the philosophy that was central to the founding of the plant. Another part lay in the innovative ways in which FMC Aberdeen organized its critical human resources. And a big part had to do with its leadership, first, Bob Lancaster, then Jeff Bust, and later, Roger Campbell. These people understood the importance of building an organization that supported people so that they could do their best. And a central part of that organization's mission was determining the critical skills that they needed to create the kind of workplace they wanted to have—many of which were the so-called softer skills of giving and receiving feedback, learning, team play, flexibility, and interpersonal relationships.

4. SUPPORTING OTHERS SO THEY CAN CONTRIBUTE

The traditional assumption mentioned earlier—that people should fit into job descriptions—limits what management expects from job incumbents. This same assumption also limits the structure, systems, and culture of organizations. Increasingly, in changing environments, organizations are having to find new, nontraditional ways of managing their people.

Two forces are shaping this redesign: the explosion of information technology and the constantly burgeoning press of people to be in control of their lives. Both forces are empowering the workforce whether management wants it to or not. Both forces demand that effective leaders find ways of supporting their people by designing new organizational forms that no longer hinder people's creativity and sense of responsibility for results but rather encourage it.

Information Age Organizational Structures

Perhaps nothing has been so influential in the organizational redesign wave that has hit the world than the explosion in new information technologies. As introduced earlier, the growing, widespread availability of accurate, voluminous, and timely data about business activity has begun to literally transform the shape of modern organizations. Colocating becomes less and less of an issue as simultaneous databases, video conferencing, net-based meetings, and e-mail become more prevalent and inexpensive. Cheap, distributed computing power for analysis and communications means that people at all levels of organizations can gather, analyze, decide, and maintain contact with people at all levels of other organizations. The need for vertical hierarchies to make good decisions is rapidly evaporating. In fact, in many cases, better decisions are being made by people who are closer to the data and the customer than those several layers up. And the layers are disappearing.

The new, emerging infocracies are looking more and more like what we used to call the informal or organic organization. In older cities such as Boston, streets eventually grew out of meandering cow paths; likewise in organizations, new lines of authority and influence are developing out of informal lines of communication where the data flow is fast and accurate. In some cases, organizational control is being swiftly shifted away from vertical hierarchies toward information-based networks. Take for instance, the case of rapidly expanding BancOne in the Midwest.

BancOne was a large and growing regional bank that had taken a different and exciting tack to managing its development. Unlike some other growing regional banks, which acquired a new subsidiary and repainted the buildings, added new signs and delivered volumes of new operating procedures in the attempt to get the new affiliates to do things their way, BancOne used information technology to manage its new partners.

First, being clear on their goals, BancOne management identified 47 key indicators of the kind of performance they wanted to see. Second, they developed an information network that allowed them to tie in new affiliates quickly. Third, they designed the information system to provide almost instantaneous feedback on results from data collected. Fourth, management decided to share the results with those managing the more than 50 banks in their system rather than keep it close to their chests. All of these features are dramatic departures from the traditional methods of planning, organizing, motivating, and controlling that grew out of the bureaucratic mind-set.[9]

With this system, a newly acquired bank president in the BancOne system suddenly found him- or herself receiving on a weekly basis a ranked listing of all of the banks in the system on each of the 47 key indicators. Now, what do you suppose happened next? If you assume that people don't care about their performance (a commonly held bureaucratic assumption that limits one's thinking), then you might think not much would happen. On the other hand, if you believe that people want to think well of themselves and to do well among their peers, then you might expect something else.

What happened was that bank presidents looked quickly to see how their banks were doing compared with the others in the system. When they saw that they weren't doing so well on a particular indicator, they looked to see who was doing well. And this led the newly acquired bank president to a critical point. If she was proud and lacking in the learning spirit, she might stonewall for a while and avoid learning from others in the system. But what happened more often than not—and in the process created a new and emerging culture—was that the bank presidents began to call one another, completely bypassing corporate management, to find out how they got such good results. Quickly, much more quickly than corporate training or quarterly review meetings could hope to accomplish it, the best practices of the organization were not filtering but *flowing* from one part of the system to the next, week by week, as each of the decision makers, the small "l" leaders throughout the organization, got timely data, compared their results with others, and sought to improve their standing. Each implemented the suggestions of others in ways that fit his organizations and people; each adjusted, modified, and recast the suggestions he got to match what he thought he could do and his current priorities.

Then the following week, each received another current listing of what was happening with his bank and the other banks in the system, and each was confronted again with the consequences, the results of whatever management steps they had taken. All this was done without negative organizational politics or the time delays of waiting for senior management analysis, decision making, training programs, and coordination. And all this would have been impossible without superb information technology and a senior management philosophy that utilized it efficiently.

This is an example of how effective leadership can redesign organizational systems to support followers and make it easier to release their potential contributions to the organization. Effective leaders are able to clarify not only what potential followers have to contribute but also how the work systems in which they operate could be reorganized to realize the workers' potential.

Empowering Systems Design

BancOne was also an example of a system that empowers people. Its tacit assumption was that the bank managers all wanted to do well, that they all knew their banks better than anyone else, and that they all would do what they could within their historical tradition and operating environment to move in the direction of improving in the direction of the key indicators. Very little was said to them about what they had to do or should not do. Senior management assumed that they would know what to do *if they had the right information and could see the direction the company wanted to go.* (To be fair to Skinnerians, given our earlier discussion, this is a fundamentally Skinnerian system that focused on inputs and outputs with little attention given to Levels Two and Three at the presidential level.)

Often, our organizational structures, systems, and cultures inhibit rather than encourage people to use their full talents. Too many have heard too often, "That's on a need-to-know basis only" or "Don't ask questions, just do it!" or " You're not paid to think, you're paid to do what you're told" or "My job is to think, your job is to do" or some other similar comment.[10] Although this kind of language and the assumptions that the language was based on formed the foundation of the bureaucratic mind-set, the newly emerging postbureaucratic organizations or infocracies will be characterized by different kinds of language based on a different set of assumptions.

One of the changes occurring in the new, emerging infocracies is a movement away from the assumption that people should fit into the organization ("Here's my organization chart, now let's figure out who fits into it and where") and toward the assumption that talented people should be given current information and be left to organize their work to fit the need ("Here are my people, let's figure out how to organize for the moment to meet the customer's needs"). What this shift means is that, as Peter Senge has written, leaders are increasingly becoming designers of new kinds of organizational forms.[11] Many of these are built around circles or networks rather than pyramidic bureaucracies. Who has what authority is becoming less and less the organizing principle; who has the right information and insight is becoming more and more important.

So, in part, effective leadership means casting away bureaucratic assumptions that we have taught in business schools for decades and searching for and creating new organizing principles that promote the rapid use of good information and the multiple talents of the people employed.

5. BEING RELENTLESS

Effective leaders are relentless.[12] They often exhibit stamina in enormous volumes. When a person has a purpose and a vision and wants to achieve them, it is difficult to push her off that chosen track. If her commitment to the purpose and vision is weak, she can be diverted. If this happens, she becomes less effective with others and more confused even to herself. I asserted earlier that it's difficult to know what values we truly hold until they are tested among our peers and in high-stakes situations where our true (operating) basic assumptions and priorities will be manifest. The same is true of our commitment to our purpose. We often learn about how committed we are to an endeavor by watching ourselves in action. Like the other steps introduced earlier, this principle is both a reflection of and a means of clarifying our centers. We learn how much stamina we have by watching our own commitments to our goals. We clarify our centers by learning from that observation.

Life As a Motorboat or a Wood Chip

One way to think of the commitment-building or stamina-building process is to compare life and business to an ocean: vast, constantly changing, open, and inviting to the skilled sailor. At the same time, life's sea has currents, winds, storms, denizens of the deep, and the possibility of total destruction. Some people launch into life without a purpose or direction, seeking in their naïveté to experience life as quickly as they can. Not thinking beyond their prows, they push off from shore with no motor, no sail, and no rudder and become a chip upon the tide, floating to and fro without destination. It is true that sometimes such chips find themselves by luck and the wind ashore on favorable beaches and enjoying the finer things of life. Most, however, never get anywhere and sink before they realize that it could have been different.

Leaders have a purpose to which they are committed, and it provides the charts by which they sail. Their stamina becomes the large sails, and their centers become the compasses to help them move ahead. When the winds of fate blow, they adjust the trim and the rudder to utilize whatever life brings them to keep them headed toward their destination. Leaders also have internal motors that keep them moving when the external winds are calm or blowing against them. Leaders have fuel to burn and reserve bunkers to feed their motors when the going gets tough and the waves mount. Leaders are not easily blown off course.[13]

This relentlessness, the drive to get up when you're knocked down, to right yourself when capsized, is essential to achieving important goals. Without it, leaders-to-be will become followers. This may seem to be stubbornness, but there is a distinct difference between stubbornness and relentlessness. The relentless leader can still be willing to listen, willing to understand and utilize any fact, truth, or valuable information or alliance that will move toward the visioned goal. Stubborn people stick to the original vision or strategic means selected without modification. If you accept this, then you may wonder, "So how does one develop leaderlike relentlessness?"

Developing Commitment

Easily chosen goals do not lead to deep commitment. Constancy of commitment is a function of careful thought, sometimes painful scrutiny of the purpose and vision— often stimulated by the criticism of others—and an ever-clarifying sense of one's center. Commitment grows out of knowing yourself. If you know what you want and why you operate the way you do and you are willing to change your ways of operating to get what you want, you will be able to develop commitment. The more commitment you develop, the more relentless you will become.

Relentlessness is also born of confidence in oneself. If you don't believe in your goals or in your ability to achieve them, it will be easy to push you aside. Perhaps the most dramatic example of relentlessness is that of Thomas Edison, the inventor of the lightbulb. He tried over a thousand configurations before he found the one that produced light from electricity. Can you imagine how you would feel working on your goal and having just failed the two hundredth time? The six hundredth time? The nine hundredth time? Would you have the commitment to carry on? This kind of relentlessness requires a high level of confidence in the value of your purpose and in your contribution to achieving it.

6. MEASURING AND CELEBRATING PROGRESS

Few of us can carry on without some positive feedback. We all need some data that says to us, one way or another, "Okay, you're getting there! You're making progress!" Without this, our sense of forward movement, our sense of value added, our sense of the possibilities, and hence our motivation and hope begin to wither. Effective leaders recognize this principle in the way they deal with themselves and with others. Two points about this are important to make.

Focusing on the Right Measures

As the BancOne example demonstrated, a key leadership skill is focusing on the right measure. Steve Kerr's article "On the Folly of Hoping for A While Rewarding B" makes a strong point, that we can't realistically expect to get certain results while we model and reward behavior that leads people to an entirely different outcome.[14] Yet, he notes, many managers and management systems get caught up in that very misconception. Operating on the basic principle that the boss knows best, bureaucratic organizations too often have made decisions that later on actually worsened the problem they were trying to solve. We often refer to these as unintended consequences.

Unintended consequences are frequently the result of not seeing ahead clearly and of not understanding the people with whom we're dealing. A good example of this lies in the air-quality problem of Mexico City, one of the largest cities in the world. Lying as it does in a topographical bowl, Mexico City often has intense air pollution caused mostly by the huge number of automobiles there. In an attempt to alleviate this problem, city officials counseled and came up with a plan to reduce the number of cars on the roads and hence, they hoped, to reduce the air pollution. They decided that people should be prohibited from using their car at least one day a week. This regulation, they thought, would stimulate car pooling and reduce the number of cars on the roads. The simple way to do this, they thought, was to assign a day of the week to the last digit of license plates. If your license plate number ended in 1, you could not drive your car on Monday, and so on. They expected to reduce air pollution by 15 percent immediately. Instead, what happened was that most people bought an older, used car, most of which had less efficient engines and exhaust systems, and they drove that car on the restricted day, so rather than reducing the air pollution problem, the law actually almost doubled it!

The ability to focus on the right measures is a key leadership skill. If people begin to believe that they are working to create results that are trivial or diversionary from the basic goal or purpose, they will lose heart and become weak followers. On the other hand, if the leader can home in on a small set of key indicators and is able to show them how those indicators relate to the purpose and the vision, these people will be focused and clear on what they are working for.

One example of focusing on a diversionary goal is often found in monthly or quarterly profit figures. Everyone, especially investors, wants to have stable, monotonically increasing profits (meaning profits that increase steadily without any dips). Having that as the primary focus, however, can have unintended consequences among followers. I know of one facility where employees regularly shipped the next month's orders in the current month to make up any shortfall in the current month's shipping goals and in so doing eventually built up an enormous surplus in customers' warehouses. Finally, customer orders fell precipitously when customers finally said, "We can't take any more!" The short-term goal of monthly shipments diverted attention from the long-term goal of financial health and stability and ultimately caused some severe repercussions throughout the company.

Focusing on the Glass Half Full

Another common measurement-related residue of the bureaucratic mind-set is variance management. This is the willingness to let things go until there is a variance from the organization's plan, at which time management's job is to step in and get things back on track. Fundamentally, this is a negative approach and ultimately demotivating to the people involved.

First, who knows if the plan was accurate and right for the current business conditions? As business conditions change rapidly, business plans grow obsolete and out of date. More and more companies are developing flexible plans that respond more quickly than the traditional semiannual or annual reporting and management cycles. Second, if management's primary communication with the employees revolves around criticism when things aren't going well, how can employees be expected to be enthusiastic followers and coordinate their efforts smoothly with management? This is a formula for managing the downside, not the upside. Determining the right measures and developing a positive philosophy about how to administer them makes the difference between an average organization and a vibrant, leading one.

Effective leaders watch for progress on key indicators and celebrate the positive with their people. Rather than looking for how the glass is half empty, that is, how they can find the mistakes and faults of the organization, they look for ways in which the glass is half full and how to fill it further. They build on the successes rather than rail on the failures. Sure, yelling may get short-term, Level One results, but if the leader leaves for a while, have the employees learned how to carry on? Probably not. Rather, they've learned an insidious, unintended dependence on the manager as regards matters of performance and quality. The employees who've worked with a leader know when they're doing the right thing because they are celebrated. They begin to look for other ways to get positive feedback. Celebrations of forward progress bring the work up out of the mundane and routine and present it as it is, on the track of the organization's purpose and in line with the vision of what can be.

CONCLUSION

Personal leadership characteristics are not all that is necessary for effective leadership to occur. Nevertheless, who you are and what you do as an individual is a major part of a positive leadership outcome. This chapter presents six things you can do to improve your personal leadership effectiveness. Each step is an ongoing process, not something that one can do once and for all. Leadership requires a long-term commitment to personal exploration and to personal visions. Without that level of engagement, leadership is not likely to happen.

PRINCIPLES OF EFFECTIVE LEADERSHIP INTRODUCED IN THIS CHAPTER

1. Effective leaders are centered, that is, they know who they are, what they believe in, and what they want to accomplish with their lives.
2. Effective leaders have a clear view of what's possible for the organization; they have created a vision of where to go.
3. Effective leaders can see what others can contribute in their unique ways and with their unique talents to the accomplishment of the vision.
4. Effective leaders are good organizational designers; they reshape the organization to support talented people as they work toward the vision, trying to make the organization help rather than hinder the people working in it.
5. Effective leaders are relentless. They don't give up even though they are flexible enough to take different routes to their goals.
6. Effective leaders recognize progress and praise those who made it.

QUESTIONS FOR REFLECTION

1. What are your core leadership principles? If you were asked to take charge of an organization, what have you concluded thus far in life about how you'd go about leading?
2. What is your organization's purpose? Can you write it succinctly and immediately or not? Are you engaged in that purpose? Why or why not?
3. What do all of your coworkers contribute to this purpose? Can you identify contributions that each makes?
4. How would you reorganize your organization to make it more effective? How could you make your ideas happen?
5. What things in life are you relentlessly committed to? What, if anything, are you willing to spend 10 years working on? What does this have to do with your ability to lead?

NOTES

1. Nigel Nicholson, *Executive Instinct* (New York: Crown Business, 2000).
2. James Allen, *As a Man Thinketh* (New York: Crowell, 1913).
3. Mark Baker, *Nam* (New York: Morrow, 1981).
4. See, for example, Konosuke Matsushita, *As I See It* (Tokyo: PHP Institute, 1989).
5. Steve, who was my first instructor in business school, speaks of circles of concern and circles of influence in his best-selling book

The Seven Habits of Highly Effective People (New York: Simon & Schuster, 1989).

6. See Stan Davis, *Future Perfect* (Reading, MA: Addison-Wesley, 1987).

7. Covey's four-quadrant model depicts our attention to things important (or not) and things urgent (or not). Quadrant I refers to things both urgent and important, the so-called crisis zone.

8. See *FMC Aberdeen,* UVA-OB-385, www2.darden.edu/case/collection.

9. See the BancOne case, *BancOne Diversified Services,* UVA-BP-335, www2.darden.edu/case/collection.

10. Chic Thompson, in his book *What a Great Idea!* (New York: Harper Perennial, 1992),

calls these "killer phrases," statements that destroy motivation and creativity.

11. See Peter Senge, *The Fifth Discipline: The Art and Practice of the Learning Organization* (New York, Doubleday Currency, 1990).

12. See Jim Collins, *Good to Great* (New York: HarperCollins, 2001).

13. If you are interested by the sailing analogy, you may enjoy reading Richard Bode, *First You Have to Row a Small Boat* (New York: Warner, 1995), which describes learning life's lessons through sailing.

14. Steve Kerr, "On the Folly of Hoping for A While Rewarding B," *Academy of Management Journal 18,* (December 1975): 769–783.

CHAPTER

8

Leadership and Intelligence

Much evidence testifies that people who are emotionally adept—who know and manage their own feelings well, and who read and deal effectively with other people's feelings—are at an advantage in any domain of life, whether romance and intimate relationships or picking up the unspoken rules that govern success in organizational politics.

—DANIEL GOLEMAN, *EMOTIONAL INTELLIGENCE*

Although the previous chapter presented a list of six things one might do to enhance one's leadership impact, leadership is clearly much more than applying a recipe. First, recipes may or may not fit one's style and personality. Second, if one is not skilled at or genuine in using the recipe, potential followers will see through it in a New York minute. And third, formulaic approaches to managing people often run into the dilemma of what to do with the exceptions. People are organic; they keep creating variations on themes. Even in surgery, for example, doctors know that every person's anatomy will be a little bit different.

All that being said, however, most observers believe that intelligence is an important precursor to effective leadership. Smart people are generally considered to have the best potential as leaders of industry, nations, and institutions. Interestingly, a study of valedictorians, people who graduate at the top of their high school classes, indicates that after 20 years, most of them are working for their classmates.[1] This counterintuitive result prompts us to rethink our beliefs about intelligence and its relationship to effective leadership.

For more than a century, business leaders have, for the most part, tried to downplay emotions in business as unprofessional, undisciplined, and unrelated to good decision making. This stems in part from Enlightenment-era philosophy in Western civilization. Knowledge, said Sir Francis Bacon, is power. Like the other philosophers of the Enlightenment, Bacon saw emotions and passions as obstacles to knowledge, the pathway to universal liberation. Many of the leadership models taught in business schools have focused on rational decision making in which emotions are viewed as a hindrance. Students are taught to search for the right answer and to do so in a rigorous, analytic, and logical way.

Further, U.S. school systems have focused on the notion of intelligence quotient (IQ) in striving to educate millions of children. School systems designed curricula with the intent of utilizing more of students' IQs, if not adding to them. Although the validity of IQ tests have come into question in recent years,[2] other measures of purely rational thinking—the Scholastic Aptitude Test (SAT) and the General Management Aptitude Test (GMAT), for example—still wield a great deal of influence over our individual academic opportunities and those of our children.

Recently, however, some startling conclusions about the nature of intelligence—many of them directly at odds with old assumptions—have begun to emerge. Daniel Goleman points out three important inferences we can draw from recent studies:

1.   Existing standardized intelligence tests fail to predict success in life or in business because they do not tell the whole story. Intelligence is not singular; rather, it comes in a number of forms. Current thinking posits *multiple intelligences,* of which intellectual intelligence, the kind measured by IQ tests, is only one kind.

2.   Emotion, although it can sometimes sabotage clear-headed thought, has been scientifically shown to be an indispensable contributor to rational thinking and decision making. As oxymoronic as it would have seemed to Sir Francis Bacon, a range of intelligences can be called emotional—and they are important for aspiring business leaders to understand better.

3.   Despite traditional views that IQ is inherited and that one could not do much to change it, the newly recognized intelligences seem to be learned to a large extent.

NOT ONE INTELLIGENCE, BUT MANY: GARDNER'S RESEARCH

Goleman draws on the work of several researchers to demonstrate the existence of multiple intelligences. Howard Gardner, a psychologist at the Harvard School of Education, has found the longstanding notion of a single kind of intelligence both wrongheaded and injurious. He blames this belief, which he calls the "IQ way of thinking," largely on the IQ test: People are either smart or not, they are born that way, there's nothing much you can do about it, and tests can tell you if you are one of the smart ones. The SAT test for college admissions is based on the same notion of a single kind of aptitude that determines your future. This way of thinking permeates society.[3] Statistically speaking, though, IQ measurements, SAT scores, and grades turn out to be relatively poor predictors of who will succeed in life and who will not. (Goleman puts the contribution of IQ to a person's success at about 20 percent.)

Gardner's groundbreaking 1993 book *Frames of Mind* repudiates the IQ way of thinking by identifying seven kinds of intelligence: verbal, mathematical-logical, spatial (as demonstrated by painters or pilots), kinesthetic (as seen in the physical grace of a dancer or athlete), musical, interpersonal (upon which a therapist or a diplomat might rely), and intrapersonal (something akin to self-awareness). Gardner's perspective explains why traditional tests have been ineffective in predicting success: They measure only one or two of many necessary and important kinds of intelligence.

Goleman took Gardner's interpersonal and intrapersonal intelligences and cited hundreds of studies to create a story that describes what he calls emotional intelligence

(EQ). Goleman asserts that EQ is just as important as IQ in helping people become effective leaders. As Gardner points out, "Many people with IQs of 160 work for people with IQs of 100, if the former have poor intra-personal intelligence and the latter have a high one. And in the day-to-day world no intelligence is more important than the interpersonal. If you don't have it, you'll make poor choices about who to marry, what job to take, and so on. We need to train children in the personal intelligences in school."[4] It's a compelling argument. Let's examine IQ and EQ and some related concepts in more detail.

INTELLIGENCE QUOTIENT

IQ (which we will use as a substitute for mental capacity in general) is largely genetic but can be honed or made more manifest by curiosity, by discipline in studying, and by adding a range of experiences to a person's life (see Table 8-1). You may not be able to change your IQ score much, but you can learn to do more with what you have been given. If you don't know your IQ, don't worry about it, for broadly speaking, although standardized tests have some predictive power (those with very low IQs often end up making little money, and those with high IQs frequently take demanding, high-powered, better paying jobs), other kinds of intelligence are equally if not more important to being successful and developing leadership influence.

EMOTIONAL QUOTIENT

Emotional intelligence, as introduced by Goleman, is basically the ability to manage your own emotions (see Table 8-2). It begins with the ability to recognize your emotions, then to understand them, and finally to manage yourself out of what Goleman calls "emotional hijackings." In this view, IQ is your brain power, whereas EQ is your emotional control power.

The first step to developing your EQ is to learn to recognize your emotions. Many people are not very aware of their emotions although they often say they are. Have you ever talked with someone who seemed visibly upset, whose neck veins were bulging, whose face was red, whose voice was raised, and yet, when you asked him to

---

TABLE 8-1   Characteristics of IQ

1. Genetic
2. Revealed in curiosity
3. Honed by discipline in study
4. Supported by a range of experiences

TABLE 8-2   Components of Emotional Intelligence

1. Recognizing your own emotions
2. Managing your emotions appropriately
3. Productive self-talk out of emotional hijackings

calm down, he screamed, "I *am* calm!" This person was not in touch with his own emotional reality. Another manifestation of the difficulty people have in recognizing their emotions appears when you ask people how they are feeling; they often will describe behaviors or thoughts. Many are not skilled in paying attention to their own emotional state. many people have learned that the emotional world is not legitimate, and after years of practicing to suppress or subdue their emotions, they have lost touch with how they feel. I'm repeatedly surprised how few talented, practicing managers and leaders are able to identify and talk about their emotions.

Aware of them or not, people can often become prisoners of their emotions. In Goleman's terms, they get hijacked by them and thus lose control of their rational processes. An emotional hijacking occurs when a person begins with a little emotion that then builds and builds in intensity until the person is overwhelmed by it. The most common emotional hijackings are related to anger, fear, and depression. A person hijacked by anger, for instance, may be a little irritated at first, but as time passes, she becomes more and more angry until she is bursting at the seams and acting openly hostile, whether the situation calls for such behavior or not. People with a low EQ who become angry, afraid, or depressed find themselves in an ever-widening spiral of emotions to the point where they are unable to think clearly or to make good decisions.

Consider a hijacking by fear. Modern equipment has given us much greater insight into how this hijacking occurs, because we can trace with increasing accuracy the electrical impulses that course through the brain during different events. We used to think that when a person saw something dangerous, such as a snake, the eye would send a signal to the thinking part of the brain, the brain would consciously register danger, and send signals to the muscles to move quickly, and then he would jump. In fact, we've learned that a short circuit, as it were, bypasses the thinking part of the brain and transmits danger signals directly to two small, almond-sized structures called the *amygdala* that sit atop the human brain stem.

The amygdala is old in terms of the human brain's development; it evolved earlier than the neocortex above it—the area that handles conscious thought—and its functioning is largely beyond the control of the thinking brain. When it receives a short-circuit signal from the optic nerve that you've seen a snake, the amygdala immediately begins a complex chemical process that pumps muscle stimulants into the blood stream, and you literally jump *without* thinking. If a person's ability to manage these chemical outbursts is underdeveloped, this can create a growing whirlpool of fear so strong that you could jump when you should hold still or be paralyzed by the fear when you should jump. When you're so enraged that you can't think straight or so blue in the face that you can't function, you could blame your amygdala and its partners in the limbic system.

Dr. Antonio Damasio, a neurologist at the University of Iowa, has studied patients with damage to the circuits between the amygdala and the brain's memory center. These patients show no IQ deterioration at all, yet their decision-making skills are amazingly poor. They make disastrous choices in their careers and personal lives, and the most mundane decisions—white bread or wheat?—often leave them paralyzed with confusion. Damasio has concluded that their decision making is impaired because they have no access to their *emotional* learning. Searching their memories for the last time they had been in the present situation, they don't remember how they *felt* about the outcome because the emotional lessons, stored in or regulated by the amygdala, apparently are out of reach.

One of the most dramatic examples was of a man working with dynamite on a road crew. In an accident, the steel tamping rod he used to pack the dynamite in a hole drilled into rock was propelled out of the hole and through his brain, leaving him miraculously alive and physically well. But as time passed, it became clear that the limbic portion of his brain had been damaged so that although he could calculate numbers and solve equations, he could not express a preference for meeting time, sock color, or any of the other myriad decisions you and I make every day. He had lost the emotional value of alternatives and became unable to make even simple choices.[5]

Damasio's research (and that of others like him) suggests that the conventional wisdom imparted to us by the Age of Reason and the intervening years of scientific and business experience was wrong at least part of the time: Emotions are in fact *essential* for rational decisions. Memories of ecstatic successes and painful failures help us steer our course every day.

By contrast, people who have a strong connection between the amygdala and the neocortex seem to be better equipped to make good decisions—decisions that are based on a balancing of rational and emotional input rather than one without the other. Applying this insight to business and organizational life, it seems clear that people who have learned over the years to manage their emotions have learned to manage their behavior and their relationships better—and that this translates into more success in the social world of business.

To a certain extent, just as with IQ, we're stuck with the emotional cards we're dealt at birth: Depression, for instance, has been shown to have a hereditary component. But the good news is that EQ seems to be more responsive to learning activities than IQ. You can develop emotional skills that will help enrich both your personal and professional life. Following the outline in Table 8-2, let's explore some ways one can improve one's EQ.

Recognizing Your Own Emotions

The first step toward building your EQ, of course, is being aware of your emotions. It may seem that your feelings are self-evident and that this point is hardly worth making, but closer examination reveals otherwise.

We all sometimes lose sight of our emotions. Goleman offers examples of situations we all recognize, for example, getting up on the proverbial wrong side of the bed and being grouchy all day long. What we would call "getting up on the wrong side of the bed" might actually have stemmed from kicking your toe on the bathroom door, from a curt exchange with your significant other, bad news on the radio, and a bad night's sleep stemming from heavy dinner or some modest chemical imbalance. Perhaps rainy weather was involved, too. Whatever the source, with this initial emotional set, many people are unaware that they are behaving crossly or are seemingly depressed throughout their work day.

Being aware of emotions requires reflection. If one learns to pause, to focus inward, and to seek one's emotions, one can become more aware of them. You might begin asking yourself several times during a normal day, "What am I feeling now?" If you do this for a week, you will probably be able to notice what you feel more readily.

Then the challenge, one accepted by people with high EQs, is to manage those emotions in a more positive way. People who have developed a high EQ do not yield to their emotions easily; rather, they seek to manage them.

Managing Your Emotions

Maybe the thought of managing your emotions is too rational for you, too contrived. Perhaps you prefer to allow your emotions to ebb and flow, and you like their spontaneity. That's fine. The point here is that the data suggest that if you manage your emotions, not just suppress and ignore them but become more aware of them and deal with them, you are more likely to have a positive impact on yourself and the people around you at work or elsewhere. This is particularly true in the case of potentially debilitating emotions such as anger, fear, and depression. We'll see later how this principle might apply to the more positive emotions of resonance and high performance.

To a person with a low EQ, an emotional hijacking may seem like an irresistible call to action: Anger leads to shouting, fear leads to flight, depression leads to crying or withdrawal. But with practice, the amygdala's urgings can be overcome through what Goleman calls productive self-talk (borrowing from Albert Ellis among others).[6] In other words, when someone cuts you off on the highway, you don't have to respond by yelling, pounding on the steering wheel, and clenching your jaw and arm muscles. There *are* options.

To manage one's emotions, one must first decide that one wants to be in control of them. This is not to say that one can manage emotions by willpower alone, but it is to say that unless one decides to do so, one is not likely to increase one's EQ. If you say to yourself, I want to learn how to not be angry so often (or not to be depressed so often or to be more courageous), this is a start.

Next, we begin to develop productive self-talk—recognizing our emotions and then examine the perhaps irrational links that we make between an external event and our emotional reactions to it. Consider the rude driver again. If you imagine that maybe, just maybe, the driver who cut you off is in a hurry to get to the hospital, suddenly there seems to be less to get angry about. Even if you conclude that driver is just being self-centered and rude, you can still say to yourself, "Well, I may wish that he weren't that way, and I cannot control the behavior of others, so why should I let a complete stranger ruin my moment or day?"

In the case of anxiety, the analytical thought process is itself often the source of trouble: Some people can worry about almost anything. If you choose, however, to look at your pessimistic assumptions critically ("Is this bad outcome really inevitable? What other possible outcomes are there? Isn't there something constructive I could do to improve my chances for a favorable outcome?"), you may be able gradually to break them down. People with a high EQ have learned over the years how to do this. Sometimes they use productive self-talk; at other times they might even use physical relaxation methods, such as meditation or prayer, as means to help stem the onset of anxiety once it has been recognized.[7]

All of this is a personal challenge. Do you think you can manage your emotions? Would you like to be able to do so? Are you willing to try? I think if you can, not only will you feel better about your life, but you'll also be better able to manage your relationships. Although Goleman lumped the personal and interpersonal aspects of EQ into one concept, I'll separate them here for clarity's sake.

SOCIAL QUOTIENT

Goleman asserts that a high EQ has a positive impact on one's relationships. If EQ is the ability to manage one's emotions, then social quotient (SQ) has to do with recognizing and managing the emotions in interpersonal relationships. SQ skills are similar to those used in EQ but are directed toward others; hence, they include recognizing emotions in others, developing a concern or caring about the emotional state of others, and being able to help them manage their emotional states as outlined in Table 8-3.

Like EQ, SQ can in large part be learned. And in an organizational world that places a premium on interpersonal skills—in which you can't, as they say, fax or e-mail a handshake—a well-developed SQ can take you places that IQ by itself cannot. Similar to EQ, the skills of recognizing, caring about, and managing emotions are important in SQ.[8]

Recognizing the Emotions of Others

This is the interpersonal corollary to the EQ skill of recognizing your own emotions. The better you are at understanding your own emotions, the more likely you are to be adept at picking up on others'. The difficulty with tuning into another's emotional state, of course, is that people don't usually put their emotions into words. More often, they express them nonverbally through cues such as tone of voice, facial expression, gesture, and other forms of body language. Some research suggests that in general, women are better than men at this kind of attunement; however, the ability to see emotions in others is something that anyone can learn with a little attention and effort.

In the organizational environment, opportunities for this kind of learning are plentiful. In meetings, sales presentations, and chance exchanges with subordinates and superiors, attention to nonverbal cues can yield sharp insights into what another person is experiencing *emotionally.* Knowing how to read the signs is a valuable interpersonal skill. Practice in your conversations, in your meetings, and in group settings. While you listen, see if you can identify the emotions of the people you're talking with. At first, this may be confusing to you; however, if you practice, it will become second nature. You'll learn to listen more completely.

Listening

Lots of people give lip service to the concept of listening as an important leadership skill. Yet many don't listen well because they focus only on content. Listening, as it applies to SQ, means more than just letting someone else speak. It means listening *attentively,* with an ear—and an eye—toward recognizing emotion in addition to content. It means

---

TABLE 8-3   Components of Social Intelligence

1. Recognizing emotions in others
2. Listening
3. Caring about others' emotional state
4. Helping others manage their emotions

putting out of your mind, for a moment at least, what you plan to say when it's your turn to respond. It means seeing if you can register what the other person's heart—not just her mouth—is saying. The challenge is to be conscious of the emotions that the other person is experiencing. If you're able to see what she is feeling, then the question is, do you care?

Empathy and Caring

When you become open to and aware of others' feelings, you become able to *empathize*—to tune into their emotional experience. Empathy—and the caring for another's well-being that usually, but not always, results—is a Level Three connection that binds us in our personal lives and strengthens our attempts at leadership. When we can see and care about what others feel, we have a major opportunity to influence and to be influenced. If you are able to help others manage their emotions, you can be a Level Three leader.

Helping Others Manage Their Emotions

If you see others' emotions, if you care about that emotional reality for them, and if you have the skills that allow you to help them manage their emotions, you will have the opportunity to influence others. This is a powerful form of leadership.

In some cases, you may help others manage their internal emotions to help them out of emotional hijackings. A personal example related to my youngest child. As an eight-year-old girl, she was very talented and energetic, and she also had a tendency to become overwhelmed by daily events. When she was feeling this way, she could talk herself into a dither until she wound up a sobbing heap on the couch or in her bed. As parents, we could see this emotional storm developing almost as clearly as gathering rain clouds on the horizon outside. Armed with Goleman's insights, we tried to help her manage her emotions by talking with her and helping her to see that (1) she could get control of her feelings and could stop the downward spiral, (2) she could focus on only one thing that needs to be done and do it without worrying about the others, and (3) she could begin to feel good about herself not only for doing that one thing but also for managing her feelings. I'm happy to note that several years later (now) she has become much more adept at seeing and managing her own emotions. Perhaps it was just the passage of time. I think not. For many, the passage of time does nothing more than reinforce their earlier conclusions.

Coworkers in business are similar. You can help some of them learn to manage their emotions more effectively. You should start by trying to find out why they are feeling what they feel. Often, emotions are based on a comparison between an event and an underlying VABE. If you ask yourself or them "Why are they feeling that way?" you can begin to get insight into their basic values and assumptions. If you can understand those, you can see more clearly how they respond to the world around them. Then you may begin to help the person reexamine those assumptions. Although many managers feel ill at ease with this approach, those who have some skill at it are able to have a profound impact on their colleagues.

SQ also can come into play in helping others manage their emotions in relationships. One of the most valuable skills in the organizational environment—and one of the most striking examples of SQ in action—lies in resolving the conflicts and disputes that arise frequently in the business world, sometimes accompanied by heated feelings and accusations. All too often, solutions are handed down from above—and emotionally speaking, these are solutions in name only: Business goes on, but someone inevitably comes away feeling wronged and resentful and perhaps in search of payback. In the long run, as morale and cohesiveness breaks down, the organization as a whole will suffer.

Skill in managing emotionally charged conflict situations is a valuable personal asset. When people have low EQs and SQs, they can let their emotions get the better of them. When you are skilled in recognizing and managing your own and others' emotions, you can help balance the rational and the emotional content and influence people to make better decisions. Good mediators are not only smart; they have strong EQ and SQ skills as well.

Here's a simple example. An employee reacts to a coworker's criticism, gets hijacked, and launches a volley of defensive remarks that make matters even more volatile and charged. A person with high EQ skills would have instead turned to self-talk, interpreting the criticism judiciously to keep destructive feelings in check. In much the same way, a high-SQ mediator can explain to the injured party that the remarks may not have been intended to wound and that at any rate, the comments are only data, and not necessarily facts, and need not be internalized unless one chooses to do so. The mediator might then explain to the critic better words to have chosen if one wants to influence others.

"Common sense!" you say? Yes, common for people with high SQ but maybe not so common for people with lower SQs. One person gifted in SQ can help offset the EQ deficiencies of many others—and in so doing is likely to be seen by coworkers as an extraordinary person worthy of leadership. Needless to say, organizations find such mediators and leaders extremely valuable. And conflict resolution skills, the skills of SQ, as any diplomat or marriage counselor will tell you, can be learned.

CHANGE QUOTIENT

Another kind of intelligence should be introduced here. Neither Gardner nor Goleman identified it explicitly, but it has a big impact on leadership; I call it "change quotient (CQ) . People seem to vary in their change intelligence—their ability to recognize the need for change, their comfort in managing change, and their understanding of and mastery of the change process (see Table 8-4).

High-CQ people are the so-called lifelong learners who adapt to rapidly changing business environments much better than their more stubborn counterparts. When high-CQ people look at challenges, they see opportunities rather than threats. They are willing to learn whatever skills a situation calls for rather than look for ways to reapply what they already know. Here are a few ideas for managing your development in CQ.

TABLE 8-4   Components of Change Intelligence

1. Recognizing the need for change
2. Understanding the change process
3. Mastering implementing the change process
4. Comfort in managing the change process

Recognizing the Need to Change

Many people find it difficult to recognize signals of change that surround them. Maybe the signals are coming from customers, from significant others, from employees, from the financial indicators, or from colleagues and peers. E. C. Zeeman, an English researcher, made an interesting observation in this regard. He noted how very danger-ous drunk drivers are: They begin to steer off the road, see a tree, overcorrect, see oncoming headlights, and overcorrect again, perhaps plowing into the next set of trees. Then he noted that, paradoxically, sober drivers drive the same way. They never drive perfectly straight; they register incoming data and make small, midcourse corrections accordingly. The difference is that the drunk driver's ability to *see* the new data is impaired, and he waits until too late to make the appropriate correction. Of course, the opposite is equally dangerous; people who are hypersensitive to incoming data may get so overloaded that they become paralyzed.[9]

We can apply the same reasoning to business leaders. Effective leaders will have a high CQ, that is, they will be able to recognize the need for change before it's too late. In fact, Jack Welch, CEO of General Electric for the last 20 years of the previous cen-tury, takes as one of his six core leadership maxims, "Change before you have to."[10] The ability to sift from among a multitude of signals and pick out the ones that are impor-tant as well as a willingness to change, to consider new ways of doing things, are critical for leaders-to-be.

Understanding and Mastering the Change Process

Many people are afraid of things they don't understand. The more we understand and become competent with something, the less frightening it becomes. Change is no dif-ferent. Some predictable patterns and reactions to change can be described and under-stood. One can practice managing small change efforts and in so doing become more adept at managing larger ones. A general change process and ways of managing it are presented in a later chapter devoted to that topic.

Emotional Comfort with Change

For many of us, not much is comforting, in and of itself, about change: By definition, it means getting out of our comfort zone and experiencing different things. Although some people enjoy and seek out novel experiences, most of us seek solace in the things we know well. But one sign of a high CQ is a positive emotional attitude toward regu-lar change: the feeling that change will be for the better and ought to be embraced. In one management seminar, a participant describing one of his core leadership principles said, "Pain is your friend." He meant that learning is almost always the result of some-thing that is uncomfortable or in some way, even a small way, painful, and that learning is good because it helps enhance your competitive advantage.

This idea is consistent with the theme of the best-selling book, *The Road Less Traveled,* by Scott Peck.[11] Peck argues that most people take the comfortable road, the one they know, but that the person who learns and grows and contributes more takes the road less traveled, the one with a little discomfort, a little pain, a little learning in it. He notes that taking this path usually means a little extra effort. And it usually results in a person who is better adapted to and more influential in the world around her.

CONCLUSION

> In *Emotional Intelligence*, Goleman uses the metaphor of a journey to underscore the idea that emotional learning is not a single lesson but a course of study: "In this book I serve as a guide in a journey through these scientific insights into the emotions, a voyage aimed at bringing greater understanding to some of the most perplexing moments in our own lives and in the world around us."[12] As with most journeys, a guide can only take you so far. In the end, each traveler must make the effort to get from one place to another. The challenge and invitation presented by this chapter to each of us is to assess our emotional preparedness for leadership and to invest in our abilities to improve that kind of intelligence. This means viewing intelligence in a broader context, one that includes not only IQ but also EQ, SQ, and CQ.

PRINCIPLES OF EFFECTIVE LEADERSHIP INTRODUCED IN THIS CHAPTER

1. Although intelligence is often associated with good leaders, recent research suggests that effective leaders have many kinds of intelligence.
2. Effective leaders have a high EQ: They are able to manage their emotions appropriately.
3. Effective leaders also have a high SQ in that they are able to recognize and help manage emotions in others.
4. In addition, effective leaders have a high CQ, the ability to recognize the need for change and some comfort and skill in understanding and managing the change process.

QUESTIONS FOR REFLECTION

1. How well do you manage your emotions? If you'd like a little help in assessing your EQ, you might try having a look at Daniel Goleman's Emotional Intelligence Test at the *Utne Reader* Online site (www.utne.com/azEQ .tmpl). This site may change; if it does, you might be able to find another such instrument by searching the Web for "emotional intelligence."
2. How well can you discern the emotional states of the people you work with on a daily basis? Do you ever check with them to confirm or disconfirm your views? What emotions did you observe at work this past week?
3. When did you last help someone else manage their emotions? What did you do? How did it go? What could you have done better?
4. How is high EQ different from stuffing or ignoring emotions? What is the consequence of both approaches?
5. List the major changes you've made in your life. How well did you navigate them? What did you learn from them? What feelings were associated with those changes?
6. What signals for change do you see around you today? What kinds of changes are these signals asking you to make? How do you feel about that? Do you anticipate making changes or avoiding them?

NOTES

1. See Daniel Goleman, *Emotional Intelligence* (New York: Bantam, 1995), for more data. Many of the concepts in this chapter come from this excellent book.
2. Harvard Business School, for instance, discontinued use of the GMAT in making admissions decisions after concluding that its scores were not highly correlated with

graduate success. *Time* magazine also published a cover article in March 2001 questioning the value of the long-used SAT tests.

3. Howard Gardner, *Frames of Mind* (New York: Basic Books, 1993).

4. Ibid., 6–22.

5. Antonio Damasio, *Descartes's Error: Emotion, Reason, and the Human Brain* (New York: Avon Books, 1995).

6. Much of Goleman's approach here is similar to the rational-emotive therapy developed by Albert Ellis in which one learns to talk oneself out of dysfunctional conclusions and thoughts. See, for example, Albert Ellis, with Robert Harper, *A New Guide to Rational Living* (Los Angeles: Wilshire Book Company, 1975), or Gerald Kranzler, *You Can Change How You Feel* (Eugene: University of Oregon Press, 1974).

7. Relaxation techniques are a central part of many religious and health perspectives. See, for instance, Dr. Dean Ornish's well-known techniques for reducing risk of heart disease in *Dr. Dean Ornish's Program for Reversing Heart Disease* (New York: Ballantine Books, 1990).

8. Please note that SQ here means "social quotient" or "social intelligence." Another recent publication using that acronym explores spiritual intelligence. See Danah Zohar and Dr. Ian Marshall, *SQ, Spiritual Intelligence, The Ultimate Intelligence* (New York: Bloomsbury, 2000).

9. See E.C. Zeeman, "Catastrophe Theory," *Scientific American* 234 (April 1976): 65–83.

10. See Noel Tichy and Stratford Sherman, *Control Your Destiny or Someone Else Will* (New York: Harper Business, 1993).

11. M. Scott Peck, *The Road Less Traveled* (New York: Touchstone, 1978).

12. Goleman, *Emotional Intelligence,* xii.

Resonance, Leadership, and the Purpose of Life

I've always been interested in the mountains. The first time I went to Switzerland, I saw the mountains, and I said, "This is where I've got to be." I dropped everything and found a mountain-climbing school and spent a couple of weeks in Switzerland and learned some basics of climbing, how to cut ice steps in glaciers and basic mountaineering. I really liked that. Clearly, in technical climbing you get in situations where, if you slip, you are dead. You don't consciously seek those situations, but you reach dicey points where you basically can only go forward rather than back. And the level of concentration and thrill of operating at that level is just . . . you are alive then, and it's almost like your sense of . . . your visual acuity and sensual acuity dial up tenfold, and you can see things and you are aware of things that you are not aware of in everyday life. That is the part of rock climbing that I really enjoy.

—TOM CURREN, FORMER SENIOR VICE PRESIDENT OF STRATEGIC PLANNING, MARRIOTT CORPORATION

A world renowned musician performs in concerts all over the globe.

The world record holder in a swimming event wins the gold medal at the Olympics.

The CEO of a consumer electronics firm reports annualized growth of 40 percent per year for the last 10 years.

The head of thoracic surgery at a major teaching hospital performs a coronary bypass operation on his four hundredth patient.

What do all of these people have in common? First, and most obviously, they are performing at the peak of their professions and probably at the peak of their abilities as well.

Second, they are performing at these high levels repeatedly, not just on an occasion here and an occasion there. Third, although they come from radically different backgrounds and are performing in very different careers, they seem to be following a consistent pattern. Interestingly, what seems to work in music also seems to work in surgery; what brings success in athletics also seems to do the same in business. Each of the people described in the previous list and almost 400 others like them in a study of world-class performers conducted by Doug Newburg, a professor of sports psychology, seem to be following a remarkably consistent pattern of thinking and behaving.[1] From his interviews with these individuals, Mr. Newburg[2] has developed a powerful model of superior performance. The concepts in this model relate directly to our discussion of leadership and could help you learn how to perform better, be happier in your work, even engage a simple but powerful definition of the meaning of life, and therefore become a more powerful, centered leader.

The term *world-class performers* (WCPs), as used here, refers to people who are performing at the pinnacle of their professions. The people in Newburg's study include, for example, a world record holder and Olympic gold medalist in the 100-meter backstroke, a two-time NCAA basketball player of the year, an internationally known jazz musician, the director of training in the thoracic surgery department of a major university medical center, military personnel responsible for both the lives of highly trained pilots and their equipment, and the CEO of a high-tech retail chain that has grown at double-digit rates for the last 15 years.

Newburg saw from his interviews that first, consistently high performers have an experiential dream. Second, they are willing to work very hard for what they want. Third, they feel a strong sense of personal responsibility for creating the freedoms they wish to enjoy. Fourth, they all encounter significant obstacles. Fifth, they manage their own energy and mental state by staying in touch with their experiential dreams. Sixth, when they are performing at their best, they report feelings of harmony or wholeness, which Newburg calls "resonance." The resonance model Newburg developed is shown in Figure 9-1.

FIGURE 9-1   World-Class Performance

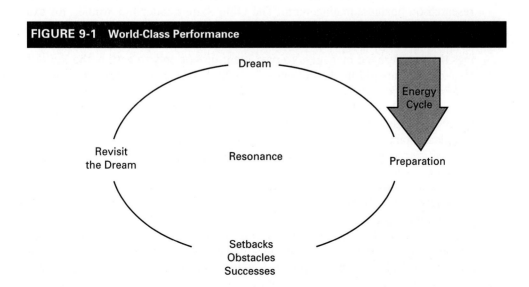

DREAMS

The WCPs in Newburg's sample often described two kinds of dreams. The first was the kind of dream that most people are familiar with, the thing they wanted to do or be when they grew up—a doctor, a musician, an Olympic gold medalist, a CEO of a rapidly growing company, or a world record holder. Typically, the WCPs referred to these as goals. Most of us have had fleeting thoughts about this kind of dream, which I will call an *external dream* or *LDext*. We envisioned being pilots or lawyers or presidents or senators. Some of us may have achieved those dreams, and some may not have. This research makes clear that there's more to fulfilling your dreams than earning a title or realizing an achievement.

Newburg's WCPs often went further and included in their comments an unusual description of an *experiential dream,* a feeling really, that characterized what was going on inside them when they were performing at their best and enjoying it the most. A two-time NCAA player of the year in basketball said, "Look, it's not about winning the gold medal. That's our goal, sure. But that's not why my dream, that's not why I play. My dream is to play to win at the highest level for as long as I can." An Olympic gold medalist in swimming said his dream was "easy speed," the harmony he felt in the water when he tried about 85 percent but got 100 percent back. These sample definitions are experiential in that they describe feelings that people have when they are performing at their best rather than what they are doing or what they are accomplishing.

Internal Dreams

Experiential, or internal, dreams have to do with how one wants to feel. Most of us are systematically trained to ignore how we feel at the expense of what we are doing. "No pain, no gain" we're told. "I don't care how you feel, just do your job and deliver those results!" "Stop whining and do your job!" What Newburg's subjects reported, however, is that what's going on inside is not only very important but can also significantly influence results.

There is precedent for this balance between results and experience in other research on business management. The Ohio State Leadership Studies, for example, have concluded that the two main factors in effective leadership are task and process. The managerial grid developed by Blake and Mouton was one summary of these findings that encouraged managers to pay attention not only to getting the job done but also to how they did it.[3] It isn't enough to get good numbers; one must also develop relationships along the way. This dichotomy of task and process also emerged in Lawrence and Lorsch's groundbreaking study of organizational design when they noted that differentiation by task and integration across organizational boundaries was complementary and a necessary force in effective organizational designs.[4]

More recently, Mike Beer and Nitin Nohria at Harvard Business School have explored ways in which leaders of change efforts cluster into one of three categories: those who focus on economic results (task), those who focus on organizational processes (process), and those who focus on both.[5] Further, Jack Welch, during his extraordinary tenure as CEO at General Electric, used a two-by-two grid to plot the talents of his senior executives: one axis plotted results and the other, process. So, although the recognition of the need for balance between task and process is not new, Newburg's subjects clarified this distinction more sharply than many managers do:

There are two kinds of dreams, one about achievement and the other about experience and feeling.

For most people, this second kind of dream, the internal dream or *LDint,* is a difficult concept to grasp. In part this relates to our earlier discussion of emotional intelligence and the low capacity many have for recognizing their own emotional experience. Most people are not skilled at this. The basic question of the internal dream is, "How do you want to feel today?" Most people never think about this and would probably find it, at first blush, irrelevant. "It's not about how you feel," they argue, "it's about what you do." It turns out that how you feel can have a big impact on your performance.

The resonance model portrays the internal dream, or LDint. I invite you here to begin thinking about your LDint and to distinguish it from your LDext, or external dream (of doing or becoming something). What is your emotional life's dream? That is, how do you want to feel on a daily basis? A good place to start thinking about this is to reflect on how you feel when you are performing at your best. Can you describe it? Can you put into words your inner experience when you are at the peak of your capacities? Some additional concepts will help illustrate this idea of LDint.

Flow

Best-selling author Mihalyi Csikszentmihalyi (he's Hungarian; *Chick-sen-me-high* is close to the correct pronunciation of his last name), former chair of the Department of Psychology at the University of Chicago, spent his career studying a phenomenon he called "flow."[6] He became interested in this as a small boy in a Nazi concentration camp when he noticed how some prisoners found a way to tolerate and even magnify their existences while others seemed to give up easily and die quickly. Later, he found people in many walks of life who exhibited such ebullient energy. In his book by the same title, he writes that flow has several characteristics (see Table 9-1). First, time warps. To a person in flow, time either speeds up or slows down. If it speeds up, one becomes unaware of the passage of time and suddenly at some point observes, "Wow, where did the time go?" If it slows down, one becomes aware of minute detail as if life were passing by in a slow-motion film. Ted Williams once said he could see the seams on the baseball as it flew toward the plate. The opening quote of this chapter reflects a time-warp slow-down phenomenon experienced by a technical rock climber. Second, people in flow lose their self-consciousness. They are no longer worried about how they appear to others. Concerns about hair, clothing, language, and so on melt away in

TABLE 9-1   Characteristics of "flow"
1. Time warps, either speeding up or slowing down
2. One loses self-consciousness
3. One focuses intently on the task
4. One performs at the peak of one's abilities
5. Yet it seems effortless, as if it were flowing
6. The experience is intensely, internally satisfying
7. Afterward, one regains a self of stronger, more capable self

the face of the third characteristic, intense focus on the task at hand. Fourth, people in flow perform at their peak, at the limit of their capabilities, and yet, fifth, it seems effortless, as if the performance was just flowing out of them. Athletes sometimes talk about this: not straining and struggling yet performing at their best. Mathematicians sometimes say the same; there's a moment when the pathway to a solution appears almost effortlessly. Sixth, being in flow is intensely satisfying. People thoroughly enjoy it. It's a powerful psychological experience. And seventh, when a flow experience is over, one feels enlarged, more capable, more grounded in the world and able to deal with its ups and downs.

Csikszentmihalyi refers to this phenomenon as flow. Basketball players call it "being in the zone." Eastern religions and languages refer to it as *wa,* or being in harmony with one's surroundings.[7] Newburg calls it resonance, the experience of being in harmony with the situation and the events in which one is performing to such an extent that one is able to influence those events masterfully, effortlessly, and with great psychic reward.

So what is your internal life's dream? Is it "to play to win at the highest level" or "easy speed" or "light, unhurried and engaged"? If you cannot answer that question immediately, don't despair. It seems like such a simple task. The first time I heard Mr. Newburg speak and describe this phenomenon, I went home and couldn't sleep that night. It took me two years to figure mine out. Perhaps you'll be faster than I was. As you try to identify your LDint, I invite you to begin with reflection on the times in your life when you've felt flow. What were you doing? Where were you? What were the circumstances? How did you feel?

In my experience, most people have felt flow at one time or another. When I ask executive groups when they have felt flow, the room typically fills with energy and enthusiasm, with much smiling and hand waving as people describe where they were and what they were doing. Some people will mention running; others, childbirth; others, skiing; some, writing computer code; and some, even calculus![8] (We acknowledge that some will note that sex seems to have all of the characteristics of resonance, so we leave that out for propriety's sake.) Resonance comes to people from different sources.

But living your LDint is not just about playing basketball all day or quitting work to go fishing. Some people will say, "Well, I get flow when I run, but not at work. How can I get that at work?" This is a significant question. First, note that the activity and the experiencing of the activity are not the same thing. Clearly the activity and the experience are related, as we have tried to illustrate in Figure 9-2. But it is important to realize that people can and do transport their experiencing from one activity to another. In other words, one can learn to bring the resonance of basketball or fishing or music or swimming, for example, to another setting. When I was a young assistant professor at the Harvard Business School, a senior colleague who was famous for his teaching skills took me under his wing. I asked him one day if he would observe me teach. He agreed, and I prepared late the night before, tried my hardest in class, and ran to his office afterward for feedback. His summary: "You're boring!" Ouch! Then he said, "I notice that you play basketball at lunch with the doctoral students." "Yes," I said, "I love basketball." "It's apparent," he replied; "when you come back, your face is glowing, you are floating down the hall, exuding energy! You've got to figure out how to play basketball in the classroom!" When I heard that, I thought, "Hmm, that's

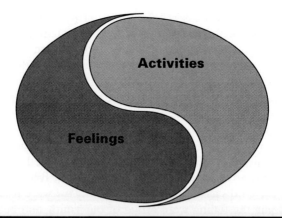

FIGURE 9-2   Internal Dreams: Experiential Feelings

dumb. You can't play basketball in the classroom." As I reflected on this, the awareness gradually dawned that yes, one can. There's a tip off. One passes the "ball." Some people fumble it, some make fancy dribbles and fancy shots, everyone oohs and aahs, and then we race down "court" in the other direction. The point is that resonant experiences are transferable, and those who learn how to do that significantly improve their performance in a variety of activities. The first challenge, though, is to recognize the sources of your resonance when it occurs so that you're able to recognize and describe it.

Regardless of where their flow came from, most people have concluded that experiencing resonance is a fleeting thing that comes and goes and cannot be recreated. One of the central and most powerful implications of Newburg's research is that lots of people are aware of this phenomenon and are working to recreate it, whether it be in sports, in music, in the operating room, or the board room, on a regular basis. If you're a heart surgeon or a performing musician, when the time comes, you cannot be wondering if you'll be "on" today or not; you need "it" to happen regularly and on cue. You may never get to the point where you can make it happen every time; however, there are at least 400 people in the world who are ramping up their percentages.

Some people seem to know immediately what their LDint is. Others struggle for some time trying to identify it. Perhaps you have a natural awareness of your peak emotional experiences. If not, you may have to work at it for a while before you can feel confident that what you've identified is what you would like to recreate on a regular basis in your life. We've included an exercise in the workbook at the back of the book to help you work through this question. But why should you want to do this?

The Universal Search for Resonance

A case can be made that much of human activity is directed toward the search for resonance. WCPs have recognized it, found a field in which they can experience it, and have invested heavily in recreating it as much as they can in their lives. Average people, too, seem to be searching constantly for resonance. Look at small children. Their curiosity and inquisitiveness is infectious. At play, they are completely engaged, absorbed in the moment, learning, growing, and stretching their boundaries. Somehow as they grow older, this magic seems to evaporate from the lives of many (not all). Robert MacCammon, in his book, *Boy's Life,* describes it this way:

> We all start out knowing magic. We are born with whirlwinds, forest fires and comets inside of us. We are all born able to sing to birds and read the clouds, and see our destiny in grains of sand.
>
> But then we get the magic educated right out of our souls. We get it churched out, spanked out, washed out, and combed out. We get put on the straight and narrow and told to be responsible. Told to act our age. Told to grow up, for God's sake. And you know why we were told that? Because the people doing the telling were afraid of our youth, and because the magic we knew made them ashamed and sad about what they had allowed to whither in themselves.
>
> After you go so far away from it though, you can't really get it back, just seconds of knowing and remembering. When people get weepy at movies, it's because in that dark theater the golden pool of magic is touched just briefly. Then they come out into the hard sun of logic and reason again and it dries up, and they're left feeling a little heavy, and they don't know why. The truth of life is that each year we get a little further from the essence that is born with us. We get shouldered burdens, some of them good, some of them not so good. Things happen to us. Life itself does its best to take that memory of magic away from us. You don't know it's happening until one day you feel like you've lost something . . . and you're not sure what it is. It's like smiling at a pretty girl, and she calls you "sir." It just happens.[9]

As you look around you, how many people do you see who are just going through the motions? How many people do you know who have lost their magic? How many people do you know who love their work and seem energized and uplifted by it? I believe that most people are knowingly or unknowingly searching for this resonance phenomenon. It strikes me that the modern addictions of drugs, alcohol, gambling, promiscuity, and thrill seeking are manifestations of this innate human drive for resonance. People naturally want to feel good, to feel productive in the use of their talents, and to do that in an effortless, flowing way. The problem with these addictions, though, is that they are shortcuts to resonance and therefore are false. They miss the seventh characteristic, a sense of growth and expanded capacity. When one gets high on alcohol, drugs, sex, or even the sterile experience of roller coasters and bungee jumping, there comes a time during "the morning after" when one realizes that the high was a false one. No growth occurred. Unless the individual has worked to make the resonance experience happen, it is nothing more than a short-term engineered artificial experience manufactured by someone else. False resonance doesn't add to your skills, your strength, or your capacity. In short, you haven't grown, so the attempts to take shortcuts to resonance don't work; they don't provide the real growth upon which one can build regular resonant experiences. This brings us, in the resonance model, to the topic of working for what you want.

PREPARATION

People who eventually performed at the world-class level moved from the formation of a life's dream (LDint) to intense, sometimes extended periods of preparation. Preparation is the *work* necessary to realize a dream, which may include schooling, training, practice, study, scheduling different experiences, travel, making appointments with experts, reading, and changing one's lifestyle or structure. The central goal in each of these activities is gaining mental, emotional, physical, and even cosmological mastery in one's chosen arena. The central question here is, "What activities will help you experience your internal dream?"

Preparation can take months, years, even decades. A well-known jazz musician told of renting a remote farm with a small barn behind the house in his early years. For more than a year, he would spend 8 to 10 hours a day in the "shed," as he called it, playing scales on a baby grand piano. His new wife said it was not a very pleasant time. He seldom bathed, changed his clothes, or got a haircut. About halfway through his 15-month "shedding" period, he decided to learn to play with his hands reversed, so he crossed them and began his self-invoked training regimen again. Coperformers observing him on stage reverse his hand position and continue without missing a note were flabbergasted at his virtuosity. So, by virtue of his preparation, when he emerged from the shed, he had developed complete freedom of expression. He could express through his fingers on the keyboard exactly what he was feeling inside, but it did take 15 months of concentrated effort on top of years of study and practice.

The time spent in preparation to excel becomes irrelevant, though, if the preparation is on target and in line with the realization of one's life's dream. But remember, the internal dream, the resonance, is different from the external dream, the goal. Good preparation provides momentary glimpses of resonance and how it might be during the real thing. Additional preparation, then, is the work required to lengthen those experiences and to make them more frequent, to increase the probability of making them happen again, to increase the glimpses of resonance to a designed recurring lifestyle in which resonance is a regular experience. What does it take to prepare that diligently? How does someone become so dedicated to excellence that she can work that hard?

The Energy Cycle

The answer lies in their management of their energy. Most people focus on time management, but WCPs focus on managing their energy. There are several aspects to developing world-class performance. First, the WCPs in Newburg's study talked a lot about freedom—the need to feel free, to be free, and to behave freely. They talked about freedoms *of,* freedoms *to,* and freedoms *from.* Although these are similar, we can see some nuances in the way WCPs talked about their freedoms.

Freedom of is a kind of release from the inability to perform. Freedom of expression for an artist or musician, for example, has to do with a developed capacity to put on canvas or into notes an accurate representation of what one sees, feels, and experiences inside. Freedom of has to do with a developed capacity for performing. There is a freedom of performance that resides in an athlete who can jump high enough to stuff a basketball in the hoop or who can swish the ball consistently from 30 feet (as Newburg can). There is a freedom of performance that resides with a surgeon who has done repeatedly and successfully what the body in front of him on the operating table needs to have done. Those of us who wrestle with our abilities to perform, whether it's at work, in conversation, in writing, in conducting a meeting, or in coordinating a complex project, are still developing our freedoms of.

Freedom to, on the other hand, has to do with overcoming and moving beyond the parameters and constraints that inhibit us from performing what we know how to do. We may have the ability internal to us, that is, the freedom of performing, but if we aren't invited to the key meeting or if we are restricted from the big tournament or if we are unable to see patients, we may not have the freedom to manifest that ability. Organizational regulations, customs, traditions, others' expectations, financial constraints, legal guidelines, and other external factors all can prevent us from doing what we are able. Unless we have developed a set of freedoms related to managing our external environment, we may not have the freedoms to be in situations where our freedoms of can be exercised. One well-known musician, for instance, says that he puts up with and is paid a lot of money for the hassles of traveling from city to city, wrestling with agents, airlines, motels, and difficult schedules all just so he can be free to perform when the lights go down and the spots come up on stage. What he does then, he says, is for free.

Freedoms from relate to conditions or states of mind that keep one from performing at the highest level. These might include lack of confidence, depression, a sense of mediocrity or anonymity, ignorance, and lack of motivation. Freedoms from are in one sense enablers of freedoms of. If one is free from doubt, fear, and analysis-paralysis, one may develop freedom of expression.

The key thing about the WCPs' view of freedom is that they accepted, fully and deeply, the responsibility for their own outcomes. There was no sense of entitlement in the interviews. Rather, these WCPs were very aware that it was their responsibility to learn new ways to prepare (practice) and to develop the determination to see that preparation through. This awareness of the freedom–responsibility link stimulated an intense desire to learn, to search for new ideas about how to expand their freedoms.

The Search for Ideas

When a person identifies freedoms that he or she wants to achieve and accepts the responsibilities that come with winning that freedom, he or she begins exploring. This may mean reading, taking courses, creating new experiences, building new relationships, or going different places. Implicit in this exploration is the understanding that, in the words of the Alcoholics Anonymous slogan, "Insanity is expecting different results while continuing to do the same thing." WCPs understand that one needs to find, learn, and do something different to get from where they are to where they want to be. They realize the connection between freedoms and responsibilities. This exploration leads to lots of new ideas that may come from conversations, films, readings, research, taking classes, new experiences in new places, or reframing old experiences in new ways and places. WCPs are open to and are always searching for new ways of framing who one is, what one wants to do, and how one can go about doing that. In a sense this search for new ideas is developing a freedom from ignorance—from not knowing who one is, what one wants to do, and what one enjoys doing.

We all, to some degree, engage in this search. In fact, one way of thinking of career development is as a series of explorations down alleys, some of them blind, in which we try things, reject the ones we don't like, and pursue the ones we do like. WCPs explore these various possibilities with a passion in the search for answers that will help them reach their dreams. Many of us unfortunately have given up on the possibility that we could experience regularly the kind of internal thrill we've had when we've been in flow.

Managing Your Energy

The second main issue in the energy cycle is becoming aware of and managing energy enhancers and energy drainers. Time management specialists focus on the hours spent on various activities and talk about balance. Heart surgeons working 100-hour weeks cannot afford the luxury of balancing time. One, Newburg's supervisor, in particular focuses much more heavily on managing his energy; he tells a story, for example, of choosing how to walk from his office to the operating room (OR). The direct route is the back way through a narrow, bare hallway, often stacked with boxes and other storage items. It's dirty, dusty, and dark—but faster. The alternative route is more circuitous, around a carpeted hallway, and then across a balcony that overlooks the large foyer that includes patients coming and going and occasionally someone playing the baby grand piano there. By careful self-observation, he noticed that when he took the direct route, his mood and energy had declined somewhat by the time he got to the OR. When he took the slightly longer route, he was more upbeat and encouraged, his spirits were higher, and his energy was enhanced.

This same surgeon has paid careful attention to how he feels after he eats. Step by step he has eliminated from his diet those things that sap his energy and retained those foods that enhance it.[10] We've included a brief exercise in the workbook to help you begin thinking about how you manage your energy. This, again, is another extension of the self-awareness concept introduced in the chapter on emotional intelligence. Most people don't pay attention to how they feel and why. The surgeon I've just described is a man who pays careful attention to his energy and what influences it.

> In truth, most of us, have a shallower understanding of the connection between freedoms and responsibilities than WCPs.

The fundamental question related to the energy cycle is "What are you willing to work for?" The word *willing* covers a lot of territory. By *willing,* we mean that you understand that your freedom in this area depends on you and you alone taking responsibility to make it happen, that you are intensely interested in learning whatever you can about how to perform in this area, and that you want to manage your energy to make it happen.

These three components of the energy cycle feed into each of the four steps in the resonance model. It takes energy to define and clarify your dream, it takes energy to practice over and over again until you can do something, it takes energy to overcome obstacles, and it takes energy to develop the mental focus that allows you to revisit your dream without external inducement.

Most of us dream about the various freedoms just discussed. We think, Wouldn't it be nice if I had Tiger Woods's endorsement contracts or if I could sing like Bette

Midler or if I could manage a business like Jack Welch. We may be envious or even frustrated because someone else has won their freedom and we haven't. What we lose sight of is that WCPs have worked for years—maybe decades—to win their freedoms. Again, we come back to the central question here: "What are you willing to work for?"

Maybe we recognize the connection between freedom and responsibility and have consciously decided not to pay the price for developing those freedoms. In this case, we may not be frustrated; we have just chosen a simpler, gentler, easier path, and if we are honest with ourselves, we will admit that we are content with the consequences—not performing at the further reaches of our potential and living with limited freedoms. This is a choice. It is, with a nod to Scott Peck's excellent book, the road more commonly traveled.

We have a colleague, Alex Horniman, who often notes that excellence is a neurotic lifestyle. Many find this statement irritating and uncomfortable. It may be so only to those who have lost an understanding of the connection between freedoms and responsibilities. What Alex means by this is that to perform at one's highest level, one must dedicate a significant portion of one's life to developing that freedom of. Michael Jordan, for instance, was cut from his school's basketball team in his early high school years but became so dedicated to improving himself that he began cutting classes in order to play the game. Surgeons spend years and years of rigorous schedules, developing almost obsessive study habits to get through medical school and then surgery residencies before finally being able to perform in the operating room. Successful chief executives in the private sector often spend longer hours than most of their colleagues, working evenings and weekends. To some, it seems that they are obsessed with their work. To the extent that a neurosis is a fixation on a particular aspect of life, then there is a striking similarity between what normal folks might call neurotic behavior and the focused existence in which world-class performers live.

In many respects this level of commitment is similar to that of effective leaders regardless of their profession or career. One simple, powerful definition of leadership, again from Horniman, is that leadership is an act of engagement.[11] That is, when a person becomes really deeply engaged in a cause, an issue, an activity, or a theme, people begin to notice and to respond even if the person is doing nothing intentionally to lead others. The commitment becomes infectious, and leadership happens. Likewise, when a WCP becomes committed to developing a freedom, he begins to work diligently on the responsibilities associated with achieving that freedom. Pretty soon he develops freedom of, then freedom to, and finally experiences freedom from. Usually, however, the aspiring WCP runs into a wall.

SETBACKS, OBSTACLES, AND SUCCESSES

Unfortunately, lengthy and intense preparation does not guarantee realization of one's dreams or goals. Many prepare intensely and then encounter major setbacks. Perhaps the preparation and training doesn't produce the result one hopes for but an injury instead. Or the research study doesn't yield new insight but disappointing statistics. Or traveling to a performance site creates fatigue rather than energy. Maybe the supposed experts you went to see didn't lend much insight. Or the hard workouts don't produce more speed or better accuracy. Or the team meetings produced nothing but heat and friction among the members.

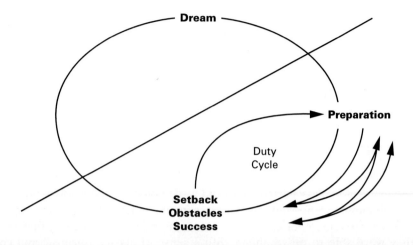

FIGURE 9-3   Losing Sight of Your Life's Dream (Internal)

What often sets in at this stage, according to Newburg's subjects, is the belief that if they only could work harder, they could win. Then they began to bounce back and forth between preparation and setbacks as illustrated in Figure 9-3. Running into an obstacle, they redoubled their efforts. Frequently this created a sort of vicious cycle—work harder, setback, work harder, setback. And in the course of this repetitive ping-ponging, the energy, commitment, and motivation for the dream became faded, fuzzy, or even lost. When the practice becomes mechanical, the study becomes drudgery, and the exploration becomes a task, a chore, and loses its energy, one is on the path to mediocrity. This is what we call the duty cycle because the language a person uses in this phase is usually sprinkled with "I have to go do this" or "I gotta go practice." Whenever you hear yourself using duty-cycle language, beware! It's a good indicator that you're caught in this ping-pong phase and that your energy is draining. It's not the way to world-class performance or to world-class leadership.

Many people, it seems, become trapped in this preparation-setback cycle, lose heart, and begin exploring other ways of making ends meet. The aspiring actor or actress becomes a waiter, then a maitre'd, and buys a car and becomes, slowly, a prisoner of obligations and paradoxically of the ancillary, distracting small successes into areas other than the dream's. When one experiences some small positive feedback in other areas, the temptation to divert energy from the dream and into the alternative activity grows slowly and insidiously. Then one day in a moment of clarity, one wonders how one got where one is and how one had let go of one's original vision. Maybe one never realizes the loss and never asks. The key question related to setbacks and obstacles is, "What keeps you from experiencing your internal dream daily?"

There's another way in which, paradoxically, succeeding at one's external dream can lead to alienation from one's internal dream. Often, people who succeed in their external dream are promoted. This may be a good thing or a bad thing. Golfers, for example, who win tournaments are suddenly put upon for corporate outings, endorsement meetings, requests to design courses, invitations to appear on late-night television shows, and so on. If they are not careful, they find themselves playing less often and less well. Perhaps they have realized their LDext, but they may be losing sight of their LDint, the feeling they get when they play well. Only if they do what the WCPs in Newburg's study reported as common means of breaking through the setback/obstacle/success barrier can they be assured of continuing to live their internal dream.

REVISITING THE DREAM

When WCPs lost sight of their dreams, their efforts became mechanical and something less than world class. Perhaps they did well enough to make a living or to continue on in their chosen profession but at a more mediocre level. On the other hand, when they were able to remember and focus on their internal dream, the way they wanted to feel, they were able to move ahead with a sense of clarity, purpose, and commitment. Distractions became less enervating, obstacles became less formidable, and setbacks became less depressing. The difference is that the WCPs came back to the hard work, the preparation *from the dream side instead of the setback side,* as illustrated in Figure 9-4. It's much easier to work hard when you have mentally and emotionally connected with how you want to feel, with your vision of what you're seeking, rather than another disappointment.

There is a mental or perhaps an emotional discipline here, and it may be an aspect of emotional intelligence. It is not easy to consciously change your mind-set, to refocus on your external and internal dreams and find renewed energy for the preparation. Nevertheless, people who do this report an infusion of enthusiasm, a more relaxed approach, and a certain "letting go" that allows them to perform better. One Olympic swimmer who had previously set a world record listened to the media and became convinced that unless he won the gold medal, his career would be lacking. In

FIGURE 9-4 How You Approach Preparation Makes All the Difference

his final heat at the Olympics, he tried hard to win and ended up losing by 0.06 second. Although the silver medal is nothing to sneeze at, he was very disappointed. The next day, prior to a 4-by-100 medley race in which he had the lead leg, a teammate reminded him, "You should go swim the way you did to get here; don't worry about winning." At that point, he said he decided to focus on how he felt in the water, the easy speed he had enjoyed frequently while training, and not to focus on winning. A few moments later, less than 24 hours after losing the day before, he broke his own world record on his leg of the medley, and his team won the gold medal. This demonstrates the way in which revisiting one's LDint can have a better influence on performance than focusing on one's LDext.

When the preparation doesn't seem to be working and the setbacks and obstacles seem insurmountable, WCPs are consistently able to break through the barrier. This means pausing, getting out of the vicious failure-try-harder duty cycle, revisiting one's definition of the internal dream, refocusing one's mind and attention on the joy that the dream brings, and letting go of the outcome. Paradoxically, by doing this, one performs better. Golfers often recognize this concept. If one tries too hard to do all the things that one must do to hit the ball well, one becomes paralyzed. George Plimpton, as a writer for *Sports Illustrated,* was once allowed to play three PGA tour events as research for a story, which later became a book. The following excerpt makes the point that focusing on the outcome and trying harder often leads to disastrous results:

> When I am playing badly, far more massive speculation occurs: I often sense as I commit myself to a golf swing that my body changes its corporeal status completely and becomes a *mechanical* entity, built of tubes and conduits, and boiler rooms here and there, with big dials and gauges to check, a Brobdingnagian structure put together by a team of brilliant engineers but manned largely by a dispirited, eccentric group of dissolutes—men with drinking problems, who do not see very well, and who are plagued by liver complaints.
>
> The structure they work in is enormous. I see myself as a monstrous, manned colossus poised high over the golf ball, a spheroid that is barely discernible 14 stories down on its tee. From above, staring through the windows of the eyes, which bulge like great bay porches, is an unsteady group (as I see them) of Japanese navymen—admirals, most of them. In their hands they hold ancient and useless voice tubes into which they yell the familiar orders: "Eye on the ball! Chin steady! Left arm stiff! Flex the knees! Swing from the inside out! Follow through! Keep head down!" Since the voice tubes are useless, the cries drift down the long corridors and shaftways between the iron tendons and muscles, and echo into vacant chambers and out, until finally, as a burble of sound, they reach the control centers. These posts are situated at the joints, and in charge are the dissolutes I mentioned—typical of them a cantankerous elder perched on a metal stool, half a bottle of rye on the floor beside him, his ear cocked for the orders that he acknowledges with ancient epithets, yelling back up the corridors, "Ah, your father's mustache!" And such things, and if he's of a mind, he'll reach for the controls, (like the banks of tall levers one remembers from a railroad-yard switch house) and perhaps he'll pull the proper lever and perhaps not. So that, in sum, the whole apparatus, bent on hitting a golf ball smartly, tips and convolutes, and lunges, the Japanese admirals

clutching each other for support in the main control center up in the head as the structure rocks and creaks. And when the golf shot is on its way the navy-men get to their feet and peer out through the eyes and report: "A shank! A shank! My God, we've hit another shank!" They stir about in the control center drinking paper-thin cups of rice wine, consoling themselves, and every once in a while one of them will reach for a voice tube and shout: "Smarten up down there!" Down below, in the dark reaches of the structure, the dissolutes reach for their rye, tittering, and they've got their feet up on the levers and perhaps soon it will be time to read the evening newspaper."[12]

Preparation is essential, but like a well-used battery, eventually it runs down. Unless there is a way of reenergizing one's efforts, the obstacles begin to have more power than the dream, and they win. Take, for example, the experienced heart surgeon who one afternoon has his four hundred and third operation scheduled. That morning he had lost a patient. Does patient 403 understand the frame of mind the surgeon is in just before her operation? If the surgeon is not able to get past the setback experienced earlier in the day, he may not be able to perform at the world-class level that afternoon, something that you or I as patient 403 would like to know in advance, I'm sure. If the surgeon has a means, external or internal, of revisiting his internal dream, he may be able to revitalize his emotional, mental, and physical self before the next operation. In this case, when the patient died, a call went out to Mr. Newburg, who came in and interviewed the surgeon. His first question was, "Why did you become a heart surgeon?" This might have been perceived as an unpleasant, uncomfortable conversation at first. Most people find this line of inquiry too touchy-feely, too soft. Pushing back in time, however, with Newburg's nudging ("What will it take to regain your dream?"), eventually the surgeon was able to find his center and remember.

As a six-year-old boy, he said, he heard a commotion in the house during the night and ran to the living room. There, standing in the doorway, he watched his grandfather die of a heart attack. The boy felt helpless and vowed he'd prepare himself so that would never happen again. That's why, he said, he became a surgeon. At that point he reconnected with the emotional experience that had shaped his career. The experience of revisiting his dream gave him a new mind-set. Then the two of them, the performance counselor and the surgeon, went to visit patient 403. After several minutes of inquiry, also viewed skeptically at first, about *why* the 65-year-old woman wanted to live longer, she paused and answered that she had two grandchildren and that she wanted to go swimming with them. The surgeon at this point was able to connect his internal dream with her dream and in the process was energized. As it turned out, the surgeon reported later that in surgery he felt as if he were having an out-of-body experience—he could see his hands tying the sutures, flying nimbly, yet they didn't feel like his own. He had a resonance experience. Patient 403 survived the operation and several months later sent him a picture of her swimming with her grandchildren. After several iterations of this, the surgeon has learned to manage his own reconnection with his LDint. He keeps a drawer full of pictures of people with whom he's connected his dream and who have gone on to connect with theirs. When he's down or in an obligatory duty cycle, he pulls out the drawer and reconnects with his internal dream, the emotional reason why he's doing what he's doing. It is a powerful motivator.

By revisiting the LDint, the WCP can approach preparation with a renewed vigor and sense of purpose and more importantly, enjoyment. By developing the internal capacity to reconnect with the joy of fulfilling their LDint, WCPs bring energy, enthusiasm, and freedom of together in ways that allow them to perform at their best.

This is true, too, of people who go to work in the mundane world where we might not often think about world-class performance. Whenever we begin to think that our work is a drudgery and that our energy is lost, we can revitalize our efforts if we will pause and revisit the choices we made that got us to where we are, more particularly, how we want to feel as we are engaged in that activity. Fundamentally, if we understand and use the principles of the energy cycle, we realize that we have *chosen* to be where we are.[13] If we allow ourselves to stay in the drudgery mode, the duty cycle, we will not do our best, and our opportunities will shrink. If, on the other hand, we are able to reenergize each day by revisiting and remembering that, of all the choices we had before us, we chose this path and this work and the way that it makes us feel inside, then we can invigorate ourselves and our work. When that happens, when we remember how we are working toward a way of being, something special happens.

RESONANCE

Resonance is the sense of seamless harmony with one's surroundings so that internal experience and external experience are one, the fulfillment of performing at your best without strain (see Figure 9-5). "Happiness is when what you think, what you say, and what you do are in harmony," said Gandhi. Phil Jackson, award-winning coach of the Chicago Bulls and the Los Angeles Lakers basketball teams—a lesser philosopher to be sure—noted, "Winning is important to me, but what brings me real joy is the experience of being fully engaged in whatever I'm doing." When we tritely call this insight "the journey, not the train station," we underestimate the power of this concept. When we realize the importance of giving at least equal time and attention to our experience as we do to our attempts to achievement, we begin to see how valuable this idea is.

FIGURE 9-5   Five Key Questions for a Resonance Focus

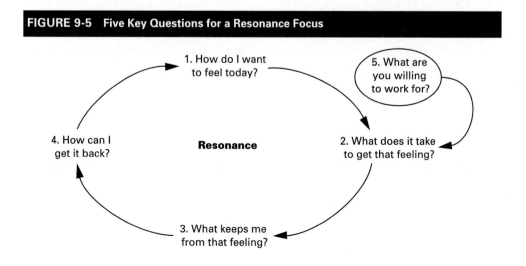

1. How do I want to feel today?

5. What are you willing to work for?

4. How can I get it back?

Resonance

2. What does it take to get that feeling?

3. What keeps me from that feeling?

CONCLUSION

It is so valuable, in fact, that I assert it gives us a powerful answer to the question, "What is the purpose of life?" (See Table 9-2.) The resonance answer to this question is fourfold: (1) to identify the area in life that resonates for the self, (2) to invest in the ability to create it and reproduce it, (3) to experience and enjoy the resonance by performing at one's highest potential, and then (4) to help others find their source of resonance. Thus, the first subquestion is, "Can you, before you die, figure out what it is for you that creates this flow or resonance experience?" In my experience, many people never do. Second, if you discover your resonance, do you have the energy and determination to invest in your capacity to recreate it? Third, when resonance occurs, will you have the presence of mind to recognize it and acknowledge that life won't get better than this? By definition, if you are focused, performing at your best effortlessly, enjoying it and learning and growing at the same time, what more could one ask for? And fourth, if you can help others discover and recreate their resonance—at home, at work, at play, wherever—what a wonderful kind of leadership that would be in the world!

Some may be concerned that this resonance model is a selfish concept. I disagree. One may resonate as Mother Theresa did in the service of others. Further, how could helping others find ways to experience resonance repeatedly be a selfish thing? Others may note that this is an antireligious view of the world, that somehow it negates deity. They say, "The purpose of life is to glorify god." I disagree. If one resonates teaching the gospel or in doing missionary work, I say, hurray. Knock yourself out! The resonance model clearly allows for religious experience as well as scientific focus, fine arts expression, and business achievement.

Sadly, it seems, too many go through life and never identify what resonates for them, the endeavor that engages them and calls on their best efforts; they never experience resonance in any more than fleeting ways. What more positive cause could there be for aspiring leaders than to find resonance in their own experience, to invest in the capacity to recreate it, to enjoy it when it happens, and then to help others find theirs?

One final question: What about people who have a dream but seem destined never to achieve it? Take, for instance, basketball players who never make the NBA or students who never get to medical school or managers who never become CEOs. In some cases, we observe almost pitiful attempts to carry on in spite of clear evidence that the dream will not happen. First, I will note that many of these people are following an LDext, not an LDint. They are concerned about becoming somebody or something *instead of* focusing on how much they enjoy their work. Who's to say that the former collegiate basketball star playing in Italy is not enjoying his work? Who's to say that the pharmacist who once wanted to be a doctor is not engaged in helping others improve their health? Who's to say that the middle manager frustrated in her attempts

TABLE 9-2 The Purpose of Life

1. To find your resonance
2. To invest in your resonance
3. To enjoy your resonance
4. To help others find their resonance

to be promoted cannot enjoy her work with her present subordinates or seek a larger job in another company? Who's to say that the writer or the artist who struggles to make ends meet (the external measures of success) are not resonating in their work? The difference lies in where we place our attention—LDext or LDint? (We have included an exercise in the workbook to help you work through the key questions related to LDints and LDexts introduced throughout this chapter.)

Yet, sometimes, we have to revise our dreams to deal with reality. Clinging to an unrealistic LDext in a way represents one's own loss of freedom and avoiding the responsibilities that come with seeking freedom. Finding resonance is also about finding what we can do and doing that to the best of our abilities. And when that happens, life is enormously rewarding. If we have experienced that ourselves and are investing to recreate it more voluminously in our lives, perhaps we can understand why some who seem to be at the end of their careers hang on for a little longer, seeking to extract that last ounce of resonance from their lives. On the other hand, we might also ask, "How could you transport your resonance to other activities?" If you don't know what it is, that's a problem. If you know what it is and repeatedly lose sight of it, that's a problem. If you haven't figured out yet how to reconstruct it and how to reconnect with it, that's a problem.

PRINCIPLES OF EFFECTIVE LEADERSHIP INTRODUCED IN THIS CHAPTER

1. There is something called flow or resonance in the world in which people perform at their best in an effortless, fulfilling way in harmony with their surroundings.
2. Most people have experienced resonance at one time or another in their lives.
3. Despite common belief, flow or resonance can be enhanced and repeated.
4. World-class performers have dreams.
5. There are at least two kinds of dreams in the world: internal dreams (LDints) and external dreams (LDexts). We need to pay attention to both kinds.
6. Some people have a natural dream, others have dreams given to them by their parents or churches, and some people have to rediscover or build their dreams.
7. World-class performers work hard to create their dreams.
8. World-class performers manage their energy as much or more than their time.
9. World-class performers are very aware of the relationship between freedoms, responsibilities, ideas, and learning.
10. All aspiring world-class performers run into setbacks, obstacles, and alternative successes that get in the way of living their dreams.
11. The way world-class performers get past their obstacles is to revisit their dreams, particularly their LDints.
12. Leaders who resonate and can help others resonate can produce extraordinary results.
13. One way to define the purpose of life is to suggest that people should find their resonance before they die, invest in their capacity to recreate that resonance, enjoy it when it happens, and help others find their resonance.

QUESTIONS FOR REFLECTION

1. When have you resonated? What were you doing? How did it feel? How might you recreate it in your work?
2. What is your internal life's dream? (See exercise in the workbook.)
3. What are you willing to work for?
4. What helps you realize your LDint?
5. What keeps you from realizing your LDint?
6. How can you reconnect regularly with your LDint?

7. What drains your energy?
8. What renews your energy?
9. What would happen in your work group if everyone were resonating regularly?
10. How might you take the lead in moving toward resonance in your work group?

NOTES

Note: To quickly access all *Harvard Business Review* reprints listed here, go to www.hbsp .harvard.edu/hbsp/adv_search.asp, insert the reprint number in the Product Number field, and click Search.

1. Mr. Newburg received his Ph.D. from the University of Virginia, where he studied under Bob Rotella. As of this writing he was employed by the University of Virginia medical school's thoracic surgery department, where he worked as a performance counselor with thoracic surgery residents. So far as I know, the University of Virginia is the only medical school with a performance counselor for its surgery residents.

2. At other institutions, Mr. Newburg might be called Dr. Newburg; however, the convention at the University of Virginia is that all faculty are referred to by Mr. or Ms. out of respect for the remarkable talents of the university's founder, Thomas Jefferson, who although he never sat for a doctorate is recognized as having been one of the brightest men of his era. In this way, University of Virginia faculty do not presume superior title or capacity to Mr. Jefferson's.

3. Robert Blake and Jane Mouton, *The Managerial Grid* (Houston: Gulf Publishing, 1969).

4. Paul Lawrence and Jay Lorsch, *Irwin, Organization and Environment* (Homewood, IL: Dow Jones-Irwin, 1969).

5. Mike Beer and Nitin Nohria, "Cracking the Code of Change," *Harvard Business Review* reprint R00301.

6. See Mihalyi Csikszentmihalyi, *Flow: The Psychology of Optimal Experience* (New York: Harper & Row, 1990).

7. In Japanese, pronounced *wah,* which is the *on,* or Chinese reading, for a character meaning "harmony," depicted as a sheaf of rice next to a mouth.

8. Yes, calculus. A participant in one executive program described how he had taken an advanced calculus class, aced all of the pre-exams, took the final exam even though he didn't have to for the sheer joy of it, and then took all the makeup exams.

9. Robert MacCammon, *Boy's Life* (New York: Pocket Books, 1991), 2.

10. If you'd like to learn more about this kind of dietary journaling, see Kathleen DesMaisons, *The Sugar Addict's Total Recovery Program* (New York: Ballantine, 2000).

11. Mr. Horniman is a full professor at the Darden Graduate School of Business Administration and teaches a variety of programs at the school and worldwide. Trained at Harvard University, he works in organizational behavior, leadership, managing change, and creating high-performance workplaces.

12. George Plimpton, *The Bogeyman* (New York: Harper & Row, 1968), 2–3.

13. See William Glasser, *Choice Theory* (New York: HarperCollins, 1998), for more details on the power of this fundamental concept.

PART

III

Strategic Thinking

CHAPTER

10

Strategic Thinking

There are two parties, the establishment and the movement.
—RALPH WALDO EMERSON

Leadership is nothing without strategy. If there is no strategic thinking, leaders have nowhere to go, nowhere to point. Effective leaders, by definition, have a strategic view and direction. The previous chapters explored various principles and concepts related to the topmost ball in our general leadership model, the self or individual leader. Now we will explore concepts related to the righthand ball in our model, the task, and to the connection between the self and the task, which, in essence, is all about strategic thinking.

To become effective leaders, we need to become strategic thinkers. This need is even stronger at the beginning of the twenty-first century because we live in a time when the Information Revolution is transforming the nature of our lives, our organizations, and our societies. Unless potential leaders can begin to make some sense of our present world and the kind of world they would like to see emerge from it, their attempts to lead are likely to be impotent.

Great leaders have great strategic dreams, visions of what could be and what they think should be. As quoted earlier, Robert Greenleaf, in his book *Servant Leadership*, makes this comment: "Not much happens without a dream. And for something great to happen, there must be a great dream. Behind every great achievement is a dreamer of great dreams. Much more than a dreamer is required to bring it to reality; but the dream must be there first."[1] Although you may not have thought of yourself as a dreamer or a strategist, I assert that unless you are able to develop powerful strategic dreams, your abilities as a leader will be greatly undermined. To be a powerful leader, you must first have a strategic dream that defines and describes what could be—or rather what you believe should be. But first, we need to establish some common language.

DEFINITIONS

A *strategic issue* is any issue that affects one's ability to develop and maintain a competitive advantage.

When people begin thinking and talking about strategy and strategic thinking, they often get confused with the terminology. I often hear senior executives interchanging *strategy, values, mission, purpose, vision,* and *goals* as if they were the same things. Some simple definitions and concepts can help us be clear in our conversations. First, the term *strategy* often conjures up thoughts of long term, broad scope," and high level. Yet all that misses an important point. A strategic issue is any issue that affects one's ability to develop and maintain a competitive advantage. If one has no competitive advantage, one does not have much of a strategic future. Eventually, organizations with a competitive advantage will exercise that advantage and put those who are at disadvantage out of business. Strategic thinking is about conceiving ways to build and sustain competitive advantages (see Table 10-1).

A *competitive advantage,* in turn, has three components.[2] First, it means that we can offer superior value to customers. If we can't offer superior value to those who use our goods and services, we have no advantage over others who would fill those customers' needs—and eventually they will do so. Superior value may be defined by the customer in terms of quality of the product or service, convenience of access to it, cost, unique features, or in many other ways. Unless we know what our customers value, we will have difficulty identifying how, if at all, we have something of superior value to offer them.

Second, competitive advantage means that our ability to offer superior goods and services is hard to imitate. If they are not, others will quickly copy what we do, and our advantage will disappear. Difficulty in imitation can come from several sources. Patent protection is a common one, although it expires after a set period of time. Financial resources can be another. Large installed base can be yet another. Quality of service based on careful employee hiring practices, intensive and consistent training, and advanced human resource management policies can also be a source of competitive advantage that can take years or decades to imitate. Brand recognition and reputation, geographic dominance, and government subsidy and support serve this purpose well, too.

Third, a paradox: Our ability to offer superior goods and services must be hard to imitate and yet enhance our own flexibility. If we learn to do things in a superior—but fixed—way and the market environment changes quickly so that we are unable to respond or adapt, our advantage vanishes. The very systems that made us hard to imitate can also compromise our ability to adapt. We want our delivery capabilities to be hard to imitate yet not hard for us to modify or adapt. Unless our management style and organizational realities include the capacity to learn and grow rapidly, we will, in a rapidly changing world, become quickly obsolete.

Strategic challenges and issues occur in three immediately relevant domains: the organization, the work group, and the individual.

TABLE 10-1   A Competitive Advantage Consists of Three Components

1. Superior value added
2. Difficulty in imitation
3. Enhanced flexibility

STRATEGIC DOMAINS

Our definition of *strategy* includes the phrase "one's competitive advantage." This brings us to the next point: Who is the "one"? Strategic issues and thinking do not just apply to large organizations. Every organism faces strategic challenges, and those that are unable to meet and surmount those challenges will lose their competitive advantage and begin to die out. In the biological world, if rabbits are unable to figure out how to live in the presence of wolves, their numbers decrease. If the wolves are unable to learn how to hunt better than cougars or to live among humans, they face extinction. In the business world, units that cannot meet their competitive challenges begin to disappear.

The concept of strategic challenge applies to at least three levels: the organization, the work group, and the individual. If our organizations cannot compete successfully against other companies, they eventually die. If our work group (accounting or sales or computing or telemarketing or production, for instance) cannot compete successfully against other, for-hire accounting units or systems consultants or telemarketing companies, it will lose competitive advantage and eventually be sold off. Virtually every function of any organization can be outsourced. This has happened a lot during the downsizing and "rightsizing" activities of the 1980s and 1990s. Finally, if we as individuals are not adding superior value to our employers, they will find others to do the work we used to do. We, as individuals, also face strategic challenge and threat.

As we consider the basics of strategic thinking, I urge you to remember that strategic issues occur at the organizational level, the work group level, *and* the individual level. Perhaps you haven't thought of yourself as facing strategic challenges before, but I hope that you can see that unless you provide hard-to-imitate superior value that leaves you more flexible for adapting to changes in the future, you are growing more and more obsolete, and your personal strategic competitive advantage will be shrinking. If you accept that concept, then you'll be interested in some others that will help you build your strategic-thinking capacity.

FUNDAMENTALS OF STRATEGIC THINKING

Bruce Henderson, founder of one of the world's great consulting firms, the Boston Consulting Group, summarized strategy succinctly this way: Strategy is the management of natural competition.[3] He then pointed out five basic elements of strategic competition:

1. The ability to understand the interaction dynamics of competitors in an arena
2. The ability to predict how action will affect those dynamics
3. The ability to commit resources to future outcomes
4. The ability to predict risk and return on those commitments
5. The courage to act

These principles relate directly to your skills and abilities at strategic thinking. As it turns out several different and related approaches have been taken over the last 50 years that build on this foundation and seek to strengthen our understanding of strategic competition. Each of these can add to your ability to think strategically. The challenge is not to memorize and regurgitate them all but rather to understand the basic perspectives of each and incorporate them into your strategic thinking and view of the world.

Fit Model

Ken Andrews was one of the earliest modern strategy observers and commentators.[4] Andrews popularized the separation of strategy formulation and implementation; he argued that corporate leaders had to first create strategy and then lead and manage so as to implement it. He proposed nine criteria for evaluating the strength of corporate strategies:

1. Has the strategy been made clear and identifiable?
2. Does the strategy fully exploit domestic and international opportunities?
3. Is the strategy consistent with current and future corporate capabilities?
4. Is the strategy internally consistent?
5. Does the strategy present a manageable risk level?
6. Does the strategy match the personal values and goals of senior management?
7. Does the strategy match the company's societal contribution goals?
8. Does the strategy stimulate to action?
9. Does the marketplace seem to be responding to the strategy?

Although these tend to be yes–no rather than descriptive questions, considering them carefully can help one assess the clarity and appropriateness of one's own strategic thinking.

Andrews's approach was essentially a fit model in that it encouraged management to find appropriate niches in the world of opportunities and to use their strengths to exploit those opportunities. Andrews's views led to a widely used model of strategic analysis commonly referred to as the SWOT (strengths, weaknesses, opportunities, and threats) model. The idea was that managers should examine all four elements carefully and find areas in which their particular strengths and weaknesses could be brought to bear most effectively. Figure 10-1 shows a diagram of how the SWOT model was often presented and conceived. The SWOT model often was used to discuss four related,

FIGURE 10-1 Four Questions That Guide Strategic Choices

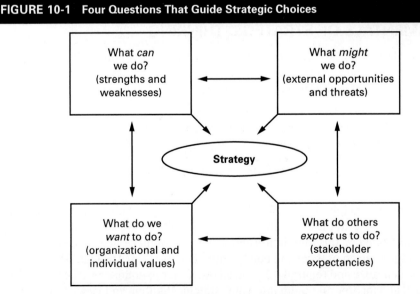

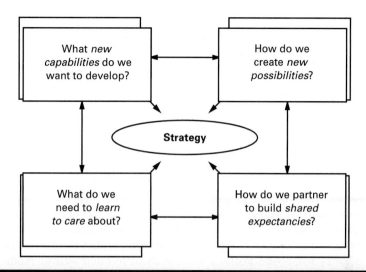

FIGURE 10-2   Four New Questions That Guide Strategic Choices

action-oriented questions: What new capabilities do we want to develop? How do we create new possibilities? What do we need to learn to develop new capabilities? How do we partner to build better? These related questions are shown in Figure 10-2.

During the 1980s, Michael Porter, also of the Harvard Business School, introduced what he called a five forces model (shown in Figure 10-3) that became very pop-

FIGURE 10-3   Porter's Five Forces Model

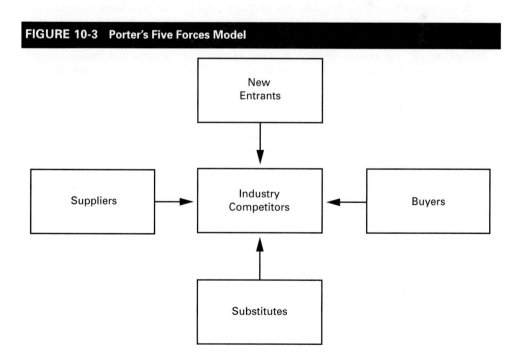

ular. Porter's economics background led him to focus more on industries than Andrews's corporate perspective. In Porter's model, one assesses one's advantages compared with other firms in an industry.[5] The five forces that shape an industry, he said, are new entrants (held at bay by barriers to entry), the power of suppliers, the power of customers, the threat of substitution, and your company's core capabilities to compete amidst the other companies in your industry and the other four forces.

Barriers to entry make it difficult for new entrants to compete in an industry and may include patent protection, geographic proximity, established share of market, and huge but necessary initial investment costs in plant and equipment. Customers have power over you to the extent that they want additional products or services that your company may not offer. Suppliers can influence your ability to compete to the extent that you depend on their outputs to meet your customers' demands. Industry innovations that leapfrog your products and services and provide substitutions for them can be a major threat to a firm's survival. Finally, if your firm's internal skills and abilities don't compare favorably with those of your competitors in an industry, your position in that industry will erode. Porter's work seemed to build well on Andrews's model and managers accepted the five forces model as a natural extension of SWOT analysis.

Value Chain

Porter also clarified another important strategic concept: the value chain, which is a stream of activities that add value to inputs and make them desirable to others. In Porter's model, each company has a value chain that enables it to compete against others. One can examine the strength of one's ability to compete by understanding the economics of each link in the value chain. In Porter's view, one can identify a generic value chain consisting of nine basic elements, which consist of five primary links and four supporting structures. The five primary links are inbound logistics, operations, outbound logistics, marketing and sales, and service. Basically, Porter asserted that every organization followed this pattern, taking something in, manipulating it, and then delivering it to others through marketing and sales groups and finally servicing it if necessary. The quality of the value added at each of those steps collectively defined the strategic competitive advantage that a company had. If value was lacking at each step or was easy to imitate, the organization had little competitive advantage.

The four secondary support structures are organizational infrastructure, human resource management practices, the technology employed and its development, and methods of procurement. These basic supporting structures make it possible for an organization to add value at each of the five links in the value chain. If any of the four supporting structures are weak or unable to contribute to the five links, then an organization's strategic competitiveness is reduced. Porter's view of the generic value chain is shown in Figure 10-4.

Revisions of the value chain concept recently have applied it to a larger, industry-based view in which one traces the major value-adding activities of a class of products or services and tries to analyze where the economic opportunities are and how one's own capabilities and strengths apply to those segments of the chain. In the automobile industry, for instance, one could develop a simple value chain that included mining, shipping, steel production, shipping, component fabrication, subassembly, shipping, assembly, storing, shipping, marketing, sales, financing, and service. Henry Ford decided in the 1920s to integrate his firm to each and every step in this chain, but over the years

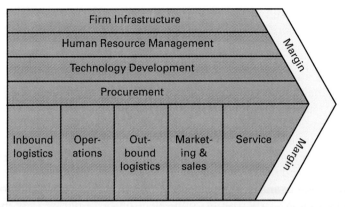

Adapted from Michael Porter, *Competitive Advantage* (New York: The Free Press, 1985), 46.

FIGURE 10-4   Porter's Generic Value Chain

he discovered that it was not a profitable venture. The skills, competencies, and capabilities demanded in each step of the value chain were different, and Ford Motor Company eventually narrowed its automobile business to focus on fabrication, sub-assembly (although many are subcontracted), assembly, and financing.

This broader view of an industry's or a class of products' value chain helps a management team decide where their organization's particular skills and abilities might best add value and hence better serve customers. If one analyzes the economics of each of the steps in an industry value chain, one may find opportunities or, alternatively, segments of the business where competition doesn't make much sense (for instance, because margins are low, barriers to entry are high, and competition is stiff).

There is no magic about deciding what the discrete links in a value chain should be. One tries to identify all of the separate activities that add value in the series of processes from raw material to consumption and then analyze the economics of each one. If an activity has trivial impact on the overall value added throughout the chain, it might be grouped with another activity until the grouping becomes a significant link in the value chain that delivers to customers. The goal is to create a sequential list of value-adding activity clusters, each of which has a significant impact on the value of the final product or service.

With such a list in place, one can then begin to analyze each link in the chain to see where the economic opportunities are. In this analysis, one looks at special skills or technology demanded by the activity, what the cost structures in that activity are, and what the related margins might be and then compares these with one's own corporate capabilities. If the skills and experience demanded by a link—say, in the Ford example just mentioned, mining—are inconsistent with the organization's core capabilities and hence ability to add significant value, then the firm should choose to compete elsewhere. If the margins in that link (mining) are narrow and shrinking because competition is high, barriers to entry are relatively high (cost of new equipment and remote location costs), and customers' power is high, as it might be in mining, then the firm should choose to compete at a different point in the value chain. James Moore, principal at GEO Consulting, for example, has developed an analytic procedure that helps organizations clarify whether they have what it takes to succeed in business at any point in a product's value chain.

Core Capabilities

Core capabilities are a key concept in fit models. First popularized by C. K. Prahalad and Gary Hamel, *core capabilities* refers to the collection of organizational skills that a firm has developed over time that enable it to compete and make it difficult for others to imitate its success.[6] Core capabilities are seen as often intangible clusters of skills or competencies that relate to technology and its development, internal organizational processes around innovation, production and financial management efficiencies, and marketing. An example of successful core capabilities identification and application would be Canon's expertise in "opto-electronics," a phrase they use to capture their ability to marry optical skills and electronic skills effectively through efficient internal organizational processes and thus create new products. The recognition of this core capability took Canon from being a camera company to being the forerunner of the laser jet computer printer industry. Recognition of one's core capabilities can transform the way you think about yourself or your company. Caterpillar's extraordinary capability for managing the production, financing, and distribution of first-rate construction equipment worldwide is an example of a cluster of organizational skills in design, manufacturing, global relationships, financing innovation, and dealer relations that complemented each other intricately to create the world's most successful construction equipment company. Wal-Mart's ability to manage inventories across a vast retail distribution system is another example of organizational core competitive capability.[7] Honda's expertise and innovativeness in designing and applying high-power, high-efficiency small engines led to competitive advantages in several industries including motorcycles, lawn care products, and automobiles. And Disney's ability to imagine and create animated stories that appealed to children and adults was the central factor in the creation of an empire of entertainment that has grown to include amusement parks, broadcasting companies, toys, hotels, golf courses, and various related items.

The central question posed to a firm's management by this kind of strategic thinking is "What are your unique core capabilities?" If a firm can identify something that it does better than anyone else and is able to focus that capability on responsive markets, the firm will have a competitive advantage—for the moment. By definition, core capabilities take time to develop, and they are so complex, weaving together competencies from various divisions of an organization, that they tend to be difficult to imitate, especially in the short run. This was one of the key findings in Jim Collins and Jerry Porras's seminal book *Built to Last.*[8] As firms tried to find places where their particular core capabilities might compete successfully, they found themselves fighting for increasingly narrow niches. This strategic fit thinking was ultimately limited, which caused some firms to begin thinking about ways of changing the relative mix of competitive advantages in industry according to their desires.

Growth Model

Most strategists are convinced that businesses must grow. Although population specialists, environmentalists, and conservationists argue whether growth is unlimited or sustainable, most business leaders actively seek to grow. This may be in part a natural

FIGURE 10-5   Every Business Is a Growth Business

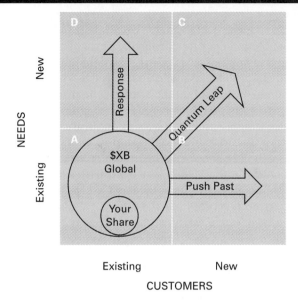

human desire to extend one's experience and boundaries.[9] Ram Charan and Noel Tichy have made a case that every business can be a growth business, even in what seems to be a saturated market.[10] They build their argument on a two-by-two grid showing old and new customers and old and new products as depicted in Figure 10-5. They point out that no matter how mature your current market with current customers and current products may be, you can find ways to identify broader ponds of opportunity. One way is to realize how much, in total, your customers are spending on products like your own and view that as your target "share of wallet," that is, the total amount of your customers' spending. In addition to seeking to gain a larger share of wallet, one can think about new customers for existing products and services. This is the route that most sales forces take, trying to find ways of pushing out what we already know, do, and make. The third route, offering new products and services to existing customers, demands a willingness to look at customers' total wallet of *all* spending, not just on products and services like your own, and your willingness to develop capabilities to capture more of that spending. This approach requires research and develeopment, close customer ties, and a strategic, innovative mind-set. The fourth avenue for broadening your pond is moving into the new customers–new products cell where both elements are new. This is a high-risk strategy in that it implies a greater leap from your current platforms of competency and customer base—and the risk of falling down in the process.

Intent Model

Although Andrews, Porter, and others emphasized finding the right time and place to compete, Hamel and Prahalad began to wonder about how to develop core capabilities as a means of developing strategic competitive advantage in the future.[11] In this, they built on the ideas of Karl Weick, who wrote about the importance of not just responding to one's environment but of *enacting* it.[12] James Bryant Quinn and others had defined strategy retrospectively as the path made apparent by a series of historical decisions ("logical incrementalism"),[13] but Prahalad and Hamel asserted that strategic thinkers should be finding ways of enacting or shaping their competitive environments by investing in and creating a set of organizational capabilities that would give them a competitive advantage at some time in the future.

This strategic intent might take years to realize, but if carefully conceived and managed, it could reshape the economics of an industry and give a firm an advantage that would take others similarly years to duplicate. In the meantime, of course, the innovative firm would continue to develop its core capabilities. This more proactive approach was called the *strategic intent model*. One shining example of this way of thinking is manifest in the history of Komatsu, the Japanese construction equipment maker, which, when they decided to take on Caterpillar in the global construction market, had neither the resources nor the core capabilities to do so effectively. Yet they formed a serious, strategic intent, and by following that intent, investing in their targeted capabilities year by year, were able to win major portions of their chosen business.[14]

The strategic intent model brings to the fore the importance of having a vision of what the organization could and should become and then the determination and resources to invest in developing the competitive capabilities that are necessary to bring that vision to fruition. If it takes years, even decades, to build an advantageous set of core capabilities, then only firms with the vision and resource to continue doing business will be able to achieve that goal.

Ecological Model

A third approach has emerged in the work of James Moore at GEO Consulting. Moore postulated that the concept of business industries was dying and that a more accurate descriptive metaphor of what was happening in the business world at the turn of the millennium was the concept of business ecosystems.[15] Moore argued that Company A may be competing with Company B in one region of the world, selling to Company B in another region, and in a joint venture alliance with Company B in yet another region. Each company, in this ecological view, was living and thriving in a complex relationship with the other, and the destruction of either might lead to disastrous results for the one that remains. In biological terms, they were in a symbiotic relationship—if either one were to die, so would the other.

This view is decidedly different from the common "business is war" mentality that most managers take to their strategic planning and that usually involves finding ways to minimize or destroy competitors' positions. In the ecological view of business, putting other companies out of business may be the worst thing for a company with multiple relationships around the world to do. The more long-term approach would be to view their businesses as ecosystems with ill-defined boundaries between industries or companies and to approach their competitors as a necessary parts of the business ecosystem rather than as enemies to be exterminated. Companies that can compete on one hand and ally on the other are developing core capabilities that allow them to deal with ambiguity, contradiction, and competing internal pressures in ways that give them an advantage, are hard to imitate, and build their flexibility for the future. Those that persist in fighting their competitors may in fact be sowing the seeds of their own destruction—naturally or through antitrust regulation as in the case of the former AT&T before the 1984 court ruling.

Strategy As Revolution

Gary Hamel offered a more radical view of strategic thinking in his book *Leading the Revolution.*[16] Hamel argued that most established businesses are at risk—from revolutionaries. Eventually, he said, revolutionary companies would steal customers and markets, then employees, and finally assets. In the spirit of the quote from Emerson that starts this chapter, Hamel posited two kinds of leaders: value squeezers who try to milk additional profits out of an "old" business model or value proposition and revolutionaries who create new value propositions and businesses. Hamel asserted that the real strategic thinkers are the revolutionaries. Eschewing continuous improvement, Hamel argued that strategic leaders should search for radically new business models regularly—and challenge and destroy their old ones. If they don't, they will find their profits getting asymptotically eaten away until they finally die as other revolutionaries find new ways to service their customers.

Hamel proposed a series of rules for designing revolutionary organizations that might be constantly reinventing themselves. First, he said, set unreasonable expectations. This was consistent with Collins and Porras's concept of BHAGs (big, hairy, audacious goals) that stretch people to do more than they think they can. Second, Hamel recommended using elastic business definitions. Don't get locked into one view of what kind of company you are. If Canon had always thought of themselves as a camera company, the laser jet printer would probably never have been invented. Third, create energy by defining your activity as a cause, not a business. People would rather work for something important and powerful than to make others wealthy. Again, this is consistent with Collins and Porras's concept of purpose beyond profits. Fourth, listen to revolutionary voices. Most companies are led by people who want more of the same and are not sensitive to or sympathetic with discordant voices. Yet those very voices (for example, Steven Jobs and Steven Wosniak at Hewlett-Packard trying to build their personal computer) may well be those of the next generation.

Fifth, create an open market for new ideas. If the organization does not systematically and openly find and reward new ideas, it will die. Sixth, create an open market for capital to fund those new ideas. Let managers invest freely in the ideas they believe will serve their customers. Seventh, create an open market for talent. Attracting and retaining talent is one of the key strategic challenges in the twenty-first century. Organizations that encourage mobility and allow highly talented people to work on projects they are moved by are much more likely to attract and keep them. Eighth, encourage low-risk experimentation. If you have free markets for ideas, funding, and talent, then the next step is to encourage rather than punish people for trying small experiments in growing revolutionary ideas. Ninth, grow by cellular division. When a little experiment succeeds, don't stifle it and bureaucratize it; let it grow naturally and independently. The Johnson & Johnson (J&J) family of businesses is a good example of this. J&J is a collection of more than 200 businesses, each formed from a new idea brought forward internally and then spun off into a separate yet affiliated business. Tenth, let the revo-

TABLE 10-2 Hamel's Rules for Designing Revolutionary Organizations

1. Set unreasonable expectations
2. Maintain an elastic business definition
3. Create a cause, not a business
4. Listen to revolutionary voices
5. Create an open market for ideas
6. Create an open market for capital
7. Create an open market for talent
8. Encourage low-risk experiments
9. Grow by cellular division
10. Share the wealth

lutionaries participate in the wealth creation. Hamel wrote, "You can't reward entre-preneurs like you reward stewards." If a revolutionary comes up with a great idea, she naturally wants to enjoy that idea's benefits.

Hamel's ideas about strategy invite all leaders to rethink their commitments to innovation and self-reinvention. The profit-squeezing leader, trying to get one last drop of juice out of a system, a process, or a business model, may be ignoring larger strategic dangers. They would do better to find and listen to the revolutionaries who exist on the periphery of their organizations and who may have a vision of the next, new, radical model of creating superior value (see Table 10-2).

DEVELOPING STRATEGIC THINKING

As you can see from this discussion, the main elements of the fit, growth, intent, ecologi-cal, and revolutionary models of strategic thinking build on and are related to each other. Modern strategic thinkers work hard to understand the influential forces in the world around them, to assess and develop their relative competitive strengths vis-à-vis their competitors, to develop clear visions of where they want to go, and to maintain the flexi-bility and even contradictory nature of countervailing relationships to develop a sustain-able, strategic, competitive advantage. Strategic thinking is hard work. One must read about and follow trends in the general and trade presses to keep current on forces that are influencing one's present and future. One must be keenly aware of the basis on which one's own unit competes with others. One must be open to learning and developing new ways of competing. One must have not only the vision but also the courage to choose a path and then the fortitude to stick to it over years of effort, perhaps with modest results at first.

Two modern strategists, Jeanne Liedtka and John Rosenblum, call strategic con-versations the building blocks of strategy.[17] Business leaders get together and talk. In the course of those conversations, they try to clarify their view of what the organization can and should become and how that might happen. Sometimes these conversations are very fuzzy, and sometimes they are quite sharp.

Strategy building is difficult in rapidly changing environments. When the context is chaotic, strategic thinkers need to develop alternative, flexible courses of action. This will only be effective if they are based on a strong value base and are consistent with what Collins and Porras called the firm's purpose beyond profits. The economic world's recurring turbulence has led to a rapid erosion of trust in strategic-planning departments. Many companies that developed strategic plans, had strategic intent, and had bet large resources on those plans discovered in the last 20 years that things often changed so rapidly that strategic plans could not be trusted.

Scenario Building

A proven, effective alternative to the practice of strategic planning is *scenario building,* a process in which strategic thinkers develop plausible stories about what could happen in the changing environmental context. True strategic scenario building is something quite different from the common practice of best-case, worst-case, most-likely-case scenarios. In scenario building, each story is plausible and has significant consequences for the firm. The challenge is to identify these likely alternatives and then find ways of scanning the environment to find out which is occurring as soon as possible.

Strategic thinkers at Royal Dutch Shell in the late 1960s and early 1970s developed the scenario-planning technique to the point where they were able to prepare their company to move from being number seven among the seven major oil companies to number one or two at the end of the millennium. By reading and thinking about economics, politics, geography, nationalism, and a host of other factors, Pierre Wack, Peter Schwartz, Les Grayson, and their colleagues were able to identify likely alternative scenarios that Royal Dutch Shell might face and then to specify the kinds of leading indicators or signals they might see in the newspapers for each one.

When small articles about Middle Eastern oil producers meeting to discuss international affairs began appearing in the newspapers that they scanned regularly, for example, they recognized a leading indicator of one of their scenarios, which included the formation of an oil cartel. What was to others a trivial item in the middle of the paper was to the scanners at Royal Dutch Shell a piece of data with enormous implications for getting stable supplies of crude. Seeing these articles and having already worked through what might happen if such a cartel were formed, Royal Dutch Shell was able to change its strategic course to one of gaining direct access to oil supplies before the energy crisis of 1973 hit and in so doing laid the foundation for the company's dramatic rise among its competitors.[18] Scenario planning, therefore, has a demonstrated capacity for helping strategic thinkers approach the process of strategy building with a discipline and grounded foresight that includes flexibility.

Broad Reading

From the previous examples, it is clear that wide-ranging reading and thinking are key activities in the development of good strategic thinking. Sometimes impending opportunity or disaster can be best seen from a different and distant vantage point. Strategic thinkers are skilled at viewing situations from multiple points of view and at collecting data on and perspectives of those different points of view. One way, for instance, that we have tried to help our MBA students develop this ability to see the alternative is by teaching them to play the Chinese and Japanese game of Go.

Go is played on a board with 19 lines on each side, creating 361 squares. Unlike chess, in which players have many different kinds of pieces to move, Go players have only stones, black and white, which they may place as they wish on the intersections of the lines. The objective in chess is to capture or kill the opposing king, but in Go the objective is to control more territory than your opponent but not to annihilate him (consistent with the ecological view of strategy). Because there are many more squares (chess has only 64) and the object of the game is different, Go turns out to be much more complex than chess. Linear thinking that anticipates several moves down the line becomes a liability. Rather, the ability to see the development of strong and weak shapes or configurations of stones as they evolve on the board becomes more important. Western students report that learning to play Go caused them to realize that the majority of the world's population, those living in Asia, might think about things in fundamentally different ways than Westerners. I offer this as only one example of ways in which you might think about developing your strategic-thinking skills.

ESSENTIAL ELEMENTS OF STRATEGIC THINKING

Jeanne Liedtka helps us summarize our discussion with her perspective on strategic thinking, which, she says, has five key elements: a systems perspective, intent focus, intelligent opportunism, thinking in time, and a hypothesis-driven basis.[19]

Systems thinking begins with a systems perspective, an ability to see how the various forces and components of an industry fit together. Systems perspective helps one get beyond satisfying one's own departmental goals to see how all parts of an organization or industry fit together and how changes in one will affect others. When and if one understand the various components, the parts of the value chain in an industry, for instance, then intelligent opportunism allows one to find the profitable places to do business. *Intelligent* refers to the ability to analyze and interpret the various parts and pieces of an industry or business segment. This is where the analytic techniques we described earlier in this chapter come in. One can use these tools to develop an intelligent view of where the opportunities might lie. This analysis provides an opportunity for strategic thinkers and leaders to make a decision about what they want to do. This choice forms the core of one's intent. Unless this intent is clear, the strategy will begin to vacillate and wander.

The implementation of an intent is based on some hypothesis about cause-and-effect relationships in the industry or business. Recognition of the hypothetical nature of this element is the difference between stubbornness and persistence. As one implements one's intent, if things don't work out, the person with a hypothesis-driven perspective will be willing to try something else. Sometimes this means a change in method; other times, a change in intent.

Finally, strategic thinkers understand the importance of timing. They understand that the right product or strategy at the wrong time will fail. One must be neither too soon nor too late, neither rushing nor delaying unduly. Good strategic thinkers develop a sense of when one should act and when one should wait.

CONCLUSION

Effective leaders are strategic thinkers. They have developed the skills of clarifying what their purpose is, what they could become if that purpose were realized, and of exploring ways and means of reaching that vision. They understand the importance of investing in and developing the core capabilities that are necessary to execute and implement their strategic intent. Increasingly, they understand the importance of managing their strategic intentions with enough flexibility to allow them to not only coexist with competitors in a global market but to thrive with them in a symbiotic way.

Strategic thinking is part art and part discipline. You can develop your strategic-thinking skills. This development, however, will require effort, study, lots of conversations, and a wide range of reading and reflection. It will require practice in articulating what may be only fuzzy thoughts occasionally illuminated by brief flashes of insight. It will mean learning to capture those thoughts and flashes in your conscious mind and on paper. It will demand revolutionary reflection and energy. And if you are to implement and realize your strategic dreams, you must develop consummate skills in leadership and managing change.

Principles of Effective Leadership Introduced in This Chapter

1. A strategic issue is any issue that affects one's ability to develop and maintain a competitive advantage.
2. A competitive advantage has three parts: superior value added, difficulty in imitation, and enhanced flexibility.
3. Strategic thinking applies to at least three levels: the organization, the work group, and the individual.
4. Strategically, one can think of one's fit in the environment (fit model) or of creating an environment in which one can fit (strategic intent).
5. Each link in the value chain for a product or service has its own strategic value or lack thereof.
6. Competitive advantage is built upon core capabilities that take time to develop.
7. Most businesses have lots of room for growth.
8. Effective strategic thinking is usually revolutionary.
9. Strategic scenario building can help position one effectively for the future.
10. Effective leaders are good strategic thinkers.
11. Strategic thinking involves an ability to analyze competitive advantages and to devise means of developing and maintaining them.
12. Strategic thinkers are familiar with several perspectives including SWOT analysis, five forces analysis, building strategic intent based on core capabilities, long-term scenario building, businesses as ecosystems, and strategy as revolution.

Questions for Reflection

1. How much time do you spend thinking strategically about your own position, your work group's position, and your company's position?
2. If you avoid strategic thinking because your job doesn't demand it or you don't have time for it, what impact will this have on your career over the next 10 to 20 years?
3. How does your organization treat its revolutionaries?
4. How, if at all, are you revolutionary in your thinking?
5. What could you do to develop your strategic-thinking skills?
6. How can you allocate regular time to strategic thinking?
7. What do you need to read to develop a different perspective on your industry, company, and work group?
8. What are the key competitive forces at play in your industry? Where are they headed?
9. What scenarios can you imagine that are plausible and yet potentially disrupting to your firm or work group? How could you prepare for those alternatives?

NOTES

Note: To quickly access all *Harvard Business Review* reprints listed here, go to www.hbsp .harvard.edu/hbsp/adv_search.asp, insert the reprint number in the Product Number field, and click Search.

1. Robert Greenleaf, *Servant Leadership* (New York: The Paulist Press, 1977), 16.
2. George S. Day, "The Capabilities of Market-Driven Organizations," *Journal of Marketing* 58 (October 1994): 37–52.
3. Bruce Henderson, "The Origin of Strategy," *Harvard Business Review,* reprint 89605.
4. Kenneth Andrews, *The Concept of Corporate Strategy* (Homewood, IL: R. D. Irwin, 1971; reprint, 1980).
5. Michael Porter, *Competitive Advantage* (New York: The Free Press, 1985).
6. C. K. Prahalad and Gary Hamel, "Core Competence of the Corporation," *Harvard Business Review,* reprint 90311.
7. See George Stalk, Philip Evans, and Lawrence E. Shulman, "Competing on Capabilities: The New Rules of Corporate Strategy," *Harvard Business Review,* reprint 92209.
8. James C. Collins and Jerry I. Porras, *Built to Last* (New York: Harper Business, 1994).
9. See, for example, Mihalyi Csikszentmihalyi, *The Evolving Self* (New York: HarperCollins, 1993).
10. Ram Charan and Noel M. Tichy, *Every Business Is a Growth Business* (New York: Times Business/Random House, 1998).
11. Gary Hamel and C. K. Prahalad, *Competing for the Future* (Boston: HBS Press: Boston, 1994).
12. Karl Weick, *The Social Psychology of Organizing* (Reading, MA: Addison-Wesley, 1979).
13. James B. Quinn, "Strategic Change: Logical Incrementalism," *Sloan Management Review* 30, no. 4 (summer 1989): 45.
14. See "Komatsu Limited," Harvard Case Services 9–385–277, for further details.
15. See James F. Moore, "Predators and Prey: A New Ecology of Competition," *Harvard Business Review,* reprint 93309.
16. Gary Hamel, *Leading the Revolution* (Boston: HBS Press, 2000).
17. Jeanne M. Liedtka and John W. Rosenblum, "Shaping Conversations: Making Strategy, Managing Change," *California Management Review* 39, no. 1 (1996): 4.
18. For more information on scenario planning, see Les Grayson and James G. Clawson, "Scenario Building," UVA-G-260, www2.darden.edu/case/collection; Paul Shoemaker, "Scenario Planning: A Tool for Strategic Thinking," *Sloan Management Review* 36, no. 2 (winter 1995): 25: Pierre Wack, "Scenarios: Uncharted Waters Ahead," *Harvard Business Review,* reprint 85516; and Peter Schwartz, *The Art of the Long View* (New York: Doubleday Currency, 1991).
19. Jeanne Liedtka, "Strategic Thinking: Elements, Outcomes, and Implications for Planning," working paper, Darden Graduate School of Business Administration, Charlottesville, VA, 1996.

CHAPTER

11

Personal and Organization Charters

Mission statement work is the single most important work because the decisions made there affect all other decisions.

—STEPHEN COVEY

Leaders involved in strategic discussions often get confused by the strategic language. They begin to use *strategy, vision, mission, business, values,* and other related terms loosely or interchangeably, and this can lead to miscommunication and misdirection. The range of strategic frameworks, introduced in the last chapter, surely contributes to this. One way you can begin developing your strategic thinking skills is to work through what we will call a personal or organizational charter.

CHARTERS

In the colonial era, charters were documents that outlined the purpose, scope, and range of authority for a particular expedition. These included geographic definitions, goals, expected outcomes, and delegated certain powers for implementation. Similarly, we can consider an *organizational charter* as a set of documents that outline the present and future intentions of the organizational expedition. As shown in Figure 11-1, they have six distinct and sequential parts:

1. A mission statement
2. A vision statement
3. A values statement
4. A strategy
5. A set of operating goals
6. A leadership that defines these

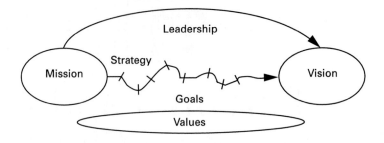

1. Mission statement   4. Strategy
2. Vision statement   5. Operating goals and milestones
3. Values statement   6. Leadership

FIGURE 11-1   Organizational Charters

Most U.S. companies seem to spend most of their time and energy attending to and working on operating goals. In fact, I have heard a senior executive tell employees that the company's "strategy" for the next six months was to curtail sales costs. I heard another executive of a major firm tell managers from around the company that their business was to make the firm's stock price rise to a certain figure by the end of the year and that if they didn't, the senior executives wouldn't get their year-end bonuses, so they needed to get their rears in gear. This was the apparent nature and sum of their strategic thinking. Although I believe that concern for profitability and stock performance are important, I also assert (along with Collins and Porras and others) that focusing on these measures to the exclusion of customer service and value delivered undermine the long-term viability of a firm and can actually harm it by encouraging people to make decisions and take actions that hurt customer relationships and, eventually, profitability.[1] The challenge for effective leadership is to clarify an organization's purpose and vision and to do that in a compelling, even inspiring way.

This is a relatively new phenomenon. Most of management research and effort during the nineteenth and twentieth centuries was directed at Level One (that is, intrinsically short-term) behavior. Job descriptions and other features of the bureaucratic management paradigm were directed at controlling the behavior of employees regardless of their thoughts and feelings. Henry Ford, for example, once declared in exasperation, "I keep trying to hire a pair of hands and they keep coming with people attached!" The new, emerging organizational forms, however, which seek to create high-performing workplaces, are increasingly and appropriately targeted at Levels Two and Three. Today's managers realize that they need to get employees' minds and hearts, as well as their bodies, engaged in their work if the organization is going to compete successfully.

Level Three leadership begins with what we may call an *organizational charter*. As presented here, organizational charters are composed of a mission statement, a vision statement, a values statement (all three of which are Level Three statements), a strategy, and short-term operating goals. Each of these elements is unique and serves a different purpose. Many organizations either confuse these terms or don't use these statements as the powerful leadership tools they can be. Furthermore, many organizations focus almost exclusively on the short-term goals. When this happens, Level Three opportunities are lost, and the leadership retreats to a Level One influence structure.

One may also consider personal charters and work group charters. In other words, if you cannot write down your personal charter, how could you expect to do so for your work group or organization? I invite you to begin this process and have included an exercise and worksheet in the workbook at the back to help you.

Mission

The mission statement is a concise declaration of the reason for the organization's existence and of the kind of activity the organization will pursue. Organizations or work groups or people don't need a mission statement to exist, and some even argue that mission statements can get in the way of doing business.[2] I argue, however, that a powerful mission statement makes a more powerful organization because it helps to concentrate the efforts of organizational members and helps preclude attention from other activities and enterprises. Effective mission statements are action oriented and revolve around a core that offers something to customers rather than something that primarily benefits the organization.

When asked to identify their company's mission, many managers today reply, "To make money!" and then look at you as if it's a dumb question. The problem with this kind of thinking is that it begins to encourage focused Level One behavior that undermines itself. Here's how. Consider a simple causal map like the one shown in Figure 11-2. You can see that many things in the map contribute to profitability, but the two immediate contributors are revenues and costs. The dotted lines are included to indicate other contributors to each node. The + and - signs on each relationship show whether the previous causal node adds to or detracts from the next node.

We all have implicit causal maps that explain our view of how the world operates, and we may or may not be able to articulate them or write them down. Sometimes, we use these mental causal maps without questioning their validity or impact. The first step in using them effectively, and perhaps in modifying them, is to make them explicit so we can examine them. Once one knows clearly what will affect profitability (or anything else), one can begin to plan interventions at various places in the map that could have strategic impact.

A critical issue is where one chooses to focus one's attention on the causal map. *Focus* here means putting a spotlight on different relationships in the map, thus highlighting one area while leaving others in shadow. We do this naturally all the time with our implicit causal maps of how the world, our relationships, or our businesses operate. Our decisions about where to focus our attention are critical to our ability to find and solve problems and to make strategic interventions. When we shine our mental spotlight on a part of our causal map, we begin attending to certain parts or processes of the organization rather than to others. This focusing of attention is a key leadership activity—and, in fact, central to purpose clarification.

When the primary and relatively exclusive focus is on profits, employees are encouraged to do things that may not be good, paradoxically, for profitability. For instance, in one $600 million firm, employees were so focused on profits and meeting their targets, period by period, that they began to ship next month's orders to customers to be able to include them in the current month's accounting figures. They

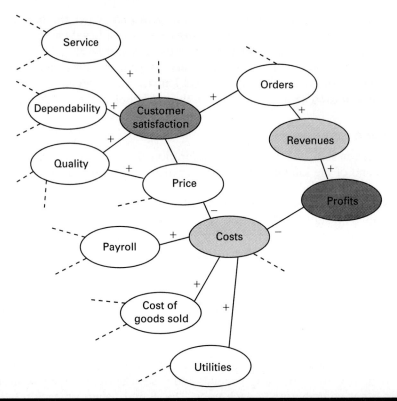

FIGURE 11-2 **A sample, simple, causal map**

began to postpone training and maintenance activities and to eliminate time spent dealing with customer complaints and inquiries to focus more time on the efficiency of their design and production processes. One month, after several years of this behavior, their orders suddenly dropped by almost 50 percent. Panicking, they called their major customer, a distribution firm, and learned after several conversations that they had shipped so much product to the distributor's warehouses under their old operating guidelines that the distributor simply couldn't carry or sell any more. Oblivious to what was happening among end users and insensitive to the realities faced by their distributors, this producer was faced with a cataclysmic realization that focusing on short-term profits had severely eroded its ability to stay in business. This is a classic example of a de facto mission statement that revolved around making money and hitting the numbers rather than serving customers.

A more productive approach is to look back in the causal chain map to the customer satisfaction node. You can see in Figure 11-2 that this node is somewhat removed from the profits node and that its impact on profits is indirect. Turning our spotlight here does not ignore the importance of profitability, but it does put it in a larger context and in a different light. If we attend to the customer satisfaction node, we can begin to think energetically about what specific customers want. Although profit is, in this light, no longer the *central* reason for the organization's existence (its mission), profitability becomes a predictable and stable by-product of the attention given to customer satisfaction.

Of course, one shouldn't ignore cost structures either. The point is that this shift in focus is a subtle but powerful one that allows us to begin leading at Level Three in that it communicates the organization's underlying purpose. The Level Three message to employees when one says "The purpose of the business is to make money" is "My work here is to make other people wealthy." This is not a very motivating purpose. On the other hand, with a mission statement presented in terms of how the organization will serve customers, leaders and employees can begin to join in a common purpose of sorting out how to fulfill the mission and organizing to accomplish it.

We call this a *service-oriented mission statement.* This way of thinking about and presenting the organization's mission is intrinsically uplifting and energizing. Most people feel larger when they are part of a morally powerful service purpose. "Service to customers" has an outward focus that speaks to an employee's sense of contribution and draws on her sense of connection to society. "Making money" as a core mission is inwardly focused and attends to what the organization can take from society and, I say, will in the long run be a less powerful motivator.

When an organization's mission is morally focused and clearly understood and people are committed to it, they may make decisions that seem, in the short run, to erode profits. Compared with our earlier example, this different focal point in the business's causal map may lead to postponing shipments rather than accelerating them to meet customer needs or to acceleration of training and maintenance activities so that customer needs can be met more quickly and with higher quality in the future. This approach may also lead to a greater propensity to listen to people who are in active conversation with the customer, people who may not have organizational status or power but who in reality have the information that the organization needs to meet customer needs. This trend is observable in many high-performing service organizations throughout the world today.

This approach suggests that a mission statement should identify a customer group. This is different from focusing on a product area. If, for instance, around the turn of the twentieth century, you had focused on a product grouping, say, "carriage accelerators" as your (overly narrow) definition of your industry, you might have continued to see your mission as building buggy whips but might also have missed the market's encouragement to do research and development on new types of transportation, such as automobiles. If you had focused on serving people who wanted to travel independently, automobile research would have easily fit into your mission and your thinking. The mental mind-sets that would-be leaders bring to their efforts to establish mission statements either allow them to respond to changes around them or inhibit their ability to see what they need to attend to. Going back to the leadership point of view, your statement of mission, for yourself, your work group, or your organization will be a powerful indicator of what you see.

A good mission statement declares what your organization intends to do and for whom. For conglomerates, each division should have a mission statement that defines these foci. Likewise, each department can have a mission statement that helps employees understand *why* they come to work each day.

Conceiving a good mission statement is not an easy thing. Perhaps you have seen corporate mission statements laminated in plastic and distributed to all employees. It's a sure sign of the statement's lack of power if you ask employees, "What's the mission of your company?" and they have to fish in their wallets for the card. Good mission statements are powerful, crisp, memorable, and easy to connect with. Writing them is more than stringing together trite clichés such as *world-class, provider, customer oriented,* and *balanced returns to all our constituencies.* If you'd like to see a whole volume of mission statements to compare and get some examples, I refer you to *The Mission Statement Book* by Jeffrey Abrahams.[3] Let me offer a couple of examples, however, that seem to me powerfully done. First, consider the mission of the Commonwealth of Virginia Department of Transportation (VDOT). How could you get thousands of people spread all over the state in a variety of roles—administration, painting stripes, laying asphalt, putting up traffic signals, doing research on roadways, putting up signs, and spreading salt—to have a common purpose when they go to work? After a year and a half of careful reflection, VDOT came up with its mission, to "keep Virginia moving." I love this. It is clear, simple, pointed, and allows anyone in the system to see how their work might connect to this purpose.

The Darden Graduate School of Business Administration where I work has a powerful mission, one that I can and do connect to daily. What do you suppose the mission of a large well-known business school might be? The formula for mission statements previously implied might suggest something like "to be a world-class provider of leading-edge research to academicians, managers, and students in a customer-oriented, six-sigma way." Blah, blah, blah. Rather, we chose the following: "The mission of the Darden School is to better society by preparing leaders in the world of practical affairs." We may on occasion fall short of that lofty mission, but I can say personally that it is clear, crisp, morally sound, and something that I can relate to every day whether I'm writing, teaching, conducting a committee meeting, or teaching in an executive program.

Another powerful example comes from the religious realm. There are many churches in the world, and many of them have diffuse or unclear mission statements. If you attend a religious organization, I wonder, can you repeat its mission? The LDS Church in contrast has a clear mission: to assist God the Father in bringing all mankind unto Christ.[4] This mission has three components, they say: perfecting the saints (teaching members to be better people), teaching the gospel (doing missionary work among all nonmembers), and redeeming the dead (performing priesthood ordinances for all those who have lived on the earth—a key reason why Mormons search their genealogies so vigorously). This mission provides a compelling purpose for the growing worldwide membership of the LDS Church and its lay ministry.

Gary Hamel, as noted in the previous chapter, asserted that mission statements should be flexible. His concern, a good one, was that narrow mission statements created mental barriers to innovation, flexibility, and seizing opportunities. The three examples I've given you here are all broad enough that they allow for multiple visions, multiple strategies, and lots of creativity; however, they are focused enough to define a purpose, a cause, and a raison d'être that any member or employee can identify with and choose to engage in.

What is your mission in life?

Before we leave this section, I invite you to consider your personal mission in life. What is your purpose on the earth? Some believe this is a silly question that has no answer. Others believe that god gives one a mission in life and the goal is to figure that out. Others believe that you can live with or without a purpose but that having one lends clarity and energy to your daily activities. I'm in the latter camp. (Duh!) Do you have a personal mission statement? If not, can you craft one that captures what you're trying to do with your life? Lily Tomlin, the comedienne, once remarked, "I always wanted to be somebody. I guess I should have been more specific." Again, there's a worksheet in the workbook at the back of this book to help you begin this process if you like. Perhaps a couple of examples will help get you thinking. I have two colleagues, both excellent instructors, who told me their mission statements: "to make people think," and "to help people create powerful futures." Both of these seem like very appropriate mission statements for university professors. Mine is "to help people find themselves." I can and do apply this to my teaching, my writing, my consulting (helping organizations find themselves), and my administrative work. For me, this is more tolerant than "helping people become what they should become" and more powerful than "to teach" and more motivating than "to publish." If you find this a compelling question, I invite you to ask a number of people whom you respect what their life's mission is. Some will have clear ones, and some will not. My educated guess is that you'll learn from the conversation who's who.

Vision

Given a mission or purpose, most people need a view of where they're going. If a mission is about what we do or why we exist today where we are, a vision is the view that we take of what the organization can and should become if it follows and succeeds in that mission. A visionary leader looks ahead, sees what the organization should be, and uses that panoramic view to guide communications with others in the organization. This is a key element in leadership.

Would-be leaders who cannot envision the future and what their organization can do in it have a very difficult time talking and behaving in ways that inspire and motivate others at Level Three. In the same way that short-term financial goals make weak mission statements, short-term financial visions of the future make weak visions. Stan Davis's book *Future Perfect* explores this concept well.[5] Davis describes how effective leaders cast their minds into the future, Merlin-like, and then look back on the organization's present state. The gap in between is the progress that the organization must make to achieve the vision. Leaders who think in this way, Davis notes, tend to talk in the *future perfect* tense; that is, they will use phrases such as "When we achieve our vision, we *will have done* x, y, and z." The x, y, and z, of course, are the things that the leader recognizes need to be done to move toward the vision. These become the shorter-term goals and objectives for the organization that are described later.

The more descriptive, detailed, and passionately held visions are, the more powerful they become. If leaders talk just about becoming a world-class organization (which has become a trite and almost meaningless phrase), they overlook the myriad details that are necessary to do that and to describe to others what world class in their business looks like. Effective leaders will imagine, see, and then painstakingly describe what they see as possible—and not just once but hundreds of times in hundreds of settings.

> Where do you believe you or your organization ought to be in 10 (or 30) years?

Often, midlevel managers and employees claim that their lack of vision is a function of the work they do and that if they had the CEO's job, they, too, would be able to see things in broader, visionary terms. We disagree. The data we've developed from the *Survey of Managerial Behavior,* a self-assessment instrument that measures in part one's interest in visioning, suggest that little correlation exists between a person's level in an organization and the time and energy they spend on creating a powerful vision. In this database were many senior managers who spent little time thinking about the future, and many lower-level employees who had worked to develop a clear picture of what they were doing. The obvious conclusion is that the mental effort to define a vision is person specific, not job specific. Those who are appropriately promoted to strategic positions have already developed personal beginnings of a corporate vision and will get the strategic jobs *because of* their demonstrated visionary capacity rather than potential to develop it. Although I don't say it's too late to develop a vision when you get a visionary job, you'll be better off in the promotion pool and more effective as a leader wherever you are if you've developed a personal image of what your department and your organization can and, in your mind, should become. This process develops in you the mental capacity for strategic, visionary thinking.

A second excuse that people offer for not being more visionary is that the world is changing so fast that no one can tell where it's going. This is a cop-out. Visioning doesn't necessarily mean being able to predict the future; rather, it means envisioning what you think it could, and should, be. Without this kind of vision, it is virtually impossible to develop the strategic intent described in the last chapter. Are you able to describe what your company should be in 10 years? Twenty years? How about yourself? Remember Lily Tomlin's line: Maybe it's time to be more specific.

Visioning is a learned behavior that can be developed, but it doesn't come easily. Visions grow out of study, reading, comparing, traveling, seeing, imagining, seeking, analyzing, and a host of other activities that give the individual a base from which to create and receive new views of what is possible. If you want to become an effective leader, you should be practicing visioning *now.* You can do this by thinking regularly about where you or your organization are going; what you or it should look like in 4, 10, 20, 30, or 100 years; by reading extensively; and by formulating your own broad answers to the pressing problems of the day, whether they be personal, national, or organizational.

You might begin by making a habit of asking yourself difficult questions such as, "How would I respond to the economic situation today if I were the nation's chief executive?" "How do I see my company operating in the next century?" "What would its reputation be?" "What do I plan to be doing when I am 45? 55? 65?" Shower time, commute time, or end-of-day reflection time are all good opportunities to pause and think about what you would do if you were in the chief strategic job in your country, region, organization, or department—or in your life. If you really get serious about this, you may begin scheduling time to read and think about these issues and developing on paper your view of what's possible. Of course, your first drafts may not be your last; the point is to get started and to develop your capacities by practice and revision. A previously mentioned but stellar example in this regard is Konosuke Matsushita, founder of Matsushita Electric (Panasonic in the United States), the global Japanese electronics firm. His vision extended 250 years into the future and was divided into ten 25-year pieces, each with its specific goals and strategic targets.

In a sense, visioning is daydreaming, but in another sense it is hard mental exercise. Like physical exercise, it is hard work. You must stretch your thinking, your view, and your basic assumptions about what could be. You must also be realistic and take into account all of the factual data available to you. If you daydream or practice visioning by assuming away thorny realities, you aren't helping your skills to develop at all.

Visions are like targets: They give organizational members something to shoot at. If the mission statement defines what we do, the vision statement puts an element of striving into it by giving people something to reach for. We present these two steps, defining a mission and creating a vision, as steps one and two of building an organizational charter. They become the bookends of the strategic manuscript of the organization; they frame what comes between. They rest, however, on the foundation of a set of values.

Values

A values statement addresses the question, "How are we going to go about accomplishing our mission and realizing our vision?" Values statements declare the principles by which an organization will work on fulfilling its mission. Values are arbitrary in that they may not be based purely on effectiveness; there are usually many ways to go about creating a future.

A values statement outlines which ways or principles we will choose and which we will not. For example, one major company recently declared, along with many others, that Southeast Asia was going to be an area of emphasis over the next several decades. The company also declared that despite the widely held rule of thumb that political payoffs and kickbacks were common practice in many of the areas in which they wanted to do business, they would walk away from business that required that kind of unethical behavior. This is a values statement and one that will surely impact profitability in a variety of ways.

In another example, the heads of the subsidiaries of a global communications firm that had grown by acquisition met to discuss strategy. As they talked about their futures, they began to discuss a small part of one business leader's activities that involved producing and broadcasting satellite programming. They discovered in the meeting that one of the firms they had acquired produced, among other things, adult films. The discussion recognized that this segment was growing and highly profitable. They talked about whether the firm wanted to be in this part of their industry's business. It was not purely a matter of making money because this subsidiary was highly profitable. This is another example of a values discussion that sets a tone for the rest of the organization as it implements its mission and strives toward its vision.

What do you and your company stand for in terms of how you conduct your business?

Many companies explicitly write down their values in published values statements; these are intended to help members and outsiders alike understand what the leadership stands for and how members of the organization should act. If these statements match the behavior of the managerial and leadership ranks of the organization, then the values are likely to become more and more instilled in the thinking and behavior of the rest of the organization. If stated values contradict actual leadership behavior, employees and outsiders alike will begin to see the hypocrisy and attempt either to find other companies to do business with or ignore the public statements and try to discern the underlying, true values that guide the leaders' behaviors. For this reason, we cannot talk about leadership without talking about values and ethics—as discussed earlier.

A major challenge for leadership is to be congruent with their stated values. Few things are more demoralizing to a work force than to see a gap between a leader's walk and his talk. When you reflect on, identify, and declare your or your company's values, you had better be sure you are a good role model for them. If you are not, it would better not to declare them.

Perhaps you have seen several values statements. One company printed a core values pamphlet that declared "Integrity, Communication, Accountability, Respect, and Excellence," with helpful statements under each about how an individual might manifest those values. (For example, "I act with integrity when I stand up for what I believe is right.") Another company prints unique cards imprinted with "create a safe involved workplace, Passion for growing with our partners, Recognize & reward strong performance, Measurement defines progress, Speed a hallmark, Motivated, productive and diversified workforce is our goal, and Honesty and integrity" as its guiding principles. One federation of tae kwon do schools offers five core values, Courtesy, Integrity, Perseverance, Self-Control, and Indomitable Will, hung for all to see on large signs in the practice area.

When thought through carefully and modeled consistently, values statements can be very useful. They can guide recruiting and promotion activities, daily decision making and work habits, product development, production activity, customer relationships, organization design efforts, government relations, advertising, and almost every other feature of an organization's activities. Although they tell us how we might make decisions, they don't tell us what to do. We still have to figure out how to get from mission to vision.

Strategy

A strategy statement is different from a mission statement, a vision statement, and a values statement. A strategy is a choice about the broad approach an organization is going to take toward executing its mission statement and in so doing will develop a competitive advantage. In that sense, it is a "how" answer to the mission statement's "why" and the vision statement's "what." Rather than focusing on principles of activity as does the values statement, the strategy states explicit, broad decisions about targets of business activity. In that sense, a strategy is more specific than a values statement— but less specific than a goals statement. A strategy distinguishes among the routes we are going to take as we move toward our vision yet allows the values we've espoused to continue to govern our activities as we move along a given route. The values statement becomes the roadbed to the strategic highway as an organization moves toward its vision.

Strategies may relate to the various functions of the firm or to its overall direction. Strategy questions must be answered in finance, operations, marketing, and human resources. Will we take the high-equity or the high-debt road? Will we go public? Will we take the make or buy road? Will we take the head-on or the niche competition road? Will we attack the high-margin or the low-margin segments? Will we source here or there? How will we attract and retain talent? And so on. Strategies, by definition, are far-reaching in their implications and cannot be changed easily. Because most organizations have functional as well as corporate strategies governing their financing, production operations, marketing, and organizational areas, the effective ones will have ways of tying these strategies together so that all are working in concert to support the overall strategy. A strategy's purpose is to create a high-value-added, difficult-to-imitate, and unique set of organizational capabilities.

> What path will you take toward implementing your vision?

So, in the end, this collection of strategies should target the development of capabilities within the firm that focus on a set of customers. Note that capabilities are not competencies. We may think of competencies as relatively discreet and individual skills existing in various parts of the organization that may have to do with technical concerns, customer relationships, process management, computer management, data collection, or other narrow functions. To become true competitive capabilities, though, competencies must be bound together and integrated in ways that augment and leverage each other in a powerful synergy. For example, a company may collect lots of data on customers; however, only when account managers are selected and trained to utilize that data in a timely fashion will the organization's potential power be unleashed. (See, for example, the story of Capital One corporation.)[6] These larger capabilities (in the Capital One case, the capability of segmenting and serving the financial credit market almost customer by customer) grow out of the individual specialized competencies, the encompassing organizational structures, the processes that bind them, and the leadership behaviors that grow them. Developed over time, these capabilities become hard to imitate and give the firm a distinctiveness and a foundation for competing in the marketplace. Clearly, effective leadership has to do with working directly in the process that defines this strategic focus and in overseeing the way in which an organization develops its competitively advantageous capabilities.

The effective leader, then, is a leader of strategic change, one who understands the mission, sees and communicates relentlessly a clear vision, stands on a solid values foundation, and knows how to initiate and effect changes that will have a long-lasting and productive impact on the organization. This perspective begins to define the most common target areas for leading strategic change efforts: interventions in mission; vision; technology; organizational design; and acquiring, developing, and deploying human resources.

Operating Goals

There are, of course, short-term and long-term goals. Long-term goals begin to approach what constitutes a vision statement, whereas short-term goals provide milestones for the organization as they move toward the vision. Short-term goals help people decide what to do today and tomorrow and help them link mission and vision statements with their own work.

For that reason, goals can be very dangerous. If organizational members don't see, understand, and connect the mission, vision, values, and strategic statements, explicit or implicit, of the firm, they can easily lock onto short-term goals and begin to focus their activities on achieving those goals. As long as the short-term goals in place are carefully aligned with the other statements, this is fine, but in a world that is changing at an increasingly frenetic pace, it is more and more difficult to select specific goals that are always aligned with meeting customer satisfaction. Political, economic, and social realities are now changing so quickly that many firms are finding it harder and harder to establish realistic annual goals, much less two- or three-year plans.

> What indicators will you use to signal progress along your path toward your vision?

Nevertheless, short-term (monthly, quarterly, or annual) goals *based on the right measures* can help guide day-to-day efforts enormously. Books and books have been written about how to select, write, and work on goals. The basic point of many of these books is that effective goals (personal or organizational) are tied directly to the mission and vision; are specific, clear, and have deadlines; and are attainable. As I noted in the last chapter, though, seeking continuous improvement through short-term, attainable goals may actually be the path to a lingering strategic death. Quarterly goals do not represent strategic vision. Quarterly results may be important, but they are not the organization's purpose. Executives who mistake quarterly goals for strategic vision lack the latter.

CONCLUSION

Leaders who confuse the concepts of missions, visions, values, strategies, and goals present an unnecessarily confusing picture to their organizational members. If you understand the differences among each of these elements of what I call a comprehensive organizational charter, you will be better prepared to create content for each, to communicate the purpose of each, and to use them in organizing and energizing your organization's members. The reason for this is diagrammed in Figure 11-3. If a would-be leader does not have a clear vision of what she thinks the organization should become, the north–east axis in our basic model is broken. Without this clarity, the leader's communications to the employees along the north–west axis will also be broken. And the result is that the employees will be unable to form their own view of what we're working on here—the east–west axis fails to form, and the leader is relegated to constant supervision in guiding the employees toward short-term goals.

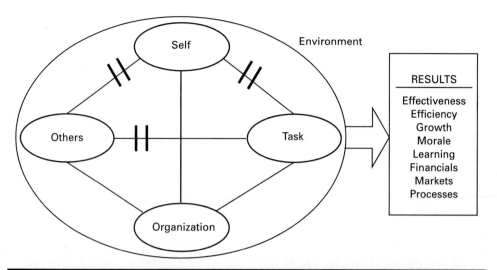

FIGURE 11-3   Key Links in Organizational Charters

> Developing an organizational charter is a powerful step toward learning and implementing Level Three leadership.

On the other hand, if the leader has a clear mission and vision in mind for the organization, she is much better prepared to talk with employees (and other constituents) at that level. Then she can talk about why we're in business and what we're trying to create here and which customers we're trying to serve. This clarity helps employees to see their work's purpose—a purpose that extends beyond the creation of wealth for other people. This vision begins to create the east–west axis and reduce the need for constant supervision. If the organizational design, including the organization's selection, work design, appraisal, reward, and learning systems, supports the vision, the east–west axis will be strengthened, and so will the ties of the employees to the organization, the south–west axis. The sixth and final element in an organizational charter, therefore, is the leadership that defines the other elements. If the first five elements are fuzzy or uninspiring or misaligned, we can only look to the leadership and ask, "Why don't you work on clarifying these?" Such a direct question can be threatening, and sometimes people will say that it is irrelevant to running the business. Usually, I find that situations like that indicate an executive who did mission work or visioning because someone convinced him that he should rather than having done it because he believed in it. At the same time, interviews with employees often reveal that they are confused about where they are going and what they should be doing other than putting in time and collecting a paycheck. This is the widely known and well-used formula for mediocrity. Sometimes people will admit that they don't know how. In such cases, there's hope. The leader may be willing to learn and to invite his colleagues to learn. As they work on developing their joint views on mission, vision, values, strategy, and goals, they build stronger teamwork and, more important, shared understanding of what the organization is all about. I have had clients who have worked through their charters and in so doing felt a renewed sense of purpose and energy for their work. From these experiences, I've concluded that developing an organizational charter is a powerful step toward learning and implementing Level Three leadership.

We have included an exercise in the workbook for you to craft your personal, work group, and organizational charters. We believe that if you continue to refine your charters, revisiting them regularly and polishing and updating the language, your clarity of strategic thinking and intent will improve, and your ability to communicate with your employees at Level Three will also expand.

PRINCIPLES OF EFFECTIVE LEADERSHIP INTRODUCED IN THIS CHAPTER

1. Many leaders get their terminology confused, often mistaking short-term operating goals for mission or strategy or even vision.
2. The concept of a charter is a good way to clarify this confusion. Charters consist of a mission statement, a vision statement, a values statement, a strategy, operating goals, and the leadership that defines them.
3. A mission statement defines the reason for the organization's existence in a memorable, artful way.
4. A vision statement is a mental and verbal picture of what the leadership believes the organization could and should become. There is no right answer to vision—it is a question of desire, faith, and values.
5. A values statement makes explicit the principles upon which the company will do business. Values statements can be dangerous if the leadership does not behave congruently with the espoused or stated values.
6. A strategy is a broad set of decisions, functional and organizational, that define how the company is going to go about working toward its vision. Strategies may change from decade to decade in established firms, but yearly or quarterly changes are hardly strategic given the time and effort it takes to mobilize resources around the development of corporate capabilities to support the strategy.
7. Operating goals are often mistaken for strategic intent. They consist of short-term, quarterly targets or key indicators of progress along the strategic pathway. Poor choice of measures can sidetrack a strong strategy by sending mixed signals to the employees and encouraging behavior that may actually be self-defeating.
8. The charters concept can be applied to an organization, to the various divisions and work groups within it, and even to individuals. A strong personal charter will help a would-be leader select career opportunities, communicate effectively to others, and build a stronger plan for the organization.

QUESTIONS FOR REFLECTION

1. What is the purpose of your life?
2. What is your vision for your future?
3. What values do you stand for—in your behavior as well as your talk?
4. What strategy are you pursuing to reach your vision?
5. What are your short-term annual goals that will indicate your progress along this strategic pathway?
6. What is the purpose of your work group? Can you articulate this in a powerful, memorable way?
7. What is your vision for your work group or your organization? What do you think they should look like in 5 or 10 years?
8. What values are you modeling in your work group? What would your associates say if they were interviewed independently?

9. What is your strategy for moving toward the vision you see for your work group or your organization?
10. Why are you waiting and letting other people set the mission, vision, and strategy statements for your work group or organization?
11. What will you have to do differently to create clearer mission, vision, values, and strategy statements for your work group or organization?

NOTES

Note: To quickly access all *Harvard Business Review* reprints listed here, go to www.hbsp .harvard.edu/hbsp/adv_search.asp, insert the reprint number in the Product Number field, and click Search.

1. See, for example, Robert S. Kaplan and David P. Norton, "The Balanced Scorecard—Measures That Drive Performance," *Harvard Business Review,* reprint 92105.
2. See Barbara Bartkus, Myron Glassman, and R. Bruce McAfee, "Mission Statements: Are They Smoke and Mirrors?" *Business Horizons* 43, no. 6 (November–December, 2000): 23.
3. Jeffrey Abrahams, *The Mission Statement Book* (Ten Speed Press, 1995).
4. The formal name is The Church of Jesus Christ of Latter-day Saints, commonly referred to as the Mormon Church.
5. Stanley M. Davis, *Future Perfect* (Reading, MA: Addison-Wesley, 1987).
6. Bharat Anand, Michael Rukstad, and Christopher H. Paige, "Capital One Financial Corp.," HBS case 700124, www.hbsp.harvard.edu/hbsp/prod_detail.asp ?700124.

Leading Others

12

Leading Others

You have to look at leadership through the eyes of the followers and you have to live the message. What I have learned is that people become motivated when you guide them to the source of their own power.

—ANITA RODDICK, *BODY AND SOUL*

L eadership eventually comes down to influencing others. Even with a strategic vision and skills in managing change, leaders must know how—and be willing—to do just that. This chapter will deal with the north–west axis of our basic leadership model, the relationship between leaders and followers. Our earlier definitions of power and leadership (repeated in the highlighted text boxes that follow), along with the discussion of levels of influence (behavior, conscious thought, and VABEs), compel us to consider how we might think about influencing others at Level Three.

Power is the ability to get others to do what you want them to do.
Leadership is the ability to influence others and the willingness to do so in a way such that they respond voluntarily. Hence, leadership has power, but not all use, or abuse, of power is leadership.

Historically, leadership was associated with one's title or position. Later in the mid-twentieth century, leadership was described in formulaic fashion, often as planning, organizing, motivating, and controlling (POMC) or as knowledge, attitude, skills, and habits (KASH). All of these approaches were designed to get others to do what the leader wanted them to do, which corresponds to our definition of power.

SOURCES OF POWER

The widely read and quoted classical view of power comes from French and Raven, who have concluded that people influence others by using one or more of five fundamental sources of power: legitimate authority, coercion, reward, expertise, and reference (see Table 12-1).[1] Legitimate influence is based on the follower's recognition of the legal authority of the leader's title. If the follower believes that people should obey the boss (or the teacher or the duke or the coach or whatever title is presented), then the follower will allow those people to influence them, in effect giving them power. This is only because to the follower, the leader has a legitimate right to have influence.

Coercion, of course, is based on fear. Coerced followers are afraid of the consequences if they do not do what the leader wants them to do. These consequences could be physical, emotional, social, or professional, like losing one's job.

Reward power comes into play when the leader influences others by offering them something in return for their conformity. These are usually if-then relationships, for example, "If you do this for me, then I'll do that for you." Reward power is based on the leader's ability to offer something of value to the follower.

Expertise influence comes about when one person knows more about a critical issue than another. If the job, for instance, is to build a bridge and there is only one civil engineer in the group, that person is likely to exert the most influence and become the group's leader. In another group or relating to another goal, of course, the engineer might have no influence. Expertise power depends largely on the task at hand—and the followers' perception of the relevancy of the leader's skills.

Finally, referent power relates to the ability to influence others because they admire, respect, and want to be like the leader. People who want to emulate a person's style will be influenced by that style. People who want to join a club will be open to influence by those who control admission to the club.

People can and do draw upon all of these sources of influence in any given situation. We don't use one source of influence exclusively. Not all sources of power are equally useful, though, depending on the situation, the people involved, and expectations for the future. In my view, reward, expertise and referent power are all more effective in the long run than legitimate and coercive power. Legitimate power relies on one's title rather than on one's expertise or willingness to exchange rewards. I have met far too many middle and senior managers who have little respect for their bosses' talents. Legitimate power and coercion often go hand in hand. Coercion may get people to comply in the short run, but it will not have the staying power of the more respectful sources of influence. Coercion is a Level One source of influence; you do what I say or you'll be punished, and I don't care what you think or feel about it.

TABLE 12-1 Sources of Power
1. Legitimate authority
2. Coercion
3. Reward
4. Expertise
5. Personal reference

Expertise power that relies largely on skills and judgments and reward power that relies on mutual exchanges can both be considered rational or Level Two sources of influence. In these uses of power, one is trying to change the thinking of the other person, to persuade him. The Level Three values of the followers come into play when they consider whether the rewards offered by the leader are attractive, but the target focus is on persuasion.

Finally, when someone follows because she wants to emulate the leader, she is responding at a VABE level or Level Three. Our identities, that is, who we think we are and who we want to be, are very much a part of a referent response. This is one of the reasons why labels and memberships are so important in the world in general and in leadership roles in particular. When we say, "I am a Christian" or "I am a Muslim" or "I am a Delta Tau" or "I want to be like John Kennedy," we are declaring to the world something about our core values and beliefs. Religious, nonprofit, political, national, regional, cult, and some business leaders all recognize the power of a Level Three referent approach. Those who ignore it may well have significant influence using the other bases of power, and they are leaving something on the table in terms of their potential for influence.

Furthermore, remember that our definition of leadership involves getting people to respond voluntarily. In this view, coercion moves one out of the realm of leadership. One may be exerting power and people may be responding, at least in the short run at Level One, but if they aren't responding willingly, then it is not leadership.

> In the long run, all enduring and effective relationships, including those between leaders and followers, are voluntary and reciprocal in nature.

Clearly legitimate power and coercion are common sources of influence used by people in positions of power today. Many people respond to others' wishes either because they assume that the boss has the right to ask, has all the answers, or has the power to hurt them in some form. Although these are common and well recognized as a means of getting things done, I assert that they are not leadership.[2] Steve Covey, my first organizational behavior instructor, once asserted that when you use your title as a means to get something done (e.g., "I'm the vice president, so you need to do what I ask!"), you're using a crutch. And very much like a walking crutch, a leadership or power crutch is unwieldy, not very nimble, and doesn't contribute much to world-class performance. So, even if you have positional power or the means to coerce others, if you use it, you're undermining your own ability to lead. One way to test this concept is to ask this central leadership question, "Are these people doing this because I told them to or because they understand why we need to do this and voluntarily agree that it's the right thing to do?" If the answer is because they understand and agree, then you're on the road to becoming an effective Level Three leader. If the answer is because you told them to, then you might rethink the long-term consequences of your approach to influencing others. In the long run, all enduring and effective relationships, including those between leaders and followers, are voluntary and reciprocal in nature.

THE CURRENCY OF RECIPROCITY

Allan Cohen and David Bradford have taken this fundamental insight several steps further and argued that relationships in which influence—with or without authority—occurs are based on reciprocal exchanges and that the currencies of these exchanges can be identified and managed (see Table 12-2).[3] These are not monetary but psychological currencies in which people will exchange, for instance, effort for praise, work for recognition, and compromise for inclusion. Cohen and Bradford assert that this exchange model implies a logical sequence to developing influence with others.

First, they say, one must assume that the other person is a *potential ally* in accomplishing your purposes. If you can't make that connection, it will be difficult to consider giving him something he wants in exchange for something you want from him. This perspective aligns with the six steps to effective leadership: A key leadership skill is to clarify what the others can contribute to your cause.

Second, they argue that you need to clarify your goals so that you know what you want. This is consistent with our principle of clarifying your vision. If you are unclear about what you want, how can you assess whether others can contribute and how to begin to invite them?

Third, they build on Kotter and Gabarro's famous article on managing your boss to assert that you need to assess carefully the other person's world so that you can understand her concerns, her priorities and goals, and her immediate needs.[4] Unless you do this, you are unlikely to be able to offer her something she wants in return for her giving you something you want.

Fourth, they suggest that you need to assess your resources to determine what you can give that she wants or needs. Sometimes this means evaluating your own willingness to give recognition or praise or other forms of interpersonal currency where you otherwise might not do so.

Fifth, Cohen and Bradford advise that you diagnose your relationship with the other person to see if the underlying foundation is there to support a series of exchanges. This is similar to our assertion that you need to have the moral foundation in place before you begin trying tools and techniques of leadership influence. If the foundations of trust and respect are not there, developing influence on an exchange basis will be difficult.

And finally, they encourage you to select a basis for exchange and begin making exchanges in the relationship until it begins to be comfortable, ongoing, and reciprocally rewarding, much like a business relationship. If you haven't established a rela-

TABLE 12-2   Bradford and Cohen's Principles of Influence Without Authority Through Exchange Theory

1. See others as potential allies.
2. Clarify your goals, what you want.
3. Determine what the other person wants.
4. Determine what of value you can give to the other.
5. Determine if you have a relationship foundation for exchange.
6. Select a basis for exchange and begin exchanging until it is reciprocal.

tionship with the other that will support exchanges of mutually valuable currencies, trades or interactions are not likely to occur.

The focus in the Cohen and Bradford model is on the medium of exchange between people, a set of various kinds of psychosocial currencies that are ethereal but very real. People value these currencies differently. If one is skilled in identifying them, determining which ones a person values, and exchanging them, one can significantly enhance one's ability to influence regardless of title or authority. Cohen and Bradford identify several currencies in which people can trade influence: inspiration based, task related, position related, relationship based, and personal related.

Inspiration-based currencies include vision, excellence, and moral correctness. If you have a vision with a larger significance for your department, organization, community, or society, the other person may wish to be a part of that and therefore will do what you ask in exchange for being included. If you are part of a team that is recognized for being outstanding at what you do, the other may be open to influence to associate in some way with this reputation for quality. Or the other may be inspired by the moral rectitude of your activity and wish to participate to be a part of that. The inspiration currencies that the leader exchanges for followership are a new view of where to go, of how good that could be, and of how right that is.

Task-related currencies include new resources, opportunities to learn, home job support, rapid response, and information. If you can offer the other additional resources such as money, personnel, or facilities, they may be open to your requests. If you can offer them an opportunity to learn something new, they may respond. If you can lend them support for their work, they may be willing to support yours. If you can promise them quicker response times in your relationship, they may be willing to adjust the way they do things. And if you can give them better access to key information that they need, they may be willing to follow your lead.

Position-based currencies are recognition, visibility, reputation, insider importance, and network contacts. If your recognition of their good work, even if they don't work directly for you, could be influential in their world, you could exchange this for their help on your work. If you have access to people who are viewed by the other as important, you could trade introductions to these people (visibility) for response. If your comments on your organization's social network has an impact on reputation in the firm, you could exchange reputation-enhancing comments for another's willingness to help out. If you are a member of an inside group and the other person values membership in that group, you could trade this sense of belonging by including them in the group for followership. And if you know people who could benefit the other, you could exchange your introductions as a means of expanding the other person's networks in return for them helping you out.

Relationship-based currencies are related to the quality of your relationship with the other person and include understanding, acceptance, and personal support. If you are willing to take the time and emotional energy and have the skills of reflective listening and empathy, you can exchange your willingness to attend to and understand the other person's point of view or situation for their willingness to assist you in meeting your goals. Further, if you can genuinely express a sense of acceptance and friendship with the other person, you will likely have more influence on him than if you cannot. And if you can extend your friendship to include personal and emotional support in times of need for the other person, he is more likely to help you when you need it.

Finally, Cohen and Bradford identify *personal-related currencies* such as gratitude, ownership, self-concept building, and comfort levels as means of influencing others through exchange. When you express your gratitude to others, they often feel closer to you and more bonded—and more likely to assist you in your endeavors. If you can acknowledge the ways in which others might own or be the key figure in a project, they are likely to be open to your influence. If you can honestly affirm their personal values, their sense of self, their definition of who they are, they are likely to be more responsive to your requests. And finally, if you can manage your relationship in a way that minimizes the hassles that the others experience, then you are more likely to get their attention and willingness to respond.

As you read down through these influence currencies, you probably thought that they could be used in many, perhaps manipulative, ways to get others to respond when your own feelings might not be genuine. A word of caution here. Although this may be true in the short run, I argue again that unless you have the moral foundation in place to begin with, use of any technique of influence to manipulate will eventually be perceived, and your ability to influence will be greatly eroded. If you give praise to someone who wants it but do so insincerely, the day will come when the other person figures this out, and your ability to influence at that point will be undermined.

> After every exchange, ask yourself, "As a result of that encounter, am I viewed as more of an adversary or an ally?" If the answer is adversary, your influence declined; if the answer is ally, your influence has increased.

One major advantage of an exchange model is that it helps us to consider how we might manage our boss or others with whom we have no formal authority. The steps just outlined include searching for the basis for alliances. In my experience, most people approach relationships with a strong though sometimes well-masked intention of changing the other person. Even if a person says, "My boss is doing the wrong thing, but I need to go in and learn his way of seeing things," they will typically begin trying to change the boss's mind within minutes. Usually this means that the person ends up being viewed by the boss as more of an adversary than an ally. The challenge is to present oneself as complementary to the other person's goals and aspirations. Unless you can do that, you will be perceived as something of a hindrance rather than a help.

Of course, the first challenge in this approach is to assess and understand the other person's goals, challenges, visions, dreams, and motivations. If you can do this through careful listening (a great use and application of active listening, by the way) and observation, then the challenge is to find out how you could help that person achieve what they want to accomplish. This simple construct is the basis for the highly successful careers of many people.[5] If one cannot in good conscience align oneself with another's goals, then you may not be able to influence using Level Three approaches.

A major, potentially negative aspect of exchange models is that they can create resentment in people if they sense that one is doing favors primarily to establish influence rather than out of a genuine concern for their well-being. In this case, recipients feel beholden or obligated to respond in kind, but although they may meet their obligations to relieve their sense of it, this effort may not come with the quality or long-term consequences that an aspiring Level Three Leader would hope for.

The primary solution for this dilemma is to have a deep, honest, and genuine interest in others' well-being and in helping them achieve their wants and goals. Without this, one's leadership will eventually be seen for what it is, self-serving and uncaring, and this perception will be disastrous to your ability to influence. You may say that you don't particularly like the people you work with or that you really don't have a lot of respect for the people who work for you. If that's the case, you may have to settle for Level Two or even Level One Leadership—remembering, of course, that if you compete against an organization with a Level Three Leader, you may have a difficult time keeping up.

THE ROLE OF TRUST AND RESPECT

When mutually rewarding relationships are built upon the moral foundation, trust and respect develop and have a major influence on the willingness of potential followers to be open to influence. In my own study of superior–subordinate pairs in a large insurance company, the level of trust and respect in the relationships accounted for more than 75 percent of the learning that the subordinate experienced. To the extent that learning is a substitute for openness to influence from another, trust and respect are essential in establishing a strong leader–follower relationship.[6]

Sometimes people resist the notion of looking at relationships as a series of trades or exchanges. It seems too commercial to them. Yet, a substantial momentum behind this view bears consideration. Stephen Covey, author of the best-selling book *Seven Habits of Highly Effective People,* compares relationships to the accounts that bookkeepers use to keep track of a company's finances.[7] Covey argues persuasively that we have "accounts" with other people. When we do something for them that they value, we make a deposit into our mutual account, and when we ask them to do something for us, we make a withdrawal. Likewise in reverse, if they do something for us, they make a deposit in our account, and we are likely to be responsive to them in the future because of this credit balance. If we ask them to do more for us than we have done for them, we may use up our credit with them and perhaps even overdraw the account to the point where they feel that they have been carrying us in the relationship. If they trust us, they may let us carry an overdrawn account in the short run, but this situation is unstable and probably won't last for long. The challenge in managing our relationships and our ability to influence others is to maintain at least a balanced relationship account, and if we want to have more influence in the future, to build a large credit balance.

Further, the exchange model system of credits and debits in relationships has been used in many societies and formalized in some. In the published accounts of the Mafia, for instance, or in the nation of Japan, clear rules about exchange of favors have been established. In Japan, members of society are taught to watch carefully the balance between *on* (pronounced *own*) or bestowed benevolence and *giri* (pronounced *geedee*) or duty or obligation. People will manage their obligations so carefully that they may not accept a random act of kindness from a stranger for fear of generating more responsibilities than they feel they can manage in the future.

GENERAL APPROACH TO INFLUENCE

If we consolidate the classic and exchange models of influence introduced here, we can create a general approach to influencing others. In this approach, unless you (1) have a clear purpose, (2) are able to communicate that purpose clearly and inspirationally, (3) can garner the support of others by virtue of showing them how the purpose and your relationship benefits them, (4) can manage reciprocal exchanges with others, and (5) can manage progress toward the purpose, you won't be able to have a lasting influence on others.

Purpose

Most leadership fails because it has an ill-defined or weak purpose. If you aren't clear on who you are and what you want to do, you won't be able to inspire superior effort in yourself and in others. It is essential to clarify what you want to do and to have committed your professional efforts, if not your life, to this purpose, mission, or dream. Earlier chapters have discussed various perspectives on developing a strategic vision, a charter, and of creating a personal dream. I wish to remind you here only that unless you can clarify that to yourself, you won't be able to engage others.

Clear Communication

Language is the primary medium through which we communicate with and attempt to lead and influence others. If your language is fuzzy, illogical, uninspiring, or diffuse, the odds are you won't be able to inspire others. I see at least four basic principles that govern effective leadership communications: clarity, respect, stimulation, and congruency (see Table 12-3).

Clarity is essential in leadership communications in that one must be clear about one's purpose and the role that others can play in it. If either of these two elements are fuzzy to you, they are likely to be fuzzy to others, and so will your attempts to influence them. If you can describe with focus what you're trying to do, why others should want to do that as well, and how they could help make it happen, you have taken major steps toward enlisting others in your enterprise.

Effective leadership communication is also *respectful* of others. This respect can take several forms. One is not using condescending or disparaging language. Rather, effective leaders imply by their speech the value that others have toward the leader's goals. Consider President John F. Kennedy's famous remark during his inauguration, "Ask not what your country can do for you, ask what you can do for your country." On the surface this comment might seem discouraging to listeners in that it seems like a demand, but if we consider the implied message, namely, that we all have talents and

TABLE 12-3 The Language of Leadership
1. Clear
2. Respectful
3. Stimulating
4. Congruent

abilities and our country needs us, so let's find a way to make our best contributions, the statement becomes a powerful communicator of respect. There is no sense here of manipulating the rubes, of fooling some of the people some of the time, or of getting the masses to do what we want them to do. Rather, the implication is one of profound respect for the people who, if they chose to do so, could make an enormous difference in the quality of their lives, our lives, and the reality facing our nation. When you communicate that kind of respect to others, you are much more likely to get a positive response.

Effective leadership language is also *stimulating.* Even if we are clear and respectful, if we don't deliver our message in powerful, inspiring, dramatic ways, others may not see the significance or appreciate the urgency of what we propose. Effective speakers find ways to present data in poignant ways, to make provocative statements that jar and cause listeners to pay attention and to think, and to dramatize their points with stories, nuances of speech, and emotional connections. If the others can't remember what you've said, how can they become galvanized by your strategy or sincerity?

Many potential leaders feel uncomfortable thinking about, much less working on, improving their delivery style. They believe that the content of their message should carry the day. The reality is that many stimulating messages with weaker content have carried the day in innumerable human endeavors. Consider all of the less-than-leading-edge products that have dominated their market segments because of superior promotion. Better yet, just think of the speeches and leadership invitations you can remember. What made them memorable? Why did you respond? Our guess is that many of them were because of the way in which the content was delivered.

Consider the simple eloquence and inspiring nature, for instance, of Gandhi's march to the sea to make salt. Manufacture of salt by Indians was prohibited by the British government at the time, and Gandhi's simple act, declaring his intention to walk from the interior to the sea and make salt and then doing so, captured the attention of millions of people and presented an extraordinary challenge to the government. When you want to influence others, consider carefully how you can make your message stimulating.

Congruency (walking your talk) is another principle that many would-be leaders violate and consequently fail. Hearkening back to our chapter on the moral foundation of leadership, you don't make promises that you cannot keep. Effective leaders understand deeply that unless they are willing to live what they are asking others to do, they will not be able to sustain their influence. If we ask employees to endure cost cutting and yet take a big salary increase ourselves, our ability to influence employees is greatly undermined. If we ask people to be creative and then hammer or punish or ridicule those who try it, they learn that we speak with a forked tongue. To be an effective leader means to be at one in our speech and in our actions. If you cannot do it, don't say it!

Invitations

One reason people don't do what we'd like them to do is that we don't ask them in powerful ways. Effective leaders know how to frame and extend powerful invitations. Of course, unless an invitation is based on clear purpose, clear reward, clear role for others, respect for others, and is delivered with stimulation and congruency, it may not be accepted. Effective leaders, though, don't shrink from the asking. And if they have learned how to ask powerfully, to frame the invitation in a way that is attractive and engaging to the others, their probability of getting favorable responses goes way up. The very concept of leadership extending invitations rather than issuing demands, commands, or instructions implies a different attitude toward leadership than most people in positions of power take.

An invitation is respectful and thus consistent with our basic definition of leadership, which includes a voluntary response from others. When you invite someone to do something, you acknowledge that unless you have done your homework and can present the invitation in a powerful way, they may say no. If you conclude at the moment that invitations and leadership are incompatible, then, you'll be giving instructions, commands, guidelines, and demands, and although the others' mouths may say yes, inside, at Level Two and Level Three, they may well be saying no. We invite you to consider your ability to frame and deliver powerful invitations and then practice doing so.

LEVEL THREE INFLUENCE

Given an understanding of the sources of social power, of exchange theory in relationships, and of the power of the language of leadership, we are confronted with how to use these in developing influence on others' VABEs and hence on their thoughts and behavior as well. Effective Level Three leaders understand, either intuitively or explicitly, the following basic principles: Clarify what you want, observe the VABEs of others, confirm the VABEs of others, set a probationary period, utilize your influence to invite re-examination and modification of VABEs. These principles represent a consolidation of the research and insights introduced earlier (see Table 12-4).

The first challenge, repeated elsewhere in this volume, is to be clear about what you want. Your life's dream, your mission in life, your ambitions, your definitions of success, and your short-term goals are all a part of what drive your behavior daily. Unless you're clear about what those are, it will be difficult for you to have influence on others. You won't know how you can trade with others, and you will probably be unclear as to what to ask of them.

Second, if you are watchful and can observe the apparent VABEs of others with a somewhat trained eye, you'll get a powerful insight into why they behave the way they do. We devoted an earlier chapter to this phenomenon. Every time someone says, "I should do this" or "People should do that," they are revealing to you part of their core VABE system. If you keep notes, preferably on paper because our thoughts are so ethereal and imprecise, you can begin to develop a profile of a person's Level Three motivations.

TABLE 12-4   Principles of Level Three Leadership Influence
1. Clarify what you want.
2. Observe others' VABEs.
3. Confirm others' VABEs.
4. Establish a probationary time frame.
5. Coach to the best of your skills, using effective language, listening, and invitations. Learn what you need to become a better coach.
6. Assess progress and continue or move on.

Observations are only that—they don't necessarily reflect fact. So, the third step in a Level Three influence model is to confirm your observations. By this I mean talking with the person or people to determine whether your observations are accurate or not. Politicians do this all the time to try to get the pulse of the country. Of course, one may interpret the data in self-serving ways. Nevertheless, it is important to confirm whether your inferences are, in fact, accurate. You might meet with a person you're hoping to coach or train and note, "You know, it seems to me from watching you that you really value getting positive feedback. Is that true?" Or "From watching you, it seems that you believe if you want it done right, you have to do it yourself. Is that right?" You'll find out pretty quickly whether your inferences were on target or off base.

Fourth, most leaders set time frames of some kind. They ask themselves, "How long am I willing to give to this effort?" In the case of influencing others, in singles, twos, groups, or organizations, leaders make the same assessment. They may or may not announce their time frames. Often it is better not to. Announced deadlines, particularly in change efforts, have a way of embarrassing one. But, for instance, if you wanted to coach a person toward changing her behavior, you might declare to yourself, "I'm going to give this effort six months." Then, at the end of your probationary time, you could reassess and determine whether it was worth it to carry on or not.

Fifth, with a clear goal in mind, clear understanding of the other's VABEs or Level Three realities, and a bounded time reference, you can begin coaching, or influencing. This coaching could take any number of forms, including speeches (to larger audiences), one-on-one counseling sessions, debriefings of performance, supervision of practice sessions, and so on. This effort may bring all of your best effort and skill as a leader to bear. You may have to learn along the way by reading or seeking your own counsel from other experts.

At the end of your probationary time frame, you can then pause and assess how the effort is going. Is the person making progress? Have you established a stronger relationship? Are you making more effective exchanges? Is the performance improving? If the answer is yes to these questions, then you can, with a certain sense of satisfaction, acknowledge your developing skills as a Level Three leader, one who is influencing the basic VABEs of others and doing so in a respectful way with voluntary responses. If, on the other hand, little or no change is made, you may have to conclude that the effort is not working out.

There are two basic reasons why this might happen: either your skills as a coach are insufficient to have impact on the other or the other's CQ (change quotient) is too low. In either case, you may have to conclude to leave off the effort and make a reassignment to either yourself or your counterpart(s) so that you both can move on to more productive efforts. Again, this process happens in every walk of life, in politics, in the military, in athletics, and every day in business organizations.

CONCLUSION

Leading and influencing others is a complex task, and you can go about trying to do so in many ways. If you choose to influence others using power as a base and the tools of coercion, manipulation, and force, you will get a Level One response; the body may move, but the head and the heart will be unfazed. If, on the other hand, you choose to work a bit harder on the front end to clarify your wants as well as the other person's VABEs and learn how to extend invitations to others in ways that are clear, respectful, stimulating, and congruent, you are likely to get favorable responses, not only behaviorally but also at Level Two and Level Three.

This approach implies that the ability to influence others, and to influence them deeply, is as much about attitude, philosophy, and motive—your attitude, your philosophy, and your motive—as it is about learning specific techniques and tips of leadership skills. If you truly want to be more effective in leading others, then I invite you to consider the principles introduced here and focus on your purpose, your language, and your ability to deliver what we might call Class Five Invitations, invitations that invite world-class performance at the upper end of the 1–5 performance distribution introduced in the chapter on the moral foundation of leadership.

PRINCIPLES OF EFFECTIVE LEADERSHIP INTRODUCED IN THIS CHAPTER

1. In general, we use our titles, coercion, rewards, our expertise, or our group membership to influence others.
2. In reality, virtually all relationships are based on exchanges, which must be mutual and approximately equal if a relationship is to endure.
3. Language is one of the effective leader's most powerful tools. The language of leadership is clear, respectful, stimulating, and congruent.
4. Effective efforts to influence others respect the others' goals and present oneself as an ally to the achievement of those goals.
5. Effective leaders know how to issue world-class invitations that get voluntary responses from the people they wish to influence.
6. Level Three leaders are clear on their wants; observe others to infer their VABEs; confirm their observations; bound their change efforts in time; coach as well as they can as an ally using respect, invitations, and exchanges; and then assess and either continue or move on.

QUESTIONS FOR REFLECTION

1. How do you most often try to influence others? What sources of influence do you use most frequently?
2. What are the personal goals of the people you'd like to influence? If you can't think of them, how can you present yourself as an ally? If you can't list them, how could you find them out?
3. How could you practice making your speech and communication more clear, more respectful, more stimulating, and more congruent with the way you behave?
4. Make a list of the people or groups of people you'd like to influence. Next to each person or group, note whether you've been trying to influence them at Level One or Level Two or Level Three. If you've been trying at Level One, consider the consequence of your efforts and the results you're getting. If you've been trying at Level Three, consider how you might make those efforts more effective.
5. The next five times you try to influence someone, listen to yourself speak and search for an invitation that is clear, respectful, stimulating, and congruent in what you say. Think about how you might improve your invitations.

NOTES

Note: To quickly access all *Harvard Business Review* reprints listed here, go to www.hbsp .harvard.edu/hbsp/adv_search.asp, insert the reprint number in the Product Number field, and click Search.

1. John R. P. French Jr. and Bertram H. Raven, "The Bases of Social Power," in *Studies in Social Power,* ed. D. Cartwright (Ann Arbor: University of Michigan, Institute for Social Research, 1959), 150–167.
2. See, for example, the chapter on coercion in Edwin C. Nevis, Joan Lancourt, and Helen G. Vassallo, *Intentional Revolutions* (San Francisco: Jossey-Bass, 1996).
3. Allan R. Cohen and David L. Bradford, *Influence Without Authority* (New York: John Wiley & Sons, 1991).
4. John Gabarro and John Kotter, "Managing Your Boss," *Harvard Business Review,* reprint 93306.
5. See, for example, Zig Ziglar, *On the Top* (Nashville: Thomas Nelson, 1994). One of the book's central points is that if one can help others get what they want, one can look forward to a lifetime of success. Likewise, Stephen Covey's principle, "Seek first to understand, then to be understood," conveys the same message.
6. James G. Clawson and Michael B. Blank, "What Really Counts in Superior-Subordinate Relationships," *Mentoring International* 4:1 (Winter 1990).
7. Stephen R. Covey, *Seven Habits of Highly Effective People* (New York: Simon & Schuster, 1989).

13

Leading Teams

*While not ignoring or neglecting the individual, we should devote
far more thought to teams: to the selection, development, and training
of teams, to the qualifications, experience, and achievements of teams,
and above all to the psychology, motivation, composition, and
behaviour of teams.*

—ANTHONY JAY

An information systems project leader wrestles to organize a massive change effort in an urban municipal modernization program involving hundreds of people.

An account executive for a global financial services firm wonders how to coordinate the efforts of colleagues in eight different cities on behalf of a single global client.

A wiring harness group seeks help in making up a backlog of product that a customer needs immediately.

A course head struggles to find a way to build a cohesive teaching team among colleagues teaching multiple sections of the same course.

A world-class climber tries to manage his emotions as the expedition moves up the 8,000-meter mountain despite large egos, troublesome porters, and peers jockeying for position on the summit team.

Each of these teams faces a common set of problems. How does one build an effective team, especially when time is short and the consequences are significant? The answers are not easy but increasingly important as the quote from Anthony Jay points out. The paradigm shift described in the first chapter is creating more and more team-based organizations. As a result, more and more leaders are faced with the dilemmas and challenges of managing teams—short-term teams, project teams, program teams, special function teams, ad hoc teams, and permanent, goal-oriented, profit-motivated teams. There are even national and international conferences designed primarily to help people learn how to lead teams more effectively.

Although all of the skills outlined in the chapter on leading others apply to leading teams, this chapter will introduce many more principles to help you do this, and I invite you to pay attention to them in your team experiences–whether you're designated leader of the team or not.

WHAT MAKES A TEAM?

First, every group of individuals does not necessarily constitute a team. Katzenbach and Smith offer first a definition of what a team is and then identify differences between groups and teams. In so doing, they have created a worthy target for team leaders and members alike: What do we have to do to make our work group an effective team? Simply meeting often will not be enough; effective team leaders will actively manage the principles of team dynamics to forge effective teams. Their definition of *team* is "a small number of people with complementary skills who are committed to a common purpose, performance goals, and approach for which they hold themselves mutually accountable." Katzenbach and Smith have also identified seven characteristics of effective teams that distinguish them from simple work groups:[1]

1. *Shared leadership* rather than having one, dominant leader
2. *Team accountability* rather than holding individuals accountable
3. *Distinctive purpose* rather than assuming the corporate mission is the team's
4. *Shared work* rather than simply trying to string together individual efforts at the end of a project
5. *Open-ended meetings* rather than efficient, carefully managed meetings that stifle exploration and creativity
6. *Direct, collective measures* rather than rewarding individuals on individual effort
7. *Real work* rather than busywork projects

One could use these criteria to assess whether one's work group was becoming a team or not. Some of the criteria have to do with internal affairs of the team (1, 2, 3, 4, and 5), whereas others may require changes in the surrounding, supporting organizational context (6 and 7). Much of a group's future and possible destiny as a group or a team, though, can be managed by its members. One of the first things to note is that groups evolve over time.

TEAM LIFE CYCLES

The organization that is able to form and reform multifunctional teams quickly and effectively has a distinct competitive advantage.

Short lived or long lived, groups seems to pass through a life cycle of distinct phases, each one presenting its own challenges (see Table 13-1). Perhaps you've heard the common phrase that groups go through stages of forming, storming, norming, and per-

TABLE 13-1 Stages in Group and Team Development
1. Forming
2. Norming and storming
3. Performing
4. Reforming

forming. I'd like to suggest, based on the research on group behavior and the realities of the current paradigm shift, a slightly different predictable pattern that groups exhibit and that group leaders need to understand: forming, norming, performing, and reforming. Reforming has become important because so many groups now need to reconfigure when a particular task is done. In fact, I argue that the organization that is able to form and reform multifunctional teams quickly and effectively has a distinct competitive advantage over companies that cannot.

Forming: Initiation and Orientation

When teams or groups first come together, group members spend most of their energy getting accustomed to and assessing one another. Communication is tentative as members try to answer key questions such as, "Should I be here?" "What is the purpose of this group?" and "Who is the leader?" As previously described, team members often look for a leader to instill the group with a sense of purpose. If the membership, purpose, and leadership issues are not sorted out quickly, the group's efforts to do its work will flounder. Even if the group jumps into its task prematurely (the most common team-building flaw), the membership, purpose, and leadership issues will surface again later, causing disruption and confusion.

Effective team leaders (or team members) who are willing to participate in a distributed leadership pattern will work through these three fundamental issues explicitly and early to avoid inefficient reviews of them later on. This means clarifying the task and intended output of the team, the reason why each member is there and how they might contribute to that output, and some discussion about how leadership of the team will evolve and develop.

Norming: Exploration of Procedure

As soon as a collection of individuals has sorted out what they are supposed to do, who should be there, and how they'll manage leadership, they begin sorting out the how questions: How will we work together? How will we resolve disputes? How will we relate to the outside world? Disagreements over the ground rules, the scope of the group's mission, and the best among possible courses of action make the norming stage one of the most fertile—and the most trying—for leaders and group members. Members want to know where the boundaries are and how hard they are, so they test them in myriad ways. Who speaks? How do we determine who speaks? How do we make decisions? How do we revisit those decisions? How often do we meet? What do we do before and after we meet? These are just some of the questions that members need to sort out so that they can focus on the task at hand.

In this creative but often volatile stage, members cultivate their ability to work together. The effective leader will neither take challenges as an invitation to rule autocratically nor use group upheaval as an excuse to micromanage. Rather, these times become opportunities to point out how each member's skills and abilities will contribute to achieving the team's task.

Most groups don't manage this exploration explicitly; it just happens as groups spend time together and naturally develop. In fact, that's the point. Effective leaders are aware of these developmental stages and the tasks that a group faces in each and manage the team through them. Team leaders who ignore this predictable pattern of group development may feel like they are getting ahead, but usually the issues come up later and bog the group down. So in the long run, jumping immediately to the task and ignoring the forming and norming issues makes the group less effective and less efficient.

The key way that a designated team leader can manage the early stages of group development is by spelling out and discussing the tasks of each developmental stage. Of course, the team may decide as time passes that some of the earlier discussions and conclusions don't work and then argue for change, and one may feel that the early time was lost. Nevertheless, the more a leader can help a group move through these two early stages, the sooner the group can focus on getting the work done without distraction.

Performing: Stabilization

Eventually, more quickly if the leader has managed it well, much of the uncertainty that hung over the group at the outset evaporates, and the group can get down to the actual work assigned to it. Individual roles and interpersonal relationships become clear and accustomed. Members can now look to established precedent as they draw up their plans. Members leave off challenging the purpose, membership, or leadership and focus their efforts on getting the job done. The group has progressed along a collective learning curve and now may be operating at higher levels of efficiency.

There are new dangers to face, however. Having drawn energy from the heady atmosphere of the exploration stage, members may begin to see stability as dull routine. While working with the team to ensure that efficiency is in fact being improved, effective leaders try to maintain the sense of urgency and excitement that often characterizes the early stages.

This is an ongoing dilemma. How does one reenergize long-term work groups? How does one combat the debilitating effects of day-in, day-out routines? One answer lies in the concepts introduced in the earlier chapter on resonance. If you can help your team to identify and revisit their team dream (LDint) regularly, you can help them see how today's work fits into the plan to realize that dream. If you have organized the structure and relationships of the team with solid foundations of trust, respect, and vision, then you can do much to revitalize ongoing efforts. In many respects, this becomes the work of the team leader, finding ways to remind, refocus, and rebuild the resonance that comes from doing important work well in ways that are intrinsically rewarding to the team members.

Reforming: Reassessment

Stable work groups often develop deep-seated working habits and in so doing become an organizational subculture, if you will. The more stable a group becomes, the more difficult it will be for it to respond to radical change. Sooner or later, though, something—declining profits, a transformed marketplace, different demands on the group from above, or just finishing the original job—will make reassessment and even dissolution or reforming unavoidable.

What makes this crossroads so difficult—indeed, life threatening—for the group is that the group members' feelings about it are likely to be wildly varied. Some will vehemently oppose any change in the group's mission, some will accept it enthusiastically, and some will feel betrayed by the leader or top managers. As discussed in the strategic thinking chapter, competitive advantage is based in part on flexibility. Unless the processes of understanding and dealing with change are built into the group's culture, finishing the present task can easily ruin the group. Inability to dissolve teams effectively can be a source of competitive disadvantage.

Depending on the team's culture and the quality of its leadership, several things can happen near the end of a team's life cycle. The group may emerge from this reassessment phase revitalized and refocused, it may burst from internal dissent, it may cling to its outmoded vision and die a more protracted death, or, appropriately, it may just disband with a sense of completion and its members move on to other work. Organizations that have paid attention to and developed the processes of reassessing and reforming productive work teams will have a distinct competitive advantage against those companies that have not.

TEAM ROLES

Every time you are invited to a new group (will it be a team?) meeting, you are likely to see a predictable pattern of roles being played by the group members. You'll see the person who tries to be the dominant, loud leader; you'll see the quiet mouse who never speaks the whole time; you'll see the naysayer who disagrees with everything no matter what it is; you'll see the joker who tries to make everything a laughing matter; and you'll see the skeptic who sits back with arms folded, frowning, exuding vibrations of "Prove it to me!" What other roles have you seen in your group meeting experience?

Obviously, not all of these common roles are effective and helpful. Meredith Belbin has identified a series of roles that are essential for building effective teams: company worker, chair, shaper, plant, resource investigator, monitor evaluator, team worker, and completer-finisher (see Table 13-2).[2] Company workers put company ahead of self and like to organize and arrange things to suit the larger organization. Chairs are adept at utilizing the group's resources to good advantage, calling on var-

---

TABLE 13-2   Belbin's Roles in Effective Teams

1. Company worker
2. Chair (leader)
3. Shaper (leader)
4. Plant (creative)
5. Resource investigator (creative)
6. Monitor evaluator (decision)
7. Completer-finisher

ied skills to get things done. Shapers are hard-driving, action-oriented leaders like to get things done. Plants are introverted, clever people who tend to be technical specialists with deep expertise. Resource investigators are networkers, constantly on the phone, walking around, always wanting to check on things and to be in the know on all fronts. Monitor evaluators are decision makers, usually serious minded, immune to group enthusiasm, and always testing and checking assumptions and the validity of group conclusions. Team workers are extroverts without the need to dominate, so they are willing to do what's necessary for the good of the team's efforts. Completer-finishers are those who drive to get a job done, who tolerate creative exploration but in the end push to closure. Belbin identified these seven roles from a variety of studies using psychological testing and observation matched with team results.

Effective team leaders pay a lot of attention to making sure that the jobs and tasks assigned to members fit their talents and their inclinations. Belbin's typology helps here in guiding those forming teams to ensure they have a solid foundation for team development. Sports coaches, expedition team leaders, project team leaders, and work group leaders all understand the value of this principle. Sometimes the person with the talent for a job doesn't want to do it, and unless the leader can build a process that allows for each member to do things they want to do along the way, the whole team's success can be jeopardized. Yet, if left alone, talented team members will often tend to find niches themselves, zeroing in on the work for which they're best suited and in which they are most interested. Several recent alumni report that some organizations leave the assignments of new employees intentionally ambiguous in the belief that talented people will create their own best way of making a valuable contribution.

That being said, in our experience, four general roles are essential in effective groups (see Figure 13-1). These roles can be viewed as pairs of polar opposites, with each member of a pair contributing in a way that holds his or her counterpart in check.

Task Driver

This is the results-oriented member of the group, the one who keeps the group focused on the ultimate goal of completing the task at hand. Urging his creative colleagues to get their brainchild, the Macintosh, off the drawing board and into stores, Steve Jobs was playing the role of task driver when he said, "Real artists ship."

FIGURE 13-1   Essential Roles in Effective Groups

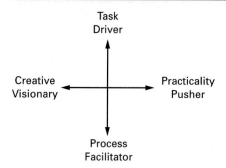

Process Facilitator

The task driver's counterpart, this member keeps tabs on the interpersonal dynamics of the group. The quality of working relationships among group members is critical—and the process facilitator watches them carefully, working hard to help the group manage misunderstandings that arise in the course of the team's work.

Creative Visionary

This member's mind is most open to creative solutions, no matter how outlandish they might sound, and is always trying to find a better way. Creative visionaries are always exploring the four basic kinds of creative thinking—risk taking, considering the opposites, relying on uncertainty, and looking for multiple possibilities.[3] Sometimes, team members, particularly the task drivers, try to squelch the creative types in the name of getting things done. In so doing, they can overlook alternative ways of doing things that might, in the end, reshape entirely the team's process or product.

Practicality Pusher

The counterbalance to the creative visionary is the practicality pusher. This is the person who attends to the practical realities of getting the job assigned the team done. Although too much attention to practicalities in finishing a job can squelch creativity, too much attention to creative alternatives can strangle a team in possibilities. Practicality pushers make sure that what the team asserts to do is doable and then push for completion.

These four roles form two polar scales, creativity versus practicality and task versus process. In effective teams, these opposites are balanced and well managed. But what if your group doesn't naturally include these roles and in a balanced way? If team members don't naturally seem to fit these four roles, they can be assigned. I have seen teams' efforts improved dramatically by simply assigning team members to attend to and be responsible for these four roles. These invitations ask group members to become "team workers" in Belbin's terms, that is, willing to do what's necessary for the group's growth and success. The recognition by all members that these roles are necessary and helpful contributes to their willingness to evolve toward becoming a team.

We've seen that effective teams have certain characteristics, evolve predictably though not necessarily through stages, and include a variety of roles. Designated or would-be team leaders understand these aspects of work groups and try actively to manage them. As a team leader, your challenge will be to recognize these aspects of effective teams and manage them well as the development of your team unfolds. But how? How does one combine all of this insight into an effective team leadership style? Well-known author Warren Bennis and his colleague, Patricia Biederman, made a very interesting study of seven of the most successful groups in history that sheds light on this question.[4] Their insights, outlined in the following sections, provide a powerful profile of effective teams and team leadership. As we describe these lessons from seven great teams, try to link them to the frameworks we've already introduced. This integration exercise will strengthen your mental map of what it takes to lead a team effectively.

INSPIRED VISION THAT CREATES . . .

Bennis and Biederman found that the groups they studied all had a leader who provided a vision that inspired the team. These leaders were able to describe this vision in such vivid and alluring detail that others could see it clearly—and wanted to join the enterprise to see it realized. For example, they cite the conversation when Steven Jobs was courting John Sculley, an executive from Pepsi, for the CEO position at Apple Computer. Jobs reportedly asked Sculley, "Do you want to spend the rest of your life selling flavored water, or do you want a chance to change the world?"

Walt Disney, as the leader of the group that produced the world's first feature-length animated film in 1937, encountered stiff opposition to his idea, so he stood up in front of the group and acted out the entire story of *Snow White and the Seven Dwarfs*. The performance was convincing and, ultimately, spectacularly successful. Those who can galvanize the efforts of groups of people will be able to articulate a clear and powerful vision. This vision, in turn, will mobilize the resources of the team.

. . . A POWERFUL SENSE OF MISSION

As a result of an inspiring vision, members of successful groups feel more zealous about their work than the average employee. They feel like they're indispensable parts of a vitally important enterprise. A leader who hopes to get peak performance out of a group must make certain that this sense of mission is clear—and clear in a way that ties in at Level Three to the goals and aspirations of the team's members.

Bennis and Biederman draw an instructive example from the Manhattan Project, the group that built the first atom bomb during the latter half of World War II. At first, the secrecy surrounding the project was so complete that the researchers themselves were not told exactly what they were doing or why. The secrecy led to declining morale and a climate of anger and confusion. The group floundered—until the leader, Robert Oppenheimer, called them together, told them what the project was trying to do and how each of their various pieces were important to the overall mission, and then explained in emotional terms that the survival of the free world was at stake. The project was suddenly a crusade, and productivity soared.

Corporate leaders face less apocalyptic challenges, but effective ones share Oppenheimer's ability to instill their followers with a sense of mission. This was one of Steve Jobs's strengths at Apple. He convinced his team that they were marauding rebels destined to defeat the IBM empire—and even flew a Jolly Roger above Apple headquarters as a playful reminder of their mission.

GETTING THE RIGHT PEOPLE

Perhaps the first step in realizing a vision is getting the right people to be a part of the team. "You can't pile together enough good people to make a great one," said Bob Taylor, one of the kingpins of Xerox Corporation's Palo Alto Research Center (PARC). Taylor looked only for great people in his recruiting efforts at PARC, which was to spend the early 1970s radically rethinking computer science.[5] Taylor's group of young mavericks refused to let any assumption about computers go unchallenged.

They were revolutionary thinkers as outlined at the end of the strategic thinking chapter. The computer that PARC created was the first to boast many features we now take for granted: a graphical user interface, a mouse, and a desktop display format with windows.

Unfortunately for Xerox, the company did not share its research lab's vision, leaving the development opportunity open for a young visitor to PARC's facility, Steven Jobs, who was so taken by the new machine that he decided to use his small upstart company called Apple to exploit these innovations commercially.

Whom do you look for when recruiting? Bennis and Biederman offer a list of attributes that the members of successful and innovative groups share: original thinking, specialized skills, fresh perspective, ability to see gaps in current thinking, good problem solving, ability to make connections across broad disciplinary gaps, and broad frames of reference. The mix of these characteristics put in the cauldron of an inspiring vision and stirred by powerful leadership has created dramatic results.

Members of a team will periodically assess their own appropriateness or worthiness to be on the team by weighing their own abilities and contributions to the group against their perceptions of those of the other members. A member who feels unworthy or inappropriately included will likely participate less often out of fear of censure or lack of interest, thus damaging the group's effectiveness in the process.

Consequently, one of the first requirements for an effective group leader is to make certain the right people are on the team and, once the team is selected, to reinforce the right of each to be on the team. This doesn't mean just including those with the best technical skills. More important, it often means paying attention to members' social, team-related skills. Further, it means that the leader should help team members solidify their sense of why they were included from early on. Mountaineering expeditions are a good example of this practice. Lou Whittaker, renowned mountain guide and leader or member of several Himalayan expeditions, concluded after years of forming and leading teams that deal with life and death situations regularly, "I came back from K2 in 1975 with this understanding: The measure of a good team is not whether you make the summit, but how well you get along during the climb."[6]

DISTRIBUTED LEADERSHIP

Once membership and purpose have been determined, most groups will naturally wrestle with issues related to leadership. There seems to be a natural human tendency to try to sort out who's in charge. Effective groups have strong leadership although it's not necessarily embodied in a strong leader. Increasingly, this means distributed leadership rather than a designated leader. By *distributed leadership,* I mean a comfortable process in which those who have the perspective, the skills, and the motivation to deal with the situation of the moment step to the fore and assume—and are granted—influence on the group. For this to happen, each team member must be comfortable with the team's purpose and each team member's role in it. Concerns about control and "who's the boss" must give way to a focus on the objective. This kind of process is not usually easily won but often develops as a result of lots of experience working together as a team.

The need to develop distributed leadership is one reason why many corporate clients use "ropes" or "adventure challenge" courses. These team-based forays into the woods for low events that occur 2 to 3 feet off the ground to high events that can occur at 60 to 90 feet in the air help team members realize that each of them can contribute something of value and that the team's goal is to figure that out efficiently and to develop a repeating process. This kind of learning can transfer to business settings and allow the team members to work together more efficiently regardless of location.

EXTRAORDINARY COORDINATION

Effective team leaders may not have the specialized technical expertise that other team members have; rather, they exhibit an extraordinary expertise in mobilizing and coordinating the team's efforts. The leader's role is to provide the best possible environment for those recruits to do their work—not to do the work personally. This is a difficult hurdle for many would-be managers and leaders to overcome. Sometimes people are promoted into positions of leadership and struggle with letting go of the work and learning new coordinating and facilitating skills. A psychological leap must be made when one becomes responsible for work that one isn't doing directly.[7] Effective team leaders don't micromanage. Instead, they have a good sense of the loose-tight paradox that allows them to guide the group without interfering with team members' initiative and talents.

CREATIVE SUPPORT

Effective team leaders also buffer the team from bureaucracy and bureaucratic processes. As Bennis and Biederman observe, "Great Groups are never places where memos are the primary form of communication. They aren't places where anything is filed in triplicate. Time that can go into thinking and making is never wasted on activities, such as writing reports, that serve only some bureaucratic or corporate function outside the group."[8]

Jewel Savadelis, a former student, was confronted one day at Atari with the prospect of managing more than a dozen highly creative software programmers, people on whom the revenues from the home video game market depended. They presented her with a list of challenges that she had to meet to be allowed to manage their team. One of the demands was that she buffer them from the organization's paperwork. Effective team leaders figure out ways to minimize the time spent by team members in organizationally originated diversions from the primary task.[9] This incident raised for Jewel a series of questions, some of which had clear moral and ethical overtones.

MORAL FOUNDATION FOR RESPECT

Effective team leaders build their influence on the moral foundation introduced earlier: truth telling, promise keeping, fairness, and respect for the individual. Jewel Savadelis knew that whatever her title was, unless she could gain the respect of the programmers, she wouldn't be able to manage, much less lead them.

Likewise, Bennis and Biederman report that Kelly Johnson, leader of the Skunk Works—the top-secret research group at Lockheed that created the U2 spy plane, the SR-71 Blackbird, and the F-117 Stealth Fighter—was an irascible man who could scare away group members and clients alike with his temper. But he made up for this weakness with the immense respect he inspired in his researchers. They knew he would not build a plane he didn't believe in, because once he returned millions of dollars to the U.S. Air Force rather than do exactly that.

THE RIGHT ROLES FOR THE RIGHT PEOPLE

Having the right team members and the right leadership processes doesn't ensure the creation of an effective team. Team organization that puts its members in the right roles is critical for success. This is akin to the concept of supporting others so they can contribute, introduced in the chapter on six steps to effective leadership. Thomas Carlisle, the English philosopher, once said that he did not believe in the "collective wisdom of individual ignorance," yet time and time again, team decision making produces better decisions.[10] This will be especially true if team members are organized so as to take the greatest advantage of their talents and abilities.

PARTICIPATION

Not all talented people are equally adept at collaboration. People vary in their introversion and extroversion, for example, regardless of their technical skills.[11] Some are active in the discussions that surround the team's purpose, and others are more reticent. Effective teams have figured out ways for all team members to participate. In effect, participation is an extension of membership. If you have the right membership, everyone should be participating. If everyone is not participating, then you may not have the right membership.

Participation is not limited to the team in effective groups. In their article "How Bell Labs Creates Star Performers," Robert Kelley and Janet Caplan summarize seven years of research into the work strategies of standouts—and their less successful peers—at AT&T's prestigious research unit. Bell engineers all agreed on nine work strategies that influenced productivity, of which fully two-thirds—networking, teamwork effectiveness, leadership, followership, show-and-tell, and organizational savvy—can be seen as varieties of group cooperation skills.

The importance of networking in particular became apparent when Kelley and Caplan investigated the actual work habits of average and "star" teams. Although both groups agreed that a network of knowledgeable colleagues was crucial to weathering a crisis on the job, much of the star teams' success could be traced to their efforts to build networks *before* those crises happened. For example, a member of an average team (still great by most standards) talked about being stumped by a technical problem. He painstakingly called various technical gurus and then waited, wasting valuable time while calls went unreturned and e-mail messages were unanswered. Star performers, however, rarely faced such situations because they did the work of building reliable networks before they actually needed them.

THE RIGHT MEASURES

The more organizations are built around teams, the more old measures of performance seem to become outdated. Traditional measurement systems often serve the top-down power structures of the Industrial Age—what Christopher Meyer has called "results measures."[12] A results measure is one that gives you information about something that happened in the past as opposed to one that gives you information about what's happening at the moment. Furthermore, results measures are usually functionally based: The marketing department monitors market share, finance keeps track of costs, and so forth.

The trouble with results measures is that although they may help top managers keep tabs on the company's or a team's past performance, they don't shed much light on the current *processes* that determine whether or not the company will achieve its goals. As Meyer says, "The fact that a program was six months late and $2 million over budget doesn't tell anyone what went wrong or what to do next."[13]

Results measures are especially harmful to groups because they tend to be function specific (market share is relevant to marketers but less so to production people) and thus undermine the advantage of group decision making, in which people from different functions develop a strategic overview together. Further, they can divert attention from the ongoing processes that a team is employing to produce.

Meyer cites the multifunctional group that recently presided over the development of a luxury automobile and whose measures were simply an accumulation of the ones the individual functions had long been using. The project was delayed for several weeks by a squabble over a new door handle design: The finance people feared it would be too expensive, whereas the design people stressed its importance to the overall design of the car. Hamstrung by their own measurement criteria, neither side thought to ask the overarching and crucial question: "Will the new handle help the car compete in the marketplace?"

The alternative to using results measures is to use what Meyer calls "process measures," which track the activities throughout an organization that help reach a given goal. Process measures are real-time indicators of key processes and their central contributors. For example, rather than simply knowing that its project is behind schedule and over budget, groups for which staffing is critical could benefit from tracking staffing levels during the course of the work—a process measure which could point to corrective fine-tuning.

> Process measures are like the gauges on an automobile dashboard. They indicate current status so that you know before you run out of gas or before a drop in oil pressure ruins the engine.

Process measures are like the gauges on an automobile dashboard, giving the driver and passengers current information on key processes: how much fuel is left, how far we've traveled, whether or not the battery is charging, and how the oil pressure is doing. All of these measures are indicators of current status and necessarily so; it doesn't help to know that you've run out of gas after the fact.

Meyer offers four guiding principles that may help in designing a measurement system to suit the needs of a group. First, the team's process measures should be designed to help the team during the process, not management after the fact. The measures should be a warning system that alerts the group when corrective action is needed. Second, the team should design its own process indicators. This principle is consistent with our earlier assertion that the key process contributors, those closest to the work, know what really needs to be done. Of course, for the team to devise the right measures, it needs to be clear on the firm's strategy: if the east–west connection in our basic model is flawed, the team's ability to create good measures will be undermined. Third, the process measures should be multifunctional and focus on the whole work of the team, not just a few aspects of it. Along with tracking receivables, for instance, the system might also gauge the percentage of new parts to be used in a product. New parts are often an unknown quantity and thus can raise issues across a number of functions—design, inventory, manufacturing, and assembly. Finally, teams should keep the number of process measures down. Meyer recommends no more than 15, or else the team will become paralyzed by evaluation. The challenge is to build a dashboard for the team's metaphorical car that will keep the driver and the passengers informed about how the car's doing while they travel.

VIRTUAL TEAMS

In today's global marketplace, business leaders are confronted increasingly with managing virtual teams, people who have a joint purpose but are spread all over the world. Many financial services as well as consulting and conglomerate organizations wrestle with the management of virtual teams. Let's be honest: It's difficult. Companies have used e-mail, Lotus Notes, faxes, telephone, videoconferencing, and other technological advances in the attempt to reduce the costs of travel and to try to weld people from all over the world into highly functional teams.

Many obstacles exist to this goal. First, people have local objectives, that is, they are focused on their work in their local region, and because it is often closer and more pressing than the global objective, they tend to ignore the larger team purpose. Australian members of a global account team for XYZ corporation may not pay attention to the XYZ account in Sydney because its presence is small there. This can be frustrating to the XYZ account manager in New York who is trying to get account managers all over the world to pay attention to his (and their) joint responsibility for XYZ. Second, people are dispersed. Studies of communication show that when people are more than 90 feet away, the level of their interactions drop off dramatically. Although technological advances have helped in this regard, most managers agree that nothing really substitutes for personal, face-to-face interactions. Third, team members often have allegiances to local leaders rather than global leaders. This is another manifestation of the power of personal contact. Distant virtual team leaders have to overcome or at least compensate for the influence of local site managers who may have different priorities and certainly have more contact with the global team members.

Despite these challenges and others, virtual team leaders struggle to build cohesion and concerted effort among widely dispersed team members. Several principles seem to help in this struggle. First, regular face-to-face meetings are important. Virtual team leaders must travel often. Getting team members to understand and remember the team's charter takes lots of personal time, particularly when team membership crosses international and cultural boundaries. The well-known difficulties of communicating with e-mail are exacerbated by cultural differences.[14] Second, active and frequent use of technology to overcome the distance gap is a growing means of team management. As noted above, though, e-mail, telephone, fax, and Lotus Notes cannot substitute for face-to-face meetings; they can only fill in the gaps between visits. Sometimes the ambiguities and misunderstandings caused by technologically mediated communication have to be addressed by personal visits. Third, conferences can help weld international groups into teams. This is clearly more expensive than having the team leader travel, yet many companies have used annual conferences or retreats as an effective means of networking and team building. Conferences of this type should include not only corporate-wide communications and training but also ample opportunity for each virtual team to meet and renew their LDints, charters, and operating principles and goals. Fourth, teleconferences built around creating and confirming a team charter can be an effective virtual team management technique. I've participated in teams from three continents, all on the line together, working through a team charter in the course of a day (as described elsewhere in this volume). We were online for a couple of hours, worked off-line to consolidate or brainstorm, and then went back online for several more hours, talking, sorting out, consolidating, and defining our common purpose, vision, values, and goals.

The research around virtual teams is thin and new. As the technology front continues to advance and we continue to wrestle with international boundaries and cultures, I'm sure we'll learn more about managing virtual teams.

CONCLUSION

Leading highly effective teams is an essential skill for the modern leader. As team-based organizations become more and more common, the challenges of leading teams become more apparent. Status hierarchies continue to break down not only in team-based organizations but also within the teams themselves. Distributed leadership becomes more important. Clarity of mission and purpose, vision, and careful attention to roles are challenges that the team leader faces. People who understand the characteristics of effective teams and how to manage them over the natural course of their development, from formation through dissolution, will become more effective leaders and better contributors to their organization's development of competitive advantage.

PRINCIPLES OF EFFECTIVE LEADERSHIP INTRODUCED IN THIS CHAPTER

1. Effective teams often display smooth processes of distributed leadership.
2. Groups and teams are not the same thing.
3. Predictable roles often appear in groups and teams: Some are necessary for effectiveness, whereas others are dysfunctional.
4. Groups and teams move through stages of development. Good team leaders understand and manage them.
5. Effective team leaders understand the importance of clarifying membership, purpose, and leadership processes early in a team's life cycle.
6. Effective team leaders will find ways to revisit the team's vision while it is performing its task to keep energy and motivation high.
7. Effective team leaders understand and are able to manage the team's response to changing environmental and internal conditions and events.
8. Effective team leaders can manage the difficult reassessment and reforming process that occurs when a team's work comes to an end for whatever reason.
9. Companies are exploring means of managing virtual teams as they become more common.

QUESTIONS FOR REFLECTION

1. Is your current group a work group or a team? How do you know?
2. What is your present work team's mission? Can you describe it verbally with energy and passion without reference to notes? Why or why not?
3. How can you ensure that you have the right members on your present work team? What does each member of the team contribute to the vision of the team?
4. How can you ensure that you have each team member working in a role that maximizes her contribution to the team's work? When the team meets, do you have a balance between task and process and between creativity and pragmatism? If not, how could you develop that?
5. How can you help your team periodically revisit the work team's dream or mission and in so doing revitalize their energy and commitment? What contribution does the team make to the organization? What

contribution does the team make to the organization's customers?
6. How do you envision the transition of the team from its present status to a new status once the team's work is done? What processes could you design that would facilitate this process? Under what conditions could you imagine the team's work being done? What would you do then?
7. How do you measure your team's work and effort? Do you have analog measures in place? What measures could you develop?
8. What roles do you commonly play in the teams you are a member of? What other roles could you learn to play? How could you help others expand their repertoire of roles?
9. How do you manage participation in your teams? Do you ensure that every team member has a chance to contribute the value for which he was chosen as a team member?
10. What is the LDint for your team?

NOTES

Note: To quickly access all *Harvard Business Review* reprints listed here, go to www.hbsp.harvard.edu/hbsp/adv_search.asp, insert the reprint number in the Product Number field, and click Search.

1. Jon R. Katzenbach and Douglas K. Smith, *The Wisdom of Teams* (New York: Harper Business, 1994).
2. R. Meredith Belbin, *Management Teams: Why They Succeed or Fail* (Woburn, MA: Butterworth Heinemann, 1981; reprint, 1999).
3. See the chapter entitled "Survey of Behavioral Characteristics," which deals with creative thinking, in James G. Clawson, John Kotter, Victor Faux, and Charles MacArthur, *Self Assessment and Career Development,* 3d ed. (Englewood Cliffs, NJ:

Prentice Hall, 1993). See also Chic Thompson, *What a Great Idea!* (New York: Harper Perennial, 1992); and Roger von Oech, *A Whack on the Side of the Head* (Menlo Park, CA: Creative Think, 1983).
4. Warren Bennis and Patricia Ward Biederman, *Organizing Genius: The Secrets of Creative Collaboration* (Reading, MA: Addison-Wesley, 1997). The seven groups were the Walt Disney studio, Xerox and Apple Computer's development groups, the 1992 Clinton presidential campaign, Lockheed's Skunk Works, Black Mountain College, and the Manhattan Project (which built the first atomic bomb).
5. Ibid.
6. Lou Whittaker with Andrea Gabbard, *Lou Whittaker: Memoirs of a Mountain Guide* (Seattle: The Mountaineers, 1994), 111.

7. See, for example, Gene Dalton, Paul
    Thompson, and Raymond L. Price, "The
    Four Stages of Professional Careers, A New
    Look at Performance by Professionals,"
    Organizational Dynamics, summer 1977,
    19–42.
8. Bennis and Biederman, *Organizing
    Genius,* 211.
9. See "Jewel Savadelis A," UVA-OB-190,
    www2.darden.edu/case/collection, for more
    details if you're interested.
10. For example, in the well-known survival
    team exercises Desert Survival and
    Subarctic Survival, team decisions are
    almost always superior to individual choices,
    even when the individuals have had survival
    training and experience.

11. See, for example, the Myers-Briggs type
    indicator as one way of measuring this.
    David Kiersey and Marilyn Bates, *Please
    Understand Me* (Del Mar, CA: Prometheus
    Nemesis Book Company, 1978), is one place
    to start.
12. Christopher Meyer, "How the Right
    Measures Help Teams Excel," *Harvard
    Business Review,* reprint 94305.
13. Chris Meyers, "How the Right Measures
    Help Teams Excel," *Harvard Business
    Review,* reprint 94305.
14. See, for example, "Intersoft of Argentina A",
    Harvard Case Services, HCS 497–025, for an
    example of the difficulties managing teams
    across cultures.

Leaders As Designers

14

Leading Organizational Design

*Most organizational designs and management practices were not cre-
ated with the current rate of change in mind. They were created to work
well in a more stable, predictable world.*

—JAY GALBRAITH AND ED LAWLER

The design of the context in which people work is an oft-ignored and underutilized
aspect of effective leadership. Even if a leader has a clear strategic vision and is
effective at communicating that to followers, unless the organization in which she is
asked to work has been designed to facilitate her contributions, little progress is likely
to be made. The north–south axis between leader and organization in our general
model represents this aspect of leadership, designing effective organizations. Good
leaders understand the nature of organizations and are insightful about how to design
and shape them. But it's not only design. There is a fit question, too. Some people have
leadership styles that allow them to function well in many kinds of organizations,
whereas others thrive only in a narrower range of organizational parameters.

Effective leaders are effective designers of organizations.

Depending on your authority and power base, you may or may not have the
opportunity to design or redesign an organization or parts thereof. If you are wise,
though, you'll recognize that you cannot get good results if your organization's hiring,
work design, appraisal, reward, and educational systems aren't aligned with your

strategic goals. As Peter Senge has pointed out, leaders are designers.[1] In fact, decisions made about organizational designs may ultimately be more powerful than subsequent decisions about allocations of resources within those designs. Further, the basic assumptions you have about people are likely to have a huge influence on your designs. If you trust people, you may design systems one way. If you believe people are lazy, you are likely to design them another way. Your leadership assumptions about people will shape the organizations you create—and thus, designing organizations is a Level Three activity. Let's see how this plays out in organizations.

A GENERAL MODEL OF ORGANIZATIONAL DESIGN AND ITS IMPACT ON RESULTS

Leaders scan an environment and make decisions about what they want to work on, as outlined in the chapter on strategic thinking. Having selected or created some goals and objectives for their business, they begin to make design decisions, some of them explicitly and others by default. These design decisions (about hiring, pay, work, benefits, promotions, information, etc.) begin to affect the people working in the organization. The interaction between design features and the employees creates an organizational culture, the way that people in the organization have agreed over time to operate, which in turn produces the organization's results. Each of the elements shown in Figure 14-1 contributes to the overall outcome of an organization's efforts and hence to the ability of an organization's leader(s) to make things happen.[2] Effective leaders need to understand how they link with each other.

Background Factors

Background factors have to do with the basic building blocks of an organization, the raw materials from which one hopes to build an effective company. Sometimes they are taken for granted and ignored; at other times they are carefully examined and managed. These background factors include such things as local labor pool, local political and economic environment, relative isolation from other hierarchical influence (as in the case of a new plant), history, and anything else that will influence the company's success. These background factors are similar to the environmental factors in our general leadership model introduced earlier.

Garage-based entrepreneurs may not give a lot of thought to these factors as they focus their efforts on developing an idea and getting it before the public. More sophisticated entrepreneurs, perhaps working through venture capitalists, may pay considerable attention to the best place to start their company in terms of availability

FIGURE 14-1 Fundamentals of Organizational Design

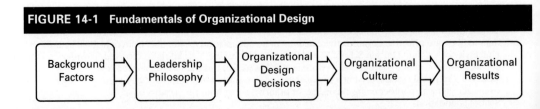

Background Factors → Leadership Philosophy → Organizational Design Decisions → Organizational Culture → Organizational Results

and cost of labor, regulatory restrictions, and local or regional tax incentives. Steve Jobs and Steve Wosniak, for example, didn't travel the country to build their first Apple computer but worked in their garage, albeit in technology-rich and soon-to-be Silicon Valley, California. In contrast, General Motors, in its attempts to build a new kind of small car manufacturing plant based on the Japanese model of high quality, lean operations, and efficient processes, searched the country before settling on relatively remote Smyrna, Tennessee, as the site for its Saturn plant. An important consideration in that decision was Smyrna's relative isolation from corporate headquarters, which tended to reduce the number of managers steeped in the old way of doing things who might raise questions and inhibit innovation in process as well as product. Removal from headquarters is a way of breaking with historic tradition.

The effective leader understands how these background factors influence attempts to create a new organization. Bob Lancaster, for instance, who was given the assignment by FMC Corporation to build a new kind of plant, chose his location very carefully so that he could create a new kind of facility without a history, based on a new philosophy, and in a place where senior FMC management were not likely to interfere. If he had chosen to build the plant in Minneapolis, accessible to divisional executives, he might have experienced a very different outcome.[3]

Leadership Philosophy

Leaders take their philosophies, their VABEs, into a context of background factors and using what they know and believe, they begin to create a business. The purpose that they define for themselves and their organizations (the north–east connection in our general model), the principles that they operate on, and the style they use in dealing with others all begin to have an effect on the organization, some of it intended and some of it not intended. Earlier chapters discussed the role of strategic thinking and of organizational charters including mission, vision, and values in demonstrating a leader's philosophy. A leader's Level Three beliefs about the purpose of the business, the way one influences others, the appropriateness of the systems in the business, and the means of managing change have an enormous impact on the way she approaches leadership opportunities, especially those related to organizational design. Consequently, a significant stream of literature today encourages leaders to reexamine not only what they want others to do but more importantly how they themselves might need to reexamine how they think about their work and role.[4]

A leader's philosophy will shape the kind of organization that leader designs. If one believes that people are basically lazy and have to be supervised, the recruiting, training, supervision, performance evaluation, and information-sharing systems will all reflect that bias. If one believes that all people are competitive or that people who work in the organization should be competitive, the leader will design its structure and reward systems accordingly. The structure and systems of an organization are Level One artifacts or manifestations of those beliefs. By studying an organization's major components, one can often discern many of present and past leaders' Level Three beliefs about how the organization should be run.

The key issue here is that your mind-set or philosophy about how organizations should work will be a key factor in determining how you would create a new organization or perhaps how effectively you would be able to work within or design changes for an existing one. Assessing that north–south connection becomes critical in understanding how a situation will turn out. By default or by design, leaders begin making design decisions that will affect how work is done.

Organizational Design Decisions

The first place many people in positions of power look is to the organizational structure. Whether on paper or simply evolving in people's minds, this is the organization's network of intended relationships for coordinating decision making across many functions. Another way of thinking of organizational structure is as the pattern of power-based relationships that help hold an organization together. When people think of organization structure, they often think of organization charts. This perspective can create problems in that when things change, people who've become accustomed to the old structure may feel betrayed or frustrated. If we accept Stan Davis's maxim that organizational structures are by definition obsolete, then we can look at organizational charts as we do financial balance sheets, as nothing more than a snapshot picture of how things were at one instant in time, and realize that they do not reflect in and of themselves the dynamic nature of what's really happening in the organization over time.[5] (In our general model, this observation suggests that the south–east relationship between task and organization is always going to be obsolete.)

Yet by law and by principle of order, organizational leaders have to figure out how important decisions will be made, and this is the crux of the attention we pay to the distribution of power throughout some kind of structure. A number of common structures were used during the Industrial Age.[6]

Military Model

One of the most common models of the Industrial Age bureaucracy was the military model, developed in large part by Frederick the Great.[7] This pyramidal structure helped clarify who was in charge and codify who could make what decisions. It was a hierarchical model in which each officer was responsible in turn to a higher officer. Each layer had its functional specialities, which were coordinated by the authority at the next highest level. Although it was a very orderly system, it slows decision making. In the rapidly changing environment of the 1980s and 1990s, the classical, bureaucratic model became too sluggish.

Divisional Model

As corporations grew in size, they developed broader interests and eventually new organizational structures. The natural outgrowth of the pyramid bureaucracy was the M-form, or divisional structure, which was an association of bureaucratic pyramids loosely coordinated toward common corporate goals.[8] As in the single-pyramid organization, M-form organizations (so called because when you put two pyramids side by side, they look like an **M**) developed great efficiency skills but difficulties in sharing and building on skills horizontally. Redundancies in special functions such as finance, marketing, accounting, information processing, and human resources and larger and larger project demands by customers led to the formation of a hybrid organization, the matrix.

Matrix Model

Matrix organizations were an answer to the problem of escalating costs on (originally) large engineering projects such as space vehicles and defense weaponry. Typically, matrix organizations had two sides: a project leader side that included a list of project managers who handled various parts of the overall project and had budgets assigned to them for reaching their goals and a functional specialist side that included technical specialty managers with the human resources needed to tackle the various challenges that the project or program leaders faced.

Matrix organizations attacked and destroyed many widely believed bureaucratic principles such as "one person, one boss." Each employee in a matrix organization usually had at least two bosses, the project leader to whom he was temporarily assigned and who paid his salary and the technical specialty boss who hired and assigned the individual based on his skills and availability. Matrix organizations heralded the beginning of the end for the Industrial Age functional bureaucracies.

Matrix organizations allowed people to be used more efficiently by moving from one project to another, but they also created a wave of confusion among those who were used to the simple orderliness of bureaucratic pyramids.[9] Soon, volumes of description and counsel about how to manage matrices emerged, and many companies tried to incorporate aspects of matrix organizations in their own structures.

Hybrids

Since the boom of matrix organizations in the 1950s through the 1970s, organizations have continued to evolve in a variety of directions. The major forces that have contributed to the speed of this evolution are the Information Revolution, the increasingly global nature of modern corporations, the sheer size of modern projects, and the necessity of managing more efficiently in the face of new competition. As people become better educated and have better information available to them, they become more aware of the business processes in their organizations and how they work. The Internet, local area networks, and personal computing give them access to the data that are necessary for making business decisions—and better educational backgrounds help them interpret those data. As a result, the power of knowing what needs to be done is rapidly dissipating downward throughout the ranks of most companies. Many senior management people are distinctly uncomfortable with this trend, but it has continued unabated for the last 20 years and likely will accelerate in the future.

This dissemination of data and the increasing reality of having to compete on a global basis has put pressure on meeting customer needs, responding to increasing competition, and doing so without raising costs. Consequently, organizations around the world for the last 15 years have been downsizing, delayering, and reengineering in an attempt to find more adaptive, distributed, empowered organizational forms that can keep up the rapid pace of change. These forces have spawned a variety of hybrid organizations.

Charles Handy described four emerging kinds of organizations: the federalist, the shamrock, the doughnut, and the clan.[10] The federalist form is akin to the M-form organization but spreads across national boundaries in global settings. Each pyramidic bureaucracy is both independent and obliged to the holding company, working together like a loose federation with some common guidelines and goals. If these federalist structures are to work, leadership has to work hard to ensure that the local pressures do not overwhelm the common goals and benefits that can be gained overall by cooperating amongst themselves. Royal-Dutch Shell, Unilever, and Johnson & Johnson are examples of federalist structures that did remarkably well in the 1990s—

and that continue to wrestle with the balance between competing interests in various parts of their organizations.

Shamrock organizations, so named because of the distribution of their employees, are about one-third full-time employees, one-third contract employees, and one-third part-time employees. This structure gives an organization more fluidity of talent, greater flexibility of managing human resource costs, and a manageable core of full-time, ostensibly dedicated employees. The challenge, of course, is to meld the efforts of the part-time and contract employees with those of the full-time force and still develop strong competitive advantages—from people who are only partially committed to the firm. Ethical issues also arise as companies utilize more and more part-time employees with the nature and allocation of benefits and the impact of lesser benefits on family structures and health.

The doughnut organization, Handy says, reflects an emerging principle in which organizations are centered around a core of key people who mobilize and focus the talents of "stringers" who operate outside and around the core. A central task of the core group is to balance its energy and activities with those of the outside groups. Part of that job is defining the boundaries that identify the core group and those who are suppliers, contributors, vendors, and contractors working in the surrounding space. In a sense, these doughnut organizations are extensions of the shamrock organization, where the focus is on the type of connection to the main organization.

The clan organization emerges from what Handy calls the Chinese Contract, a philosophical approach to relationships, including business relationships, that recognizes and values not only self-interest but also a greater common good. This Chinese Contract reminds us of our earlier discussion of the moral foundation of leadership, of the need for building a business purpose beyond profit, and of the strategic notion of a business ecosystem. A clan organization recognizes that its future lies inextricably intertwined with the futures and fortunes of other organizations and visions around it and that it must fit into this broader purpose for the well-being of all.

Perhaps the extreme form of hybrid organization was described by Tom Peters when he wrote about a Danish CEO who became so concerned about his organization's inability to break through functional boundaries that he bulldozed the walls in the head office building; put everyone's phone, computer, and other personal effects on wheeled carts; and installed electrical and data hookups all over the floor.[11] In this configuration, which he called spaghetti organization, people group together as long as they are working on a common project and then immediately move their "desk" to another group as they go on to their next assignment. This also highlights the competitive advantage to be gained by being able to rapidly form and reform project teams as outlined earlier.

Despite the wide and ever-changing array of options to choose from, organizational structure is only one of several design factors with which leaders as designers need to deal. Sometimes managers rearrange the boxes and lines in their structures while ignoring the other design factors of the organization and then are perplexed when things don't change. Unless they pay attention to all of the key organizational design features, that is likely to be the result.

Systems Design

In most organizations, several key systems have major impacts on the organization's ability to perform. Effective leaders who understand the designer role in leadership

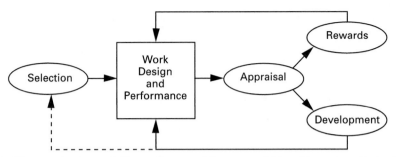

Source: Noel Tichy, et al., "Strategic Human Resource Management," *Sloan Management Review* 23:2 (Winter 1982): 47–62.

FIGURE 14-2   Human Resources Cycle

will not ignore these systems. Noel Tichy and others have described a "human resources cycle" consisting of hiring, work design, appraisal, reward, and development elements as shown in Figure 14-2. Although hundreds or thousands of systems are at play in a large corporation, these certainly are key ones.

Selection and Hiring

Every hiring decision by a company represents a significant investment and, potentially, a constraint on or boon to the company's future. People with the right talent and personality to succeed at a company and to help it succeed are hard to find and difficult to identify. The ability to attract and retain talented people who fit the organization has become an increasingly important source of competitive advantage. Some companies go through elaborate processes to screen out inappropriate applicants; others seems to hire almost as an afterthought any warm body that comes along. Whether part time, full time, contracted, or volunteer, each employee can become either a hindrance to the organization's strategic intent (assuming it has one) or a help that can push the company along in the direction it wants to go.

> The ability to attract and retain talented people who fit the organization has become an increasingly important source of competitive advantage.

Sometimes companies use traditional methods for finding new employees without realizing the consequences of their actions. Effective leaders understand that every system in the company should support and accelerate the company's strategic intent and that those that don't should be a target for reengineering or surgical removal. Hiring is one such system.

Most companies that need a certain kind of skill will advertise for it. Usually these are technical skills. If a company needs a welder, it advertises for welders and then screens applications for welding credentials. The same is true in accounting, marketing, and other technical areas. The process typically involves some personal contact with applicants in which the interviewers try to determine the applicants' "fit" with the company. This is often done by human resource professionals who may or may not know the working environment of the part of the company for which they are interviewing or by line managers who, although they know the working environment, may not see the value of paying attention to the softer criteria, the human aspects of the candidates. One problem with this approach is that although you may get the technical skills you desire, the technician may or may not have the social and leadership skills you'd like to have.

Say, for instance, that you're trying to build a collaborative, team-based organization and you hire a skilled welder, who unbeknownst to you is a loner and basically distrustful of others. Although she may have the right technical skills to contribute, her social skills will hinder the organization's goals. And if you see the development of a collaborative, team-based organization as a part of your strategic intent for building a sustainable competitive advantage, the new welder's social skills may actually inhibit your company's development more than the technical skills help it. Belbin's work on effective teams has clearly shown that teams that comprise the most clever individuals were not necessarily the best. This so-called Apollo Syndrome points out the importance of hiring for a team or organization with a broad range of criteria in mind, including social as well as technical skills.

For this reason, many firms are paying much more attention to the psychological, social, and organizational skills of new applicants than they used to. At FMC Aberdeen, for instance, new applicants undergo a four-hour psychosocial testing program administered by regular employees to see if their personal philosophies and tendencies match the plant's organizational goals. In several cases, they hired people with minor technical skills and superior social skills, the philosophy being that it was easier to teach technical skills than psychosocial skills that may be deeply ingrained.

Work Design and Performance

Although Industrial Age organizations went to great efforts to specify job demands and requirements, modern organizations are much more likely to offer more autonomy to employees to define and shape their jobs. This is especially true at the managerial level. New managers who ask too many questions about what they can and cannot do are sending signals that maybe they aren't managerial material after all. If you experience a gap in your understanding of what your job is, my advice would be to take the leadership point of view described earlier: Look around, see what needs to be done, analyze the relevant forces at play, and then initiate action. Don't wait to be told what to do. In some companies, even at the entry level, people who ask for definitions of their jobs are viewed as hiring mistakes and seldom last long.

That being said, if you are in a position to be designing jobs and shaping what people do, build on Industrial Age research.[12] People want to have some say in what they do (autonomy), a sense of doing a complete job (holism) rather than a tiny part of it (putting nuts on bolts), some variation and creativity in what they do, clear indications of how well they're doing, and a feeling that they are doing something worthwhile and important.

Appraisal

Few systems in organizations have been more maligned and misused than performance appraisal systems. The motivation for creating them is clear: If you have people working, how can you tell how they're doing? Superior–subordinate performance assessment systems attempt to identify each job's requirements (the result of the design work just discussed) and then to assess the employee on each of those requirements. It's not as easy as it may sound.

Many problems have cropped up over the last 100 years in this process. Employees felt they had little or no input into their job descriptions. Bosses felt uncomfortable giving straight or negative feedback, fearing they might be seen as being overly subjective in what is intended to be an objective process. Evaluations escalated, like the so-called grade inflation in schools: More and more people got the highest rating, and the distributions rose. Rewards may not have been tied to the evaluation—for any number of reasons—so employees saw no connection between what they did and what they were paid. Employees may have been demotivated rather than motivated by the process. Further, feedback from one's boss was clearly incomplete. What about what one's peers said? What about what customers said? What about the employee's subordinates' (if any) opinion?

Companies have tried many remedies to these problems. Management by objectives. Better training for bosses who have to give performance reviews. Designing ever tighter evaluation systems in an attempt to reduce bosses' subjectivity. Forced curves in the process ensuring that only 10 percent, for example, will get excellent ratings. Tightening up the links between appraisal and reward systems. Separating the reward announcement from the developmental conversation. Creating 360-degree feedback systems that include data from bosses, peers, subordinates, customers, and suppliers. And finally, even doing away with performance appraisal altogether![13]

Appraisal systems are powerful in that they reflect the leadership's philosophy about how an organization tries to track its internal performance. Basic assumptions about workers and their attributes, such as trustworthiness, are embodied and manifest in the appraisal systems and therefore send signals to employees about their relationship with management. Appraisal systems can also be a powerful negative influence, clogging communication and creating awkward, demotivating conversations that can harm rather than help the company. In some companies, they work well; in others, not so well. Whether they help or hinder will depend on their design, implementation, and alignment with other systems, especially the reward system.

Rewards

Reward systems play a big part in directing the attention of an organization's employees. Strangely, many organizations design or allow to remain in place reward systems that shunt employee attention away from the organization's goals or strategic intent.[14] Unless the reward systems that include the decision making related to salary increases, bonus awards, promotions, public recognitions, and other forms of positive feedback to employees are aligned with the organization's strategic goals, people will feel confused and fragmented in their efforts and in their daily labors.

Despite this logic of this simple principle, many organizations, with good intentions, put in place and continue to use reward systems that seem, perhaps unintendedly, at odds with their goals. Consider, for example, the case of a company that had in place a $500 prize for new ideas that the company used. At the same time, they had a forecasting and planning system that used demographic behavior to predict possible sales for the following year and a low-base-pay, high-bonus-for-exceeding-quota system that in effect punished people for selling more or submitting ideas that would increase quota allocations. The company's systems were working against it.[15]

In an attempt to improve customer service, another firm's senior management decreed that 80 percent of all incoming phone calls were to be answered within 20 seconds. Electronic systems were put in place to monitor calls and call length by operator. Paradoxically, to meet management's request, employees manning the phone lines began cutting their conversations short to answer the next incoming call. As a result, customers were cut off before they got their problems solved, and overall customer satisfaction actually declined. These examples of unintended consequences emerged from positively motivated design decisions intended to focus attention and reward people for behaving in one way but actually encouraged the exactly opposite kind of behavior.

The challenge is to make sure that the reward systems in operation are reinforcing strategic intent instead of being a drag on it. Although senior management or specialists in human resources may think they have the answers, there is a strong logic to the premise that people who will be working in the system should be included in its design, especially after they've been fully educated regarding the firm's goals and strategic intent.[16] Employees are deeply affected by perceived fairness and justice in their reward systems.[17] Further, reward systems seem remarkably long lived. The more a team can build flexibility into a reward system that allows it to adjust rewards for changes in behavior needed, the more likely the organization will be able to direct employee attention to the current strategic challenges that the organization is facing.

Learning Systems

In a turbulent environment, it has become a maxim that the ability to learn is the only source of sustainable competitive advantage. This is true at the individual, work group, and organizational levels. Effective leaders understand that unless people are growing, learning, and expanding their skills and talents, the firm will gradually fall into obsolescence.

An organization's learning systems, including its training programs, are therefore critical to the realization of strategic intent. The story of IBM, including its decline during the 1980s, surely is testament to the fact that mere training is insufficient. For many years, IBM had a policy that all employees should receive a certain number of hours of training annually. Despite this seemingly laudable goal with the intent of ensuring an ongoing learning culture in the company, the company became increasingly out of touch with its markets.

This points out the necessity of having training programs that are the result of and match the firm's strategic intent. Again, at FMC Aberdeen, Bob Lancaster wanted to create an organization where people could work without fear of their own management. He knew this meant that employees would have to understand their markets and the nature of their business and could therefore understand how they might fear competition and the results of not meeting or exceeding customer desires and that they would have to be able to work together in significantly more efficient and productive ways. Consequently, he designed, with the aid of a professional consultant, a training program that began with how to relate to people. Now, most adults going to work for a new company and being informed that they had to go through nine days of training on how to talk with each other might think it lunacy. But Lancaster was convinced that unless all employees understood the basic principles of the organization that he envisioned and could implement them in their daily work lives, they would be unable to build the kind of facility he wanted.

These nine days of specialized training introduced the principles of respectful, fact-based communication and taught people how to avoid judging others as well as how to engage them in mutually respectful, joint problem solving. The program dealt with responding to feedback as data nondefensively and how to manage change within oneself as opposed to trying to change others. Part of effective feedback included describing the potential consequences of unchanged continuation of dysfunctional patterns of behavior. The program was based on Level Three principles such as "All feedback is data, and no one has to respond unless they want to," "We're not trying to change anyone, we think people are fine the way they are," and "If we continue behaving this way, what will happen?" Through systematic exploration of these VABEs and how one communicates and behaves them, new employees were trained to view, to think of, and to behave in relationships in ways consistent with the organization's desired culture. Hiring the right people was an important first step in this process, and adding targeted training was an important follow-on. Regardless of their training, though, unless employees have accurate and relevant information, they will be unlikely to capitalize on that training.

Information Technology

Information processing in the Information Age has become a strategic weapon. I am surprised at how many senior managers still think of information systems as tactical tools rather than as sources of strategic capability. Poor information systems can hamstring an organization's ability to bring its high-quality resources to bear on market issues. Superior systems can enable and facilitate the application of highly talented individuals on key issues and even create a new and powerful business model.[18] The way we structure our information systems, gathering data, sifting it, disseminating it, sharing it, and making decisions based on it, will help to build and even provide a basis for or erode our opportunities for competitive advantage.

Increasingly organizations are realizing how new information systems are literally transforming their structure, culture, and other systems. Powerful information systems are flattening organizations, distributing key data to lower levels of the organization and making the vertical decision-making chain obsolete. With access to data around the world, team members can communicate instantaneously with clients and colleagues in an up-to-date and informed way. More than anything else, the Information Revolution has caused the erosion of the bureaucratic pyramid and is replacing it with a range of organic, powerful, highly responsive organizational forms as described in a previous chapter.[19] Because superior information systems are both difficult to design and expensive to implement, as companies make that investment and learn how to manage those systems' impact on their organizational cultures, they are developing a competitive advantage that will take others years to duplicate. John Galbraith and others have written extensively on how this information technology is affecting the nature of organizational design.[20]

Many other organizational systems and processes exist in addition to the ones we have mentioned here. In fact, one powerful definition of an organization is "a bundle of established processes." The elements of the human resource cycle plus information systems, however, are critical ones that bear special attention. A key point is that unless all of these systems are aligned in the organization, that is, encouraging people to think and behave in consistent ways, people will be confused, the force of the strategic intent will be dissipated, and the organization's effectiveness will be diluted.

In established organizations, the leader-as-designer work that needs to be done involves reexamining key processes and systems and, if necessary, redesigning them so that they are consistent with each other and with the corporate intent. This kind of reengineering effort takes enormous courage, conviction, and stamina. Part of the reason is that not all of these design factors have a direct impact on organizational outcomes; rather, they create an environment in which people work and develop a deep-seated set of guidelines about what is acceptable and what is not. Organizational culture—the behavioral outcome among employees of leaders' design decisions—can be enormously helpful or a huge hindrance to realizing strategic intent.

ORGANIZATIONAL CULTURE

Cultures, according to Ed Schein, develop in response to problems that confront a group of people.[21] As the group addresses, analyzes, and solves each new problem, it develops a history of acceptable ways of behaving that become a part of its culture. If the group agrees to explain thunder and lightning as a manifestation of the gods' displeasure, then this becomes a part of the group's history and culture and is passed on from one generation to the next. If the founders of a company conclude that closed architecture is the best solution to the problem of competing with clone manufacturers (e.g., Apple Computer), then the company develops a history and a culture that shapes its behavior in the future and distinguishes it from other company cultures (e.g., IBM). Organizational cultures, then, are the results of myriad decisions made over time that, when combined, make up the pattern of VABEs that distinguishes one group from the next.

These cultures, referred to in the vernacular as "the way we do things around here," may be so deeply ingrained in the way a group of people behave that they no longer recognize them as something they created but rather as just the way things are and should be. It is often not until someone from one culture visits another that one becomes aware of how cultures differ and of how much one has taken for granted about the way things "should" be done.

> None of these design factors have a direct impact on organizational outcomes; rather, they create an environment in which people work and develop a deep-seated set of guidelines about what is acceptable and what is not.

Organizational cultures can be shaped intentionally, but usually they evolve over time as decision after decision is made and the consequences are accepted and incorporated into the daily routine of doing business.[22] The challenge to the leader-as-designer is to anticipate clearly the impact of organizational design decisions on the culture that emerges from the other side of those decisions. What many seem not to realize is that *design decisions do not have a direct impact on organizational behavior.* The behavior that emerges is filtered through the existing culture. If a leader has paid careful attention to that fact, she may be better armed to avoid unintended consequences—probably by including more people who are going to be affected by the design decision–making process.

Because organizational cultures are the results of many decisions made and absorbed over time, organizational cultures are often nearly invisible to the people who work within them. Determining your organization's operating culture can be frustrating. As Schein points out, doing so requires large amounts of courage, self-reflection, the collaboration of outsiders who can recognize things that insiders take for granted and don't even notice, and extraordinary skills of observation, abstraction, and articulation. If one is able to identify some part of the present culture, one is then semiprepared to think about how it aligns with strategic intent and then to begin thinking about how design decisions might impact that culture in ways that would support the strategic intent. It is not easy to define what you might want the organization's culture to be and then to try to change it. Although many executives during the 1980s and 1990s presumed to undertake a culture change in their organizations, most learned that this was neither quick nor easy nor in the end even feasible.

Jack Welch, for instance, launched a major culture change at General Electric (GE) with his "Work Out" effort in the late 1980s. His goals were to reduce bureaucracy, to increase initiative and decision making among middle and upper-middle-level managers, and to ingrain a new set of operating principles (speed, simplicity, and self-confidence) in the company's multiple divisions. The well-publicized Work Out (from working out to reduce fat and cholesterol) effort made clear first that each division and various parts of those divisions had their own subcultures and second, that managers with 25 to 35 years of experience in GE were not going to change their fundamental way of thinking and managing just because of a few announcements, a few seminars, and a few hard conversations with the boss. After several years of effort and with some good progress in hand, GE's management had to accept more modest results on the goal of revamping the culture of some 200,000 employees.

> Attempting to change an organization's culture is an enormous undertaking.

In the end, culture is the *result* of organizational design efforts. If the design is conceived and implemented carefully, the resulting culture may reflect more, rather than less, than the leaders' original intentions. If the design is not carefully thought out, one may get a variety of unintentional outcomes that over time become cemented in the culture and make it even more intractable. In the end, the leadership, their organizational design, and the culture that emerges will all be evaluated by their results.

ORGANIZATIONAL RESULTS

Organizational design decisions create a context in which people work and perform. In the midst of that context, leaders strive to encourage and guide, and all this effort eventually produces some results. One challenge is to figure out what kind of results one wants and whether one is focusing on the results that will accurately and comprehensively reflect how the organization is doing in meeting its mission or purpose.

Historically, the most broadly accepted indicator of organizational results has been profitability. Although many have suggested variations on this theme (e.g., sales, return on equity, and growth in earnings per share), in the end the underlying focus has been on profitability. Many, if not most, executives will say that their business's primary mission is to make money. The chapter on strategic thinking explored how this view of an organization might be helpful—and hurtful. If managerial conversations and reward systems focus exclusively on profitability, leaders can find themselves paradoxically working with an organization that is becoming less and less profitable as they and their employees make short-term decisions that undermine the company's competitive advantage. In some ways, it's like the discussion on resonance earlier: There is a way in which focus on the task weakens one's ability to perform.

Ralph Waldo Emerson's oft-quoted comment about happiness illustrates the point. Emerson said that happiness is like a butterfly; the more you chase it around the meadow in the noonday sun, the more exhausted you become and the less able to catch the butterfly. The very act of running and darting about, swiping with your net, makes the butterfly more skittish and less catchable. Paradoxically, after pursuing this approach unsuccessfully for a while, when you fall exhausted on the grass and lie still, the butterfly often alights on your shoulder. In the resonance chapter we described how a focus on internal experience can enhance performance. And in the chapter on strategic thinking, we pointed out how a focus on customer service is a powerful precursor to profit when profit focus might undermine customer service—and hence profits.

When leaders focus on profitability as the organization's primary purpose, they are in danger of losing the inspiration and motivational power that resides in the expression and grasping of a high vision or purpose. When senior executives declare to their subordinates, as I heard one do one day, that unless the stock price rose to a certain number by the end of the year, he and his colleagues were not going to get their annual bonus, so the subordinates had better get to work and work quickly, they overemphasize results to the detriment of those results.

More recently, scholars and leaders have been pointing out the virtues and practical productivity of a more balanced approach to assessing organizational results.[23] The balanced scorecard approach recognizes that unless leaders understand the relationships between the reasons why people go to work every day, meeting and exceeding customer expectations, and the importance of making learning and improving one's ways of doing business part of general practice, their ability to improve results may be undermined.

The balanced scorecard approach does not ignore financial results; rather, it simply notes that other measures of success are, taken together, more accurate, more predictive, and more healthy and will lead to better leadership decisions than focusing just on profitability. Short-term profitability turned out to be a disastrous focus, for instance, for many overseas companies' efforts in Central and South America prior to the 1980s. When local governments grew tired of the exploitation of financial results and nationalized those investments, many companies lost millions in equity and in future income streams. A more balanced approach that included learning and development, community involvement, and reinvestment might have produced a lower level of profitability in the short run but a larger net present value when long-term future revenue streams were considered in the equation.

The balanced scorecard approach considers not only financials but also employee morale, learning and innovation, and regulatory relationships as key indicators of an organization's health and long-term prospects. A balanced approach would say that rather than maximize profitability, we should maximize an index of all four areas, which might mean lower levels of profitability to maintain steady levels of innovation in products, services, and the systems we use to produce them; of satisfying customers; and of building employee learning and growth over the long run.

ORGANIZATIONAL GLUE

A good colleague and former human resources executive for Circuit City stores during their phenomenal growth used to teach the importance of organizational glue.[24] Consider for a moment the glue that holds the various organizational design components together. In other words, why do people stay with organizations? What forces keep them connected as opposed to luring them away to other pursuits or enterprises? Clearly rewards are on this list; people stay in part because they're paid. Some people stay because of charismatic leadership; they identify with and want to be a part of the leader's team. Rules, regulations, procedures, and systems can also be a powerful force that shapes employees' behavior and keeps them in line. Shared values and purpose are a fourth and powerful glue that can help keep an organization together. If we array these forces in a table and consider how much of each in any particular organization seems to be contributing to its cohesion, we can see the strength of that organization.

Attracting and retaining talented employees has become an increasing strategic challenge to companies. The mix of glue that an organization offers can well determine the strength with which they bond with the company. Some of the most powerful organizations in the world offer no rewards; instead, they use leadership, rules, and common values to bind their members to them. Others may use mostly rewards to attract and retain people—and realize perhaps too late that a lack of leadership or common values or purpose have left the employees feeling flat or unmotivated. Table 14-1 shows various configurations of organizational glue, each with different strengths and weak-

TABLE 14-1 Organizational Glue				
	Percentage			
Charismatic leadership	10	60	30	
Rewards	40	10	0	
Rules and regulations	20	10	20	
Common values and purpose	30	20	50	
Total glue	100	100	100	100

nesses. What might those strengths and weaknesses be for each of the glue profiles? Take column one, for example—what are the strengths and weaknesses of an organization held together primarily by financial rewards? Or in column two, what are the strengths and weaknesses of an organization held together primarily by one strong charismatic leader?

Consider organizations you've worked for. As you think about why you worked there and for how long and why you left, how would you allocate the glue that bound you to the organization across these categories? Use the last column to estimate the glue that generally held your organization together. Perhaps you saw other kinds of glue; if so, you could add one or more rows to the exhibit to complete the cohesion you experienced.

CONCLUSION

The shape and construction of the organizations that leaders intend to lead have an enormous impact on the outcomes of any leadership situation. Effective leaders understand the importance of their job's design demands and work hard to craft contexts in which their visions can be realized. Their Level Three philosophies about business and people inform those decisions and in turn influence the company's culture. Leaders also understand that they do not have direct impact on their companies' results or even on the development of the dominant cultures that operate in those companies. Rather, they make design decisions that not only address the immediate problems at hand but also leave a legacy that adds to, augments, or shifts the momentum of the organization's cultures and subcultures. When reviewing the results that emerge from any organizational or leadership situation, effective leaders realize that a balanced perspective may not optimize profitability in the short run but in fact produce a more stable and therefore larger net present value of that profitability over the long run. To realize that stream of profits, organizations need to survive and thrive. Leaders pay attention to the glue that holds their organizations together and manage it to strengthen the bonds between employees and organizations (the south–west axis of our general model).

PRINCIPLES OF EFFECTIVE LEADERSHIP INTRODUCED IN THIS CHAPTER

1. Effective leaders are effective designers of organizations and their components.
2. Leaders scan the environment and pay attention to the background factors that affect their organizational planning.
3. Effective leaders develop a clear organizational philosophy and mission or purpose and work to align the organization and its various components with that purpose and vision.
4. Effective leaders realize that their decisions about organizational structure and the internal systems and procedures that define the principles by which work is done in the organization will have only an indirect effect on organizational outcomes and that they need to pay attention to how the organizational culture is affected by those decisions.
5. Effective leaders carefully include others in their design decisions to avoid as much as possible the debilitating effects of unintended consequences.
6. Effective leaders understand the strategic value of information systems and design organizations that revolve around those systems.
7. Effective leaders work hard to review and reengineer organizations or their parts (systems, processes, procedures, etc.) that divert them from achieving their visions and strategic intents.

8. Effective leaders pay particular attention to systems that often seem unimportant, such as hiring, training and development, reward, and information systems, because they know that these all have big impacts on their people and the culture they develop.
9. Effective leaders understand that an overemphasis on profitability can actually undermine their ability to produce profits and that a more balanced approach to assessing organizational outcomes is paradoxically more powerful in the long run.
10. Organizations, particularly in today's global and virtual world, require some kind of cohesion. Mixing the forces of strong leadership, rewards, rules and regulations, and common values and purpose appropriately for the company and its industry can help ensure an organization's longevity.

QUESTIONS FOR REFLECTION

1. Describe your personal leadership philosophy and how it relates to your vision of what your organization could or should become.
2. What, if any, organizational structures, systems, or procedures in your organization inhibit you from doing the quality of work you believe you can and should?
3. Describe the core elements of your organization's culture. What are your organization's VABEs? Use outsiders to check and confirm your description. Ponder and then describe how you think the culture should evolve if your organization is going to be increasingly competitive in the future.
4. Assess your organization in terms of its ability to learn and adapt to changing market conditions. What could you do to enhance the learning atmosphere or culture in your organization?
5. Describe how your organization does or does not use a balanced scorecard in assessing its results. What would be necessary to take a more balanced approach, and what would that look like?
6. What is the glue that holds your organization together? What are the strengths of this mix? What are its weaknesses?

NOTES

Note: To quickly access all *Harvard Business Review* reprints listed here, go to www.hbsp .harvard.edu/hbsp/adv_search.asp, insert the reprint number in the Product Number field, and click Search.

1. Peter Senge, *The Fifth Discipline: The Art and Practice of the Learning Organization* (New York: Doubleday Currency, 1990).
2. Although this is an older viewpoint, the connections are powerful and still generally applicable. This view was adapted from Anthony G. Athos and Robert E. Coffey, *Behavior in Organizations: A Multidimensional View* (Englewood Cliffs, NJ: Prentice Hall, 1968).
3. See "FMC Aberdeen," UVA-OB-385, www2.darden.edu/case/collection, for a description of Lancaster and his work in establishing this plant.
4. See, for example, Chris Argyris, *Improving Leadership Effectiveness* (New York: John Wiley & Sons, 1976); and Robert E. Quinn, *Deep Change* (San Francisco: Jossey-Bass, 1997).
5. See Stan Davis, *Future Perfect* (Reading, MA: Addison-Wesley, 1987). He argues that because all organizational designs follow a strategy in some sense, by the time the organization has been built, the surrounding environmental factors have changed sufficiently enough that the strategy has shifted

and the organization has become out of date. The challenge, of course, is to build organizations that will respond to environmental changes more quickly.

6. For more details on various organizational forms see the technical note, "Organizational Structure," UVA-OB-0361, www2.darden.edu/case/collection.

7. See the earlier chapter on the context of leadership for more details.

8. See Alfred Chandler, *Strategy and Structure* (Cambridge, MA: MIT Press, 1962), for a detailed account of how this form evolved, and William Ouchi, *The M-Form Society* (New York: Avon, 1984), for a good overview.

9. For more information on managing matrix organizations, see Stan Davis and Paul Lawrence, *Matrix* (Reading, MA: Addison-Wesley, 1977).

10. Charles Handy, *The Age of Paradox* (Boston, MA: Harvard Business School Press, 1994).

11. See Tom Peters, *The Tom Peters Seminar* (New York: Vintage Books, 1994), 29.

12. For a brief summary of the research on job design, see "An Introduction to Job Design," UVA-OB-0091, www2.darden.edu/case/collection.

13. See, for example, "SAS Institute," (Stanford case study HR-6, January 1998), a highly successful software company that has done away with performance appraisals on the grounds of their inaccuracy and ineffectivness.

14. See Steve Kerr, "On the Folly of Hoping for A While Rewarding B," *Academy of Management Journal* 18 (1975): 769–83.

15. See the Hausser Foods Company case written by David Nadler of Columbia University for more details on this nonaligned system. Available from the author.

16. See C. Meyer, "How the Right Measures Help Teams Excel," *Harvard Business Review*, reprint 94305.

17. See, for example, Joe Harder, "Organizational Reward Systems," UVA-OB-0667, www2.darden.edu/case/collection.

18. A fine example is the Capital One Financial Services corporation, whose sophisticated, intentionally designed information system provides the very basis for their highly customized line of credit card products and services.

19. See also James G. Clawson, "Leadership Implications of the New Infocracies," *Ivey Business Journal* 64, no. 5 (May–June 2000): 76–83.

20. See *Designing Complex Organizations* (Reading, MA: Addison-Wesley, 1973); Jay R. Galbraith and Ed Lawler, *Designing the Organizations of the Future* (San Francisco: Jossey-Bass, 1993); and Charles Savage, *Fifth Generation Management* (Bedford, MA: Digital Press, 1990).

21. See Edgar Schein, *Organizational Culture and Leadership,* 2d ed. (San Francisco: Jossey-Bass, 1992).

22. See again, for example, the FMC Aberdeen case (UVA-OB-385, www2.darden.edu/case/collection), which describes the intentional construction of a unique organizational culture by an extraordinary leader.

23. See R. S. Kaplan and D. P. Norton, "Balanced Scorecard: Measures That Drive Performance," *Harvard Business Review*, reprint 92105.

24. Thanks to Bill Zierden for this perspective.

CHAPTER

15

Leading Change

It's not the critic who counts. It's not the man who points out where the grown man stumbles, or how the doer of deeds could have done them better. The credit belongs to the man who actually is in the arena, who strives violently, who errs and comes up short again and again, who knows the great enthusiasms, the great devotions, and spends himself in a worthy cause, who if he wins knows the triumph of high achievement, but who if he fails, fails while daring greatly, so his place will never be with those cold and timid souls who know neither victory nor defeat.

—THEODORE ROOSEVELT, TWENTY-SIXTH PRESIDENT OF THE UNITED STATES

Leadership is nothing if not about change. If there is no change, one could argue that there is no leadership; we don't talk about leadership for the status quo or maintenance leadership. Change and its related concepts and principles are inextricably intertwined with leadership. In a world that continues to change rapidly, effective leaders are masters of the change process; they understand, embrace, and lead change. Ineffective leaders struggle with change and find that many of their efforts at managing change fail. It behooves every aspiring leader, therefore, to understand her own attitudes toward change and to become a master of the change process and how to manage it.

A GENERAL MODEL OF CHANGE

Over the course of our lives, we become comfortable with a certain set of behaviors. We have used them before, they seem to work well enough, and thus they become a part of our common routines. This is also true of organizations. This set of comfortable routines becomes a box for us, a box that allows us to be productive and to move forward efficiently without testing every thing we do but that also constrains us and

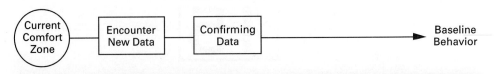

inhibits our thinking about and trying new things. We can call this set of routines at the personal level our *comfort zone* or our *baseline behavior* and in the organizational sense, our *organizational culture* (see Figure 15-1).

As long as we continue to get confirming feedback from the outside world about our baseline behavior, we have little motivation to change it—unless, of course, we are simply curious and want to learn and grow. We can in that context speak of internally motivated and externally motivated change. Internally motivated change generates from our innate curiosity and desire to improve things. Externally motivated change is forced upon us by external agents (such as parents, teachers, bosses, investors, competitors, governments, etc.). The dangers of externally motivated change—that is, of responding rather than leading—are many: being too late in the market, taking a compliance instead of an excelling mind-set, missing a market altogether, and half-hearted or haphazard implementation.

This is also true in business. Many managers, especially those with Industrial Age methodologies, ascribe to the maxim "If it ain't broke, don't fix it" and see in stable, historically successful routines a way of generating steady cash flows, building leverage, managing margins, and realizing returns of past investments. The danger is that these comfort zones can reduce our flexibility—in which case it's just a matter of time until the market shifts and we're left behind. Unless these investments in our historical means to success build an enhanced ability to adapt to our environment into our personal and organizational systems, they become strategic blockades rather than sources of competitive advantage.

Let's acknowledge here that we all want to think well of ourselves. Our minds develop remarkable techniques for maintaining a positive self-image. If what we did in the past worked and helped us succeed in some sense, then we seek naturally to maintain that modus operandi. This desire to think well of ourselves connects to our view of the outside world. If, after long periods of time receiving confirming data about our baseline behavior, we get some *dis*confirming data, we are faced with a choice about what to do about them.

Disconfirming data are a challenge to our self-concept because it says that what we used to do doesn't work any more. These data try to pull us away from our baseline behavior and signals to us that we should try something new. The data may be in the form of a monthly profit report, the establishment of a new competitor, feedback from a spouse or peer, angry facial expressions from a subordinate, a weak performance review, or an appointment request turned down. Whatever the source of the disconfirming data, they challenge our view of ourselves and invites us to do something about it.

We decide in a variety of ways whether to accept or reject this invitation. Accepting it can be painful because we will have to rethink our self-image, perhaps change our behavior, move out of our comfort zone, and experiment with untried and unproven behaviors that also may or may not work. This is risky business.

Accepting disconfirming data or, even prior to receiving them, breaking out of the comfort zone and trying to do difficult, somewhat painful, new things is the subject of Scott Peck's best-selling book *The Road Less Traveled.*[1] Because most of us want to stay in our comfort zone, we persist in our baseline behavior. Breaking out of it is uncomfortable and threatening. Peck argues that the road less traveled is the path that leads to this discomfort; this is the road to learning and growth. Without it, he argues, we are destined to become little more than we presently are. A few of us welcome disconfirming data because we view them as an opportunity to learn, to break out of our comfort boxes, and grow larger.

Many people, however, choose to stay in their comfort zone and respond to disconfirming data by systematically discounting them, distorting them, or ignoring them altogether; then one can continue behaving as one always did without interruption. It's as if our behavior, like a rubber band stretched from the baseline, snaps back; we fall once again into our old behavioral patterns. These concepts are shown in Figure 15-2.

Of course, the strength of the disconfirming data will have something to do with whether or not we can discount, distort, or ignore them. If they are very strong, we may not be able to ignore them. At the same time, we all know of people who have received enormous disconfirming data and been quite able to put them out of mind. Our attitudes about and comfort levels with change may shape our response to disconfirming data. At some level, though, we can choose whether to accept them.

If we recognize the need to change our behavior, then we have to do something about it. This will involve, by definition, some experimentation on our part. We will elect to try out things we haven't done before. For most people, that's threatening, scary, and undertaken with trepidation. We undertake the experiment and that, in turn, generates more feedback data. If the data call the experiment's validity into question, even if we didn't do the experiment correctly, we are likely to abandon the new approach, and our behavior will snap back to the former baseline.

Think about your personal efforts to change, whether it be losing weight, stopping smoking, studying more frequently, exercising regularly, writing to family more often, or whatever it is. If the new behavior didn't bring some positive results to you,

---

FIGURE 15-2   How Most People Deal with Disconfirming Data

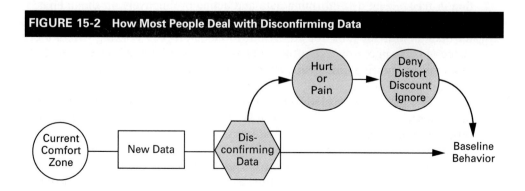

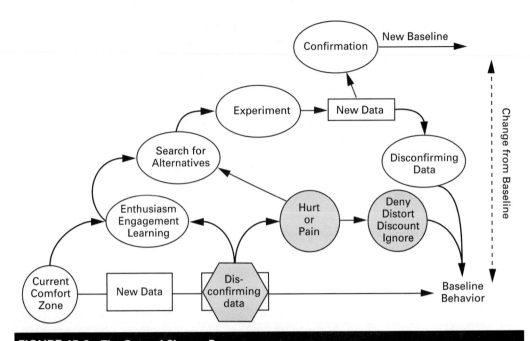

FIGURE 15-3 The General Change Process

you probably concluded that it didn't work and thus slipped back into the former comfort zone.

If the new behavior produces positive results, though, then a new pattern begins to be established. With reinforcement, one begins to see that the new approach works. As the positive feedback continues to come in, the new baseline is established, and one continues on it until new disconfirming data comes in. This general model of change appears in Figure 15-3.

THE ROLE OF OUTSIDE HELP IN MANAGING CHANGE

There are several places where outside help can greatly assist a person or an organization in recognizing disconfirming data and acting productively on them. First, assembling and presenting the disconfirming data is something that others can often do better than an individual or, for an organization, employees working within a firm. By virtue of living in our own comfort zones, it's often hard to see how we might be overlooking (discounting, distorting, or ignoring) bits of disconfirming data. Our long-established behaviors, our habits, become invisible to us. If we tend to be defensive (again, as a person or an organization), outside infusions of information from consultants, physicians, friends, and so on can help us to view the data differently, with more seriousness and a greater sense of validity.

A second place where outside help is of great assistance is in identifying alternative courses of action. Because we have been operating in our comfort zone, we don't see clearly how else to do things. Getting a consultant or a new executive from another industry can be very helpful in developing a new view of what's possible.

A third place where external viewpoints are helpful is in interpreting the data from the new experiment. If we are defensive, we may interpret the new data negatively and even subconsciously manage the experiment so that it fails. This happens in business, too. Outside monitors can help us be honest in our evaluations of the data from the new experiments until we get our own bearings and are able to see things more objectively.

In fact, all of the circles marked with an L in Figure 15-4 show places where leaders can influence the general change process. If you understand this process and the vantage points where external influence can make a difference, you can have a big impact on change efforts.

Given these points of influence in the change process, we can infer some steps for managing change. These are (1) clarifying disconfirming data, (2) building a change team, (3) designing and leading change experiments, and (4) relentlessly reinforcing results with the vision.

Clarifying Disconfirming Data

Effective leaders are able to clarify and publicize, even popularize, disconfirming data. Many organizations have massive capacity for discounting, distorting, and denying disconfirming data (see Table 15-1). Even natural scientists have been shown to be remarkably resistant to new data that disconfirm their old views of the world.[2] Depending on the resistance to change, a would-be leader may have to expend enormous energy to get people to see disconfirming data and their implications.

FIGURE 15-4   Where Leaders (L) Can Affect the Change Process

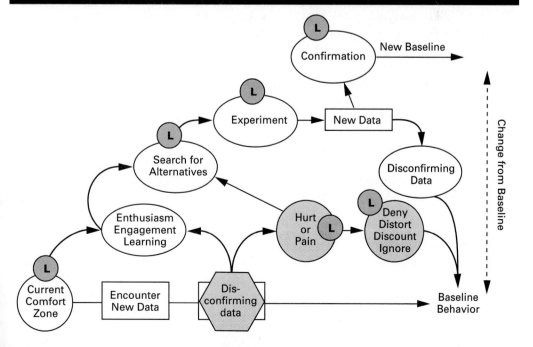

TABLE 15-1   Leading the Change Process
1.   Clarifying disconfirming data
2.   Building a change team
3.   Designing and managing change experiments
4.   Relentlessly reinforcing the results with the new vision

Disconfirming data may not necessarily be negative, though. Faced with a leadership opportunity, you may want to create a new vision of what could be possible for an organization. This doesn't mean that you have to create what is often called a "burning platform" or some false third-party enemy; rather, it may mean that you see a new vision of what could be if the company were able to transform itself. There may be no immediate threat. Obviously, this kind of change is difficult to sell in an organization, so the strength of the leadership's vision is critical to getting organizational members to accept this kind of new information. An excellent example would be the shift in strategy at Kimberley-Clark in the mid-1990s when the CEO and his staff decided to sell off their paper mills, including the namesake mill in Kimberley, Wisconsin, and focus on consumer products.[3] Employees generally are not likely to buy into this kind of new data, especially when things seem to be going well.

It's much easier to see and accept an immediate threat such as declining profitability, losses in market share, rising costs, or unmanageable levels of debt. The leader who bears this kind of disconfirming data may get a more willing response from employees or the unions that represent them. Unfortunately, disconfirming data like this often appear very late in the competitive game, and the company may or may not be able to recover.

So asserting disconfirming data doesn't just mean bringing bad historical news; it also means creating new visions of what's possible and then galvanizing people in that direction; another good example of this kind of strategic vision–driven "disconfirming data" would be Enron, the energy management firm. This was a company that once held a vast network of pipelines and transmission lines and then, led by a team with a different vision, decided to move from the pipeline business to an energy brokerage business. This vision-led change resulted in wonderful financial results and the company being named by *Fortune* magazine as the most innovative corporation in the United States for six years running. In this kind of example, the disconfirming data lie in the vision presented by leadership. Employees are then challenged to let go of their historical ways of doing business and learn new ones–because their leadership sees something new. Now, Enron has collapsed, but the collapse had to do with dishonest management practice. The strength of their vision in leading change remains.

Building a Change Team

Carol Rubin was for a time the chief operating officer of the Chicago Park District during a period when the district underwent dramatic changes from a highly dysfunctional patronage system to an organization that was dramatically improved on virtually every measure. The general superintendent of this change team was Forrest Claypool.

During an interview about this change process, Rubin commented on Claypool's approach:

> The first thing that he did was that he spent a lot of time recruiting good people. As soon as he knew that he had this job, he spent months recruiting good people. And that is the only way that you could turn a bureaucracy around. I know people who have gone to other bureaucracies here and in other cities and it's always a telltale sign for me that whether they will succeed or fail, if they brought in a good team. I've had people say, you know, "I'm the only one that the new director brought over." Well, if I hear that I know they're really not going to get to do anything because, to turn a place around, you need a band of revolutionaries and you need a lot of people. One person can't do it alone, and there is so much to do that you really need to spend time bringing in a good team of people. Because if you have good people, you know, while strategic planning is great and it's very important, if you have good people, the job will get done. They have to share your vision; they have to share your values; they have to be *your* people. But they will come in and they will be the ones that will get the job done. They will also bring in good people.[4]

Leading change is like dropping a pebble in a pond; there is an initial splash, and then, if it is to be successful, concentric waves emanating out from the center. The leader with the vision is that center, and the team he has assembled becomes the waves that affect the rest of the pond. It's like guerilla warfare: The leader assembles a small band of revolutionaries, imbues them with a common vision and purpose, organizes their efforts, and relies on them to spread the word. You cannot lead change by yourself.

Designing and Leading Change Experiments

Change means doing something new. By definition, these are experiments for the people who try. If the experiments aren't well designed and managed, participants can come out the other end and conclude, "See, I told you! I knew it wouldn't work!" This was the experience of many companies who over the years tried the latest managerial process as a bandage stuck on the surface of the underlying, persistent organizational culture. Management by objectives, nominal groups, self-managed teams, total quality management, and benchmarking, to name a few, worked in some companies and not in others, in part because the experimental trials were not well designed or even led in the first place. I'm reminded of a situation where a general manager was asked by his boss to delegate more because he was trying to do too much. A year later, after the manager had tried his definition of delegating, the company's financial indicators were down. His probably erroneous conclusion was that delegation didn't work. The experiment for him was unsuccessful. We might have asked his boss how he had designed the change attempt and how much coaching and guidance he gave to others during the experiment. Announcing a change and then disappearing does not constitute experimental design and leadership.

Well-designed experiments require clear goals and objectives, substantial training for how to achieve those goals, coaching and support when fledgling attempts don't go well, and lots of positive reinforcement when the behavior moves in the desired direction.

Relentlessly Reinforcing Results with the Vision

People want and need positive reinforcement, especially when they are trying something new. Although I am not a strict Skinnerian, as you can tell from the chapter on human behavior, positive reinforcements clearly have a powerful effect on behavior. Sometimes the innate, natural results of a situation (the final score in a game, the ability to ride a bike, the quarterly results) will be sufficient to reward people for their efforts. Few would argue, however, that positive reinforcement, even in small doses, can have a powerful influence on people.[5] Hard-core Skinnerians would argue as well that positive reinforcement is the only kind that has lasting power—punishing may teach someone what not to do, but it does not teach them what to do—there are too many options beside the one that the leader may be desiring.

Given these fundamentals of a basic change process, we can explore the popular and documented change models used in business organizations today.

CLASSIC AND CURRENT CHANGE MODELS

Historically, probably the most popular change model has been to order people to do something different. If there was an army, a police force, a dungeon, or a guillotine behind the leader, many would comply. Although compliance is not a Level Three response and certainly not the route to world-class performance, telling or threatening as a means of initiating change remains a powerful, simple model today.

In the business world, a dominant change model was the simple three-step one articulated by Kurt Lewin. He noted that a change effort began with an unfreezing process, contained a transformation process in the middle, and ended with a refreezing stage. Nowadays, with the rapid rate of change taking place around us, most observers agree that the refreezing is dangerous and that we probably should think more in terms of gelling the new processes; The gel image is more flexible and responsive to future change while still giving some stability. Others argue we should simply give up on unfreeze-retrain-refreeze and accept the reality of today as unfreeze-change-change. This implies that each new baseline in our general change model will constantly be challenged by the events changing around it.

In today's changing world, unless an individual or organization has a deep-seated Level Three appreciation for change, life will be a constant series of irritations and frustrations. People who have or develop a value for change, on the other hand, will understand this process and manage it to their benefit.

A more recent, widely used change model comes from Michael Beer at the Harvard Business School. Beer asserts an equation that suggests that the amount of change in a system is equivalent to the amount of dissatisfaction with the status quo times the clarity of the model of where we want to go times the strength of the change process when that product exceeds the cost of making the change.[6]

$$Cv = D_{sq} \times M_f \times P_c > C_c$$

where

$$Cv = \text{volume of change}$$
$$Dsq = \text{dissatisfaction with the status quo}$$
$$Mf = \text{model of the future}$$
$$Pc = \text{Process of change, and}$$
$$Cc = \text{Cost of the change.}$$

This is a very useful model because it tells us that unless people are unhappy with the way things are, they aren't likely to change, and even so, unless they can see a way to change things as they'd like, chances are that nothing will happen. Change leaders can see in this approach specific things they can do to raise the probability of success.

Hal Leavitt at Stanford adds a provocative thought by suggesting that the role of effective leaders in today's environment is becoming more about *creating* problems for satisfied employees. Historically, leaders have been viewed as problem finders and problem solvers.[7] In a rapidly changing environment, though, waiting until the signals are crystal clear may be too late. Leaders must challenge employees and associates before it's too late to do something constructive.

ROLES IN THE CHANGE PROCESS

There are other roles besides problem creator that we can identify in the change process: change leader, change agent, change manager, and change model.[8] Any one person may or may not play all of these roles. A *change leader* is one who initiates a change process. This may have come about by virtue of a significant event or a bolt of inspiration or simply doing one's strategic homework. Senior executives are often change leaders in corporations. They may, for instance, commission studies, request a new process for developing company strategy, or decide to acquire new kinds of businesses.

A *change agent* is one who actually causes the change to begin in a person or an organization and may or may not be the change leader. Consultants are often change agents as are senior staff members, both of whom respond to a change leader's request or initiative.

A *change manager* is the person with the day-to-day responsibilities of implementing and overseeing the change effort. This could be a staff or a line person. This is the person to whom the change leader will look for reports and progress and who has to influence others in the organization so that the changes take place.

A *change model* is a person who exemplifies the change effort. Change models are consistent in their repetition of the disconfirming data (the need for change), in their language in encouraging the change, and in their behavior in acting consistently with the change objectives and principles.

These various change roles interact. For instance, if the change leader is not a change model, that is, if the senior executive recommending an organizational change does not manifest the requested changes, the change effort's strength is greatly undermined. Identifying each of these roles in a change effort and assessing how their behavior and communications are consistent or inconsistent can help explain why many change efforts succeed or fail.

We could and should also recognize the *changee,* the person or people who is being asked to change what she does and how she does it. This is as difficult and as important a role as any of the others, yet it is often overlooked by those in the first four roles. People being asked to make significant changes often go through some predictable phases.

RESPONSES TO CHANGE—DYING LITTLE DEATHS

When a person or an organization changes, they let go of some part of their historical comfort zone and begin to embrace a new pattern. This letting go, in a significant way, is like letting a part of oneself die. We can speak of experiencing change, then, as if it were like dying a little death.

There are powerful parallels between the research of Elizabeth Kübler-Ross on the stages of terminally ill cancer patients' experience and the experience of individuals and organizational members during the change process. [9] Although neither individuals nor groups of employees go through all these stages in exactly the same way or even in the same sequence, a general pattern can inform the leader desirous of managing change processes better.

People experiencing significant change typically go through periods of denial, anger, bargaining, despair, experimenting, resignation, and integration. Again, please note that not everyone experiences these in this order, and certainly not everyone goes through all the stages. Some, for instance, get hung up in denial.

The Many Faces of Denial

Many people react to disconfirming data by denying them. There are many forms of denial as shown in Figure 15-5.[10] First, one can discount the data source's validity. If one rejects the message before even considering the content because of its source, one is easily able to avoid thinking about that content. If one is able or forced to admit that the messenger is credible, one can then deny the content of the message, holding on to a belief that the data are false. Again, it's easy to avoid doing anything about data that one

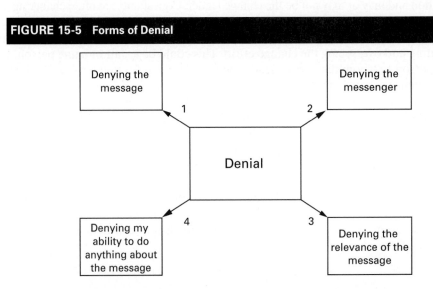

FIGURE 15-5 Forms of Denial

doesn't believe. If one is forced to accept both the message and the messenger, one can deny the relevance of the message to one's own situation. "Yes," we may say, "it's true, and I acknowledge that you brought this to my attention, but it really doesn't concern me." Finally however, if we are forced to acknowledge that the data source is credible, that the data are true, and that they relate to us, we may then deny our ability to do anything about it. These four successive hurdles to receiving and seriously considering disconfirming data are defense mechanisms that we often use to protect our self-image.

People can stay locked in denial for long periods of time. Some refuse ever to come out. Addictions are, in part, a form of denial inasmuch as they are an attempt to seek alternative forms of peace or resonance to what the nonaddictive world presents. People who ignore health warnings from the surgeon general's office are in a form of denial. And employees or managers who ignore competitive signals from their industries and persist in old routines are in a form of denial, too.

If the disconfirming data are strong enough to pierce a person's denial, the first typical emotional response is anger, which arises when the changee realizes that the new information must be dealt with. This understanding forces one to leave the comfort zone and move into a new, unknown arena and, if navigated successfully, will require giving up something of the old self and moving on. To change, one gives up an investment of time, energy, and emotion in a pattern that no longer works so well. This anger caused by this disappointing reality may be vented at any number of targets that may or may not have anything to do with the problem's real source. Employees may get mad at employers instead of the competition. They may get irritated at customers instead of trying to serve them. They may get angry at their colleagues, their families, their counterparts in other departments, and so on. As outlined earlier, people with higher EQs and CQs are more likely to be able to manage this anger and succeed in social situations like businesses.

Anger in response to a recognized need for change often leads to bargaining. Having been forced to recognize that the old way doesn't work so well anymore, people will often try to bargain their way out of the change. "Maybe if we just cut back on expenses, we could continue as we are" is one common bargaining ploy. Another is "Maybe we can work harder, and the data will get better." One also hears "This is a short-term phenomenon; we'll get back to the old way soon," "We've managed changes before, and we'll manage this one doing what we've been doing," "The customer doesn't really know what he wants; we need to educate him," and so on.

Bargaining is an attempt to reverse the disconfirming data and retreat to the original baseline. In the resonance model presented earlier, bargaining is related to the ping-pong effect between preparation and SOS barriers in the resonance model. Disconfirming data are manifestations of barriers. If short-term bargains are made and the data begin to show some responsiveness, bargaining can be very dangerous to change efforts because people *want* to believe that things will get better without their changing. When bargaining fails though, as it will in all fundamental change situations, one realizes that one truly has to change, and this realization often leads to despair.

Despair for most is a watershed transitional stage between attempts to go back and willingness to go ahead. In this hopefully brief period, one realizes that there is no going back, that the former comfort will not be had again, and that however uncomfortable, one must go ahead.

Some argue that people need time to grieve at this point, to vent their despair, to cry, to reflect on the good old times, and to lend a sense of completion to the past before going on to the next stage. I don't disagree with this; at some point one must say, "Enough crying for the past. I must live in the present preparing for tomorrow." The sooner one completes one's grieving for the past and begins to see possibilities for the future, the sooner progress will be made. Making changes in our lives and in our organizations is like dying small deaths, and like deaths, these changes require some grieving and attention if we are to move ahead with psychological wholeness.

When the grieving is coming to an end, most people begin, however timidly, to see possibilities, which is the beginning of exploration and experimentation. As mentioned previously, this is a place where outside, less involved, expert assistance can be of enormous help as one begins to see new, manageable routes of progress, as one takes a few steps in that direction and begins to see the possible results. These alternative directions help generate some hope that the despair of the recent change will be replaced with a new sense of comfort and capability.

Hope is the anticipation that one's efforts can yield results. If people in the midst of a major change cannot see how the world will get better, it will be difficult for them to find something to work for in the new state of things, and they will begin to look to the past for comfort and support. False hopes aren't any help. If management deviates from the moral foundation described earlier and allows or constructs false hopes, employees will soon become disenchanted and disengaged and will slip back into despair. Realistic, achievable, and small but tangible hope is better than promises made lightly and without much expectation of fulfillment.

As hope is realized and the data coming in from the new experiments begin to be positive, people begin to integrate the new way of doing things into their network of assumptions and values. Ghosts of the old assumptions begin to fade, and the new principles start to take their place. Often this integration occurs so subtly that one doesn't even notice it. Although equally powerful as anger and despair, integration is much less obvious. One day, one might notice that one had been using the new principles for a while and things have been going okay. The new order seems *almost* comfortable. Celebrating this ethereal transition is an important part of helping people understand what has happened, that they are veterans of managing change and that they with you have together created a new reality.

The process just described can be diagramed as shown in Figure 15-6. It represents an oscillation between behavior and emotion, each in turn typically triggering the next. Overcoming denial leads to anger. Overcoming anger leads to bargaining. Overcoming bargaining leads to despair. Working through despair leads to new options. Working those options can generate new hope. And hope and work together produce the kind of behavior that leads to a new pattern of doing things. Effective leaders not only understand this process but also actively plan for and anticipate the reactions so that their downside effects are minimized and their upside possibilities are maximized.

Another way to depict this process of change is shown in Figure 15-7. Here, the early complacency of past successes is represented by a smooth, flat line. Disconfirming data become like rocks in a river causing chaotic rapids. Despite the evidence, people resist the need for and efforts to introduce change. If leadership is strong and good processes are put into place, short-term positive results begin to emerge. Then, lest the new efforts snap back to the old way, a repeating, iterative consolidation of the new way into a habitual way of doing things establishes a new baseline, which, unless it includes processes of continuous change, can before long become its own complacency–and the process begins again.

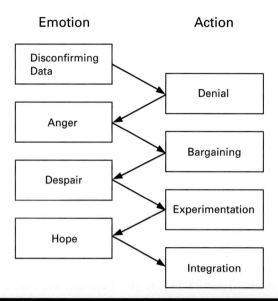

Emotion | Action

Disconfirming Data → Denial

Anger → Bargaining

Despair → Experimentation

Hope → Integration

FIGURE 15-6   Reaction to Change: The Balance Between Action and Emotion

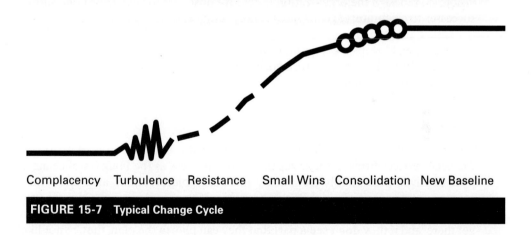

Complacency   Turbulence   Resistance   Small Wins   Consolidation   New Baseline

FIGURE 15-7   Typical Change Cycle

LEVELS IN CHANGE

Similar to the way that we earlier talked about Level One, Two, and Three leadership, we can talk about Level One, Two and Three change. If the target of our change effort is behavior only, we are working on a Level One kind of change effort, but these can often have unintended Level Three consequences if the formal changes requested affect people at a deeper level. Effective leaders recognize that powerful change invites people to alter not only their behavior but also their thoughts and beliefs, so they target their attempts at Level Three. A Level Three change modifies the basic values and assumptions of an individual or organization.

TABLE 15-2   Kotter's Model of Change
1.   Create a sense of urgency.
2.   Create a guiding coalition.
3.   Create a clear vision and strategy.
4.   Overcommunicate.
5.   Reorganize to remove barriers to change.
6.   Celebrate short-term wins.
7.   Consolidate little wins into initiatives.
8.   Incorporate changes into the culture.

JOHN KOTTER'S MODEL OF CHANGE

John Kotter, of the Harvard Business School, would refer to the Level Three change as "anchoring the changes in the culture of the organization." Kotter's research has outlined eight reasons that corporate change efforts fail—and eight corresponding ways of managing them (see Table 15-2).[11] Kotter's counsel was that change leaders should (1) establish a sense of urgency; (2) create a guiding, powerful coalition; (3) develop a clear and powerful vision and strategy; (4) communicate at every point possible the change vision; (5) redesign the organization to remove obstacles to change; (6) find short-term successes to celebrate; (7) consolidate short-term wins into new change initiatives; and (8) ensure that the changes are incorporated into the underlying organizational culture. These eight steps correspond well with principles introduced earlier in this book. Although Kotter has a well-informed, empirically based view, here's a similar supporting perspective from industry.

THE FOUR P'S

The president of the largest divisions of one of the United States' most successful financial services firms summarizes the change process as the Four P's of change: purpose (derived presumably from some felt pain), picture, plan, and part. This is, in essence, a manager's view of Beer's equation: If people don't see a purpose for the change, if they don't see where they're trying to go, if they don't see a plan for how to get there, and if they don't see a part that they can play in the plan, they're not likely to participate in the change effort—and it will flounder or founder.

THE MIT MODEL

Just down the road from Kotter's Harvard office, researchers at MIT have developed a powerful seven-step model of managing change.[12] They suggest that change is a three-dimensional phenomenon involving a developmental process, seven tools for effecting change, and the importance of managing resistance to change (see Table 15-3).

According to the MIT team, major change efforts typically progress through four clear phases. In the first, employees and management are just learning that the old ways aren't working any more. They are coming to grips with disconfirming data from the environment. Once this realization has set in, management begins searching for

TABLE 15-3   The MIT Change Management Skill Sets

1. Persuasive communication
2. Participation
3. Use of expectations
4. Role modeling
5. Using extrinsic rewards
6. Making structural and organizational changes
7. Coercing

new approaches in the exploratory phase. Next is the generative phase, in which key pieces of the change effort are generated out of new processes and approaches so that they become the source of energy for change. Finally, in the internalization phase, the new processes become so well ingrained that they become a natural part of the organization.

Nevis and his colleagues argue well that successful change efforts utilize not one or two but seven sets of skills related to change: persuasive communication, participation, the use of expectations, role modeling, reward systems, structural or organizational changes, and finally coercion. Each of these skill sets has its strengths and weaknesses, and each might be more or less appropriate at each of the four phases. The challenge for effective change managers is to understand and be able to use each of these tools as appropriate—and to avoid using them inappropriately.

Nevis and colleagues include coercion in the list of change management skills. I have argued that coercion is a use of power that moves one out of the realm of leadership. You may or may not feel that coercion is necessary for a short period of time. I know managers who say that sometimes you have to force people to do what they don't want to do when you know that the effort will eventually lead to their acceptance of the right way of doing things. My concern here is that if you get comfortable using coercion as a crutch, as a last means of creating change, then there is a danger that it will become easier and easier to use the next time—and soon you're leading almost exclusively at Level One. It's faster in some sense, but in the mid to long runs, it's less effective.

Finally, the MIT team notes that many change efforts fail because they ignore predictable resistance to change. Using the learning organization work that's been done at MIT by Peter Senge and colleagues, they suggest that a powerful way of recognizing this common feature is to encompass the principle of multiple realities. In other words, lots of subgroups in an organization will see the change efforts differently. Some will be in favor, and some will be opposed to the changes—each for their own reasons. If change leaders can recognize that each of these groups have good reasons for their viewpoints, they are better armed to select and use change tools that fit that group's perspective. The keys to this approach are to legitimize diverse perceptions rather than to demand a singular view. If management takes this approach, they can find richer solutions through using these various viewpoints and thus reduce resistance.

CONCLUSION

Understanding and managing change is an integral part of effective leadership. Leadership seeks to change what people do, and if it is effective, it will change what people think and believe. People naturally tend to settle into a comfort zone using personal, interpersonal, and organizational techniques that have served them in the past. Changing out of or from this historical pattern usually begins with disconfirming data. Those who attend to these data and interpret them as meaningful begin a change process. In so doing, they leave behind a part of their former self, as if they were dying a little death. Making real change, especially Level Three change, triggers a common response pattern of denial, anger, bargaining, despair, experimentation, hope, and integration. Leaders who understand this process and can develop some skill at managing people through it can work to get through these predictable stages and manage their mutual changes more effectively.

PRINCIPLES OF EFFECTIVE LEADERSHIP INTRODUCED IN THIS CHAPTER

1. Leadership by definition is about managing change.
2. Effective leaders understand and have masterful skills in managing the change process.
3. Changing is like dying a little death; part of us must be let go, and a new part must be born.
4. Change begins with disconfirming data. We have a choice about how we respond to that data, whether to ignore them or consider them.
5. Recognizing and managing various change effort roles—including change leader, change agent, change manager, change model, and changee—are helpful in mounting a successful change effort.
6. Disconfirming data often lead to a series of predictable reactions to the change process: denial, anger, bargaining, despair, experimentation, hope, and integration into a new way of doing things. People can get stuck all along the way, and often outside help is useful in moving through each phase.
7. People need strong and consistent reinforcement in the experimentation phase to settle on the new way of doing things.
8. Outside agents are often very helpful in managing change because they can see habits that have become invisible to those in the change arena.
9. Level Three, or value-level change, is the most enduring.

QUESTIONS FOR REFLECTION

1. What kinds of disconfirming data have you encountered either personally or in your work group over the last six months? What was your response to them?
2. What change roles are you playing in your work group? What data do you see, which maybe others don't see, that invite you to become a change leader?
3. What has been helpful for you in the past when you have needed support getting through the reactions to change process? How could you provide those functions to others?
4. List the most significant changes you've made in your life. Think through the process that you used to navigate each change. How well did you manage those changes? What did you learn from them and what would you like to know how to do better?

Notes

Note: To quickly access all *Harvard Business Review* reprints listed here, go to www.hbsp .harvard.edu/hbsp/adv_search.asp, insert the reprint number in the Product Number field, and click Search.

1. M. Scott Peck, *The Road Less Traveled* (New York: Touchstone, 1978).
2. See Thomas Kuhn, *The Structure of Scientific Revolutions,* 3d ed. (Chicago: University of Chicago Press, 1996).
3. Jim Collins, "Level Five Leadership," *Harvard Business Review,* reprint R0101D.
4. "Chicago Park District A," UVA-OB-0618, www2.darden.edu/case/collection, teaching note.
5. See, for example, Ken Blanchard, *The One Minute Manager* (New York: William Morrow, 1982).
6. See Michael Beer, "Leading Change," Harvard Case Services, 488–037.
7. See Harold Leavitt, *Corporate Pathfinders : Building Vision and Values into Organizations* (Homewood, IL: Dow Jones-Irwin, 1986).
8. I credit my colleague Alex Horniman for introducing me to these ideas.
9. See Elisabeth Kübler-Ross, *On Death and Dying* (New York: Collier Books, 1993).
10. Thanks again to Alex Horniman.
11. John Kotter, *Leading Change* (Boston: Harvard Business School Press, 1996).
12. Edwin E. Nevis, Jon Lancourt, and Helen G. Vassallo, *Intentional Revolutions* (San Francisco: Jossey-Bass, 1996).

Suggestions for Additional Reading

Collins, James. *From Good to Great.* New York: HarperCollins, 2001.

Hammer, Michael, and James Champy. *Reengineering the Corporation.* New York: Harper Business, 1993.

Kotter, John. *Leading Change.* Boston: Harvard Business School Press, 1996.

Nevis, Edwin E., Jon Lancourt, and Helen G. Vassallo. *Intentional Revolutions.* San Francisco: Jossey-Bass, 1996.

O'Toole, James. *Leading Change.* San Francisco: Jossey-Bass, 1995.

Quinn, Robert. *Deep Change.* San Francisco: Jossey-Bass, 1997.

Schein, Edgar. *Process Consultation.* Reading, MA: Addison-Wesley, 1969.

Watzlawick, Paul, John H. Weakland, and Richard Fisch. *Change.* New York: Norton, 1974.

Conclusion

CHAPTER
16

Summary

L evel Three leadership is about making a difference below the surface. Whereas Level One leadership focuses on short-term behavior, Level Three leadership attempts to influence what people think and believe. Level One leadership has worked well enough for a very long time—well enough to guide the Industrial Age and to form large corporations that have supplied the world with a plethora of products and services. Level One leadership gives a manager a sense of accomplishment. She can *see* what people are doing and doesn't have to worry about what they're thinking and feeling. Level One leadership is inherently visible; you can see what people do, and most people can see what the consequences are if they don't respond. In a relatively orderly world, Level One leadership works well enough.

In our turbulent, fast-changing world of today, where decisions need to be made throughout an organization and where the information needed to make those decisions can be rapidly distributed, the principles and consequences of Level One leadership are breaking down. One person, one boss; vertical hierarchies; limited spans of control; clear functional and organizational boundaries; certainty about what to do; limited sharing of information; and clear repositories of expertise are fading. In their place, multiple "bosses," including suppliers, customers, people from various functions, and even subordinates; much flatter organizations based on ever-forming and reforming teams and the importance of current databases; very broad spans of influence rather than control; fuzzy boundaries between functions and organizations; mounds of uncertainty about what to do; widespread information sharing and exchange; and constantly shifting pools of knowledge and insight are taking their places.

In this kind of environment, the Industrial Age leadership notions of command and control or planning, organizing, motivating, and controlling are becoming absurdly out of date. Huge political entities in the former Soviet Union have broken down and been replaced with widely distributed, self-determined, more democratic countries. Large industrial corporations have been disassembled and reorganized into smaller, more independent firms. Although the political and industrial borders will continue to be mapped and melded in various ways, the people of the world in large part will no longer accept circumstances in which they have less control over their lives and choices of futures. Controlling is giving way to coordinating, and coordinating implies a respect for underlying beliefs and values in a way that controlling did not.

There will continue to be Level One leaders (although in our lexicon this phrase is a misnomer because to the extent that a person with power exercises that power without regard for the followers' voluntary responses, I have argued he is no longer a leader but merely a person who exercises power) in the world. Part of the reason for this will be psychological. Many people grow up with a need to control their environment and will view people as a part of that environment. Further, there will continue to be Level One companies in the world run by Level One Leaders. These companies' cultures will continue to care little for the thoughts and feelings of the people who work within them, and they will continue to focus on short-term financial goals, many of which will hinge upon the shareholders' rewards to the subversion of other worthy objectives. Many of them may even survive for lengthy periods of time.

But increasingly, the organizations that will thrive and grow in the Information Age will be based on Level Three leadership. Their employees will not only do what they are asked to do but will also believe in it and believe in it deeply. Successful Information Age organizations will borrow from the not-for-profit organizations of the Industrial Age to understand why people will work hard yielding their best efforts for little or no pay. These Level Three firms will understand the causal networks that encourage people to work their hardest and brightest voluntarily and will know that unless they can successfully elicit this kind of work, they will fall farther and farther behind their competitors that understand how to do it.

People in Level Three organizations will be bonded to their companies by more than paychecks and fear of unemployment. They will believe in what the company is doing. They will have information available to them about how the company is doing. They will understand the importance of delighting the customer in a world where alternatives sources are proliferating. And they will understand that unless the employees are delighted, the customers will not be.

Those who desire to create Level Three organizations will face many challenges. First, there is the historical momentum of the Industrial Age and the principles that it taught. If Thomas Kuhn is right about the nature of scientific revolutions and the time it takes to realize one, it will take one or more generations in each organization before a new Level Three model of leadership will take hold.[1] This process will spread slowly through each industry. Richard Walton, a long-time researcher of high-performance workplaces, has noted the slowness of this transition.[2]

Second, the poverty endemic to many parts of the world will slow the spread of the Information Age. When people are unable to access and use computer-based information links, they are left to the information-sharing processes of the Industrial Age and remain subject to its Level One characteristics. Yet education and the resultant power to access the Internet, to become facile with intra-organizational networks, will accelerate this process. Already television and nearly global satellite-based broadcasting has changed the way people in hitherto isolated areas see the world and their personal possibilities. A major challenge of the Information Age will be to manage the increasingly obvious differences between the haves and the have-nots. When people in Eastern Europe or Southeastern Asia view "Lifestyles of the Rich and Famous" on television and see the opulent homes that they live in, the lovely places they visit for vacations, and total lack of care they have for things financial, aspirations, desires, and even demands are born. Increasingly, people will insist on self-determination, first politically and then economically.

The Information Age will make this possible. Unlike the Industrial Age, in which people could be kept in the dark about options, the Information Age will inform poor people about how others live—and therefore about how *they* could live. The challenge then will be to manage the perceived gaps in effort and reward, to create a world in which fairness based on contribution will guide reward systems. Level Three leaders will understand this and, with help from the moral foundation of leadership, will recognize and codevelop reward systems in which all can participate.

A third challenge to face in the Information Age will be the flexibility given to invade and protect people's lives. With cell phones, faxes, and Internet connections, people can work from any venue. This can be a help or a hindrance. Some people will allow their work to control their lives no matter where they may be. Others will face the dilemma of balancing their personal and professional lives. When one has access to growing volumes of work-related data from any location, it becomes more difficult to manage the other aspects of life—health, family, rejuvenation, and relationships. The messages sent when one says, "Hang on for a moment. The other line is ringing" or "I'll be out in a minute dear, I just need to clear my [58] e-mail messages" are decidedly more invasive to personal and family life than some overtime during the Industrial Age.

Fourth, Information Age leaders will need to find ways of developing Level Three influences in a population that might not be so willing to respond. Our graduate school of business administration is a good example of this. During construction of a new building during the early 1990s, the decision was made to put Internet and e-mail connections at each seat in the new classrooms. Later, in a case discussion–oriented environment, the entire tenor of the classroom was changed. Instructors entering the room found that they were not looking at the faces of 60 students. Rather, the faces had been replaced with 60 laptop lids. Some joked that the students should be required to paste a photograph of themselves on their laptops so the faculty could tell who they were. Furthermore, the faculty soon discovered that the students were e-mailing each other back and forth during class. While one student was speaking, several others were commenting and carrying on a simultaneous live discussion. Not only that, they were e-mailing their friends in other sections, learning what was going on in other classes at the same time. The faculty began worrying about this loss of control, and a similar phenomenon has hit leaders of corporations. Whether they want it to or not, the Information Age has changed the face of power in institutions by distributing it more widely and deeply than ever before. People at lower ranks of organizations are now able to communicate with each other and to get information about the business that makes it much less easy for leaders to control them. Orwell's fear of Big Brother should have been, according to many a disgruntled modern manager raised in the Industrial Age, a fear of Little Sibling.[3] For many managers living during the present transition from the Industrial Age to the Information Age, coming to terms with this loss of control is a major career and professional issue.

Level Three leadership also implies getting below the surface by not just accepting the first acceptable solution that comes along. Although Herb Simon won a Nobel Prize for his clarification of the concept of satisficing, Level Three leaders are not willing to settle for the first tolerable solution they hit upon. Forcing people to go to work, to break a strike, to stay late, or to do anything may be the easiest thing at the moment, but in the mid and long runs, this Level One approach creates much more difficulty. Level Three leaders will think beyond the immediate and work hard, mentally and emotionally, to identify other avenues that ultimately impinge on their associates' hearts and heads as well as their bodies. If all human interaction is some form of exchange in which the currencies may be ill defined, what kind of currency is necessary for a person to exchange part of her innermost motivations?

Herein lies a paradox. On the one hand, one may argue that if all human interactions are exchanges, then they are all intrinsically Level One phenomena. On the other hand, I argue that if we accept that each human is the ultimate controller of his own motivations and values and beliefs, then the question is, What currency does that person need to voluntarily exchange part of those central motivations and values and the efforts that are associated with them with an institution or leader? It seems apparent to me that only when the institutional offerings are consistent with the individual's underlying motivations and values will that individual give her utmost for the institution. Consider all those who work for little pay in rescue squads across the country. In Albemarle County, Virginia, most of the rescue squads are completely voluntary. People have full-time jobs and then offer to serve on the rescue squad vehicles, which often involves lengthy training and long night hours and weekends. Consider the PJs, the rescue swimmers who work with the U.S. Coast Guard and are willing to risk their lives and families' livelihoods (modest as they are) for the lives of others (the smart and the not-so-smart alike) at sea.[4] Consider the volunteer nurses and hospital aides throughout the world who give their own time and talent and energy to help others, many of whom are admittedly dying. Why do these people do this? Because they believe in what they're doing. These activities match their highest values for human life and service. These are extraordinary commitments. These are the kind of commitments that yield world-class service.

Perhaps you believe that this kind of commitment is not possible in business, and in many corporations, you may be right. How can one compare saving people's lives at sea in a storm with making ball bearings or fire extinguishers? On the other hand, what is the alternative? If a competitor in your industry can figure out a way to create a working environment in which people can bring their bodies, minds, and hearts to work and in which they can work wholeheartedly for a bigger purpose, what will your organization do? Over time, unless you find a similar way to engage people, your company will fall behind. The service, the quality, the customer focus, the enthusiasm, all of which characterize a Level Three organization, will not be there, and your customers will slowly at first and then more rapidly migrate to the companies that can give superior value for the same cost.

This is why I have written this book: to outline a structured set of ways in which one can begin to think about and perhaps begin to practice leading below the surface. Level Three leadership is not about trying out the latest fad and sticking it like a Band-Aid over a deep wound. Rather, it's about thinking beyond the superficial and developing a set of skills that will allow one to create a strong vision when none is apparent, to develop deeper relationships where none historically have been invited, and to organize in a way that will tend to perpetuate those deeper connections when one moves on.

To this end, the book describes the changing context in which we now find ourselves. This description outlines the ways in which deep underlying beliefs about business and enterprise are shifting. It includes a consideration of the way in which rapidly changing information technology is shaping the new organizational forms. And it implies the need for a sturdy, general model of leadership that incorporates much of what we learned in the Industrial Age and yet leaves room for the new realities of the Information Age.

This four-wheel-drive model of leadership includes four main elements: self, task, others, and organization. The book argues that who you are makes a big difference as to whether you can lead or not but that this alone is not enough. A big part of an effective leadership outcome is the view that the leader, you, take of the strategic tasks facing you, your work group, and your organization. The book offers a summary of historical ways of thinking about strategy and some newer principles of strategic thinking and invites you to practice them. The book maintains that unless you are able to develop these strategic thinking skills, you will be at a disadvantage compared with your peers.

The book then posits that the quality of your relationships with others has a major impact on whether they will accept your view of the strategic challenges facing them. If you are able to build your attempts to influence on a moral foundation and then to communicate clearly and effectively with some stamina, you might be able to make something happen.

Finally, the book argues that unless you are an organizational designer, your efforts at influencing and guiding others will be hampered by the constraints that every organization imposes on its employees. The book states that unless you can not only design organizations that fit your view of the strategic challenges but also understand and master the change process that is continually necessary to move collections of people from one way of doing things to another, your efforts at leadership will fail.

These three thrusts, strategic thinking, leading others, and leading by design, are presented as critical causes of positive leadership outcomes. I hold that outcomes can be measured in terms of effectiveness, efficiency, learning and growth, and satisfaction. And I argue that unless you can see below the surface and develop deeper skills in each of these three areas, your efforts will tend to be superficial and fleeting.

My sincere hope is that the concepts, ideas, models, and principles presented in this book will help you become a more effective leader in your personal life, in your professional life, and in your community. I believe this will happen if you think about and accept the principle of Level Three leadership, that world-class leaders are values leaders, that they think about and intend to influence the central values, assumptions, beliefs, and expectations of those they work with. They understand that unless they do this, their efforts will be like small meteor showers, scarring the surface but leaving no deep and lasting change.

SUMMARY OF BASIC PRINCIPLES INTRODUCED IN THIS BOOK

1. We are in the midst of a major managerial paradigm shift that is transforming what it means to be an effective leader.
2. Leadership is a function of many elements working together. These include individual characteristics, forces in the environment, strategic opportunities envisioned by the leader, quality of relationships with followers, and appropriateness of the organization for the leader, task, and followers.
3. Leadership is the ability and the willingness to influence others to do what you want them to do voluntarily.
4. Leadership is about change, and change requires persistence in the development of new habits and routines. Effective leaders understand and use the mechanics and processes of managing change.
5. Leadership is also about ethics and moral behavior. You cannot be an effective leader without taking a moral stand. Effective leadership and extraordi-

nary performance are based on a foundation of moral principles: truth telling, promise keeping, fairness, respect for the individual, and respect for demonstrated competency.

6. Leadership occurs at three levels: behavioral, cognitive, and value. Level Three leadership is more difficult and more powerful.

7. Your personal leadership emanates from your central beliefs and core values and assumptions. In effect, who you are as a leader defines who you are as a person.

8. Individual leadership skills can be clustered into three groups: visioning, garnering commitment, and managing progress toward the vision.

9. People's behavior is a function of their genetics and memetics. Their underlying values, assumptions, beliefs, and expectations shape what they do. Level Three leadership understands and uses this perspective.

10. Motivating leadership is, in large part, a function of clear and compelling vision of what could be. This applies to yourself in terms of your life's dream and purpose as well as to your work group and your organization.

11. Leadership is an act of engagement. When you truly engage in something, you become a leader. Engagement is a function of personal commitments usually based on personal resonance.

12. Leadership involves mobilizing the talents of others, which means clarifying what others have to offer and offering attractive invitations to them to engage in your cause.

13. People work at things they are rewarded for; they work hard for things they believe in.

14. Leadership is closely related to time. Although many speak of future-oriented leadership, much of leadership is about getting people to deal with the present.

15. Language is the primary tool of leadership. Effective leaders know, understand, have skill with, and can use with wisdom various forms of language.

16. Interpersonal leadership skills are based on respect for competency, trust in consistent caring, fair exchanges, and genuine willingness to be influenced.

17. Level Three leaders are effective strategic thinkers. They are able to articulate the mission, vision, values, and strategy as well as the short-term operating goals of their organizations. They realize that these elements are essential to connecting with their followers.

18. Leadership is about designing organizations that support what others have to offer to the leader's enterprise. Most of these organizational forms are different from the forms developed in the previous era.

19. Leaders are first and foremost leaders of themselves. They work hard to see a higher vision and to make it come to pass.

These principles have certain implications for your individual behavior as a leader. They suggest that if you are to be an effective leader, you will be

1. Clarifying your center
2. Clarifying what is possible and desirable
3. Clarifying what others can contribute
4. Supporting others so they can work
5. Relentless
6. Measuring and celebrating progress

The first three of these implications involve clarifying, which means bringing into sharper focus, developing, realizing, and using. Thus, the action implied is not a one-time thing but rather an ongoing process of discovery and utilization. An effective leader does not, for instance, simply clarify her center and then leave it for the rest of her career. Rather, she must be periodically reviewing, renewing, and recommitting to what lies at her core. The participial form of the verbs was used to imply this meaning.

Leadership is demanding and draining. It requires intense mental, physical, emotional, spiritual, and social effort. Many retreat from these demands, and our world, our businesses, and our communities are the worse for it. We hope that your exploration of leadership through this volume will have challenged you, changed you, and motivated you to reach for higher ideals and visions. We hope it will have tested and stretched your leadership skills. I hope that as a result of this effort, you see more clearly yourself, your visions, the value others have to offer, and ways and means of combining those to make the world, your business, your community, and your life a better place. Each of us can make a difference, can be effective within our circles of influence, and can improve the situation around us. I hope you will make the choice to do so.

NOTES

Note: To quickly access all *Harvard Business Review* reprints listed here, go to www.hbsp .harvard.edu/hbsp/adv_search.asp, insert the reprint number in the Product Number field, and click Search.

1. In *The Structure of Scientific Revolutions*, 3d ed. (Chicago: University of Chicago Press, 1996), Thomas Kuhn discovered that even after irrefutable scientific evidence backing up a new paradigm had been amassed, scientists who had been raised in the old paradigm literally had to die off before the new one was accepted and incorporated into general scientific thought. This may also be true of business organizations, especially given the larger and therefore stronger momentum of organizational culture that exists in many corporations. Although scientists often work in smaller organizations and even in relative isolation, corporations have a strong institutional learning process that propagates former thinking through myriads of processes and policies.

2. See Richard Walton, "From Compliance to Commitment," *Harvard Business Review*, reprint 85219.

3. *1984,* written by George Orwell (whose real name was Eric Blair) and published in 1949, at the birth of the Information Age, by Harcourt, Brace and Jovanovich in New York, told a story of how information was supposed to give control to a centralized authority, nicknamed Big Brother by the masses.

4. See Sebastian Junger, *The Perfect Storm* (New York: W. W. Norton, 1997), for a description of the training and professional lifestyles of these extraordinary men.

Supplementary Materials

Level Three Leadership Program Workbook

General Leadership Model 258

Strategic Challenges I'm Facing 258

Leadership Implications of My Strategic Challenges. 259

Organizations I Expect to Lead 260

My Core Leadership Principles 260

Self-Assessment on the Six Steps to Effective Leadership 261

Charter for My Organization 262

Charter for My Work Group. 263

Charter for Myself 264

Keep, Lose, Add 265

Systems and Processes That Need Redesigning 266

My Life's Dream. 267

Activities in Which I Resonate 268

Ways to Bring Resonance to Work. 268

Ways I Want to Improve My Leadership Language. 269

Leading Change 270

Intelligence Self-Assessment. 271

Building Commitment 272

What Do I Want to Do This Year? 273

Central Point 274

GENERAL LEADERSHIP MODEL

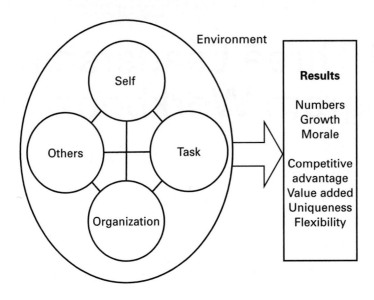

STRATEGIC CHALLENGES I'M FACING

A *strategic challenge* is anything that affects my own, my work group's, or my organization's ability to develop and maintain a competitive advantage.

A *competitive advantage* is defined by (1) superior value added, (2) difficulty in imitation, and (3) enhanced flexibility.

Organization _____
_____
_____
_____
_____

Work group _____
_____
_____
_____
_____

Self _____
_____
_____
_____
_____

LEADERSHIP IMPLICATIONS
OF MY STRATEGIC CHALLENGES

What kind of *leadership traits* and abilities will be necessary to meet the strategic challenges mentioned above?

Organization leadership   _____

_____

Work group leadership   _____

_____

Self-leadership   _____

Organizations I Expect to Lead
(from now until I pass)

1. _____
   _____
   _____
   _____

2. _____
   _____
   _____
   _____

3. _____
   _____
   _____

4. _____
   _____
   _____
   _____

5. _____
   _____
   _____
   _____

6. _____
   _____
   _____
   _____

7. _____
   _____
   _____
   _____

8. _____
   _____
   _____
   _____

9. _____
   _____
   _____
   _____

10. _____
   _____
   _____
   _____

My Core Leadership Principles
(that will guide me as I assume
responsibility)

1. _____
   _____
   _____
   _____

2. _____
   _____
   _____
   _____

3. _____
   _____
   _____

4. _____
   _____
   _____
   _____

5. _____
   _____
   _____
   _____

6. _____
   _____
   _____
   _____

7. _____
   _____
   _____
   _____

8. _____
   _____
   _____
   _____

9. _____
   _____
   _____
   _____

10. _____
   _____
   _____
   _____

SELF-ASSESSMENT ON THE SIX STEPS TO EFFECTIVE LEADERSHIP

Give yourself an honest self-assessment on each of these personal leadership characteristics and note the basis for your assessment. Read Chapter 7 before responding. In case you wish to use it, a more detailed assessment instrument follows later.

Scale: 1 = I am not very good at this, 2 = I am below average on this, 3 = I am average on this, 4 = I am above average on this, 5 = I am very good at this.

Clarifying my center	1	2	3	4	5
Clarifying what's possible	1	2	3	4	5
Clarifying what others have to contribute	1	2	3	4	5
Supporting others so they can contribute	1	2	3	4	5
Relentlessness	1	2	3	4	5
Celebrating progress	1	2	3	4	5

CHARTER FOR MY ORGANIZATION

Review Chapter 10 and particularly Chapter 11 before responding to the next three exercises.

Mission
_____
_____
_____
_____
_____
_____
_____

Vision
_____
_____
_____
_____
_____
_____

Key operating values
_____
_____
_____
_____
_____
_____

Strategic path
_____
_____
_____
_____
_____
_____

Key operating goals/
milestones
_____
_____
_____
_____
_____
_____
_____

CHARTER FOR MY WORK GROUP

Mission
_____
_____
_____
_____
_____
_____
_____
_____
_____

Vision
_____
_____
_____
_____
_____
_____
_____

Key operating values
_____
_____
_____
_____
_____
_____
_____

Strategic path
_____
_____
_____
_____
_____
_____

Key operating goals
and milestones
_____
_____
_____
_____
_____
_____
_____

CHARTER FOR MYSELF

Mission _____
_____
_____
_____
_____
_____
_____
_____

Vision _____
_____
_____
_____
_____
_____

Key operating values _____
_____
_____
_____
_____
_____
_____

Strategic path _____
_____
_____
_____
_____
_____

Key operating goals
and milestones _____
_____
_____
_____
_____
_____

KEEP, LOSE, ADD

Managing Personal Change and Blind Spots

Following your class discussion of personal blind spots and the personal change process, consider your own leadership style as you now understand it and note the aspects of your leadership style that you'd like to keep, lose, or add.

Keep	Lose	Add

SYSTEMS AND PROCESSES THAT NEED REDESIGNING

After reading the chapter on leading organizations, think about the systems and processes in your organization that aren't working well. List these and begin thinking about how you'd redesign if given the chance.

Dysfunctional systems

A better design would be

MY LIFE'S DREAM

After participating in the session on resonance or reading the chapter on resonance and leadership, consider what your internal life's dream is and write it down. Don't be frustrated if you find this difficult. It may take you some time, even months or years, to clarify it. As a way of moving toward this clarification, use this page to note times and experiences when you felt resonance. If you wish a more detailed exploration of this concept, refer to the exercise included later in this volume. Remember to distinguish between dreams and goals.

ACTIVITIES IN WHICH I RESONATE

After listening to the class or reading the chapter on resonance and leadership, list activities in the past in which you've experienced resonance. Note what you were doing and how it felt. You may wish to use the "Life's Dream's Exercise" that appears later in this workbook.

_____
_____
_____
_____
_____
_____
_____
_____
_____
_____
_____
_____
_____
_____
_____
_____
_____
_____
_____
_____

WAYS TO BRING RESONANCE TO WORK

_____
_____
_____
_____
_____
_____
_____
_____
_____
_____
_____
_____
_____
_____
_____
_____
_____
_____

WAYS I WANT TO IMPROVE
MY LEADERSHIP LANGUAGE

After a discussion of leadership language as outlined in the chapter on leading others, think about the basic concepts and consider how you'd like to strengthen your ability to communicate as a leader.

Clear: _____

Respectful: _____

Stimulating: _____

Congruent: _____

LEADING CHANGE

After the discussion of CQ (in Chapter 8) and reading the chapter on leading change, consider what you need to change to become a more effective leader. Note your thoughts here.

What Needs to Change in

Myself: _____
_____
_____
_____
_____
_____
_____
_____
_____
_____
_____
_____

My work group: _____
_____
_____
_____
_____
_____
_____
_____
_____
_____

My organization: _____
_____
_____
_____
_____
_____
_____
_____
_____
_____

INTELLIGENCE SELF-ASSESSMENT

Following the discussion of Leadership and Intelligence and/or reading the chapter, assess your intelligence in each of the following categories.

	Low	**Medium**	**High**
Intellectual Intelligence (IQ):			
Inherited abilities			
Curiosity			
Discipline			
Range of interests			
Emotional Intelligence (EQ):			
Recognizing emotions in yourself			
Ability to manage your emotions			
Using productive self-talk			
Avoiding emotional hijackings			
Social Intelligence (SQ):			
Recognizing emotions in others			
Caring about the emotionality of others			
Counseling others in managing their emotions			
Change Intelligence (CQ):			
Recognizing the need to change			
Understanding the change process			
Skill in managing the change process			

BUILDING COMMITMENT

After the discussion of leading organizations, organizational glue, and the importance of aligning organizational factors (the southern ball in the general model), consider what you can do to build commitment to your work in yourself and those you work with.

Things I can do to build commitment in

Myself: _____

_____

_____

_____

_____

_____

_____

_____

_____

_____

_____

My Work Group: _____

_____

_____

_____

_____

_____

_____

_____

_____

My Organization: _____

_____

_____

_____

_____

_____

_____

_____

_____

WHAT DO I WANT TO DO THIS YEAR?

What are the most important things you want to accomplish this year with regard to developing your leadership skills and outcomes?

1. _____

   _____

2. _____

   _____

3. _____

   _____

4. _____

   _____

5. _____

   _____

6. _____

   _____

7. _____

   _____

8. _____

   _____

9. _____

   _____

10. _____

    _____

CENTRAL POINT

What's the most important thing you learned from the book or the course you used it in about becoming a more influential leader to yourself, to your work group, and to your organization? If you focus on too many goals, you may not reach any of them. If you pick one and stick to it, you may make some real progress.

Survey of
Managerial Style

Managers constantly identify desirable behavior both in themselves and in others with whom they work. Much of this behavior takes on a characteristic pattern. Knowing something about these different patterns may help us to become more productive professionals. This instrument measures an aspect of managerial style. Please complete all items, then score and interpret them according to the instructions that follow.

Note that people will often rate questions like those included in this packet in terms of how they think they **should** answer or in terms of the way that they would **like** to be. This is not what is wanted here. Please answer the items in terms of how much you agree with a statement as it applies to what you *actually do.* Give careful thought to your answers and remember that your results are only valuable to the extent that they reflect what you do, not what you think you should do. If you are a student now, consider the last job you held as you answer these questions. If you have not worked before, think about what you think your first job experience will be like.

As you complete the survey, please answer *ALL* items. You will probably note that some of the items on the survey are very similar; this is necessary to insure that the survey information is statistically reliable. Please rate each item INDEPENDENTLY without regard to your responses to previous items. Finally, please note that there are no right or wrong answers on this survey.

SURVEY OF MANAGERIAL STYLE

Section I: General Information

1. How many major organizational levels are there in your organization from the chief executive to the lowest rank? In figuring the numbers of levels in your organization, it may help to sketch out the levels on the back of this page.

   Number of Major Levels in Your Organization: _____

2. If the chief executive is at level one in your organization, at what numerical level are you?

   Your Organizational Level: _____

3. How many people report directly to you?

   Number of Direct Reports: _____

4. Overall, how many people are in your reporting line of authority? For example, in item 3, if you mentioned four direct reports and the first has 30 employees, the second has 49, the third has 12, and the fourth has 29, and none of their subordinates has subordinates, then the overall number in your line of authority is 120.

   Overall Number in Your Reporting Line of Authority: _____

Section II: Management Style Items

Directions: For the 30 items below, read each item and rate it in terms of how much you agree that the item describes you. On the scale, SA = strongly agree, MA = moderately agree, LA = slightly agree, LD = slightly disagree, MD = moderately disagree, and SD = strongly disagree.

Item	Agreement			Disagreement		
	SA	MA	LA	LD	MD	SD
1. Managing company progress toward a vision represents a major portion of what I do in my job.	( )	( )	( )	( )	( )	( )
2. I am methodical in the way that I carry out my job responsibilities.	( )	( )	( )	( )	( )	( )
3. Most of my work-related activity is in thinking about the future of my organization.	( )	( )	( )	( )	( )	( )
4. I am a real take-charge type of person.	( )	( )	( )	( )	( )	( )
5. Garnering commitment in people toward meeting some organizational goal represents a major portion of what I do in my job.	( )	( )	( )	( )	( )	( )

Item	Agreement			Disagreement		
	SA	**MA**	**LA**	**LD**	**MD**	**SD**
6. I am very decisive. When I must make a decision, I stick to it.	( )	( )	( )	( )	( )	( )
7. Whenever I must present information to a group, I typically speak without notes or outlines.	( )	( )	( )	( )	( )	( )
8. I focus my professional energies on envisioning the future of the organization.	( )	( )	( )	( )	( )	( )
9. Whenever I must present information to a group, I write out the speech, then read it to the group.	( )	( )	( )	( )	( )	( )
10. I am self-confident.	( )	( )	( )	( )	( )	( )
11. I focus my professional energies on getting people in my organization to build their commitments to our organization and its goals.	( )	( )	( )	( )	( )	( )
12. I learn best by diving in and seeing if something works or doesn't work.	( )	( )	( )	( )	( )	( )
13. Most of my work-related activity is watching and managing indicators of organizational activity.	( )	( )	( )	( )	( )	( )
14. I spend most of my professional time considering views of what my organization can become.	( )	( )	( )	( )	( )	( )
15. Most of my work-related activity is in pulling people together for the purpose of attaining an organizational goal.	( )	( )	( )	( )	( )	( )
16. I think that the most important aspect of my job is preparing for future needs of the organization.	( )	( )	( )	( )	( )	( )
17. I manage my professional time efficiently.	( )	( )	( )	( )	( )	( )
18. I think that the most important aspect of my job is persuading people to accept my vision for our organization.	( )	( )	( )	( )	( )	( )
19. I make an effort to participate in group activities.	( )	( )	( )	( )	( )	( )
20. I focus my professional energies on managing and monitoring my organization's progress toward a goal.	( )	( )	( )	( )	( )	( )
21. Thinking about what my organization might look like in the future represents a major portion of what I do in my job.	( )	( )	( )	( )	( )	( )
22. I am a predictable person. I think that people know what to expect of me.	( )	( )	( )	( )	( )	( )
23. At work I try to foster close personal relationships with my coworkers.	( )	( )	( )	( )	( )	( )

Item	Agreement			Disagreement		
	SA	MA	LA	LD	MD	SD
24. I spend most of my professional time in managing company progress toward a vision.	( )	( )	( )	( )	( )	( )
25. Solving problems in unstructured situations is an important part of what I do.	( )	( )	( )	( )	( )	( )
26. I would rather do something myself than delegate responsibility to someone else.	( )	( )	( )	( )	( )	( )
27. I learn on my own first, then apply what I have learned.	( )	( )	( )	( )	( )	( )
28. I spend most of my professional time convincing others in my organization to carry out a plan.	( )	( )	( )	( )	( )	( )
29. Whenever I must present information to a group, I speak while using an outline as a reference.	( )	( )	( )	( )	( )	( )
30. I think that the most important aspect of my job is looking at how my company is performing and determining what it needs to do to stick to the company plan.	( )	( )	( )	( )	( )	( )

NOTE! Do not read the rest of this note until you have completed the questions that come before!

Scoring and Interpreting Your Data

The Theory

This questionnaire was designed to measure aspects of your leadership style and preferences. Measuring leadership is not easy. Social scientists have been arguing for decades, even centuries, about the answer to the question, "What makes a good leader?" Out of this debate have emerged numerous theories about what makes a good leader. But these theories are often contradictory and confusing. We believe that, in spite of the controversy about what the concept of leadership comprises, a practical, immediate model of leadership would help focus the developmental efforts of managers on things they can begin doing now.

Given our reading of leadership studies and our observation of leaders in the world, we have concluded and suggest that leadership includes three fundamental clusters of skills and abilities: creating vision, garnering commitment to that vision, and monitoring and managing progress toward the realization of that vision.

Vision

Powerful leaders have a clear vision of where they want their organization to go. Vision is the view a person holds about what the organization will look like and be doing in the future. Obviously, some people have greater visions than others, and some have visions that extend further into the future than others, and some have visions that don't work or come to fruition. Each manager can, and we believe, ought to have a vision of his or her organization, what they think it can become, where they think it is going, how it should be operating, and what it should be like to work within it.

Vision is an essential part of leadership. Having a vision requires creativity; one must be able to think and see beyond the present time frame and beyond the usual options. The ability to see ahead and to see non-traditional alternatives are creative parts of leadership. So is the ability to frame the context of a business problem in broader terms that question current assumptions. The ability to incorporate these often unusual thoughts into a cohesive vision of the future of the company defines the first set of leadership skills.

Commitment

The ability to garner the commitment of others to one's vision is a key cluster of leadership skills. A leader may have a vision of what an organization can become, but unless others receive and become committed to that vision, it is unlikely to be realized. Leaders can create visions, but commitment, on the other hand, is offered by followers. It is this commitment of a group of followers that allows leaders to build their visions into organizational realities. A key task of the leader, then, is to garner commitment from those people who are critical to his or her success.

Leaders may foster commitment in a variety of ways: public communications, one-on-one interactions, involving others in the decision-making process, and by modeling commitment to an idea to name a few. However the successful leader goes about it, he or she is able to develop and maintain strong commitments from others to his or her vision for the organization.

Monitoring and Managing Progress Toward the Vision

The third cluster of skills in leadership that we see is the ability to monitor and manage progress of the organization toward the vision. For us, this is the bulk of "management" education today: ascertaining what the right measures are to monitor and the techniques and tools of getting those indicators to yield the right results. This aspect of leadership focuses on the **details** of the business. That we place monitoring and management as a subset of leadership does not denigrate it. Rather it points out that while managers can indeed be leaders, in our view they need to augment their skills with the visionary and commitment building skills outlined above. To us, management is a component of leadership. Ensuring that deadlines are met, objectives are achieved, and budgets are used appropriately are valuable and necessary (but not sufficient) leadership skills.

LEADERSHIP AND THE SURVEY OF MANAGERIAL STYLE (SMS)

Although some writers have drawn a provocative and dichotomous distinction between leadership and management, we believe they are closely related and that a consideration of the fluid relationship between them is more productive. Hence, we assert that leadership is not so much a question of whether someone is either a manager or a leader, but rather how much emphasis one places on the component skills of leadership of which management is one. Knowing something about how one tends to emphasize creating vision, garnering commitment, and monitoring and managing progress toward the vision can help one in several ways. We'll outline some of those, but first, let's score the data you have generated.

Parts I and II of the SMS are designed to gather general information about you and to measure your self-perception of your work behavior with regard to each of the three clusters mentioned above. From these data, you can begin to construct a picture of your leadership profile, that is, how much you emphasize leadership overall and how much you emphasize the three different clusters of leadership as outlined previously. With these data, you can begin to consider how strong your desire to be a leader is and how your behavior is distributed across the three dimensions of leadership.

SCORING YOUR DATA

Step 1.   On the scoring form on that follows, you will see that values are associated with each point on the scale used in Section II of the survey:
For each section of the scoring form, indicate the score for each of the items listed. For example, if you checked "slightly agree" for item 3 and "agree" for item 8, your scores for these items would be 4 and 5, respectively. Please note that in Section II scoring, not all items are scored. The extra items in Section II of the survey are included to control measurement error and are not included in the individual scoring procedure.

Step 2.   Sum the scores in each column to derive scores for vision, commitment, and management.

Step 3.   Sum the scores for vision, commitment, and management to derive your total score.

Step 4.   Compute proportional values for vision, commitment and management by dividing the scale score by the total score.

Step 5.   Next, complete the SMS Profile two pages hence. The concentric circles represent varying strengths of leadership: the larger the circle, the greater the interest in leadership. The letters associated with each circle correspond to the total score obtained in Section II of the survey. Find the circle that corresponds to your total score in Section II and trace the circle with a heavy marking pen.

Step 6.   In the scoring profile, there are 16 pie segments that you can use conveniently to create your profile. First, starting anywhere, draw a solid line from the center of the profile diagram out to the circle corresponding with your total score. (A, B, C, D, or E). Then, note that each dotted pie segment represents about 22 degrees (22.5* exactly) out of the 360 degrees in a circle. If your V score were 40% of your total score, then .40 of 360 = 144 degrees. 144/22 degrees for each dotted segment = 6.5, so you would count 6.5 segments around the circle from your first line and draw a second one from the center to the circumference. This will be your "V" segment. Do this for one of your other scores to produce a pie chart with three segments, one each for V, C, and M. Label each segment with their corresponding V, C, or M.

Note: When you have finished scoring your data, you should have a pie chart with three divisions in it. The size of the pie reflects your overall interest in being a leader. The size of each of the three wedges (one each for creating vision, garnering commitment, and monitoring and managing progress toward the vision), indicates the relative strength of each leadership skill area. When you have completed the profile, proceed to the interpretation section.

SMS Scoring Form

Score your responses as shown below.

Strongly agree	= 6
Moderately agree	= 5
Slightly agree	= 4
Slightly disagree	= 3
Moderately disagree	= 2
Strongly disagree	= 1

Item	**Score**	**Item**	**Score**	**Item**	**Score**
Item 3	_____	Item 5	_____	Item 1	_____
Item 8	_____	Item 11	_____	Item 13	_____
Item 14	_____	Item 15	_____	Item 20	_____
Item 16	_____	Item 18	_____	Item 24	_____
Item 21	_____	Item 28	_____	Item 30	_____
Total Vision	_____	Total Commitment	_____	Total Management	_____

TOTAL SCORE SECTION II (Vision + Commitment + Management) = _____

Note: Maximum Scale Score = 30, Minimum Scale Score = 5

Score divided by Total Score =	*% Score*	*× 360 = Degrees*	*/by 22 = Segments*
Vision			
Commitment			
Management			

Survey of Managerial Style Profile

Total Score: A = 15–29 B = 30–44 C = 45–59 D = 60–74 E = 75–90

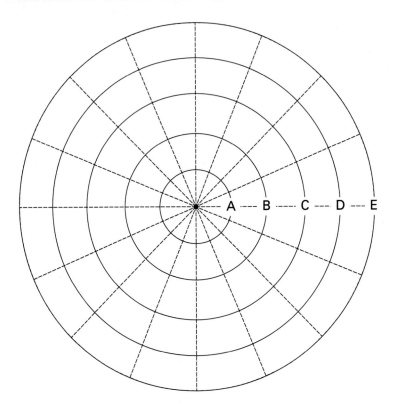

INTERPRETING YOUR PROFILE

The SMS Profile shows a graphical image of your current, self-assessed interest in leadership overall (the size of the circle you highlighted) and the relative strengths of your self-assessed skill clusters in visioning, garnering commitment, and managing progress toward your vision. Let's begin with the size of your circle.

The first thing to note is that it is not necessarily good or bad to desire to be or not to be a leader. People play different roles in life and in fact have influence in a wide variety of different situations. Leadership roles place demands on individuals just like all positions in life do; some people enjoy that set of demands while others do not. Regardless of how superficially attractive the recognition and apparent influence of leadership roles may be (e.g. "Wouldn't it be nice to be the divisional president?"), unless one's personal skills and interests fit the demands of a particular leadership position, one is not likely to be happy or successful in that position. Thus, the size of your leadership pie is not a value judgment about you or your worth in your organization or in society. Rather, it is a description of your present preferences regarding leadership activities and as such can be used by you to make more sound decisions about you and your work. If your pie is smaller than you "want" it to be, you might consider the various demands placed on leaders as reflected in the items in the survey. Do you really enjoy doing those activities? If not, perhaps you are not as enamored with being a leader as you may think at first blush. If you conclude you want your pie to be bigger, that is, that you'd like to have more interest in leadership activities, you might lay out a plan for involving yourself in more of those activities. Practice in leadership is like practice in other skill arenas—there's no substitute for it.

As for the relative strength of your V, C, and M segments, knowing something about your relative skills at visioning, garnering commitment, and managing progress can certainly help you to clarify where you're strong and where you might want to create a developmental plan. If your three V, C, and M segments are roughly the same size, you might conclude that your development as a leader so far has been relatively balanced. If one of the segments is in your view too large or too small, you might begin thinking about how you could develop that side of your leadership skill set. We offer some suggestions below.

Remember that these relative strengths are NOT fixed nor are they necessarily equally desirable. Each profile, of course, will have different implications for your planning, development activities, and perhaps for the way you manage your work. Each profile will have certain strengths and weaknesses. The goal here is to be more aware of your leadership skill set and to be consciously managing your development in each arena.

Sometimes people will generate a small V score and comment that, "Well, my current job doesn't require me to be visionary or to think strategically, so it's more a function of my job than of my personal characteristics." This is an interesting hypothesis. If it were true, we might expect to find a highly correlated relationship between "level in your organization" and "V score." The hypothesis seems to be that the higher our level, the more visioning our jobs will demand and the more V we will manifest. In fact, after collecting data from some 600 business executives over several years, and testing this hypothesis, it seems not to be true. A scatter diagram of the data points on "level in the organization" and "V score" shows points all over the quadrant, nothing approaching a diagonal trend line. This suggests that there are people with strong visioning skills and habits at virtually every level in most organizations. If this is the case, we might surmise that when it comes to being promoted, presumably to higher level jobs that require more and more visioning skills, all things being equal, the candidate with the stronger visioning skills is likely to be chosen. The implication here is clear: It's never too early to begin developing and strengthening your visioning skills.

Let's review some of the common VCM profile patterns. Look at the sample profiles shown below. What are the strengths and weaknesses of each of the profiles? Can you think of people, either at your work or in the public business eye, who seem to fit those profiles?

Now, compare your profile to the ones shown below and your analysis of them. What strengths and weaknesses did you list for "your" profile? If you wanted to "strengthen" your profile, what could you do?

INTERPRETIVE ALTERNATIVES

For each of the alternative profiles below, write your interpretation of what they might mean to the individuals or corporations that have them. See if you can identify individuals who fit each pattern.

SUGGESTIONS FOR STRENGTHENING YOUR SMS (VCM) PROFILE

If one of your VCM segments is smaller than you'd like, you may be thinking about things you could do over time to "round out" that flat spot on your profile. Again, this is a choice you make, not something you "have" to do in any sense. If you set this goal, here are some ideas for helping you do that.

Skill Cluster	Suggestions for Strengthening
Visioning	• Read journals and magazines on future trends (e.g., *Futurist*). • Spend five minutes a day thinking about where your organization should be in 10 years. • Read books on strategic thinking (e.g., *Every Business Is a Growth Business, Leading the Revolution, The Art of the Long View*). • Engage in conversations with colleagues about where you and they think the business should go in ten years. • Clarify where you'd like to be in ten years. • Think about where your business was ten years ago and the changes that have occurred, then try to project the same volume of change over the next ten years. • Identify the strategic challenges facing your firm and then think through what you'd do to manage each of them and why.
Garnering Commitment	• Reflect on your reputation among your peers. What is it? What would it take to clarify it? • What techniques do you usually use to influence your peers? How many different techniques do you use? What new ones could you add? • Practice listing and discussing the major pros and cons of key issues in the next several meetings you are in. See if you can demonstrate a balanced view to your peers on each topic/ issue rather than just buttressing your opinion with a one-sided view. • Try listening for complete understanding of your peers' ideas before you present your own. • Pay attention to how often you interrupt people. Try to reduce that frequency.

Managing Progress
Toward the Vision

- List on paper at the end of each day what you did, however small, that moved your organization toward its goals.
- List your goals (personal and professional) for the next three months.
- Invite those who report to you to do the same and then discuss them.
- Read your company's annual report in detail. Can you see progress? If not, what can you do to improve it?
- What could you delegate to others so you could focus on getting the important things done?
- How clear are you in performance reviews about exactly what you want the other person to do? How well do you listen to what they want to do and how you can help make that happen?

CONCLUSION

Leadership is comprised of many skills. This exercise was intended to help you identify your current self-assessment on three clusters of key leadership skills: visioning, garnering commitment toward your vision, and managing progress toward it. We hope that the scores on the V, C, and M scales and the graphical portrayal of their size and relative strengths will help you think about your own leadership profile and how you might go about strengthening it if your goal is to do so. This is only one instrument. There are many others. We encourage you to utilize all the data you can as you continue your quest to strengthen your leadership.

Group: _____   *VCM DATA FORM*   Date: ____/____/____

Directions: If asked to do so by your instructor, please fill out this data form, remove it from the survey packet, and give it to your instructor. Your data will be added to the SMS database for aggregate analysis.

1. **Number of Major Levels in Your Organization:**   _____
2. **Your Organizational Level:** (please express level as a number.)   _____
3. **Number of Direct Reports:**   _____
4. **Overall Number in Your Reporting Line of Authority:**   _____
5. **Your Age:**   _____
6. **Gender:** (please circle.)   Male   Female

Source	Score	Source	Score	Source	Score
Item 3	_____	Item 5	_____	Item 1	_____
Item 8	_____	Item 11	_____	Item 13	_____
Item 14	_____	Item 15	_____	Item 20	_____
Item 16	_____	Item 18	_____	Item 24	_____
Item 21	_____	Item 28	_____	Item 30	_____
Total Vision	_____	Total Commitment	_____	Total Management	_____

Life's Dream Exercise

This exercise is designed to help you identify your life's dream(s). We presume you have participated in an in-class discussion on resonance. To recap, we will explore two definitions of "life's dream." First, we refer to an "external life's dream" or LDext based on achievements and accomplishments. This is the typical definition that most people understand. LDext relates to one's early dreams in life to become something or accomplish something. Sometimes people refer to their LDext as, "what I want to be when I grow up." The central question for LDext is, "What do you dream of doing or becoming?" Examples might be "CEO of a company," or "a pilot" or "wealthy" or "a good parent." Many people refer to their life's dream when they mean their "goal in life." Goals are not dreams, especially as we are using the term here.

Second, we will also refer to "internal life's dream" or LDint. An internal life's dream is defined by our emotional experiencing. In other words, the target for understanding LDint is to focus on your feelings. For LDint, the question is, "How do you want to feel?" Examples might be "fully engaged" or "easy speed" or "productive" or "peaceful."

There is a danger in focusing too much either on LDext or LDint. If you focus on LDext to the exclusion of LDint, you may find yourself one day wealthy and miserable. If you focus on LDint to the exclusion of LDext, you may find yourself peaceful and poor. The challenge is to pay attention to both LDext and LDint. In our experience, most people focus heavily on LDext, so the more common error is to ignore and live relatively unaware of one's experience.

The questions below are designed to help you identify your LDext and LDint and to distinguish between them. In our experience, it is more difficult to define LDint than LDext. So, if you cannot write satisfactory answers on your first try, don't despair. It may take considerable thinking and reflection before you settle on a LDint that you are comfortable with. Some people seem to figure them out quickly, others may take a year or more to find the "right" wording and comprehensiveness.

IDENTIFYING YOUR LDEXT

Use the table below to draft your external life's dream or LDext.

1. What do you want to be doing at age
   (add 15 to your current age)?

   _____

2. What do you want to be at age
   (add 15 to your current age)?

   _____

3. What do you want people to
   remember you for?

   _____

4. What do you want to have written
   as your epitaph?

   _____

5. When you were little, what did you
   want to become? What happened
   to that dream?

   _____

6. If you were independently wealthy
   now, what would you Do?

   _____

7. Meld all of the answers above into
   one description of your LDext.

   _____

Note that all of these questions focus on things that you do or positions or titles that you hold. These can all be measured externally, that is, by observation by others.

IDENTIFYING YOUR LDINT

The next set of questions asks you to consider your emotional dream by focusing on feelings. Again, we presume you have had a discussion in class exploring the concept of resonance. Try to be as descriptive as you can while being concise. Finding the right words is key. Short answers like "happy" may be true, but not very helpful. How do you feel when you are happy? Long answers may be confusing and obfuscating. Try to distill your descriptions down to a phrase.

1. When in your life have you experienced "flow" or "resonance"? What were you doing?

_____

2. How did you feel when you were in flow? What aspects of it were satisfying to you?

_____

3. How are you feeling when you are performing at your peak and enjoying it?

_____

4. When were you most productive in your life? How did it feel?

_____

5. What kind of experience are you willing to work for?

_____

6. When you are "successful," how do you feel?

_____

7. Use your answers above to help you distill a single LDint here, HOW DO YOU WANT TO FEEL ON A DAILY BASIS?.

_____

8. What does it take to feel that way? (Preparation)

_____

9. What keeps you from feeling that way? (Obstacles)

_____

10. What does it take to get that feeling back? (Revisiting Your Dream)

_____

11. What are you willing to work for? (Energy Cycle)

We expect that this will not be your final draft of either your LDext or your LDint. We encourage you to keep these definitions handy and to reflect on them regularly and revise and refine them as your "eyes open" dreaming becomes clearer. The table below may help you track your life's dreams as they evolve over time.

Date	External Life's Dream (LDext)	Internal Life's Dream (LDint)

IMPLEMENTING YOUR LIFE'S DREAM (LDINT)

The next challenge after identifying your LDint will be to utilize it. In my experience, I have been so conditioned to focus on "to-do" lists and external achievements, it has become difficult to remember to focus on LDint and then refer to it regularly. In other words I, like millions of others, get caught in the "duty cycle" bouncing back and forth between work/preparation and obstacles and forget to "revisit my dream." Here are a couple of suggestions that will help you recognize how much you focus on LDext and to focus more on LDint.

1. Keep your LDint definition posted somewhere in your morning routine, perhaps in your bathroom to remind you of it.
2. Every time you find yourself making a "to-do" list for the day or week, be sure to add the full definition (not just "Live LDint") to your list.
3. If you keep a daybook or a PDA schedule, mark each day that you live your LDint with a symbol (perhaps an "LD" or "D"). At the end of the month as you scan your daybook, you can see how many days out of the month you lived your experiential dream and whether you're getting better at it or not.

Leadership Steps Assessment (LSA)

Leadership has many different components. This exercise offers the opportunity to assess your leadership activity on several of these dimensions. You will be asked in Part I to rate a series of descriptors (adjectives) for how well they currently describe you, and then in Part II to rate a number of sentences as to how well they apply to you. Note that you should answer regarding how you *currently* see yourself, not how you think that you should be or would like to be. There is no benefit to trying to "game" the assessment, just make the best assessment you can of how you *currently* are on items in the inventory.

Important: Please do not read ahead. After you have completed all of the items, then you can go on to the theory, scoring, and interpretation sections of the packet. These will explain the nature of the instrument and what it is measuring. If you read ahead, you may bias your responses and reduce the value of the data to you.

The instrument will take between thirty and sixty minutes to complete. Please leave yourself enough time to complete the instrument and work through the scoring and interpretation. When you are ready, please turn the page and begin.

This instrument was prepared by James G. Clawson, Ewan McNay, and Greg Beran. Adapted from UVA-OB-0733. Copyright © 2001 by the University of Virginia Darden School Foundation, Charlottesville, VA. All rights reserved. To order copies, send an e-mail to dardencases@virginia.edu. No part of this publication may be reproduced, stored in a retrieval system, used in a spreadsheet, or transmitted in any form or by any means—electronic, mechanical, photocopying, recording, or otherwise—without the permission of the Darden School Foundation.

PART I: DESCRIPTORS/ADJECTIVES

For this part, please reflect on your activities at work and your relationships with your colleagues at work. This section consists of eighteen items that are descriptors: adjectives that may or may not describe you. Rate yourself on the seven-point scales below where

1 means "does not describe me at all"
2 means "describes me rarely"
3 means "describes me occasionally"
4 means "describes me half of the time"
5 means "describes me more than half the time"
6 means "describes me usually" and
7 means "describes me all of the time"

		Never			**Half**			*Always*
1	Anchored	1	2	3	4	5	6	7
2	Dreamer	1	2	3	4	5	6	7
3	Encouraging	1	2	3	4	5	6	7
4	Supportive	1	2	3	4	5	6	7
5	Relentless	1	2	3	4	5	6	7
6	Congratulatory	1	2	3	4	5	6	7
7	Centered	1	2	3	4	5	6	7
8	Visionary	1	2	3	4	5	6	7
9	Sees the good in others	1	2	3	4	5	6	7
10	Reorganizer	1	2	3	4	5	6	7
11	Determined	1	2	3	4	5	6	7
12	Praising	1	2	3	4	5	6	7
13	Self-aware	1	2	3	4	5	6	7
14	Trend Spotter	1	2	3	4	5	6	7
15	Good coach	1	2	3	4	5	6	7
16	Organizational architect	1	2	3	4	5	6	7
17	Persistent	1	2	3	4	5	6	7
18	Rewards Others	1	2	3	4	5	6	7

This completes Part I of the assessment. Please go on to complete Part II without skipping ahead.

PART II: DESCRIPTIVE PHRASES

The items in this section are statements, which you may or may not agree describe you or your current beliefs. Remember that you are assessing your ***current behavior and beliefs,*** not how you think you should behave, ought to believe, or any other measure. As with Part I, you should rate each item on a scale from 1 to 7. Here, a score of 1 means "I disagree completely with this statement" or "I do not behave like this" while a score of 7, conversely, should be given to statements which you fully agree with, or behaviors that match very much with how you behave.

There are 18 statements in total; it will take you about fifteen minutes to complete this section. Be honest with yourself. If in doubt, remember that first impressions are often the best guide. If you are not now working, answer with regard to your last job.

		Does NOT describe me or my beliefs.				*Describes me or my beliefs VERY well.*		
19	I am clear on what I stand for.	1	2	3	4	5	6	7
20	I spend time envisioning what our company should become.	1	2	3	4	5	6	7
21	I look for the talents others have to offer.	1	2	3	4	5	6	7
22	I try to remove the barriers to getting good work done.	1	2	3	4	5	6	7
23	I am determined to achieve my goals.	1	2	3	4	5	6	7
24	I like to congratulate people on a job well done.	1	2	3	4	5	6	7
25	I could write down my core beliefs and values.	1	2	3	4	5	6	7
26	I enjoy imagining where we should be going.	1	2	3	4	5	6	7
27	I try to see what others have to contribute.	1	2	3	4	5	6	7
28	I often reorganize trying to find a better way.	1	2	3	4	5	6	7
29	I am persistent in my pursuits.	1	2	3	4	5	6	7
30	Good leaders reward progress openly.	1	2	3	4	5	6	7
31	I am clear on what I will and will not do to succeed.	1	2	3	4	5	6	7

32	I have a clear picture of what the company should be.	1	2	3	4	5	6	7
33	I look for people's strengths rather than their weaknesses.	1	2	3	4	5	6	7
34	Good leaders work hard to support their people and their efforts.	1	2	3	4	5	6	7
35	I never give up.	1	2	3	4	5	6	7
36	One should always praise progress however small.	1	2	3	4	5	6	7

This concludes Part II. Read Part III to learn about the theory underlying the instrument and how to score your responses.

PART III: THE THEORY

There are many theories about the elements that make up leadership. The exercise you completed, and the scoring you will do in a moment, are based on a model of leadership designed not only to describe necessary components of leadership but also to provide a framework for improving one's own leadership ability. This framework identifies six key leadership principles:

1. Clarifying your center,
2. Clarifying what's possible,
3. Clarifying what others have to contribute,
4. Supporting others so they can contribute,
5. Relentless assertion, and
6. Celebrating progress.

Let's make sure the six concepts are clear, then we'll lay out the scoring system. We use the term "clarifying" in the first three concepts because we believe that one may never really finalize one's core values, vision for the future, or the ways in which others can help achieve that vision. Each of these will continue to emerge and evolve as we progress through life. The clarifying measures here refer to on-going processes of leadership.

1.   CLARIFYING YOUR CENTER. We use the term "center" in the sense in which it is often used in Asian philosophy to refer to one's center of gravity or one-point either physically (as in martial arts traditions) or spiritually (as in meditative practices). By "clarifying your center," we mean becoming clearer and clearer about what you stand for, what you value, and your personal ethical and moral rules. Clarity of core values is a key leadership characteristic because if one is not internally clear about priorities, what is good to do, what is ethically acceptable, etc. the influence of others may sway one's behavior away from achieving one's goals or from ethical means of achieving them. A clear set of personal values helps one have confidence in one's chosen course. The absence of a

well-defined center is likely to encourage one to respond to others rather than to lead them.

2.   CLARIFYING WHAT'S POSSIBLE. Leadership efforts will go nowhere if there is no target, no direction, no vision of where one believes the organization (or one's part of an organization) should be headed. As with one's core values, seldom is a vision of the future fully formed at any one time. Rather, it emerges and evolves the more one thinks about how one wishes the future to be. Often, this visioning is intentional. Leaders work to clarify the futures they want to see created, first in their minds and later in reality. This clarification is not so much trying to identify what will be as it is identifying what one wants to be.

3.   CLARIFYING WHAT OTHERS CAN CONTRIBUTE. Leaders are not leaders without followers. People with a tendency to immediate and negative judgments about others may miss what others have to contribute to their visions. The ability to see a wide range of possibilities in what others might add to your team is a key part of effective leadership. The challenge is to assess others in terms of their potential and capabilities rather than with a hyper-critical eye. The question is, "What can they do?" rather than "What can they not do?" An initial critical and negative interpretation of others will tend to shut down possibilities and perhaps significant support for one's goals and visions.

4.   SUPPORTING OTHERS SO THAT THEY CAN CONTRIBUTE. By "support" here we mean reorganizing the surrounding work context in a way that removes barriers and frees up employee creativity, energy and productivity. Effective leaders understand that even the best vision and the most motivated work force will be hampered by poorly designed organizations. Consequently, they are working hard to make sure that organizational barriers to high performance are minimized or eliminated. Structure and the various organizational systems including recruiting and selection, reward, appraisal, and education need to be aligned and synchronized for the people in them to be working efficiently.

5.   BEING RELENTLESS. Powerful leaders don't give up. Persistent striving for your goals in the face of adversity requires a high level of self-confidence and belief in the value of your goals. Without such strong commitment and an internal drive to achieve, one can become diverted from one's goals. Clarifying one's center is important here: If you know what you are aiming for and why, your commitment will likely be stronger and relentless pursuit of that ideal easier. Although there is a fine line dividing relentlessness and stubbornness, they are not the same. Good leaders are flexible especially on means, but fixedly determined when it comes to outcomes. Without a strong internal drive, however, would-be leaders falter before achieving their goals.

6.   MEASURING AND CELEBRATING PROGRESS. Most people need encouragement as they work. It's hard to keep plugging away at a distant goal without ever getting some sign that you're on the right track. Without some measure of progress, motivation dies. Strong leaders continuously identify and set appropriate intermediate

goals on the path toward their vision or goal, and celebrate them when reached with the people who contributed to the achievement. The central feature of such celebration is the recognition of a job well done, and achievement and of the joy of doing, rather than necessarily a tangible reward.

These six principles of effective leadership constitute values of leadership, that is, principles that effective leaders hold to be true. The next section describes how to score your responses on items designed to measure these six principles.

PART IV: SCORING PROCEDURE

To calculate your scores, flip back to Parts I and II and record the score for the items as numbered in each column below. When you have completed adding your scores, fill in the graph in Part V to create your profile.

CYC	CWP	CWOCC	RTS	R	CP
1 =	2 =	3 =	4 =	5 =	6 =
7 =	8 =	9 =	10 =	11 =	12 =
13 =	14 =	15 =	16 =	17 =	18 =
19 =	20 =	21 =	22 =	23 =	24 =
25 =	26 =	27 =	28 =	29 =	30 =
31 =	32 =	33 =	34 =	35 =	36 =

Totals =

Note that the maximum score possible in each column is 42 and the minimum possible score is 7. After you have calculated your total scores, turn the page and display them graphically.

PART V: DISPLAYING YOUR SCORES

Chart your score on the table below to develop a graphical profile of your scores.

	0	5	10	15	20	25	30	40	45
Clarifying Your Center									
Clarifying What's Possible									
Clarifying What Others Have to Contribute									
Supporting Others So They Can Contribute									
Being Relentless									
Measuring and Celebrating Progress									
	0%	12%	24%	36%	48%	60%	71%	95%	107%

PART VI: INTERPRETING YOUR SCORES

The six concepts that we have used as the basis for this self-assessment measure have been tested and discussed for many years in the classroom with practicing executives. We do not doubt their validity and usefulness as elements of leadership. However, this measure itself is a new tool, and we are in the process of establishing the 'norms' for responses from people of different leadership abilities and strengths. That means that it is not possible to give peer comparison results (e.g., "You fall in the top 20% of respondents on clarifying your center.") However, you are still able to get a general sense of whether your scores in each area are "high" or "low" and can compare them with your classmates.

The graphical chart on the previous page shows a percentage scale on the right hand side. Using this scale, you can think of your scores as falling in a high, medium or low range. For each of the concepts below, consider your score and if you feel you would like to work on that aspect of your leadership, read that section for suggestions on how to do that.

Clarifying Your Center

People with strong core values have a calmness about them, tend to be less defensive, and are more likely to stand firm in a storm than those whose core values are more ambivalent or uncertain. People with clear values are more likely to adhere to those values in situations where they are pressured to depart from them. In Stephen Covey's terms, people who have clarified their core values have won the private victory before the public battle.[1] If your score on clarifying your center was lower than you would have liked, you might consider some exercises that would help you clarify your core leadership values and principles.

First, you might begin by sitting down when you have, or make, some free time and writing out a list of the core beliefs you have developed thus far in your life. Putting them on paper makes it easier to "see" them and to examine them—and subsequently to modify and polish them.

Second, you might complete the *Life's Story Assignment* (UVA-PACS-0092) exercise in which you are invited to write your life's story in 400 words or less, chart your ups and downs, and then draw some conclusions about the lessons you learned from those experiences. These major turning points in life tend to reveal our core values or to shape them.

Third, you might ask those who know you well, perhaps family members or work associates, to make a list of the things that they believe you stand for. Their take will be a behavioral one in that they will infer your values from what you do and how you behave around them. This may vary from your "espoused values" above. Reviewing the gaps if any can be very enlightening as one considers what one thinks one's core values are and what others observe them to be.

Fourth, you might take a week or a weekend and enroll in a seminar devoted to values clarification. These are taught in many large cities periodically and can be very helpful in guiding you to a deeper understanding of just what is important to you.

Fifth, you might pursue a specific values clarification exercise like the *Life and Career Values Card Sort* which is a chapter in the book *Self Assessment and Career Development,* that will ask you to lay out cards in a matrix and arrange them repeatedly until you get a "comfortable" picture of your values and their relative strength.

Clarifying What's Possible

This concept, ironically, is about "reflecting on the future." Higher scores indicate that you spend time thinking about what the future should hold for you and your company. Lower scores may indicate a lack of time or interest for such thinking, or a tendency to restrict thoughts and plans to short-term goals or continuation of the present. People without a view of what they want to achieve will have a hard time convincing others of where to go. Clarifying for yourself and others where you want to go is in itself an act of leadership. Some call this dreaming. Robert Greenleaf describes it this way:

> Not much happens without a dream. And for something great to happen, there must be a great dream. Behind every great achievement is a dreamer of great dreams. Much more than a dreamer is required to bring it to reality; but the dream must be there first.
>
> —Robert Greenleaf, Servant Leadership, p. 16

Clarifying the future in part requires a willingness to break out of current thinking. As Edward Deming once said, "Every system is perfectly designed to produce the results it is achieving." To get somewhere else, leaders must see a new and different future. If your scores here are lower than you would like, you might consider the following suggestions:

1. Set aside time weekly, perhaps an hour, to focus just on thinking about what your company, your part of the company or you will look like in five years.
2. Read a futuristic novel like *The Gate to Women's Country* or *A Canticle for Liebowitz* or *Dune*. Then reflect on what kinds of changes must have happened to have created those worlds and whether or not you see signs of them around you.
3. Learn about scenario planning and begin to practice its principles. This is much more than simply guessing about "best-case, worst case" outcomes. *The Art of the Long View* by Peter Schwartz is a good place to start.
4. Think of your parents or grandparents. What changes have they seen in their lives? What changes might you expect during your lifetime? What changes would you *like* to see?
5. Subscribe to a new magazine, for example *Future,* that you feel will stimulate your thinking about societal trends that may or may not affect your industry. Commit to reading one or two articles each issue.
6. Go visit some places you've never been before, a soup kitchen, a rehab center for children, a ballet, a country with a different culture, or a business you've never been inside of. Ask yourself why things are working they way they do and what the underlying assumptions must be to make them so.
7. Seek out people very unlike yourself at social functions and ask them about their view of the world and what they see. This is a very easy thing to do, most people are quite happy to talk about their views; the challenge will be to listen to their new ideas without interrupting or tuning out.

Clarifying What Others Have to Contribute

This principle has to do with looking for what people can do rather than what they cannot do. Higher scores tend to indicate that you are willing to listen to a wide range of people, see their ideas for what they are worth, and look for abilities in people ('seeing the glass half-full' rather than half empty) rather than their faults.

Many of us are trained professionally to find fault. Perhaps we learned this at an early age from our parents for whom our work was never quite good enough. Perhaps we learned this from our education where we learned systematic ways of striving for perfection or "six sigma quality" programs. Whatever the source, if we have learned a habit of seeing what's not there as opposed to what is there, our attempts to lead may be thwarted. Followers who feel constantly "not good enough" find it difficult to be enthusiastic and motivated. If you would prefer higher scores on this dimension, you might consider the following:

1. For the next five conversations, consciously focus in your mind on the positive qualities of the person you're talking with. Find occasion in the conversation to compliment them even if the conversation doesn't seem to call for it. For example, if at the end of a conversation you haven't found an opportunity to compliment someone, try something like this, "You know Elliott, I just wanted you to know that I really admire your ability to manage so many things. You do a great job at being organized."

2. You might also at the end of a day consider the subordinates who work for you and make a written list of their strong points. A simple list will do, but it's important to

write it down. There's a translation that occurs between thought and expression that is important to cross.

3.   In five conversations this week, discuss with your subordinates their potential skills. You might begin by asking what goals they have for developing skills in the coming year and then you might suggest one or two that you think they could achieve and that would make them much more valuable to the organization.

4.   Identify ways in which you would like to see your subordinates grow, describing the specific skills that you'd like them to develop. Then, in a private conversation, mention to them your desires and beliefs that they could, in fact, develop those skills. Offer to help them if you can.

5.   The next time you face a difficult task, identify those who could help you accomplish it and ask them if they feel up to it. Give them a significant responsibility and comment on how you are confident that they might accomplish the task. Most people will work hard to rise to this kind of occasion.

6.   Think of the people at work of whom you may have a modest opinion. Stop for a moment and think of their strong points. Why did they get the jobs they have? What skills do they bring to their jobs? Can you identify what they CAN do as opposed to what they cannot do?

Our guess is that you may find some of these suggestions "silly" or "hard to do." That's the point. If they came naturally to you, you would have scored higher on "clarifying what others have to contribute." Try these three simple suggestions for a week and see if they don't make a difference in what you "see" in your colleagues.

True followership is a voluntary process; unless your followers are responding voluntarily, you are not really leading them. The challenge here is to see what others have to offer your goals. Some people in leadership roles are fundamentally negative, searching for things to criticize and ways to find fault with others. This tendency can overlook underlying strengths and skills and be de-motivating for the people involved. The powerful leader looks and listens for possibilities in the people they work with, asking themselves, What can these people do rather than what can they not do?

Supporting Others So That They Can Contribute

Sometimes organizational structures or systems can inhibit the efforts people make to accomplish the organization's goals. Jack Welch's well-known Work-Out effort in the late 1980s and early 1990s was an attempt to remove the bureaucratic red tape that many said was slowing down decision making and development cycles. Effective leaders look for ways to remove these organizational barriers by redesigning the systems that create them. Perhaps the reward system encourages behavior A while management hopes that behavior B will occur.[2] Or the information system produces a volume and range of reports that few can interpret and use. Or the decision-making structure stifles innovativeness and creativity. The list is potentially limitless. Leaders who are oblivious to the ways in which their organizations constrain the people who work within them tolerate the resulting cynicism and frustration in their work force.

If you would like to improve your scores on this dimension, you might consider the following suggestions.

1.   Survey your direct reports and have them survey their direct reports and find out what organizational systems they believe get in the way of getting the key tasks in the organization done. Then, ask them to come up with better designs, sooner rather than later.

2.   Walk around your organization and ask, "What process, policy, or procedure recently has gotten in the way of you doing your best work? How could we change it?"

3.   Include in your performance reviews a series of questions that focus on the efficiency of your organizational processes, procedures and systems. Expect that each subordinate will pay attention to this and be making suggestions, specific suggestions, for how to mend them. This is consistent with one of the four corners of the so-called "balanced scorecard."[3] If you pay attention to this aspect of your organization, so will your subordinates and you'll find yourself repeatedly acknowledging organizational adjustments here and there that you had no idea before were getting in the way.

Being Relentless

Relentlessness is a hallmark of effective leadership. Powerful leaders don't start and easily give up. If you find that your score on this dimension was lower than you would have liked, you might try the following:

1.   On your current to-do list, mark the items that are overdue. Ask yourself why, and write down the reasons. If you've over committed, consider the old saw, "Less is more." While it's true that people who do more often get more assignments, there is a divide over which one's ability to produce declines. Pay attention to this divide.

2.   Review your New Year's resolutions and how often you've made them and not followed through. Spend some time thinking seriously about why that is. What do you need to do to follow through on a goal?

3.   Identify a small thing you'd like to try doing differently (perhaps from the lists of suggestions above) and commit to yourself to try it for three days. If three days is too long, try one or two. Then pick another just to see if you can commit to something for more than a short period of time. Broken promises to ourselves on any dimension undermine our self confidence and capacity for following through.

4.   Identify the longest project or endeavor you have stayed with in your life. Reflect on why you stayed with this project or endeavor rather than others. What about it captured your intensity and determination? How could you carry those characteristics to other endeavors?

Measuring and Celebrating Progress

Followers need to know that they are doing well. A few can make that assessment themselves, but most people thrive on positive feedback whether it be from others or from the results of their work. Few of us have the stamina to persist in very lengthy pursuits without some encouragement from positive feedback—whether it be social or natural. If you'd like to strengthen your skills in this area, consider the following:

1.   List the celebrations you have at home or at work. What do you celebrate? How often do you celebrate? How long do you typically wait between celebrations?

2.   How often do you praise the people around you? When was the last time you praised someone, a family member or a co-worker?

3.   When someone you know achieves something, how long do you spend congratulating them? Do you tend to skim over their accomplishments and point to the next hurdle? Or assume that their progress was "normal" or "expected?"

4.   How do you celebrate when you accomplish something you're working on? How long does your celebration last? How do you make the transition from accomplishment to commitment to the next objective?

Conclusion

We hope that this exercise has been of value to you by adding to your insights about leadership and your own leadership skills. Perhaps it has helped you identify an area or two in which you wish to work to improve your leadership abilities. Your instructor or session leader can provide additional information on any of the elements discussed here, as well as suggestions for further reading if you wish to explore the ideas a little more deeply.

Please take a moment to fill out the data page that follows and hand it in or send it in. This anonymous data collection is invaluable as we set population norms for the concepts measured here. Alternately, you can go to the web site http://faculty.darden.edu/clawsonj and click on the LSA SURVEY button to input your data there. Thank you!

LSA DATA COLLECTION

If you are willing to have your scores included in our database to provide norms for others who take the test, please remove this page from the packet, fill it in and hand it to your instructor or session leader. Thank you for your willingness to add your data. Alternatively, you can input your scores on http://faculty.darden.edu/clawsonj/.

Date and Group: (course or program)

Age:

Gender: Female   Male

College Major:

Job Title:

Job Functional Area: (student, finance, marketing, operations, IT, etc.)

Number of people who report to you in
your responsibility cone (all the way down).

Scores:

Clarifying Your Center:

Clarifying What's Possible:

Clarifying What Others Can Contribute

Supporting Others So They Can Contribute

Being Relentless

Measuring and Celebrating Progress

You can send your data to any of the following:

Fax: 434-243-7680
E-mail: JimClawson@virginia.edu
Web site: http://faculty.darden.edu/clawsonj
Mail: Jim Clawson, Box 6550, Charlottesville, VA 22906

1. See *The Seven Habits of Highly Effective People,* by Stephen Covey, Simon and Schuster, New York, 1989, chapter two.
2. See Steve Kerr, "On the Folly of Hoping for A While Rewarding B," *Academy of Management Journal,* August 15, 1988, p. 298.
3. See R.S. Kaplan and D.P. Norton, "Balanced Scorecard: Measures that drive Performance," *Harvard Business Review,* January, 1992, reprint number 92105.

Team Self-Assessment

The following 17 items invite your assessment of your work team in terms of characteristics shown in the current literature to describe highly effective teams. The references for these characteristics are shown at the end (feel free to tear off and keep that page for your reference if you wish).

Please rate your current working group/team on each item as to how well the item describes what your team/organization does. Then follow your facilitator's instructions for developing aggregate indicators.

Scale: 1 = Never true about your team or organization,
2 = Occasionally true about your team or organization,
3 = Sometimes true about your team or organization,
4 = True half the time,
5 = Often true about your team or organization
6 = True most of the time about your team or organization
7 = Always true about your team

ITEM	Never True			Half True			Always True
1. We share leadership roles rather than relying on one strong, clearly focused leader.	1	2	3	4	5	6	7
2. We hold the team accountable rather than holding just individuals accountable.	1	2	3	4	5	6	7
3. We have developed a team purpose that we deliver rather than just assuming the team's purpose is the same as the organization's.	1	2	3	4	5	6	7
4. We have real collective products rather than a collection of individual products (strung together at the end).	1	2	3	4	5	6	7

5. We encourage open-ended discussion and active problem solving in meetings rather than trying to be "efficient."	1	2	3	4	5	6	7
6. We measure our team performance directly by assessing our team's collective work products rather than measuring performance indirectly (e.g. financial performance of the business as a whole).	1	2	3	4	5	6	7
7. We discuss, decide, and DO real work together rather than delegating real work to others to do.	1	2	3	4	5	6	7
8. We try to establish links with key resource organizations well BEFORE we need them rather than waiting for an emergency to make contact.	1	2	3	4	5	6	7
9. We only do real "teamwork" in teams rather than trying to get lots of people involved on basically individual tasks.	1	2	3	4	5	6	7
10. We have team-based rewards rather than individual rewards.	1	2	3	4	5	6	7
11. Our "leaders" only specify the desired end states and leave the means to the team members rather than trying to specify both means and ends.	1	2	3	4	5	6	7
12. We have a good and appropriate mix of talent on our team.	1	2	3	4	5	6	7
13. We insure that our team has a whole, discrete, identifiable job to do rather than dividing the work into such tiny pieces that team members cannot see the "whole" that they are building.	1	2	3	4	5	6	7
14. The things we "have to do" and "cannot do" are clear and unambiguous to all team members.	1	2	3	4	5	6	7

15. We insure that the team has the appropriate organizational support it needs to get its job done rather than demanding big, difficult goals, but skimping on organizational support.	1	2	3	4	5	6	7
16. We assume that all team members need to be learning and growing rather than assuming that we have all the talent and learning we need.	1	2	3	4	5	6	7
17. We have devised internally real time, analog measures of our performance which we monitor and watch continuously rather than relying on measures others have developed that only show historical performance.	1	2	3	4	5	6	7

References

The items above were taken from principles and findings reported in the following literature. If you're interested in the characteristics of effective teams as measured here, you may wish to read the primary sources to get more insight.

"Why Teams Don't Work," Richard J. Hackman, *Leader to Leader,* winter 1998, p24 ff, Peter Drucker Institute, Claremont College, adapted from author's chapter in *Applications of Theory and Research on Groups to Social Issues,* edited by R.S. Tinadale, J. Edwards, and E.J. Posavac. Plenum Publishers.

"The Discipline of Teams," by Jon R. Katzenbach and Douglas K. Smith, *Harvard Business Review,* reprint 93207 and the book by the same title.

"How Bell Labs Creates Star Performers," Robert Kelley and Janet Caplan, *Harvard Business Review,* (HBR 93405, July-August 1993.)

"How the Right Measures Help Teams Excel," *Harvard Business Review* (HBR 94305)

Assessing the Moral Foundation of Your Leadership

After you have discussed the moral foundation of leadership, use this form to begin your leadership team assessment. First, make copies of the form and give one to each member of your team and have them assess your team. Second, answer each question according to your view of your current management team and its interactions. Third, collect each team member's answers (anonymously if you wish) and summarize the data. Fourth, hold a team meeting in which you discuss the results (average scores, variation, difference from expectations or hopes) and make joint plans for how to improve your scores. To answer, circle the number that represents the percent of the time that each principle describes your leadership team.

Cornerstone Principle:
Percent of the Time That This Principle Describes Our Team

1. **Truth Telling**: We tell the truth to each other and don't hide things or talk behind others' backs. We know where each person stands.

10	20	30	40	50	60	70	80	90	100

2. **Promise Keeping:** We keep our promises to each other no matter how large or small.

10	20	30	40	50	60	70	80	90	100

3. **Fairness:** We treat each other fairly and do not try to take advantage of each other.

10	20	30	40	50	60	70	80	90	100

4. **Respect for the Individual:** We show respect for each other and other members of our organization in our speech, action, and courtesy.

10	20	30	40	50	60	70	80	90	100

We invite you to note again that each of these principles is really only a different window onto the same central concept. In other words, if you tell the truth, you have to keep your promises. If you are fair, you'll have respect for the individual. Best wishes in confirming this essential foundation.

Balancing Your Life

*Then one evening I phoned home to tell the boys I wouldn't make it
back in time to say good night. I'd already missed five bedtimes in a
row. Sam, the younger of the two, said that was O.K., but asked me to
wake him up whenever I got home. I explained that I'd be back so late
that he would have gone to sleep long before; it was probably better if I
saw him the next morning. But he insisted. I asked him why. He said he
just wanted to know I was there, at home. To this day, I can't explain
precisely what happened to me at that moment. Yet I suddenly knew I
had to leave my job."*

*The central paradox is this: Most of us are earning more money and
living better in material terms than we (or our parents) did a quarter
century ago, around the time when some of the technologies on which
the new economy is based—the microchip, the personal computer, the
Internet—first emerged. You'd think, therefore, that it would be easier,
not harder, to attend to the parts of our lives that exist outside paid
work. Yet by most measures we're working longer and more frantically
than before, and the time and energy left for our non-working lives are
evaporating.*

—ROBERT REICH, FORMER SECRETARY OF LABOR,
THE FUTURE OF SUCCESS, PP. 3, 5

Leaders in the modern era face the significant challenge of finding the right kind of
balance in their lives between work, family, self, and other interests. The constantly
growing and competing demands of life on many fronts push us all to make daily
behavioral decisions about how we spend our time and talents, often without taking
the time to think clearly about the consequences of those decisions. Making those decisions without a clear picture of their consequences can be devastating for us all—leaders, managers, and employees.

Some people naturally seem to find a balance that fits them and their own definition of success over the years. Others have a more difficult job of it. Far too many at middle or late middle age find that they are deeply dissatisfied with the way their lives have turned out. Erik Eriksson in *Childhood and Society,* for example, outlined eight ages of humankind, each characterized by binary dilemmas. While this is admittedly and primarily a Western approach, his eighth stage in which people in their mature years wrestle with feelings of despair or integrity is instructive. His observation is that later in life we see that it's too late basically to change much in our lives and we come to a realization that either life has come together much in the way that we had hoped and dreamed it would (integrity in the sense of integration into a complete whole) or we realize that life hasn't turned out like we thought it would and since it's too late to change, we begin to despair. Eriksson's assertion is confirmed in the publication of books like *The Failure of Success, Must Success Cost So Much?*, *Career Success/Personal Failure, Workaholics, Work, Family and the Career, Tradeoffs: Executive, Family and Organizational Life* and the former secretary of labor's book, *The Future of Success,* quoted above, all of which examine the ways in which our daily, weekly, and yearly choices repeated over and over again structure our lives; sometimes in ways that we later deeply regret. And this is the potential tragedy; to have made those choices without thinking or anticipating their outcomes.

What we can learn from this is not to seek a common "right" balance. Rather, to be aware of our current choices of time and energy allocation and to make adjustments that point us toward our personal definitions of success, and by that I mean success in life, not just "career." The oft-quoted line, "How many of us, on our deathbeds, with our last gasp will breathe, 'If only I had spent more time at the office!'" makes the point. The tragedy lies in making daily decisions that add up over a lifetime to a balance that one realizes, in retrospect, was not what one would have consciously chosen.

This exercise is designed to help you see your current behavioral allocation of time and how that matches up with your personal definition of success. The exercise is built upon some fundamental assumptions:

1. We all have a limited, but equal 168 hours per week of time.
2. We all have some freedom in choosing how we spend that time.
3. We all have some talent to apply to the time we have.
4. We all have various dimensions to our lives that we choose, consciously or unconsciously, to develop or ignore.

A list of these dimensions is given in Table 1. Some of the definitions may not be just what you immediately think, so please look at the parenthetical definitions so you'll know what we mean for each dimension. You may be able to think of other dimensions of life that should be added to the list. The point is that, like cut diamonds, there are a number of facets to our lives, and that by choosing to spend time and energy and talent in some areas, we necessarily neglect others. My colleague, Alex Horniman, often declares that "excellence is a neurotic lifestyle" suggesting that to excel most of us have to focus our time and attention in powerful ways. When we do this consciously, as in the case of an Olympic hopeful athlete, we acknowledge the sacrifice that we are making in other aspects of life and become singular in our focus. Others prefer to have a more rounded lifestyle, and in so doing, may recognize the sac-

TABLE 1 Dimensions of Adult Life

Professional (working, earning in career and job)
Financial (managing money affairs)
Material (collecting things)
Recreational (playing)
Physical (exercising)
Sleep
Intellectual (learning, committing to memory, thinking)
Emotional (feeling, sensing, being aware of emotions)
Spiritual/Philosophical (praying, meditating, communing, reflecting)
Marital (with your spouse)
Parental (with your children)
Familial (with your parents)
Social (with your friends)
Societal (community work)
Political (political work)
Ecclesiastical (church work)

rifice of excellence in any one area. The challenge is to know what your choices are and what they mean for you. Perhaps this exercise can help.

There are several steps to completing the exercise:

1. **Clarify your personal definition of success.** Write it down in the space below. What does it mean to you now to be "successful?" Research shows that one's definition of success may vary over one's lifetime, but we need a place to start. You may or may not have thought about this before, so it may take some reflection to clarify what it means to you to be "successful." Approach this broadly, that is, consider what it means to be successful in **life,** not just your career. It's your life, only you can live it, and you are the primary shaper of it. What do you want it to be? Try to be specific as you can. "To be happy" may be true, but it's not very helpful. What will make you happy? The clarity of the definition will be make the exercise more powerful for you.

Success is: _____

_____

_____

Keep your definition where you can refer to it often; revise it as you feel it necessary. For the ship with no destination, any port will do, but the ship with a destination has a course and a purpose to its sailing. You may wish to consider the various aspects in Table 1 again as you write your personal definition. I like the comment the famous comedienne, Lily Tomlin, once uttered, "I always wanted to be somebody. Maybe I should have been more specific."

FIGURE 1 Personal Level of Development

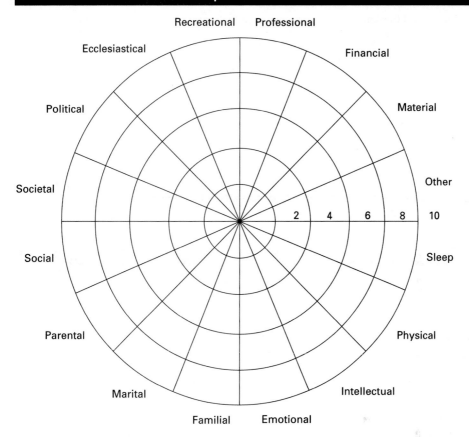

2. **Assess your current level of development.** On the wheel diagram in Figure 1, assess your current level of personal development on each dimension. Use a scale of 1 to 10, where 1 is completely undeveloped and 10 is perfectly developed, that is, at a world-class level. A "10" on the physical dimension, for example, would be an Olympic medalist; a "1" would be can't walk around the block comfortably. The zero point is at the center of the diagram. When you have marked your level of development on each dimension, shade in the area of your development across all dimensions. This will produce **your perception** of your life's developmental balance at this point. You may find the shape of your profile instructive as you think about how it compares with your definition of success. This is the central piece of this exercise.

The definitions in Table 2 suggest another way of delineating your development. You may wish to keep these definitions in mind as you determine how to assess and shade in your development profile.

3. **Assess your current allocation of time.** Return to the list of aspects of life in Table 3, and estimate how much time a week you spend on each one. Without reviewing your day planner, just estimate in Column A how much time you spend on each dimension.

TABLE 2 Stages of Growth

One way of thinking about movement from the center of the diagram or embryonic level of development is in terms of "maturity." Using the definitions below, you can gauge your development on each dimension. These terms are intended to be descriptive not evaluative.

1. **Embryonic.** Unaware that the dimension exists and therefore pays no attention to it.
2. **Youth.** Aware that the dimension exists but does little intentional about developing it.
3. **Adolescent.** Aware that the dimension exists but believes that it can be developed later; therefore, does a little about developing it now and then moves on.
4. **Young Adult.** Aware that the dimension exists and concerned about developing it; has a superficial awareness that one must work at developing it all along and makes modest efforts to develop it.
5. **Mature Adult.** Aware that the dimension exists and concerned about developing it; has a deep awareness of the need to develop the dimension constantly and is working hard to develop it.

TABLE 3 Personal Allocation of Time

	Time Spent Last Week	
Aspect of Life	*Estimated*	*Total (from Table 5)*
Professional	_____	_____
Financial	_____	_____
Material	_____	_____
Recreational	_____	_____
Physical	_____	_____
Sleep	_____	_____
Intellectual	_____	_____
Emotional	_____	_____
Spiritual/Philosophical	_____	_____
Marital	_____	_____
Parental	_____	_____
Familial	_____	_____
Social	_____	_____
Societal	_____	_____
Political	_____	_____
Ecclesiastical	_____	_____
Total	(168?)	_____

If you have time, you may wish to actually keep track of your time for a week. Like our perceptions of our spending habits, our perceptions of how we spend our time do not often match up with the realities. You can use the form in Table 4 to keep a weekly time diary and then transform your results in Table 5 to show how much time you spent during the week on each dimension. Then enter the totals in Column B in Table 3.

TABLE 4　Time Diary for One Week

Note daily your use of time in each of the following life dimensions: Working, Sleeping, Exercising, Managing Personal Hygiene (dressing, eating, bathing—you might include this in Physical if you don't want a separate look at your exercise), Reading and Learning (Intellectual), Managing Finances, Recreating (including most TV), Attending to Material Things, Parenting, Being with Significant Other, Being with Parents, Being with Friends, Working in the Community, Working in Political Events, Being in Church, Meditating/Communing/Praying. Include your "shadow hours" in parentheses. Then summarize the results in Table 5.

Time	*Mon*	*Tue*	*Wed*	*Thu*	*Fri*	*Sat*	*Sun*
12:00 midnight	____	____	____	____	____	____	____
2:00 A.M.	____	____	____	____	____	____	____
4:00 A.M.	____	____	____	____	____	____	____
6:00 A.M.	____	____	____	____	____	____	____
8:00 A.M.	____	____	____	____	____	____	____
10:00 A.M.	____	____	____	____	____	____	____
12:00 noon	____	____	____	____	____	____	____
2:00 P.M.	____	____	____	____	____	____	____
4:00 P.M.	____	____	____	____	____	____	____
6:00 P.M.	____	____	____	____	____	____	____
8:00 P.M.	____	____	____	____	____	____	____
10:00 P.M.	____	____	____	____	____	____	____
12:00 midnight	____	____	____	____	____	____	____

As you do this, you will notice that some dimensions overlap, that is, you could be working on more than one dimension at the same time. If you work construction, you are probably getting lots of exercise while you are working. Likewise some aspects of work may involve new learning that stretches your mind intellectually and spending time socially can be emotionally powerful as when you are comforting grieving friends. You might deal with this overlap by first allocating the 168 hours that you have each week to the dominant aspect and then returning to add "shadow hours" in parentheses to indicate time spent elsewhere really had developmental impact in another area. For instance, if you find that your work requires you to be learning (not just repeating what you can already do), you might assess how much of your work time is like that and add that number to the Intellectual box in parentheses. In this way, your week of 168 hours is leveraged; you can assess how rewarding on how many dimensions your time choices are. If you play golf with your peers, for example, you can count that time as recreation, but probably not include any shadow hours in parental time. If you play golf as a family, you could have recreation time and shadow time with marital and parental aspects. You may find it interesting to see how much of your work time has shadow benefits to other aspects of life, that is, are you learning at work? Are you growing socially at work? etc. You may find that you have no time either shadow or otherwise for a particular dimension or that the only time you have for a dimension is shadow time. It may be that your shadow time is not as productive as "hard time" in which your attention and efforts are concentrated. You decide what to include and how effective both hard

TABLE 5 Allocating Time Over the Aspects of Adult Life

Time Spent during the Week of   /   /

Aspect	Mon	Tue	Wed	Thu	Fri	Sat	Sun	Total
Professional	___	___	___	___	___	___	___	___
Financial	___	___	___	___	___	___	___	___
Material	___	___	___	___	___	___	___	___
Recreational	___	___	___	___	___	___	___	___
Physical	___	___	___	___	___	___	___	___
Sleep	___	___	___	___	___	___	___	___
Intellectual	___	___	___	___	___	___	___	___
Emotional	___	___	___	___	___	___	___	___
Spiritual	___	___	___	___	___	___	___	___
Marital	___	___	___	___	___	___	___	___
Parental	___	___	___	___	___	___	___	___
Familial	___	___	___	___	___	___	___	___
Social	___	___	___	___	___	___	___	___
Societal	___	___	___	___	___	___	___	___
Political	___	___	___	___	___	___	___	___
Ecclesiastical	___	___	___	___	___	___	___	___
Other:	___	___	___	___	___	___	___	___
Actual Total	24	24	24	24	24	24	24	168
Shadow Time	___	___	___	___	___	___	___	___
Total Time	___	___	___	___	___	___	___	___

and shadow times are. When you're done, you can add up your total hard hours and your shadow hours on the table in Table 5.

If you don't have time to do this (that, too, is interesting—it's all data), think back on the previous week and try to allocate the time you spent on each dimension. Use Table 4 and Table 5 to help you do this and then enter your retrospective look in column B in Table 3.

4. Create a profile of your current time allocation. There are two ways you can do this. First, you could use the second wheel diagram in Figure 2 to mark and fill in your time allocations. The wheel is the same size and shape as the one in Figure 1, but the scale is now "five times the hours of time" so that "10" means you spend 50 hours a week on this dimension. Include your shadow time in this calculation. I realize that some of you may be working 60, 70, 80, or even 90 hours a week. If so, extend your Professional pie segment beyond the outer circle in scale to your current level of work.

An alternative approach here would be to use a spreadsheet graphing program, if you have one, to create a pie chart of how much time you spent on each dimension last week using the data from step 3. The result won't match the format of your develop-

FIGURE 2   Time Allocation Wheel Diagram

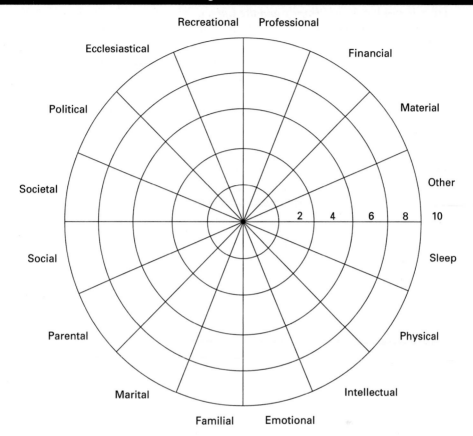

mental profile, but you can use it to compare mentally. (You could also do this by hand using a compass and protractor by drawing a circle and calculating the percentage of time for each dimension (number of hours / 168 * 100) and multiply by 360 to get the number of degrees around the circle for each dimension. For example, if you spent 55 hours working, then 55/168*100 = 33% times 360 degrees = 120 degrees of arc around the circle for that dimension.)

5.   **Compare and reflect.** Now, consider the relationships between your definition of success, your self-assessed level of development and your current time allocations. The following questions may help guide your reflection.

a. What connections do you see? What disparities?
b. Are there "flat spots" on either wheel diagram that concern you?
c. How do they relate to your definition of success and your allocation of time?
d. Do you want to do anything about them? How much time and talent will it take?
e. What will be the impact of your current time allocation on your development over the course of your life? That is, where logically does your present time allocation pattern take you 20 or 30 years into the future?

References

Derr, Brooklyn, *Work, Family and the Career,* Praeger Special Studies, New York, 1980.

Evans, Paul, and Bartolome, Fernando, *Must Success Cost So Much?,* Basic Books, New York, 1980.

Fassel, Diane, *Working Ourselves to Death,* New York, HarperCollins, 1990.

Greiff, Barrie S. and Munter, Preston K., *Tradeoffs: Executive, Family and Organizational Life,* New American Library, New York, 1980.

Korman, Abraham K., *Career Success Personal Failure,* Prentice Hall, New York, 1980.

Lee, Mary Dean, and Kanungo, Rabindra N., *Management of Work and Personal Life,* Praeger Special Studies, New York, 1984.

Machlowitz, Marilyn, *Workaholics,* Addison-Wesley, Reading, Mass., 1977.

Marrow, Alfred, *The Failure of Success,* Amacom, New York, 1972.

Reich, Robert, *The Future of Success,* New York, Alfred Knopf, 2001.

Energy Management Exercise

In the midst of busy lives, most people focus their organizational efforts on time management. Books and books have been written about how to help people do this (e.g., *How to Get Control of Your Life and Your Time,* and *The Time Trap*). Many consultants make a nice living advising people how to manage their time. Indeed, whole companies have sprung up and made a profitable existence trying to advise people about how to manage their time (e.g., Franklin-Covey, Inc.). Clearly, time is a critical resource and an important input into our productivity and enjoyment of life. But your productivity and enjoyment do not depend on your time management alone. There are many factors that impact our outputs and satisfactions in life. These include our talents, our choices, and surely, our personal energy level. In fact, the amount of energy we bring to our allotted time on the earth (beginning with the fixed 168 hours per week) may well determine much more how much we give and get in life than our allocation and use of time.

The choices we make about how we eat, how we use our time, how we sleep, how we exercise, and how we manage our relationships all contribute to the amount of energy we have in life. We would probably be better off if we paid more attention to our energy management than to our time management. Consider, for example, the case of physicians. A typical emergency room attending physician or a typical thoracic surgeon might work up to 100 to 110 hours a week. How is it that they have enough energy and stamina to live this kind of life, year after year? How would their energy level compare to that of an assembly line worker who spends 40–45 hours a week on the job? Is it just because physicians are dealing with life and death situations? Are they workaholics? Or are they managing their personal energy levels more effectively?

The goal of this exercise is to help you begin to clarify those things in your life that energize you and those that de-energize or debilitate you. Use the table on the following page to begin to be more aware of how your choices affect your energy level. You may find the references at the end interesting in helping you to learn more about how you might manage your energy on a regular basis.

This case was prepared by James G. Clawson and includes some ideas of Dr. Curt Tribble, M.D. This case was written as a basis for class discussion rather than to illustrate effective or ineffective handling of an administrative situation. Copyright © 2000 by the University of Virginia Darden School Foundation, Charlottesville, VA. All rights reserved. To order copies, send an e-mail to dardencases@virginia.edu. No part of this publication may be reproduced, stored in a retrieval system, used in a spreadsheet, or transmitted in any form or by any means—electronic, mechanical, photocopying, recording, or otherwise—without the permission of the Darden School Foundation.

Energy Management Table

	CATEGORY OF ACTIVITIES	THINGS THAT ENERGIZE ME	THINGS THAT DEBILITATE ME
Activities			
Foods			
Sleep			
Relationships			
Entertainment			
Exercise			
Other			

ENERGY ACTION ITEMS

Once you have listed as many items as you can under the categories above, reflect on the two columns. Identify one to five things you could do to increase your energy level. Try one or two of these things for the next week, and make daily, written observations about how your daily energy level is affected by them. These self-observations will be important in helping you see the connection between your choices and your energy level.

Energy management goals for the coming week:

1._____

_____

_____

2._____

_____

_____

3._____

_____

_____

Reflections

Once you have tried one or two things for a week, make some written inferences about their impact on you and your energy level. Write these down so you can see them and refer to them.

Which ones do you want to continue?

What makes it difficult to continue doing them?

What can you do to insure that these become positive, repeating habits?

References

Stephen Covey, *Seven Habits of Highly Effective People,* New York: Simon & Schuster, 1991.

Alan Lakein, *How to Get Control of Your Time and Your Life,* New York: Dutton, 1974.

James B. Maas, *Power Sleep,* HarperCollins, New York, 1999.

R. Alec MacKenzie, *The Time Trap,* New York: AMACOM, 1997.

Anthony Robbins, *Unlimited Power,* New York: Simon & Schuster, 1997.

Life's Story Assignment

People who are willing to share their life's story with others often find that this simple approach has powerful results. These short, biographical sketches help associates and subordinates understand the leader's background and "where they are coming from." These sketches also tend to be easy to remember and strong communicators of the storyteller's basic beliefs. In this sense, telling your life's story can be a powerful Level Three leadership tool. This assignment is designed to help you clarify your Level Three Leadership story and has three parts.

1. Write your life's story in 400 words or less. This will require you to condense focus on the highlights and major events. You can use the blank sheet provided if you wish.

2. In the table on page 324, list the key events you mentioned in the 400-word story in the left hand column, one event per row. Then note the extent to which each event was an emotional "up" or "down" or neutral. Then try to summarize the key learning from that event in the third column. How did this experience shape your life? What did it teach you? What did you learn from each experience about leadership? How did this event contribute to your current model of leadership?

3. Using the blank chart on page 324, chart the key events in your life in terms of their emotional height, chronological from left to right. Then label the peaks and valleys with the events they represent.

4. Be prepared to hand this exercise in. The instructor will use this as a chance to get better acquainted with you, but your primary use for this will be at various times and places in the future when, as a leader, you have a need to connect with your people and let them know why you believe what you do and where your motivations come from.

MY LIFE'S STORY IN 400 WORDS OR LESS

MY LIFE'S STORY KEY EVENTS TABLE

Key Event	Emotional Impact (–5 to 0 to +5)	Key Learning or Insight

Life Story Emotional Impact Chart

Source: Adapted from Noel Tichy, *The Leadership Engine* (New York: Pritchett, 1998).

Leadership Theories

Leadership has been widely studied over a long period of time, yet it remains an elusive phenomenon to understand and develop. This note is intended to offer a relatively quick overview of some of the major leadership theories. The theories are grouped according to the research approaches behind them (as in *Leadership in Organizations, 4th Edition,* by Gary Yukl, Prentice-Hall, New Jersey, 1998). The six categories are the Trait, Behavior, Power and Influence, Situational, Charismatic, and Transformational Approaches. Simple direct statements of the main assumptions and/or conceptual points related to each theory comprise the bulk of the note. This note does not intend to portray these theories in their entirety nor to reflect their complexity, only to give you an introduction to the key points.

1. TRAIT APPROACH

The trait approach—one of the earliest used to study leadership—emphasizes the personal traits of leaders. The underlying assumption is that certain people possess innate characteristics that make them better leaders than others.

The "Great Man" Theory of Leadership

Leaders are born, not made. Leadership ability arises from innate, internal traits. Some have them, and some don't. It is our job to figure out what these characteristics are so we can use them to identify potential leaders. No amount of training or coaching will make a leader out of someone who does not possess these traits.

Stogdill's Leadership Traits

from *Stogdill's Handbook of Leadership,* revised and expanded by Bernard M. Bass, The Free Press, New York, 1981. Summarizes over 3,000 books and articles on leadership spanning the period from 1947 to 1980. Most attempts to pursue the "Great Man" avenue of research found difficulty in identifying specific traits. However, Stogdill was able to summarize some generally common traits among effective leaders:

"The leader is characterized by a strong drive for responsibility and task completion, vigor and persistence in pursuit of goals, venturesomeness and originality in problem solving, drive to exercise initiative in social situations, self-confidence and sense of personal identity, willingness to accept consequences of decision and action, readiness to absorb interpersonal stress, willingness to tolerate frustration and delay, ability to influence other persons' behavior, and capacity to structure social interaction systems to the purpose at hand." (1974 edition, p. 81)

"Great Man" Theory Traits

(We offer a simple 10-point scale here in case you wish to assess yourself on some of these dimensions.)

Adaptable to situations	1 2 3 4 5 6 7 8 9 10
Alert to social environment	1 2 3 4 5 6 7 8 9 10
Ambitious and achievement oriented	1 2 3 4 5 6 7 8 9 10
Assertive	1 2 3 4 5 6 7 8 9 10
Cooperative	1 2 3 4 5 6 7 8 9 10
Decisive	1 2 3 4 5 6 7 8 9 10
Dependable	1 2 3 4 5 6 7 8 9 10
Dominant (desire to influence others)	1 2 3 4 5 6 7 8 9 10
Energetic (high activity level)	1 2 3 4 5 6 7 8 9 10
Persistent	1 2 3 4 5 6 7 8 9 10
Self-confident	1 2 3 4 5 6 7 8 9 10
Tolerant of Stress	1 2 3 4 5 6 7 8 9 10
Willing to assume responsibility	1 2 3 4 5 6 7 8 9 10

Skills

Clever (intelligent)	1 2 3 4 5 6 7 8 9 10
Conceptually skilled	1 2 3 4 5 6 7 8 9 10
Creative	1 2 3 4 5 6 7 8 9 10
Diplomatic and tactful	1 2 3 4 5 6 7 8 9 10
Fluent in speaking	1 2 3 4 5 6 7 8 9 10
Knowledgeable about group task	1 2 3 4 5 6 7 8 9 10
Organized (administrative ability)	1 2 3 4 5 6 7 8 9 10
Persuasive	1 2 3 4 5 6 7 8 9 10
Socially skilled	1 2 3 4 5 6 7 8 9 10

Maccoby's Leader

from *The Leader,* by Michael Maccoby, Ballantine, New York, 1981.

"I need hardly say much to you about the importance of authority. Only very few civilized persons are capable of existing without reliance on others or are even capable of coming to an independent opinion. You cannot exaggerate the intensity of man's inner irresolution and craving for authority." Quoted from Sigmund Freud

"The best of all leaders is the one who helps people so that, eventually, they don't need him. Then comes the one they love and admire. Then comes the one they fear. The worst is the one who lets people push him around. Where there is no trust, people will act in bad faith. The best leader doesn't say much, but what he says carries weight. When he is finished with his work, the people say, 'It happened naturally.'" Quoted from Lao Tzu

There are four main ideal types of character orientation to work, each with positive and negative potentials:

TYPE	POSITIVE POTENTIAL	NEGATIVE POTENTIAL
Craft	Independent and Hard-Working	Inflexible and Suspicious
Enterprise	Entrepreneurial and Daring	Instrumental and Uncaring
Career	Professional and Meritocratic	Bureaucratic and Fearful
Self	Experimental and Self-developing	Escapist and Rebellious

"**Craft** is the traditional orientation to independent, inner-directed, skilled work . . . **Enterprise** is at best an entrepreneurial, risk-taking orientation . . . **Career** is the orientation of the technical expert, at best with professional standards and a meritocratic belief that measurable performance should be rewarded by promotion . . . **Self** is the orientation of the new man in an age where abundance is taken as a right and technology provides limitless possibilities. The self-oriented person sees himself in a world of constant change and few roots, where he must create his identity and relationships and use himself as an instrument at work. At best he is experimental, tolerant, willing to be involved in an equitable enterprise that promises enriching experience and continued personal growth. At worst, the self-oriented are indeed rebellious, disloyal, centerless, and escapist into an unproductive inner world of fantasy." (Preface)

Maccoby names four main types of leaders:

Administrators: traditional expert engineer, accountant, lawyer/craftsman
Strongmen: Distrust can be overcome by bearing down: "jungle fighter"
Gamesmen: risk-taking, innovative, adaptable, inspiring in competition
Developers: New products, develop people, participative

"The new social character is evolving most rapidly in the affluent, technically educated, large urban populations here and in the other industrial democracies as well. Like all social characters, it contains both negative and positive tendencies. It is a social character more oriented to self than to craft, enterprise or career." (p. 42)

Characteristics of the New Leader: intelligent, ambitious, willful, optimistic, persuasive, influenced by religious and political thought, an able competitor, critical of traditional authority, willing to take risks, but—most importantly—possessed of:

1. caring, respectful and responsible attitude
2. flexibility about people and organizational structure
3. participative approach to management: willingness to share power

John Gardner

John Gardner, *On Leadership,* New York, Free Press, 1990.

John Gardner is a widely known and well respected essayist and author on the topic of leadership. In this volume, he explores the leadership challenges in large organizations, in political arenas, in government, and in integrating them all. He posits a series of leadership attributes drawn from other researchers as essential to good leadership:

1. Physical Vitality and Stamina
2. Intelligence and Judgment-in-action
3. Willingness (Eagerness) to Accept Responsibilities
4. Task Competence
5. Understanding of Followers/Constituents and their needs
6. Skill in Dealing with People
7. Need to Achieve
8. Capacity to Motivate
9. Courage, Resolution, Steadiness
10. Capacity to win and hold trust
11. Capacity to manage, decide, set priorities
12. Confidence
13. Ascendance, Dominance, Assertiveness
14. Adaptability, Flexibility of approach

Jim Collins

Jim Collins, "Level Five Leadership," *Harvard Business Review,* December, 2000.

Coauthor of the best selling book, *Built to Last,* describes here his new findings about the kind of leadership that has taken mediocre companies to greatness. The results of a five year study of 1,500 companies on the NYSE, *Good to Great* was published in the fall of 2001. Collins found that only 11 companies in 30 years made this jump from average to extraordinary, and that all their leaders had two traits in common: a self-effacing humility and a dogged persistence, what he called, "humility + will." He argues that Level One is the highly capable individual, Level Two is contributing team members, Level Three is competent manager, Level Four is effective leader and Level Five is the executive who builds enduring greatness through a paradoxical combination of personal humility and professional will.

2. BEHAVIOR APPROACH

The behavior approach first rose to prominence in the 1950s as researchers grew frustrated with the trait approach. They switched their emphasis to observations of what effective and ineffective leaders actually *do* on the job.

Mintzberg's Ten Managerial Roles

from *The Nature of Managerial Work* by Henry Mintzberg, Prentice Hall, 1980. Interviews and observations of five chief executives.

1. Figurehead Role
2. Leader Role: integrating the organization, motivating
3. Liaison Role
4. Monitor Role
5. Disseminator Role
6. Spokesman Role
7. Entrepreneur Role
8. Disturbance Handler Role
9. Resource Allocator Role
10. Negotiator Role

Kotter's Leadership Factor

from *The Leadership Factor,* by John Kotter, The Free Press, New York, 1988 (data from 900 senior executives in 100 American corporations), and from "What Leaders Really Do," by John Kotter, *Harvard Business Review,* May-June 1990, p. 3. See also *The General Managers* and *Power and Influence* by the same author.

"...leadership is defined as the **process** of moving a group (or groups) in some direction through mostly noncoercive means. Effective leadership is defined as leadership that produces movement in the long-term best interest of the group(s)." (*The Leadership Factor,* p. 5)

Using Lee Iacocca as an example, Kotter outlines this pattern:

1. Development of a bold, new vision.
2. An intelligent, that is workable, strategy for implementing the vision.
3. Eliciting the cooperation and teamwork from a large network of essential people.
4. Relentless work to keep key people in the network motivated toward the vision.

"Great vision emerges when a powerful mind, working long and hard on massive amounts of information, is able to see (or recognize in suggestions from others) interesting patterns and new possibilities." (*The Leadership Factor,* p. 29)

> **Effective Senior Management:**
> Industry and Organizational Knowledge
> Relationships in the Firm and the Industry
> Reputation and Track Record
> Abilities and Skills (keen mind, interpersonal skills)
> Personal Values (integrity)
> Motivation (high energy level, strong drive to lead)

"A surprisingly large number of the items [on the skill list] are developed on the job as a part of one's posteducational career. Almost all the knowledge, relationship, and background requirements fit this generalization . . . " (*The Leadership Factor,* p. 34)

Management is different from leadership. Management is about coping with complexity, and leadership is about coping with change. Both are invaluable to the well-being of an organization. Management and leadership are both focused on providing three crucial functions, but they accomplish these tasks in different ways, as outlined below:

Function	Management	Leadership
Deciding what needs to be done	Planning and budgeting (short-term focus)	Setting a direction (long-term focus; communicating a vision)
Creating networks of people and relationships to accomplish the agenda	Organizing and staffing	Aligning people (by communicating with them)
Ensuring that the job gets done	Control mechanisms (compare results to plan and make corrections)	Motivating people (appeal to human needs like self-esteem and recognition)

("What Leaders Really Do," p. 3–9)

Companies with weak leadership show these characteristics:

1. Managers who leave frustrated with neglect and/or abuse.
2. Middle management jobs are mostly fire-fighting.
3. Managers who wanted to be leaders were stymied by bureaucracy.
4. Without depth of management, people were promoted into positions they weren't prepared for.
5. Managers could not be moved across organizational boundaries.
6. Managers were rarely coached or mentored.
7. Managers had one chance only at promotion, regardless of whether that made sense.

In short, such companies manage by responding to short-term financial imperatives, and their efforts are often hampered by parochial internal politics.

Companies with strong leadership tend to have:

1. Sophisticated recruiting efforts.
2. Attractive work environment.
3. Challenging opportunities.
4. Early identification.
5. Planned development.

We need to:

1. Abandon the notion of professional leadership.
2. Think of leadership with a small "l", something we all must do better.
3. Think more carefully about managerial careers.
4. Realize that Human Resource Professionals are not professionals but rather advisors to the line management.

5. Think about how to manage global businesses and develop that talent.
6. Realize that the sources of competitive advantage have changed from the past.

Stewart's Three-Part Theory of Management

from *Managers and Their Jobs,* by R. Stewart, MacMillan, London, 1967; *Contrasts in Management,* by R. Stewart, McGraw-Hill UK, Maidenhead, Berkshire, England, 1976; and *Choices for the Manager: A Guide to Understanding Managerial Work,* by R. Stewart, Prentice-Hall, Englewood Cliffs, NJ, 1982.

Stewart outlines three forces which affect individual managerial roles to varying degrees, helping to shape the nature of those jobs:

Demands: These are duties and responsibilities, imposed by others in positions of power, which the manager must uphold. For example: standards, deadlines, bureaucratic procedures.

Constraints: These are elements in the organizational and external environment which limit the manager's options. For example: policies, regulations, and labor laws, as well as the limited funds, supplies, and personnel available for a task.

Choices: These are the things a manager *may* do, at his or her own discretion. For example: objectives for the business unit being managed, prioritizing of tasks, and strategy.

The relative influences of these three forces affect managerial behavior, and can make one management position very different from another.

Kouzes and Posner's Leadership Challenge

The Leadership Challenge, by James M. Kouzes and Barry Z. Posner, San Francisco, Jossey-Bass, 1987.

In a three year study of about 1,500 managers, Kouzes and Posner inferred five practices and ten behavioral commitments that characterized effective leaders. They developed a self-assessment and leadership assessment tool, the *Leadership Practices Inventory,* to measure these ten dimensions. The *LPI* has become widely used in many schools and businesses.

The five practices and their ten related behavioral commitments are

Challenging the Process
  1. Search for Opportunities
  2. Experiment and Take Risks

Inspiring a Shared Vision
  3. Envision the Future
  4. Enlist Others

Enabling Others to Act
  5. Foster Collaboration
  6. Strengthen Others

Modeling the Way
  7. Set the Example
  8. Plan Small Wins

Encouraging the Heart
  9. Recognize Individual Contribution
  10. Celebrate Accomplishments

Results Focused Leadership

Dave Ulrich, Jack Zenger, Norm Smallwood, *Results Based Leadership,* Boston, Harvard Business School Press, 1999.

Ulrich and his co-authors assert here that whatever a person's characteristics might be, in the end, one must focus on results, on outcomes of an organization. They point out that at least four entities perceive results from an organization: employees, organizational capabilities, customers, and investors. A results-oriented leader will pay attention to all four of these. Then they offer 14 suggestions to help one become a more results-oriented leader:

1. Begin with an absolute focus on results.
2. Take complete and personal responsibility for your groups' results.
3. Clearly and specifically communicate expectations and targets to the people in your group.
4. Determine what you need to do personally to improve your results.
5. Use results as the litmus test for continuing or implementing leadership practice.
6. Engage in developmental activities and opportunities that will help you produce better results.
7. Know and use every group member's capabilities to the fullest and provide everyone with appropriate developmental opportunities.
8. Experiment and innovate in every realm under your influence, looking constantly for new ways to improve performance.
9. Measure the right standards and increase the rigor with which you measure them.
10. Constantly take action; results won't improve without it.
11. Increase the pace or tempo of your group.
12. Seek feedback from others in the organization about ways you and your group can improve your outcomes.
13. Ensure that your subordinates and colleagues perceive that your motivation for being a leader is the achievement of positive results, not personal or political gain.
14. Model the methods and strive for the results you want your group to use and attain.

3. POWER AND INFLUENCE APPROACH

This school of research studies the influence processes at work between leaders and other individuals. In general, the aim is to gain insight into leadership effectiveness by studying the power possessed by a leader, as well as the way that power is wielded.

Two Faces of Power

from David McClelland, "The two faces of power." *Journal of International Affairs,* 1970, 24(1), 29–47.

Dominating Power: Seeks to subjugate others by keeping them weak and dependent on the leader.

Empowering Power: Seeks to enable the weak. Power is exercised cautiously; the aim is to build commitment to the organization and its ideals rather than to oneself.

Winter's Theory of Leadership

Unpublished doctoral dissertation, Harvard Business School, circa 1978.

Leadership is a function of the ability of the leader to empower the followers: to make them feel that they are more capable, more powerful, more able than they were.

"If you think about it, people love others not for who they are, but for how they make us feel. We willingly follow others for much the same reason. It makes us feel good to do so. Now, we also follow platoon sergeants, self-centered geniuses, demanding spouses, bosses of various persuasions and others, for a variety of reasons as well. But none of those reasons involves that person's leadership qualities. In order to willingly accept the direction of another individual, it must feel good to do so. This business of making another person feel good in the unspectacular course of his daily comings and goings is, in my view, the very essence of leadership." Irwin Federman quoted in *Leaders,* by Bennis and Nanus, p. 62–63.

The West Point Way of Leadership

The West Point Way of Leadership, by Larry Donnithorne, Col Ret., Currency/ Doubleday, New York, 1993.

Colonel Donnithorne describes the leadership principles that West Point cadets are taught in each year of their education at the Academy. These lessons taken sequentially and carefully, comprise, he said, the West Point Way of Leadership. Donnithorne's lessons are:

First Year
    Followership is Job One
    Finding Courage in Fear
    Honor is the Language we speak
    Being a team member

Second Year
    Positioning the leader inside the group/team
    Just and Unjust leadership
    Face-to-Face Leadership

Third Year
    Acquiring Self Reliance to lead leaders
    Pushing character to the extreme
    Leading Leaders

Fourth Year
    Executive Leadership
    Serving as the Organization's Eyes and Ears

Social Exchange Theory

from E. P. Hollander, "Conformity, status, and idiosyncrasy credit," *Psychological Review,* 1958, 65, 117–127; E. P. Hollander, "Leadership and social exchange processes," in K. Gergen, M. S. Greenberg, and R. H. Willis (Eds.), *Social Exchange: Advances in Theory and Research,* 1979, Winston-John Wiley, New York; and T. O. Jacobs,

Leadership and Exchange in Formal Organizations, 1970, Human Resources Research Organization, Alexandria, VA.

"**Social exchange**" exists between a leader and the other members of the group: the leader champions a course of action, and the group affords the leader a greater (or lesser) degree of status and influence based on the perceived success (or failure) of the plan.

When an innovative plan succeeds, the leader wins not only greater power and influence but also "**idiosyncrasy credits**"—the allowance of greater latitude to deviate from normal procedures in the future. In other words, the group becomes more receptive to radical-sounding proposals, thanks to the trust which the former success has engendered.

When the leader's plan fails, social exchange theory predicts that the leader will experience a loss of status and influence. The loss will be greater if the failure appears to be due to poor judgment, rather than factors beyond the leader's control; if the leader is thought to have pursued selfish motives; if the plan was especially divergent from group norms; or if the leader had a particularly high degree of status beforehand.

Strategic Contingencies Theory

from D. J. Hickson, C. R. Hinings, C. A. Lee, R. S. Schneck, and J. M. Pennings, "A strategic contingencies theory of intra-organizational power," *Administrative Science Quarterly,* 1971, 16, 216–229.

Strategic contingencies theory looks at organizational subunits, and their relative abilities to influence strategic decisions for the organization as a whole. In other words, what makes some subunits more powerful than others? The theory names three factors:

1. Expertise in dealing with important problems. This expertise is especially valuable when the problem is critical (essential for the survival and well-being of the organization) and when the subunits are highly interdependent.

2. The subunit's centrality in the work flow of the organization. This factor is particularly important if the subunits are not highly interdependent.

3. The extent to which the expertise of the subunit is unique and not easily substitutable.

4. SITUATIONAL APPROACH

The situational approach pays special attention to contextual factors: the nature of the work performed by the leader's unit, the individual characteristics of the followers, or the nature of the external environment. How, it asks, does the larger situation affect the leadership task?

Hersey and Blanchard's Situational Theory of Leadership

from *Management of Organizational Behavior* by P. Hersey and K. H. Blanchard, Prentice-Hall, Englewood Cliffs, NJ, 1977.

This is an extension of the leadership theories presented by Blake and Mouton (in the Managerial Grid approach) and Reddin's 3-D Management Style Theory. Hersey and Blanchard, like Blake and Mouton, use a two-dimensional grid with Task Orientation and People Orientation axes. They also argue that the maturity of the subordinate determines what mix of people vs. task orientation is appropriate for that subordinate. Immature subordinates require a more directive, task-oriented leader, while mature subordinates who are willing to take responsibility will respond better to a more relationship- and people-oriented leader. The four Blanchard leadership styles are directive, managing, coaching, and delegating (from leading less mature to more mature subordinates).

House's Path-Goal Theory of Leadership

from R. J. House, "A path-goal theory of leader effectiveness," *Administrative Science Quarterly,* 1971, 16, 321–339.

"... the motivational function of the leader consists of increasing personal pay-offs to subordinates for work-goal attainment, and making the path to these pay-offs easier to travel by clarifying it, reducing roadblocks and pitfalls, and increasing the opportunities for personal satisfaction en route." (p. 324)

Path-goal theory is related to Expectancy Theory—the belief that people are motivated by their level of expectations that they can do the work, be rewarded, and value the reward offered, in that the leader must understand the subordinates' expectancies and clarify and magnify them towards the desired result. The latest version of the path-goal approach includes four basic types of leader behavior: supportive, directive, participative, and achievement-oriented.

Fiedler's Contingency Model of Leadership

from F. E. Fiedler, *A Theory of Leadership Effectiveness,* McGraw-Hill, New York, 1967.

Fiedler's work revolves around the collection of data on a "Least Preferred Coworker (LPC)" scale. Individuals are asked to name the person with whom they have worked least well in the past, and then to rate the personality of that person; those who do so critically receive low LPC scores, while those who are more positive in their evaluations receive high scores. The interpretation of the scores has changed over the years. Fiedler's belief is that one particular score is not necessarily a better indicator of leadership effectiveness; rather, that effectiveness is a function of the individual's score and several other factors in the situation. Hence, some leaders will be more effective in certain situations, while others will do better in other situations. Fiedler argues that leader-member relationships, positional power, and the structure of the task all contribute to the degree of fit between an individual and a situation.

Leadership Substitutes Theory

from S. Kerr and J. M. Jermier, "Substitutes for leadership: their meaning and measurement," *Organizational Behavior and Human Performance,* 1978, 22, 375–403.

This theory explores aspects of a work situation which can reduce the importance of leadership by "formal leaders" such as managers. There are two situational variables:

Neutralizers: factors in the work situation which hamper the effectiveness of a leader's actions.

Substitutes: factors which make the very role of a formal leader unnecessary.

Neutralizers and substitutes may be found in three different dimensions of the work situation. A few examples of each:

1. **Subordinate characteristics.** Subordinates who arrive with extensive training (doctors, for example) or who have high internal motivation may serve as substitutes for leadership: they may not require, or even want, supervision. Subordinates' values may serve as neutralizers for leadership: if they value time spent with their families highly, they may not respond to "time-and-a-half" payment incentives for working overtime.

2. **Task characteristics.** Certain tasks, by their nature, do not call for much leadership. Simple, repetitive tasks which can easily be mastered make leadership unnecessary. Extremely rewarding tasks, too, can serve as substitutes for certain types of leadership, by ensuring job satisfaction and enthusiasm without the presence of a formal leader.

3. **Group and organization characteristics.** Highly formalized organizations, with extensive regulations and policies, can serve as substitutes for leadership: once subordinates learn the rules, there is little need for the direction of a leader. Such formalized settings can also become neutralizers for leadership, if the inflexibility of the rules impedes the leader's efforts to make strategic changes.

The Multiple-Linkage Model

from G. Yukl, "Toward a behavioral theory of leadership," *Organizational Behavior and Human Performance,* 1971, 6, 414–440.

This model builds on several earlier theories, particularly the Leadership Substitutes Theory (above). A leader attempts to influence the performance of a group, but with a class of **intervening variables** ultimately determining the performance outcomes. There are six intervening variables:

1. Subordinate effort
2. Subordinate ability and role clarity
3. Organization of the work
4. Cooperation and teamwork
5. Resources and support
6. External coordination

Like the Leadership Substitutes Theory, this model includes two additional **situational variables:** neutralizers and substitutes. Here, they exert influence at three points: they impact the behavior and effectiveness of the leader; they impinge directly on the intervening variables; and they determine the relative importance of the intervening variables. As an example of the last, a situation which requires subordinates to work in close quarters for long periods of time will make intervening variable #4, cooperation and teamwork, especially crucial.

Leaders can take actions to influence the variables and thereby bring about better outcomes. In the short term, they can correct deficiencies in the intervening variables. For example, they can affect intervening variable #2 by setting specific goals and giving feedback on performance. In the long term, they can modify the situational variables. For example, they can institute new recruitment systems to attract highly-skilled people to the organization.

Cognitive Resources Theory

from F. E. Fiedler, "The contribution of cognitive resources to leadership performance," *Journal of Applied Social Psychology,* 1986, 16, 532–548, and F. E. Fiedler and

J. E. Garcia, New Approaches to Leadership: Cognitive Resources and Organizational Performance, New York: John Wiley, 1987.

This theory explores the conditions in which two cognitive resources of a leader—**intelligence** and **experience**—have a bearing on group performance. The theory has three propositions:

1. Leader ability contributes to group performance only when a) the leader has a directive style, and b) subordinates require guidance in order to perform. When a task is complex, an intelligent leader will be able to devise a better strategy for performance than an unintelligent leader, and should use a directive style to convey it. When the task is more routine, subordinates will not need much leadership, and leader intelligence will not have any bearing.

2. **Stress** affects the relationship between **intelligence** and group performance. In a low-stress situation, a high-intelligence leader will generate better strategies and decisions than a less intelligent leader. But when stress is high, there is a negative relationship between leader intelligence and the quality of decisions.

3. **Stress** affects the relationship between leader **experience** and group performance. In high-stress situations, leaders look to their own past decisions for guidance. Experience is positively related to decision quality in these situations, but is unrelated to decision quality when stress is low.

5. CHARISMATIC APPROACH

Charisma was rarely studied in a managerial context before the 1980s, but since then it has attracted a good deal of attention. In Greek it means "divinely inspired gift," but theorists use a less colorful definition: the result of follower perceptions which are influenced by actual leader traits and behavior, situational context, and the needs of the followers.

House's Theory of Charismatic Leadership

from R. J. House, "A 1976 theory of charismatic leadership," in J. G. Hunt and L. L. Larson (Eds.), *Leadership: the cutting edge,* Carbondale: Southern Illinois University Press, 1977.

Charismatic leadership is measured by the following:

1. Followers' trust in the correctness of the leader's beliefs.
2. Similarity of followers' beliefs to the leader's beliefs.
3. Unquestioning acceptance of the leader by followers.
4. Followers' affection for the leader.
5. Followers' willing obedience to the leader.
6. Emotional involvement of followers in the mission of the organization.
7. Heightened performance goals of followers.
8. Belief of followers that they are able to contribute to the success of the group's mission.

Given these factors, charismatic leaders:

have high self confidence, strong conviction in their own beliefs.
create the impression that they are competent.
articulate ideological goals for subordinates.

appeal to the hopes and ideals of the followers.
use role modeling where they can. "Be like me."
communicate high expectations.
arouse motives related to the group's mission.

Attribution Theory of Charisma

from J. A. Conger and R. Kanungo, "Toward a behavioral theory of charismatic leadership in organizational settings," *Academy of Management Review,* 1987, 12, 637–647, and J. A. Conger, *The Charismatic Leader: Behind the Mystique of Exceptional Leadership,* San Francisco, CA: Jossey-Bass, 1989.

This theory describes five leader traits and behaviors which help make the leader seem charismatic in the eyes of followers:

1. Championing a vision that is **radically different** from the status quo—although not so different that followers will find it unacceptable.
2. Employing **unconventional** methods and strategies to realize the vision.
3. Taking personal **risk** and making **sacrifices:** followers trust a leader who may incur personal loss if the undertaking fails.
4. Projecting **confidence.**
5. Using **persuasive** appeals toward followers, rather than an authoritative or consensus approach.

The theory outlines two processes by which charismatic leaders actually influence followers:

1. **Personal identification.** Followers admire the leader, and as a result want to become more like him or her.
2. **Internalization of values and beliefs.** This process runs deeper than personal identification, which is often limited to the imitation of superficial leader traits. Followers who internalize the values and beliefs of the leader become motivated on their own to perform.

Finally, the theory names **dissatisfaction** as an important situational contributor to charismatic leadership. A charismatic leader is more likely to emerge when there is a crisis calling for drastic measures.

Self-Concept Theory of Charismatic Leadership

from B. Shamir, R. J. House, and M. B. Arthur, "The motivational effects of charismatic leadership: A self-concept based theory." *Organization Science,* 1993, 4, 1–17.

This theory, which builds on some earlier, related works, attempts to explain how charismatic leaders are able to compel followers to put aside their own self-interest for the sake of the organization's betterment. It identifies four processes:

1. **Personal identification.** As in the Attribution Theory above. The Self-Concept theory further says that those with low self-esteem are most likely identify in this way with a leader.

2. **Social identification.** More important than personal identification, this involves defining oneself in terms of one's membership in the group. High social identification leads followers to put the group's needs ahead of their own. Charismatic leaders

inspire social identification through appeals to group values, and through the use of flags, uniforms and other symbolic devices.

3.   **Internalization.** In this theory, follower adaptation (internalization) of the *leader's* values is uncommon. More often, the leader plays up existing *follower* values by linking them to task objectives.

4.   **Self-efficacy.** This is the belief in one's own competence and ability. By holding high expectations and projecting confidence that followers can live up to them, a charismatic leader inspires this trait in individuals and also in the group as a whole (*collective* **self-efficacy**).

Facilitating conditions. Charismatic leaders are more likely to motivate when:

1.   Leader's vision harmonizes with existing follower values.
2.   Organizational mission can be linked to follower values (ex: defense-contractor employees believing they are helping to defend the country).
3.   Work is unstructured and hazy.
4.   Organization is facing difficulties.

6. TRANSFORMATIONAL APPROACH

Transformational leadership is seen as a process in which leaders and followers both inspire one another to elevated moral conduct. It can be used to influence both superiors and subordinates. Those under its influence feel they are "bettering themselves."

Warren Bennis' Theory of Leadership

from Warren Bennis and Burt Nanus, *Leaders: The Strategies for Taking Charge,* New York: Harper and Row, 1985. Ninety interviews with 60 successful CEOs; 30 with outstanding public-sector leaders.

Leadership occurs in a context defined by three elements: 1) Commitment of the culture to excellence and improvement, 2) Complexity of the culture/society (swirling maelstroms of technology, social, and business change), and 3) Credibility: the willingness of a people to place trust and respect in public figures. With regard to the second element, the authors maintain that we are at a pivotal point in the world's industrial history: a transition from the Industrial Society to the Information Society.

" . . . power is the basic energy needed to initiate and sustain action or, to put it another way, the capacity to translate intention into reality and sustain it." (p. 17)

"Present problems will not be solved without successful organizations, and organizations cannot be successful without effective leadership." (p. 20)

"Managers are people who do things right and leaders are people who do the right thing." (p. 21)

Four leadership strategies were found to be used by all 90 interviewees:

1.   **Attention Through Vision.** "Vision animates, inspirits, transforms purpose into action." (p. 30)

2.   **Meaning Through Communication.** Regardless of how articulate they are in a conventional sense, leaders find a way to convey their visions and meanings in unmistak-

able terms to their constituents. "The main clue is that leadership creates a new audience for its ideas because it alters the shape of understanding by transmitting information in such a way that it "fixes" and secures tradition." (p. 42)

3.   **Trust Through Positioning.** "Trust is the lubrication that makes it possible for organizations to work." (p. 43) Trust is a function of constancy.

"Every organization incorporates four concepts of organization . . . the manifest organization (on the charts) . . . the assumed organization (what we think we have) . . . the extant organization (what we really have), . . . the requisite organization (what we should have)." (pp. 50–51)

4.   **The Deployment of Self Through Positive Self-Regard.** "To have self-respect is everything. Without it, we are nothing but unwilling slaves, at everybody's mercy, especially those we fear or hold in contempt." (p. 58) "Recognizing strengths and compensating for weaknesses represent the first step in achieving positive self-regard." (p. 58) "The second element is positive self-regard is the nurturing of skills with discipline—that is, to keep working on and developing one's talents.." (p. 59) " . . . the third aspect of positive self-regard, the capacity to discern the fit between one's perceived skills and what the job requires." (p. 60)

Five characteristics of Emotional Wisdom:

1. The ability to accept people as they are.
2. The capacity to approach relationships and problems in the present rather than in the past.
3. The ability to treat those who are close with the same respect and courtesy reserved for those who are strangers.
4. The ability to trust others even if the risk is great.
5. The ability to do without constant approval and recognition from others.

James MacGregor Burns' Theory of Leadership

from James MacGregor Burns, *Leadership,* New York: Harper, 1973.

"No matter how strong this longing for unanimity, however, almost all leaders, at least at the national level, must settle for far less than universal affection. They must be willing to make enemies—to deny themselves the affection of their adversaries. They must accept conflict. They must be willing and able to be unloved. It is hard to pick one's friends, harder to pick one's enemies." (p. 34)

" . . . transforming leadership ultimately becomes moral in that it raises the level of human conduct and ethical aspiration of both leader and led, and thus it has a transforming effect on both." (p. 20)

"I define leadership as leaders inducing followers to act for certain goals that represent the values and the motivations—the wants and needs, the aspirations and expectations—of both leaders and followers. And the genius of leadership lies in the manner in which leaders see and act on their own and their followers' values and motivations." (p. 19) "Leadership over human beings is exercised when persons with certain motives and purposes mobilize, in competition or conflict with others, institutional, political, psychological, and other resources so as to arouse, engage, and satisfy the motives of followers." (p. 18)

"We must see power—and leadership—as not things but as relationships. We must analyze power in a context of human motives and physical constraints." (p. 11)

Moral leadership "is the kind of leadership that operates a need and value levels higher than those of the potential follower (but not so much higher as to lose contact)." (p. 42)

"Second, it is the kind of leadership that can exploit conflict and tension within persons' value structures." (p. 42)

"But the ultimate test of moral leadership is its capacity to transcend the claims of the multiplicity of everyday wants and needs and expectations, to respond to the higher levels of moral development, and to relate leadership behavior—its roles, choices, style, commitments—to a set of reasoned, relatively explicit, conscious values.." (p. 46)

Transforming leadership must be distinguished from **transactional** leadership. Both appeal to values, but the latter only to values related to exchange (fairness, reciprocity). Some types of transforming leadership and their corresponding transactional types:

TRANSFORMING LEADERSHIP	TRANSACTIONAL LEADERSHIP
Intellectual leadership	Legislative leadership
Heroic leadership	Group leadership
Executive leadership	Bureaucratic leadership
Ideological leadership	Reforming leadership
Revolutionary leadership	

Bass' Theory of Transformational Leadership

from B. M. Bass, Leadership and Performance Beyond Expectations, New York: Free Press, 1985.

This theory, which builds on that of Burns above, distinguishes **transactional leadership** from **transformational leadership.** Transactional leadership is based on an exchange: the leader offers rewards for performance of a desired behavior. Transformational leadership (which differs from Burns' transforming leadership in that it does not necessarily have to appeal to *positive* moral values) lies in the leader's ability to inspire trust, loyalty, and admiration in followers, who then subordinate their individual interests to the interests of the group.

Transactional behaviors:
1. **Contingent reward.** The use of incentives and rewards to induce task performance.
2. **Passive management by exception.** The use of punishments and other measures to correct deviations from expected performance.
3. **Active management by exception.** Monitoring subordinates to ensure that deviations from expected performance do not occur.
4. **Laissez-faire leadership.** Not managing much at all; ignoring problems.

Transformational behaviors:
1. Idealized influence (charisma).
2. **Individualized consideration.** Support, guidance, encouragement.
3. **Intellectual stimulation.** Increasing follower awareness and understanding of problems.
4. **Inspirational motivation.** Conveying a compelling vision; using symbols and slogans to unite followers and intensify their efforts.

Differences between charismatic and transformational leadership:
1. Bass sees charismatic leadership as the ability to inspire *superficial* identification only. Charisma is an ingredient of transformational leadership (see "transformational behaviors," above); transformational leadership encloses it and goes beyond it. Transformational leadership arouse stronger emotions and appeal to values.
2. Charismatic leaders often try to keep followers dependent and weak. Transformational leaders offer empowerment.
3. Charismatic leaders are rare. Transformational leaders can be found at any level of an organization.
4. Charismatic leaders inspire extreme love and extreme hate. Transformational leaders inspire a less polarized response.

Tichy and Devanna's Transformational Leadership Process

from N. M. Tichy and M. A. Devanna, *The Transformational Leader,* New York: John Wiley & Sons, 1986.

Transforming and revitalizing an existing organization involves the following sequence:

1. **Recognizing the need for change.** Transformational leaders must identify significant changes in the environment, and then be able to convince others that major organizational changes, rather than small adjustments, are needed. Four ways to increase the sensitivity of the organization to environmental change:

   a. Encourage dissenting opinions.
   b. Listen to outsiders who can objectively critique the organization.
   c. Visit with and learn from other organizations.
   d. Measure performance against the competition, and not simply against the previous fiscal year.

2. **Managing the transition.** Determine what changes are necessary, and help followers deal with the emotional upheaval that accompanies them.

3. **Creating a new vision.** Communicate (through a mission statement as well as other means) a vision for the future which can inspire and unite followers. Express it not just as numbers but as ideology. Make it conducive to greater follower self-esteem.

4. **Institutionalizing the changes.** Ensure that the new vision has the support of top management and other key players in the organization. Develop a coalition of people who are committed to the vision, replacing people where necessary. Revise the structure of the organization itself if the current structure is an impediment to realization of the vision.

Seven attributes of transformational leaders:
1. They see themselves as agents of change.
2. They are not afraid to take risks, but are not reckless.
3. They believe in people and are attentive to their needs.
4. They are able to identify and articulate their own set of core values.
5. They are flexible and open to new ideas.
6. They are careful, disciplined thinkers.
7. They trust their own intuitions.

Schein's Model of Organizational Culture and Leadership

from Edgar Schein, *Organizational Culture and Leadership,* San Francisco: Jossey-Bass, 1985.

Culture is invisible. Only its manifestations are visible. Culture stems from the enduring solutions to problems that have arisen historically. It also contains and reduces anxiety. "Leaders create cultures, but cultures, in turn, create their next generation of leaders." (p. 313) " . . . the unique and essential function of leadership is the manipulation of culture." (p. 317)

In early stages of culture formation, leaders need vision, the ability to articulate it, and the ability to enforce it. They need persistence and patience. They need the ability to absorb anxiety when things do not go as well as originally planned or hoped. They must also be able to provide temporary stability and emotional reassurance.

In mature organizations, leadership is defined by culture. The leaders of such organizations must understand their cultures insightfully. They must be able to skillfully motivate their followers. They must also have emotional strength to get the organization through periods of change. In order to do so, they must be able to change the culture's assumptions. This requires the paradoxical abilities to listen and to create involvement. They must be able to see the deepest parts of the assumptive framework of the organization.

The leader is a culture manager. He/she must understand culture formation and maturation. Cultures form around assumptions relating to humanity's relationship to nature, the nature of reality and truth, human nature, the nature of human activity, and the nature of human relationships. (p. 86)

Cases That Apply

This list is intended as a sampling of some cases available at Harvard and Darden that apply to various aspects of the general model introduced in this book. As with the bibliography, the list is not comprehensive but a good starting point for building a course or a series of discussions. Harvard cases are available from Harvard Case Services (HCS), whereas Darden School cases (denoted with the prefix UVA) are available from Darden Educational Materials Services (DEMS). See also the accompanying volume, which includes many of these cases (*Practical Problems in Organizations: Cases in Leadership, Organizational Behavior, and Human Resources*, James G. Clawson, Prentice Hall, 2002).

INTRODUCTION

Peter Browning and Continental White Cap A and B (HCS-486-090-091)
Jewel Savadelis A and B (UVA-PACS-022, 023)

Self

John Wolford A–C (UVA-OB-167, 168, 169)
Jackie Woods A and B (UVA-BP-330, 331; with CD-ROM)
Stewart Glapat A–F (UVA-OB-348-354)
Peter Woodson A and B (UVA-OB-390, 391)
"The Life and Career of a Senior Executive Officer" (UVA-PACS-023; with videotape)
Hassan Shahrasebi (UVA-OB-590; set in Iran)
"Greenland" (UVA-OB-581; set in Greenland, involving Scandinavians)
"Tetsundo Iwakuni: The Case of Japanese Leadership" (UVA-OB-627)
"The Hyundai Group's Chung Ju Yung: A Profile in Leadership" (UVA-OB-555; Korea)
Robert O'Neill (UVA-OB-0702; Fairfax County, VA, leader wrestles with change in government)
Carolyn Hendricks (UVA-OB-601; young woman defines leadership and her life's dream)
"Louis Gerstner and Lotus Development" A–C (UVA-OB-0696; new CEO addresses the acquired troops.)

Task and Strategic Thinking

Walt Disney Productions A (UVA-BP-332)
"The Walt Disney Company: The Arrival of Eisner and Wells" B (UVA-BP-0339)
"Stewart-Glapat vs. Caljan" A–D (UVA-OB-628, 629, 630, and 631)
"Charlotte Beers at Olgivy Mather" (HCS 495-031)
"British Air-USAir" A (UVA-OB-584; creating strategic alliances)
"Comparing Organizational Charters" (UVA-OB-663; industry dyads to compare the
    elements of a charter)
"The Credit Acceptance Management Division" (UVA-OB-0634)

Leading Others

Warner Cable A–C (HCS 9-489-092, 093, 094)
Alvarez A and B (UVA-OB-660, 661)
"Great Expectations" A and B (UVA-OB-742; set in Nepal)
"Old Colony Associates" (HCS revised case 495-034, with individual cases associated)
"Jerry Caldwell at MOEX" (UVA-OB-0691)
Robert Jones (UVA-OB-0369; traveling engineer wrestles with traveling with a
    female companion)
Cheryl Young (UVA-OB-0383; young woman wrestles with discrimination)
James Carroway (UVA-OB-0688; young man deals with discrimination against his
    subordinate)
Marsha Harris A (UVA-OB-562; new woman manager faces downsizing challenges)
Ray Hagen A–D (UVA-OB-0262; CEO faces laying off older, ill employee before
    retirement)
"The Chicago Bulls and Michael Jordan" (UVA-OB-0727)

Leading Teams

"Crossroads" A and B (UVA-OB-0665, 0666)
"GE FANUC NA" A and B (UVA-OB-437, 438; with videotape)
"Meeting of the Overhead Reduction Task Force" (HCS-9-478-013 with videotape)
"Making the Tough Team Call" A (UVA-OB-0705; European team needs help in
    performing)

Leaders As Designers

"FMC Aberdeen" (UVA-OB-385)
"Organizing the Comanche Program" A–C (UVA-OB-432, 433, 434)
"Park Nicollet" (video case available from DEMS)
"Charge of the Nueces Task Force" A and B (UVA-OB-304, 305)
"The Kao Story: A Case Study" (*International Management Journal* 10, no. 2 (June
    1992): 179–91.
"Genetronics" A–C (UVA-OB-0306; fast-growing retailer wrestles with human
    resource management systems design)
"Johnson & Johnson: The Live for Life Program" A (UVA-OB-0412)
"Levi Strauss & Co.: The South Zarzamora Street Plant" (UVA-OB-0427)

Managing Change

"Chicago Park District" A–D (UVA-OB-618, 619, 620, 620; with CD-ROM)
"NYT PUB COM" A–C (UVA-OB-591, 592, 593; with CD-ROM)
"Big Sky Company: Magasco Mill" A and B (UVA-OB-396, 411)
"Goodwin House, Inc." (UVA-OB-704)
"Paragon Corporation and Its Flight Department" (UVA-OB-0668)
"Shell Italia A" (UVA-OB-0586)

SELECT BIBLIOGRAPHY

For more information see the Web site http://faculty.darden.edu/clawsonj

GENERAL PERSPECTIVES

Gardner, John. *On Leadership.* New York: Free Press, 1990. Well-known leadership author's summary concepts.

Hersey, Paul, and Ken Blanchard. *Management of Organizational Behavior.* 4th ed. Englewood Cliffs, NJ: Prentice Hall, 1982. General overview of organizational behavior concepts.

Savage, Charles M. *Fifth Generation Management.* Boston: DEC, 1991. Management in the information age.

Schein, Edgar. *Organizational Culture and Leadership.* San Francisco: Jossey-Bass, 1985. *Superb* insight; requires careful reading.

Wheatley, Margaret J. *Leadership and the New Sciences.* San Francisco: Berrett-Koehler, 1992. Every event is a potentiality; what can you make of it?

INDIVIDUAL PERSPECTIVES

Clawson, James G. "Why People Behave the Way They Do." Darden Technical Note OB-0183, Darden Educational Materials Services, Darden School Foundation, Charlottesville, VA. www2.darden.edu/case/collection. Summarizes the VABE model often used in class.

Covey, Stephen. *Seven Habits of Highly Effective People.* New York: Simon & Schuster, 1989. A bestseller for over a decade on core principles of effectiveness.

Csikszentmihalyi, Mihalyi. *The Evolving Self: A Psychology for the Third Millennium.* New York: HarperCollins, 1993. One of the most profound books ever written: How can we rise above millennia of genetic and cultural momentum?

———. *Flow: The Psychology of Optimal Experience.* New York: Harper & Row, 1990. Defines peak experience.

Ellis, Albert, and Robert Harper. *A Guide to Rational Living.* North Hollywood, CA: Wilshire Book Company, 1975. All about learning to speak without creating defensiveness in others—and yourself. Classic.

Fassel, Diane. *Working Ourselves to Death and the Rewards of Recovery.* New York: Harper Paperbacks, 1990. Workaholism is real and deadly. Don't ignore it.

Fromm, Bill, and Leonard Schlesinger. *The Real Heroes of Business and Not a CEO Among Them.* New York: Currency Doubleday, 1994. Often the real heroes don't have big titles and incomes.

Gallwey, W. Timothy. *The Inner Game of Work.* New York: Random House, 2000.

Glasser, William. *Choice Theory.* New York: HarperCollins, 1999. The basic motivations in life and the importance of dealing with the present, not the past.

Goleman, Daniel. *Emotional Intelligence.* New York: Bantam, 1995. It takes more than IQ to succeed.

Kouzes, James M., and Barry Z. Posner. *The Leadership Challenge.* San Francisco: Jossey-Bass, 1987. Ten steps to effective leadership.

Kranzler, Gerald D. *You Can Change How You Feel.* Eugene: University of Oregon, 1974. Goes with Ellis on how to manage your own thoughts and feelings.

McCarthy, Kevin W. *The On-Purpose Person: Making Your Life Make Sense.* Colorado Springs: Pinon Press, 1992. Don't get sidetracked.

Miller, Alice. *The Drama of the Gifted Child.* New York: Basic Books, 1990. Learning to manage the "gifts" our parents give us.

Peck, M. Scott. *The Road Less Traveled.* New York: Touchstone, 1978.

Viorst, Judith. *Necessary Losses.* New York: Fawcett, 1986. Some things you have to give up to grow.

STRATEGIC THINKING (TASK VISION)

Charan, Ram, and Noel Tichy. *Every Business Is a Growth Business.* New York: Times Books, 2000. Excellent basic strategic model for growing a business.

Davis, Stanley M. *Future Perfect.* Reading, MA: Addison-Wesley, 1987. Excellent insight on how leaders think.

Hamel, Gary. *Leading the Revolution.* Boston: Harvard Business School Press, 2000.

Hamel, Gary, and C. K. Prahalad. *Competing for the Future.* Boston: HBS Press, 1994. Two of the most influential strategic analysts today.

Porter, Michael. *Competitive Strategy.* New York: Free Press, 1980. Classic on strategic thinking.

Schwartz, Peter. *The Art of the Long View.* New York: Doubleday Currency, 1991. Excellent summary of scenario planning.

CREATIVITY

Gelb, Michael J. *Learning to Think Like Leonardo da Vinci.* New York: Delacorte Press, 1998. Seven mental habits of the world's greatest genius.

Thompson, Charles. *What a Great Idea!* New York: Harper Perennial, 1992. Charlottesville native shows how to increase your creativity.

Von Oech, Roger. *A Whack on the Side of the Head.* Menlo Park, CA: Creative Think, 1983. Easy to read, humorous, with lots of exercises.

INTERPERSONAL PERSPECTIVES

Bennis, Warren. *Organizing Genius.* Reading, MA: Addison-Wesley, 1997. Analyzes seven effective teams in recent history.

Cohen, Allan R., and David L. Bradford. *Influence Without Authority.* New York: John Wiley & Sons, 1991. How can you develop influence from the middle?

Garner, Alan. *Conversationally Speaking.* Los Angeles: Lowell House, 1997. Real tips and techniques for developing influence in relationships.

Keirsey, David, and Marilyn Bates. *Please Understand Me.* Del Mar, CA: Prometheus Books, 1984. Explains the Myers-Briggs Type Indicator.

Tannen, Deborah. *You Just Don't Understand.* New York: Ballantine, 1990.

ORGANIZATIONAL PERSPECTIVES

Beer, Michael, Bert Spector, Paul R. Lawrence, D. Quinn Mills, and Richard E. Walton. *Managing Human Assets.* New York: Free Press, 1984. Human resource management concepts the Harvard way.

DeGeus, Arie. *The Living Company.* Boston: HBS Press, 1997. Another in the line of Royal Dutch Shell strategists describing new visions of organizations and strategy.

Galbraith, Jay R., Edward E. Lawler III, and Associates. *Organizing for the Future.* San Francisco: Jossey-Bass, 1993.

Pfeffer, Jeffrey. *The Human Equation.* Boston: Harvard Business School Press, 1997. Latest summary of how human resources can be a source of competitive advantage.

Schein, Edgar H. *Career Dynamics.* Reading, MA: Addison-Wesley, 1978. Classic on career management and career anchors.

Senge, Peter. *The Fifth Discipline: The Art and Practice of the Learning Organization.* New York: Doubleday, 1990. Excellent, classic originator of the learning organization concepts.

Tichy, Noel M., and Stratford Sherman. *Control Your Destiny or Someone Else Will.* New York: HarperCollins, 1994. Story of Jack Welch and General Electric by the then-head of GE training in Crotonville, NY.

MANAGING CHANGE

Collins, James. *Good to Great.* New York: Harper Business, 2001.

Hammer, Michael, and James Champy. *Reengineering the Corporation.* New York: Harper Business, 1993. Classic on revolutionary organizational redesign.

Kotter, John. *Leading Change.* Boston: Harvard Business School Press, 1996.

Nevis, Edwin E., Jon Lancourt, and Helen G. Vassallo. *Intentional Revolutions.* San Francisco: Jossey-Bass, 1996. The MIT model of change.

O'Toole, James. *Leading Change.* San Francisco: Jossey-Bass, 1995. Excellent historical perspective on what it takes to change.

Quinn, Robert. *Deep Change.* San Francisco: Jossey-Bass, 1997. Michigan founder of competing values framework describes a huge project at Ford.

Schein, Edgar. *Process Consultation.* Reading, MA: Addison-Wesley, 1969. The classic on managing facilitation.

Watzlawick, Paul, John H. Weakland, and Richard Fisch. *Change.* New York: Norton, 1974.

Index

A

Abrahams, Jeffrey, 164
Age of Reason, 114
Air Force, U.S., 200
Allen, James, 95
Amygdala, 113–14, 115
Andrews, Ken, 146, 148, 151
Anger, change and, 237
Apollo Syndrome, 216
Apple Computer, 197, 198, 211, 220
Appraisal, performance, 20, 216–17
Argyris, Chris, 51
Aristocratic Age, 9–11
Aristocratic authority, legitimate
        authority versus, 12
Art of the Long View, The
        (Schwartz), 100
Association memes, 72
Association VABEs, 44–45
Assumptions. *See* VABEs
Atari, 199
AT&T, 153, 200
Autonomy, 66, 74, 216

B

Bacon, Sir Francis, 110, 111
Baker, Mark, 95
Balanced scorecard approach, 30,
        222–23
BancOne, 15, 103, 104
Bargaining, change and, 237
Baseline behavior, 228, 229–31
Beer, Michael, 124, 234–35, 240
Behavior. *See also* Leadership,
        Level One; Skinner, B. F.
    culture and, 71
    defined, 81
    early bases for, 67–72
    generation and, 70
    genetics and, 69–70

REB and, 81
    reward and, 47
Belbin, Meredith, 194–95, 196,
        216
Beliefs. *See* VABEs
Bell Labs, 200
Bennis, Warren, 18–19, 196, 197,
        198, 199, 200
Biederman, Patricia, 196, 197, 198,
        199, 200
Big picture, 5–6, 9, 16
    motivation and, 19
    strategy and, 144
Blake, Robert, 124
Body and Soul (Roddick), 177
Boston Consulting Group, 145
Boundaryless organizations, 16,
        18
Box, as leadership focus, 33–35
Boy's Life (MacCammon), 128
Bradford, David, 180
Built to Last (Collins and Porras),
        20, 150
Bureaucracy, defined, 11
Bureaucratic mind-set, 7, 8, 17
    organizational control and, 103
    variance management and, 107
Bureaucratic society, 11–14
Bust, Jeff, 102

C

Campbell, Roger, 102
Canon (opto-electronics manufac-
        turer), 150, 153
Capital One, 169
Caplan, Janet, 200
Carlisle, Thomas, 200
Carrot-and-stick approach, 47, 73
Caterpillar (construction equip-
        ment maker), 150, 152
Causal map, 161–62

Center for Creative Leadership
        (North Carolina), 28
Centering, 95–98, 100–101
Change
    cycle, 239
    experimentation and, 238
    Four Ps of, 240
    general model of, 227–30
    as leadership focus, 33–35
    levels of, 239, 240
    models of, 234–35, 240–41
    outside help and, 230–31
    quotient, 118–19, 187, 237
    rate of, 14–15
    responses to, 236–39
    roles in process, 235
Changee, 235
Character, centering and, 97
Charan, Ram, 151
Charters
    defined, 159
    individual, 161
    Level Three leadership and,
        171–72
Chicago Park District, 232
Chinese Contract, 214
Circles of concern, 36–38
Circles of influence, 36–38, 59
Circuit City, 223
Clan organizations, 213, 214
Claypool, Forrest, 232–33
Coast Guard, U.S., 250
Coercion, 178, 179, 241. *See also*
        Manipulation
Cohen, Allan, 180
Cohesion, of organizations,
        223–24
Collins, James C., 20, 28, 150, 153,
        154, 160
Comfort zone, 228, 229–31, 236
"Coming Death of Bureaucracy,
        The" (Bennis), 18

Commitment. *See also* Visioning, commitment, and management
  leadership and, 105–6
  motivation and, 250
Communication
  fact-based, 219
  influence and, 184–85
Competitive advantage, defined, 144
Conclusions, REB and, 78
Conscious thoughts. *See* Leadership, Level Two
Context
  environmental, 30
  of organization, 29–30
Control theory, 73
Coordination, team leadership and, 199
Core capabilities, 150
Covey, Stephen, 36–37, 38, 98–99, 159, 179, 183
CQ. *See* Change, quotient
Csikszentmihalyi, Mihalyi, 46–47, 125
Culture
  behavior and, 71
  organizational, 71, 220–21, 233, 248
  VABEs and, 77
Curren, Tom, 122
Currencies of reciprocity, 180–83, 249–50

D

Damasio, Antonio, 113–14
Darden Graduate School of Business Administration, 164
Davidow, Bill, 20
Davis, Stan, 29, 98, 165, 212
Deceptive manipulation, 56. *See also* Manipulation
Deci, Edward, 66
Defense mechanisms, 84–85, 88–89
Denial, change and, 236–39
Design. *See* Organizational design
Despair, change and, 237
Diamond, Jared, 9
Diamond model, 27–32, 33–35
Disconfirming data, 228, 229–32, 235, 236–39
Disney, 8, 150
Disney, Walt, 197
Distinction memes, 72
Distinction VABEs, 44–45
Distributed leadership, 198–99
Diversity, 21, 25, 71
Divisional model, of organizational design, 212

Doughnut organizations, 213, 214
Duty cycle, 133, 135, 136, 137

E

Ecological model, 152–53
Edison, Thomas, 106
Eisner, Michael, 8
Ellis, Albert, 74, 115
Emerson, Ralph Waldo, 54, 143, 153, 222
Emotional
  intelligence, 111–15, 125, 131
  learning, 113
  quotient, 112–15
Emotional hijacking, 112, 113, 115, 117
Emotional Intelligence (Goleman), 110, 120
Emotions, REB and, 79
Empathy, social quotient and, 117
Empowerment, 16, 48
  defined, 100
  systems design and, 104
Energy cycle
  managing, 131–32
  resonance model and, 131
  WCP and, 129–30
Engagement, centering and, 96
Enlightenment philosophy, 110
Enron, 232
Environmental context, 30
EQ. *See* Emotional, quotient
Ethics
  defined, 54–55
  leadership and, 33
  morality versus, 54–55
  organizational design and, 214
  privacy and, 42, 56, 249
Events, REB and, 75
Exchange currencies, 179–83, 249–50
Exchange model system, 183
Expectancy theory, 47
Expectations. *See* VABEs
Experimentation, change and, 233, 238
Expertise
  as leadership focus, 33–35
  power, 178, 179

F

Fads, in management, 48, 51, 52, 233
Fairness, moral leadership and, 57, 59, 60, 61
Farkas, Charles M., 33
Farmer power, 9
Federalist organizations, 213

Fifth Discipline, The (Senge), 24, 30
Fit model, 146–50
Five forces model, 147–48
Flattening of organizations, 16–17
Flow, 125–27. *See also* Resonance
FMC Aberdeen (South Dakota), 101, 102, 216, 218
FMC Corporation, 211
Followers. *See also* Others
  memes of, 72
  point of view, 3–4
  reciprocity and, 179
  respect and, 63, 97, 183
  trust and, 63
  willingness to follow, 34, 38, 47, 56
Ford, Henry, 43, 148–49, 160
Ford Motor Company, 149
Fortune (magazine), 232
Frames of Mind (Gardner), 111
Frederick the Great, 11, 212
Freedoms, WCP and, 129–30, 130–32
French, John R. P., Jr., 178
Future Perfect (Davis), 29, 98, 165

G

Gabarro, John, 180
Galbraith, Jay, 209, 219
Gandhi, Mohandas K., 3, 56, 137, 185
Gardner, Howard, 111–12, 118
General Electric (GE), 17, 119, 124, 221
General Motors, 211
Generation, behavior and, 70
Genetics, behavior and, 69–70
GEO Consulting, 150, 152
Glasser, William, 71, 73–74, 75
Goals statement, 168, 170
Go (game), strategic thinking and, 155
Goleman, Daniel, 110, 114, 115, 116, 117, 118, 120
Good breast/bad breast phenomenon, 68
Grayson, Les, 155
Greenleaf, Robert, 93, 143
Grief, change and, 236–38
Growth model, 150–51

H

Hamel, Gary, 150, 151–52, 153–54, 164
Handy, Charles, 213–14
Harvard Business Review, 33
Harvard Business School, 124, 126, 147, 234, 240

Harvard School of Education, 111
Henderson, Bruce, 145
Hewlett-Packard, 153
Hiring, 215–16
Hitler, Adolf, 56
Holes, in personality, 68–69, 74, 84
Honda, 150
Hope, change and, 238
Horniman, Alexander, 97, 132
"How Bell Labs Creates Star
    Performers" (Kelly and
    Caplan), 200
Human resources, as leadership
    focus, 33–35
Human resources cycle, 215, 220
Hunting and gathering, 8, 9
Hybrid models, 213–14

I

IBM, 197, 218, 220
Individual level of leadership, 39,
    145
Industrial Age, 8–9, 11–14
    assumptions about others in, 100
    leadership, 247–48
    Level One leadership and, 43
    traditional measurement sys-
        tems and, 201
Industry Week (magazine), 16, 63
Influence
    definition of leadership and, 36
    developing, 25
    force versus, 56
        (*See also* Leadership, power
        versus)
    general approach to, 184–86
    learned strategies for, 69
    Level Three, 186–87
        (*See also* Leadership, Level
        Three)
Infocracies, 5, 18, 99, 102–4
Information Age, 8–9, 14–21
    leadership, 248–49
    organizational structures of,
        102–4, 213
    strategic thinking and, 143
Information technology, systems
    design and, 219
Inspiration-based reciprocity, 181
Integration, change and, 238
Integrity, 62
Intelligence. *See* Emotional, intelli-
    gence; Intelligence quotient;
    Social quotient
Intelligence quotient
    predictive power of, 112
    standardized testing and, 111
Intent model, 151–52
Invitations, Class Five, 188

Invitations, influence and, 185–86
IQ. *See* Intelligence quotient

J

Jackson, Phil, 137
Jay, Anthony, 190
Jefferson, Thomas, 55
Jesus, 3
Jobs, Steven, 153, 195, 197, 198, 211
Johnson, Kelly, 200
Johnson & Johnson, 153, 213
Jordan, Michael, 132

K

KASH (knowledge, attitude, skills,
    and habits), 177
Katzenbach, Jon R., 191
Kelley, Robert, 200
Kennedy, John F., 184
Kerr, Steve, 106
Kimberley-Clark, 232
King, Martin Luther, Jr., 98
Kissinger, Henry, 3
Klein, Melanie, 68, 69
Knowledge, attitude, skills, and
    habits (KASH), 177
Komatsu (construction equipment
    maker), 152
Kotter, John, 180, 240
Kübler-Ross, Elisabeth, 236
Kuhn, Thomas, 248

L

Lancaster, Bob, 101, 102, 211,
    218–19
Lawler, Ed, 209
Lawrence, Paul, 9, 124
LDS Church, 164
Leadership
    commitment and, 105–6
    defined, 34, 36, 47, 177
    elements of, 27–30
    ethical, 33
    Level One, 42–46, 48–49, 51–52,
        67, 73, 100–101, 247–48, 250
    Level Two, 42–44, 46, 50–51, 52
    Level Three, 42–52, 86, 160–61,
        186–87, 247–51
        (*See also* VABEs)
    manipulation versus, 38, 39, 56
    moral foundation of, 57–59,
        62–63, 97
    outcomes of, 30
    philosophy, 211–12
    potentialities, 32–33
    power versus, 48, 179, 187, 241,
        247–48

refusing, 25, 36, 38, 54, 55
    relentlessness and, 104–6
    seniority versus, 3
    steps to, 94
    target levels of, 39
Leadership and the New Science
    (Wheatley), 32
Leadership point of view, 3–7, 46
Learning organization (Senge), 18,
    24. *See also* Boundaryless
    organizations
Learning systems, 218–19
Leavitt, Hal, 20, 235
Legality, 55
Legitimate authority (Weber), 12
Legitimate power, 178
Levinson, Harry, 73
Lewin, Kurt, 234
Liedtka, Jeanne, 154, 156
Lifelong learning, 14–15, 118
Limbic system, 113, 114
Listening, social quotient and,
    116–17
Livingston, Sterling, 62
Logical incrementalism, 152
London Business School, 70
Lorsch, Jay, 124
LPV. *See* Leadership point of view

M

MacCammon, Robert, 128
Malone, Mike, 16, 20
Management. *See* Visioning, com-
    mitment, and management
Manhattan Project, 197
Manipulation
    defined, 56
    leadership versus, 38, 39, 56
Marriott Corporation, 122
Massey, Morris, 70
Matrix model, 212–13
Matsushita, Konosuke, 96, 99, 167
Matsushita Denki (Panasonic
    Electronics), 99
Matsushita Electric Company, 96,
    167
Matsushita Seikei Juku (leadership
    institute), 96
McColl, Hugh, 20
Meaning chains, 82
Measurement, of progress, 106–7.
    See also Right measures
Meditation
    centering and, 97
    to manage emotions, 115
Memes, 72, 74
Meyer, Christopher, 201, 202
M-form organizations, 212, 213
Midler, Bette, 131–32

Military model, 212
Miller, Alice, 69, 70
Mission, sense of, 197
Mission statement, organizational, 159, 161–65
  individual, 163, 164–65
Mission Statement Book, The (Abrahams), 164
MIT model, 240–41
Models of change, 234–35, 240–41
Models of leadership, purpose of, 35
Moore, James, 149–50, 152
Morality
  communication and, 185
  defined, 54
  ethics versus, 54–55
  leadership and, 57–61, 62–63, 97
  mission statement and, 163
  organization design and, 214
  reciprocity and, 180
  respect and, 199–200
Morgan, Gareth, 13
Mormon Church, 164
Mother Theresa, 3, 138
Motivation, intrinsic, 74
Mouton, Jane, 124

N

Nam (Baker), 95
NationsBank, 20
Navy, U.S., 101
Neocortex, 113, 114
Nevis, Edwin E., 241
Newburg, Doug, 123, 124, 126, 127, 129, 131, 133, 134, 136
Nicholson, Nigel, 9, 70, 94
Nohria, Nitin, 124
Nonprofiit organizations, 16, 248

O

Object relations theory, 69
Observations, perceptions versus, 75
Obstacles, WCP and, 132–37
Ohio State Leadership Studies, 124
"On the Folly of Hoping for A While Rewarding B" (Kerr), 106
Operant conditioning, 47
Operating goals, 170
  charters and, 160
Oppenheimer, Robert, 197
Organization
  context, 29–30
  strategic challenge and, 145
Organizational charters. *See* Charters

Organizational cohesion, 223–24
Organizational culture, 71, 220–21, 233, 248
  defined, 51
  VABEs and, 85
Organizational design
  background factors, 210–11
  decisions, 212–14
  divisional model of, 212
  ethics and, 214
  general model of, 210–20
  hybrid models of, 213–14
  leadership philosophy and, 211–12
  matrix model of, 212–13
  military model, 212
  morality and, 214
Organizational level of leadership, 39
Organization charts, 212
Orwell, George, 249
Others, 29, 55. *See also* Followers
  contributions of, 100–102
  emotions of, 116, 117
  supporting, 102–4
  truth telling and, 57–58
  understanding of, 182
Outside help, managing change with, 230–31
Overwork, 50

P

Panasonic Electronics, 99
Participation, in teams, 200
Patriarchy
  aristocracy and, 10
  bureaucracies and, 13
Peck, Scott, 119, 132, 229
Pepsi, 197
Perceptions, observations versus, 75
Performance
  appraisal of, 20, 216–17
  work design and, 216
Personal-related reciprocity, 182
Peters, Tom, 20, 214
PJs (rescue swimmers), 250
Planning, organizing, motivating, and controlling (POMC), 177
POMC (planning, organizing, motivating, and controlling), 177
Porras, Jerry I., 20, 150, 153, 154, 160
Porter, Michael, 147–48, 151
Position-based reciprocity, 181
Post-Industrial Era. *See* Information Age

Potentialities, of leadership, 32–33
Power
  defined, 35–36, 177
  leadership versus, 48, 179, 187, 241, 247–48
  Level One leadership and, 48
  referent, 179
  sources of, 178–79
Prahalad, C. K., 150, 151, 152
Preparation, for WCP, 129–32
Privacy, 42, 56, 249
Process measures. *See* Right measures
Productive self-talk, 115
Progress, measurement of, 106–7. *See also* Right measures
Promise keeping, moral leadership and, 57, 58, 60, 61
Punishment, as motivation, 73–74
Purpose, influence and, 184
"Pygmalion in Management" (Livingston), 62

Q

Quadrant I, 99
Quinn, James Bryant, 152

R

Rate of change, 14–15
Rational-Emotive Behavior (REB) model. *See* REB
Raven, Bertram H., 178
REB, 80
  behavior and, 81
  conclusions and, 78
  emotions and, 79
  events and, 75
  leading change and, 82
  VABEs and, 76–78
Reciprocity, 179–83, 249–50
Referent power, 178
Relationship-based reciprocity, 181
Relationships, leadership and, 30–32. *See also* Followers; Others
Relentlessness, leadership and, 104–6
Resonance. *See also* Flow
  defined, 137
  energy cycle and, 131
  growth and, 128
  model, 123, 237
  shortcuts to, 128
  transferable, 127
  universal search for, 127–28
Respect, 247
  communication and, 184

moral leadership and, 57, 59, 60, 61, 62, 63, 199–200
role of, 183
Responsibilities, WCP and, 130–32
Results
balance scorecard measures, 30, 222–23
organizational, 222–23
reinforcing, 234
Results measures. *See* Right measures
Revolutionary model, 153–54
Reward
appraisal and, 217
behavior and, 47
as motivation, 73–74
power, 178, 179
right measures and, 106
systems, 217–18, 222
Right measures
goals and, 170
reward and, 106
of team performance, 201–2
Road Less Traveled, The (Peck), 119, 229
Roddick, Anita, 177
Roles
in change process, 235
in teams, 194–96
Roosevelt, Theodore, 227
Rosenblum, John, 154
Royal Dutch Shell, 155, 213
Rubin, Carol, 232–33

S

Satisficing, 249
Savadelis, Jewel, 199
Scenario building, 100, 154–55
Schein, Ed, 46, 51, 220, 221
Schwartz, Peter, 100, 155
Sculley, John, 197
Self-concept, 83–84
Self-esteem, 101
Senge, Peter, 18, 24, 30, 104, 210, 241
Seniority, leadership versus, 3
Servant Leadership (Greenleaf), 93, 143
Setbacks, WCP and, 132–37
Seven Habits of Highly Effective People (Covey), 183
Shamrock organizations, 213, 214
Sheehy, Gail, 69
Simon, Herb, 249
Skinner, B. F., 42–43, 47, 73, 79, 104, 234
Skunk Works, 200
Smith, Douglas K., 191

Social quotient, 116–18
Spaghetti organizations, 20, 214
Spherical performance evaluations, 20
Sports Illustrated (magazine), 135
SQ. *See* Social quotient
Stalin, Joseph, 56
Standardized testing, 111–12
Stanford, 235
Strategic
domains, 145
dreams, 143
intent model, 151–52
issue, 143–44
Strategic thinking
elements of, 156
fundamentals of, 145–54
models of, 146–53
Strategy
as leadership focus, 33–35
memes, 72
statement, 168–69
VABEs, 44–45
Strengths, weaknesses, opportunities, and threats (SWOT) model, 146, 148
Survey of Managerial Behavior (self-assessment instrument), 166
SWOT (strengths, weaknesses, opportunities, and threats) model, 146, 148
Systems design, 214–20

T

Task-related reciprocity, 181
Taylor, Bob, 197
Taylor, Frederick, 13, 43, 73
Team-based organizations, 190, 216
Teams
characteristics of, 191
early use of, 11
forming, 192
life cycles of, 191–94
members of, 200
norming, 192–93
performing, 193, 201
reforming, 193–94
roles in, 194–96
shift to, 17, 190
virtual, 202–3
Team spirit, 101
Theory of Social and Economic Organization, The (Weber), 12
Think (magazine), 18
Thoreau, Henry David, 42
Tichy, Noel, 151, 215

Time frames, influence and, 187
Tomlin, Lily, 165, 166
Trait model, 28
Trust. *See also* Respect
followers and, 63
role of, 183
Truth telling, moral leadership and, 57–58, 60, 61

U

Unilever, 213
University of Chicago, 125
University of Iowa, 113
U.S. Air Force, 200
U.S. Coast Guard, 250
U.S. Navy, 101

V

VABEs, 42, 44, 45, 46–47, 52. *See also* Leadership, Level Three
culture and, 77
influence and, 186–87
memes and, 72
organizational culture and, 85, 220
REB and, 75, 76–78, 82
Value chain, 148–50
Values. *See* VABEs
Values statement, 167–68
Variance management, 107
VCM. *See* Visioning, commitment, and management
Virginia Department of Transportation (VDOT), 164
Virtual Organization, The (Davidow and Malone), 16
Virtual organizations, 16, 18
Virtual teams, 202–3
Vision
clarifying what is possible, 98–100
of leader, 4–5, 29
statement, 165
VCM and, 36
Visioning, commitment, and management, 36–39

W

Wack, Pierre, 155
Wal-Mart, 15, 150
Walton, Richard, 248
WCPs. *See* World-class performers
Weber, Max, 12, 14
Weick, Karl, 152
Welch, Jack, 17, 119, 124, 132, 221

West Point Way of Leadership, The
    (Donnithorne), 36
Wetlaufer, Suzy, 33
Wheatley, Margaret, 32
White, Rod, 9
Whittaker, Lou, 198
Why We Do What We Do (Deci), 66
Williams, Ted, 125
Woods, Tiger, 131
Work design, performance and, 216

Work group level of leadership, 39,
    145
WorkOut program, 17, 221
World-class effort, 16, 52
World-class performers, 60, 63
    defined, 123
    freedom and, 129–32
    resonance and, 127
    setbacks and, 132–37
Wosniak, Steve, 211

Wosniak, Steven, 153

X

Xerox Corporation, 197–98

Z

Zeeman, E. C., 119